Art versus industry?

Manchester University Press

also available in the Studies in Design and Material Culture series

The matter of art
Materials, practices, cultural logics, c.1250–1750
EDITED BY CHRISTY ANDERSON, ANNE DUNLOP AND PAMELA H. SMITH

Bringing modernity home
Writings on popular design and material culture
JUDITH ATTFIELD

Design and the modern magazine
EDITED BY JEREMY AYNSLEY AND KATE FORDE

The culture of fashion
A new history of fashionable dress
CHRISTOPHER BREWARD

'The autobiography of a nation'
The 1951 Festival of Britain
BECKY E. CONEKIN

The culture of craft
Status and future
EDITED BY PETER DORMER

Material relations
Domestic interiors and the middle-class family, 1850–1910
JANE HAMLETT

Arts and Crafts objects
IMOGEN HART

Representations of British motoring
DAVID JEREMIAH

Interiors of Empire
Objects, space and identity within the Indian subcontinent, c. 1800–1947
ROBIN JONES

The Edwardian house
The middle-class home in Britain 1880–1914
HELEN C. LONG

The birth of modern London
The development and design of the city
ELIZABETH MCKELLAR

Interior design and identity
EDITED BY SUSIE MCKELLAR AND PENNY SPARKE

The material Renaissance
MICHELLE O'MALLEY AND EVELYN WELCH

Bachelors of a different sort
Queer aesthetics, material culture and the modern interior
JOHN POTVIN

Chinoiserie
Commerce and critical ornament in eighteenth-century Britain
STACEY SLOBODA

Material goods, moving hands
Perceiving production in England, 1700–1830
KATE SMITH

Crafting design in Italy
From post-war to postmodernism
CATHARINE ROSSI

Establishing dress history
LOU TAYLOR

The study of dress history
LOU TAYLOR

STUDIES IN DESIGN & MATERIAL CULTURE

general editors
Christopher Breward
and
Bill Sherman

founding editor
Paul Greenhalgh

Art versus industry?

New perspectives on visual and industrial cultures in nineteenth-century Britain

Edited by
Kate Nichols, Rebecca Wade and Gabriel Williams

Manchester University Press

Published by Manchester University Press
Altrincham Street, Manchester M1 7JA
www.manchesteruniversitypress.co.uk

British Library Cataloguing-in-Publication Data
A catalogue record for this book is available from the British Library

Library of Congress Cataloging-in-Publication Data applied for

ISBN 978 0 7190 9646 4 *hardback*

First published 2016

The Henry Moore Foundation

PAUL MELLON CENTRE
for Studies in British Art

Typeset in Linotype Compatil with Transat display by
Koinonia, Manchester

Contents

List of figures

at the University of Leeds. Previous books include (with Dorothy Rowe) *Architecture and design in Europe and America, 1550–2000* (Oxford, 2006) and *Fraud, fakery and false business: rethinking the Shrager versus Dighton 'old furniture case'* (London, 2011).

Lara Kriegel is Associate Professor of History and English at Indiana University, Bloomington, where she also directs the Victorian Studies Program. She has also served as the Associate Editor of the *American Historical Review.* Her first book, *Grand designs: labor, empire, and the museum in Victorian culture*, was published by Duke University Press in 2007. She is now completing a monograph called *War without heroes: the Crimean conflict and its Victorian legacies.* Kriegel is, additionally, the author of published and forthcoming essays in such venues as the *Journal of British Studies, Victorian Studies, Victorian Review, Labor, Historical Reflections*, and *19*, as well as of several book chapters considering exhibitions, empire, militarism, and social class.

Kate Nichols is a postdoctoral research fellow at the Centre for Research in Arts, Social Sciences and Humanities, University of Cambridge (2012–17). Her publications include *Greece and Rome at the Crystal Palace*: *classical sculpture and modern Britain 1854–1936* (Oxford, 2015), and a co-edited collection (with Sarah Turner) *After 1851: the material and visual cultures of the Crystal Palace* (Manchester, 2015).

Frances Robertson is a lecturer in the Forum for Critical Inquiry at Glasgow School of Art. Her cross-disciplinary research embraces art and design theory and history, visual culture, cultural history and histories of science and technology, examining drawing as practice and discourse, and as a means of shaping the three-dimensional world. Recent publications include: 'Electric pastorale', *The Drouth*, 47 (2014); *Print culture: technologies of the printed page from steam press to eBook* (Routledge 2013); 'David Kirkaldy (1820–1897) and his museum of destruction: the visual dilemmas of an engineer as man of science', *Endeavour* 37:10 (2013): 125–32; 'Science and fiction: James Nasmyth's photographic images of the moon', *Victorian Studies* 48:4 (2006): 595–623.

Colin Trodd is Senior Lecturer in Art History at the University of Manchester. He co-edited *Victorian culture and the idea of the grotesque* (Aldershot, 1999), *Governing cultures* (Aldershot, 2000), *Art and the Academy in the nineteenth century* (Manchester, 2000), and *Representations of G. F. Watts* (Aldershot, 2004). He is the author of *Blake's shadow* (Manchester, 2008) and *Visions of Blake: William Blake in the art world 1830–1930* (Liverpool, 2012).

Rebecca Wade is a postdoctoral research fellow at the Henry Moore Institute (2013–15) working on the plaster casting business and sculptural practice of Domenico Brucciani. Her research interests are situated at the intersection between teaching collections, art and design education and cultures of display in nineteenth-century Britain. She completed her PhD at the School of Fine Art, History of Art and Cultural Studies at the University of Leeds and went on to work with the collections of the Museum of Classical Archaeology, University of Cambridge, as part of the Arts and Humanities Research Council project

Connecting with collections. She is a visiting lecturer at Christie's Education and a board member of the Museums and Galleries History Group.

Gabriel Williams has recently completed a PhD at the University of York, which focussed on the relationship between ideal sculpture, modern industry and new technologies at the early International Exhibitions. From 2010–13 he was a member of 'Displaying Victorian Sculpture', a collaborative research project involving the Universities of York and Warwick and the Yale Centre for British Art. He has recently published the article, 'Italian tricks for London shows: Raffaele Monti at the Royal Panopticon', *Sculpture Journal* 23:2 (2014), which looks at intersections between sculptural style, technical display and exhibition culture in 1850s London.

Contributors

Jasmine Allen is Curator of the Stained Glass Museum, Ely. She completed her doctorate in the History of Art Department at the University of York. Her thesis explored the exhibition and display of nineteenth-century stained glass at International Exhibitions, c. 1851–1900. She has published articles on stained glass in *Vidimus* and *Visual Culture in Britain.* Her research interests focus on nineteenth- and twentieth-century stained glass, and she is particularly interested in the relationship between stained glass, architecture and other related art forms. She is an advisor to the London Stained Glass Repository and a Research Affiliate of the University of York.

Nicole Garrod-Bush completed her doctoral research in the Department of English Studies, Durham University, where she is also a teaching assistant. Her thesis explores the pre-history of cinema in the mid-Victorian period, looking specifically at moving-image technologies such as the phenakistiscope, kaleidoscope, and zoetrope, and examines how the mechanical operation and animated display of these devices offered popular literature new ways to represent the physiology of visual perception, cognition, and the working of memory. She has an article forthcoming which traces the metaphorical use of the kaleidoscope throughout the nineteenth century and addresses the phenomenological issues raised by the experience of making and watching the moving technological image.

Ann Compton is a Senior Fellow of the Paul Mellon Centre for Studies in British Art (2014–15) and the originator and Project Director of *Mapping the Practice and Profession of Sculpture in Britain and Ireland 1851–1951*. She is also an Honorary Fellow in the School of Culture and Creative Arts, University of Glasgow and a Visiting Scholar at the Victoria and Albert Museum. Prior to moving into writing and research, Compton worked for many years as a curator in Cambridge, London and Liverpool. Her recent publications include *Facing the future: sculpture from the Harrogate collection* (Harrogate, 2014), *Garth Evans sculpture: beneath the skin* (editor) (London, 2013) and *The sculpture of Charles Sargeant Jagger* (London, 2004).

Renate Dohmen is Associate Professor in Art History at the Open University. She is currently writing her book *Colonial art in British India: power, gender and race under the Raj* (London, 2017) which explores women's visual culture, representations of empire, race and exhibition in British India. Her recent book *Encounters beyond the gallery: relational aesthetics and cultural difference* (London, 2015) examines issues of contemporary art, aesthetics, anthropology and the global. She has also published on cosmopolitanism in contemporary art, women's scrap albums and British India, and the tradition of threshold drawings in Tamil Nadu.

Natasha Eaton is Reader in the History of Art at University College London. She has recently published two monographs to do with the visual and material cultures of British imperialism – *Mimesis across empires: artworks and networks in India, 1765–1860* (Durham, NC) and *Colour, art and empire: visual culture and the nomadism of representation* (London). She is currently at work on a study of the visual culture of the Indian Ocean which is provisionally entitled *The conditional image: art, indenture and colonial miasma in the Indian Ocean, c. 1780 to the present.*

Lara Eggleton received a PhD from the University of Leeds and specialises in Islamic art and architecture and its Western reception. In 2012 she was awarded a Wingate scholarship for independent research to work with the Victoria and Albert Museum's prints collections, and she has published a number of articles and book chapters on the subject of the Alhambra palace in Granada and its impact on nineteenth-century visual culture and art historiography. She is currently investigating the role of early tourism in shaping conceptions of global art history, particularly through Victorian encounters with the Islamic West. Alongside teaching and research, she publishes exhibition essays and reviews, runs workshops and provides arts consultancy on a freelance basis.

Graeme Gooday is Professor of the History of Science and Technology and Head of School in the School of Philosophy, Religion and History of Science at the University of Leeds. He works on the social and cultural experience of new electrical technologies of lighting and communication in the late Victorian period and his books include *Domesticating electricity* (London, 2008) and *Patently contestable* (Cambridge MA, 2013).

Tom Gretton is Honorary Research Fellow in History of Art at UCL. He works on nineteenth-century print culture, particularly on the work of J. G. Posada and on general-interest upmarket illustrated weekly news magazines in the UK and France from 1840 to 1914. Recent publications include 'From *La Méduse* to the *Titanic*: Géricault's raft in journalistic illustration up to 1912', *19: Interdisciplinary Studies in the Long Nineteenth Century*, 16 (2013), and 'Calaveras and commodity fetishism: the unhallowed supernatural in the work of José Guadalupe Posada', in W. Carter, B. Haran and F. Schwartz (eds.) *Re/New Marxist art history* (London, 2013).

Abigail Harrison Moore is a Senior Lecturer in Art History and Museum Studies and Head of the School of Fine Art, History of Art and Cultural Studies

Preface and acknowledgements

> a familiarity with the beautiful sculptures of antiquity ... must have an enduring effect upon the manufacture of a Worcester tea-cup or a Paisley shawl.[1]

A connection between ancient Greek sculpture and contemporary domestic manufactured commodities might seem peculiar – surreal, even – to twenty-first-century eyes. *Art versus industry?* is bursting with such apparently irreconcilable differences, and it aims to show how such sentiments were constructed in nineteenth-century Britain. The editors are all art historians, working on the intersections between sculpture, art and design education, and international exhibitions. The conference out of which this volume has grown was our attempt to engage with the complex and surprising negotiations between art and industry across different media, disciplines, and across geographical boundaries. The conference 'Art versus Industry?' took place at Leeds City Museum in March 2012, supported by the Henry Moore Foundation, the Paul Mellon Centre for Studies in British Art, and the Centre for Modern Studies at the University of York. Many of the ideas which form the basis of this volume were debated and rethought there, and it is our pleasure to thank the following participants for their papers and contributions to discussion: Patrizia di Bello, Danielle Child, Steve Edwards, Alistair Grant, Kate Hill, Anne-Marie Millim, Angus Patterson, Ben Russell, Sally Tuckett, Sarah Victoria Turner, and Mark Westgarth. Staff at Manchester University Press have been unstintingly helpful, going out of their way to assist with our various queries. The illustrations are published thanks to generous funding from the Henry Moore Foundation and the Paul Mellon Centre for Studies in British Art.

Note

1 C. Knight, *Pictorial gallery of the arts* (London, 1845), p. 2.

1

Art versus industry? An introduction

Kate Nichols and Rebecca Wade

In the winter of 2013 the British artist Jeremy Deller staged the first iteration of the touring exhibition *All That Is Solid Melts Into Air* at Manchester Art Gallery.[1] Advertised as 'a personal look at the impact of the Industrial Revolution on British popular culture', the exhibition displayed photographs of nineteenth-century miners and ironworkers, trade union banners, and paintings and etchings of factory interiors and dramatic industrialised landscapes. It positioned nineteenth-century industrialisation in conversation with twentieth-century industrial-promotional film, album covers and a soundtrack of musicians from former industrial heartlands, alongside images of contemporary workplaces such as the Amazon picking plant in Staffordshire, and Deller's graphic representations of, for example, text messages sent to workers on zero-hours contracts, and motivational acronyms displayed on the walls of call centres. It presented the Industrial Revolution as a brutal, dehumanising force, against which culture (past and present) only appears through struggle.[2]

All That Is Solid Melts Into Air reinforced the trope of an unassailable opposition between industrial and artistic production, an opposition embedded in the historiography associated with John Ruskin and William Morris. The exhibition could even be read as an illustration of Ruskin's seductive aphorism, 'industry without art is brutality', most often quoted without the preceding half of the sentence, 'life without industry is guilt'.[3] Deller's selection of artefacts from the nineteenth and twentieth centuries operated as a polemic against the factory, the archetypal site of the deskilling, brutalisation and alienation of an undifferentiated working class without complexity or nuance. It presented the achievements of those who were able to transcend industry through cultural production as anomalous and heroic creative responses. Art, according to this narrative, is intrinsically opposed to industry.

Deller's exhibition is one recent, prominent and emphatically public evocation of this apparently adversarial relationship, demonstrating its well-established position within British culture. As announced by the question mark in its title, however, this volume queries the opposition between art and industry. It disrupts and expands the construction and reconstruction of this persistent singular narrative of 'The Industrial Revolution' as something opposed and prohibitive to art, by investigating a more complex set of relations between art and industry, production and consumption, and education and display.

The concepts of art and industry as they are understood today emerged towards the end of the eighteenth century. Throughout the nineteenth century, both categories were in the process of definition. The term 'Industrial Revolution' (usually ascribed to the period 1750–1850), for example, was not widely used or understood as historically significant in Britain until the 1880s. Up until this point, 'industry' usually meant hard work, the opposite of idleness. Factories and mills, unquestionable sites of Victorian industry to our eyes, were most commonly referred to as sites of manufacture. The publication in 1884 of Arnold Toynbee's influential *Lectures on the industrial revolution of the eighteenth century in England* set up the association between industry and appalling new urban working conditions, a new workforce, new technologies such as the steam engine and machinery for working cotton, and mass production.[4] Art too was undergoing redefinitions in this period. The 'division of the arts', divorcing the 'fine arts' of painting and sculpture from supposedly less intellectual crafts, is usually attributed to the eighteenth and early nineteenth century; the foundation of the Royal Academy of Arts in 1768 in particular marked off fine art from the undertakings of the earlier Royal Society for the encouragement of Arts, Manufactures and Commerce, founded in 1754.[5] The divergent senses of the term 'art' used by these two eighteenth-century institutions – in one case to separate practices like painting and sculpture from other trades and in the other to connect them – both remained in use well into the nineteenth century, persistently complicating debates about art's relation to manufacture.[6]

'Art' and 'industry' are used in such varied ways across nineteenth-century culture, that an attempt to give a precise definition of each runs the risk of being misleading and reductive. Instead, the chapters in this volume, and particularly those in the first section, aim to show the range of meanings of these two terms in various nineteenth-century contexts. This is not a semantic study, but one which shows these keywords in motion as part of a broader interrogation of their relationship to each other. Here, abiding as much as possible by nineteenth-century terms, 'fine art' refers to painting and sculpture (though we are conscious of the problems of keeping these art forms distinct), while art-manufacture (a term commonly used in nineteenth-century discussions on art and industry, and accordingly by several contributors to this volume) indicates – in the words of the 1855 catalogue of the Museum of Ornamental Art, 'all art which finds its material expression in objects of utility, or in works avowedly decorative'.[7] This museum was initially (1852–53) known as the Museum of Manufactures, its changing name testimony to the variety of ways of labelling art-manufacture in the nineteenth century. Industry is defined differently in each chapter; throughout, however, there is a sense that industry is related to new modes of manufacture, to mass production, consumption and communication and new networks of collaboration and exchange.

Industry can operate as shorthand for – or at least is often perceived to be inextricably bound up with – commercialism, capitalism, or economics altogether. All three of these broad categories have had problematic relationships with art when it is understood as a creative process distinct from the profit motive.[8] The nineteenth-century opposition between commerce and culture evident in authors such as Matthew Arnold has been reinforced in the twentieth century by research in cultural studies, anthropology and history on ideas and practices of consumption, often regarded as commerce's close relation. These studies have similarly tended to dwell on the difficulties of reconciling consumption with any sort of 'authentic' culture.[9]

The notion of an 'industrial culture' in nineteenth-century Britain seemed paradoxical in the wake of Raymond Williams's *Culture and society 1780–1950* (1958) and Martin Wiener's *English culture and the decline of the industrial spirit* (1981). Both suggest a seemingly non-negotiable opposition between 'culture' and 'industry'. They emphasise those writings of Ruskin, and later William Morris, which decry the crossover of art and mechanical or industrial production. Morris and the Arts and Crafts Movement in general offer potent – and well-known – period invectives on the deleterious impact of capitalism, mechanisation and the division of labour on art and creative life, and have often been taken by twentieth-century scholars as testimony to a general conflict between Victorian industry and art. Recent scholarship on the Arts and Crafts has provided a more nuanced and complex picture of the objects and ideas involved, looking beyond a homogeneous 'movement' to trace connections with earlier, overtly pro-industrial design reforming ideas and manufactures.[10] This volume guards against a selective and distorting emphasis on Arts and Crafts as only oppositional voices, and highlights period discussions of art and industry that the dominant vision of the Arts and Crafts Movement has overshadowed.

In *Manufacturing culture* (2003), Joseph Bizup looks beyond Ruskin and Morris to analyse the development of a 'pro-industrial rhetoric' among nineteenth-century critics, scientists and authors. *Art versus industry?* adds a visual arts perspective to Bizup's important work, building on and around Tim Barringer's investigation of the relationship between art and labour in mid-Victorian culture in *Men at work* (2005). The wide-ranging essays contained in this volume uncover the complexities of nineteenth-century industrial culture, spanning histories of art and design, production and consumption, science and technology, gender, and imperialism.

Deller's exhibition clearly sets out its Marxist credentials in its quotation of the Communist Manifesto in its very title *All That Is Solid Melts Into Air*. A reassessment of the relationship between art and industry, however, is by no means an endorsement of unfettered capitalism or an explicit rejection of leftist critique. To a certain extent, the work of Karl Marx and Friedrich Engels underpins this volume, through their identification of the revolutionary potential of industry, the social changes that they attributed to industrial modes of production and its role in the formation of the industrial proletariat. Their critique of industrial production forms the intellectual background against which twentieth-century critics like Raymond Williams formulated the opposition of industry and culture. Yet essays here do not engage in any great detail with Marx, or Marxist art-criticism. This was by no means a prescribed editorial decision, but perhaps indicates a shift in contemporary scholarship engaging with art and industry, quite distinct from the narrative traced in Francis Kligender's *Art and the industrial revolution* (1947). This is an enormously significant publication, but one which adopts a Marxist historical scheme so dogmatically that, as Barringer points out, its vision of 'a unified triumphalist bourgeoisie' which 'torments a likewise unified heroic, and ultimately victorious proletariat' fails to acknowledge the complexity of either class, while the dominance of class as a category of analysis almost entirely obscures 'questions of gender, religion, and empire'.[11] *Art versus industry?* demonstrates the various allegiances of the art-industrial worker.

The volume concentrates primarily on Britain for several important reasons. Its British focus grows partly out of Marxist constructions of Britain as the 'classic soil' of the industrial revolution.[12] The volume's emphasis is not an endorsement of the idea that Britain *was* the unique or most important site of nineteenth-century industrial development, especially considering recent research in global history that suggests the generative roles played by China and India in early British industrialisation.[13] But it takes seriously the nineteenth-century *claims* that there was something particular about Britain and industry, and asks how the notion of this unique relationship inflected notions of an industrial art-culture.[14] And, as we explore below, the volume looks not just at the British Isles, but at art and industry in Britain's imperial networks, and at its dissemination in international exhibitions.

The peculiar British relationship with the Victorians post 1901 further intensifies the British art-industrial case. In British culture the Victorians appear as either (and sometimes both) cosy nostalgic forebears, or reprehensible others from which contemporary Britain has made terrific social progress.[15] This tendency is, for example, evident throughout Deller's installation; the title of one section, 'The Shit Old Days', attempts to subvert any sort of nostalgia for the Victorian past. Art, to return to the other half of our couplet, is (at least in theory) not exclusively connected to any time or place. But for a long time, art historians and cultural critics found little artistic merit in Victorian Britain, especially compared to the supposedly avant-garde, proto-modernist movements across the Channel in France.[16] Nineteenth-century art and industry continue to seem natural opponents because British culture has habitually set up the Victorians as its other/same, identified the Victorians with industrialisation, and nineteenth-century industrialisation with largely negative connotations. The combination of a supposedly unique association with industry, and an often under-valued artistic cache makes Britain and its imperial networks fundamental locations for a re-evaluation of the relations between art and industry.

The art–industry divide: nineteenth-century representations

Chapters in Part I, 'The art/industry divide', provide a glimpse into some nineteenth-century representations of this emergent relationship, spanning lace, stained glass, medals and works usually today regarded as fine art, such as William Blake's drawings. The divergent voices and practitioners foregrounded here, from elderly Irish women and French and British glass painters, to more familiar thinkers on art and industry associated with the Arts and Crafts Movement, demonstrate the importance of rethinking the art/industry divide. If we continue to tell a story of nineteenth-century art and industry based only on the (mostly) anti-industrial writings of John Ruskin and William Morris, and mediated through twentieth-century anti-industrialist writers, we not only distort understandings of nineteenth-century creative production, we also lose the opportunity to hear the stories of nineteenth-century arts and crafts practitioners, many of whom hail from already marginalised groups: women, the elderly, the working and lower middle classes, the colonised.

In the nineteenth century, factory owners and workers, social reformers, painters, sculptors, lace makers, inventors of optical instruments, and students at newly formed design schools were all part of the conceptual formation and distinction of both art and industry. But at the same time, their ideas and practices blurred any such division between the two. In 1835 and 1836, for example, a House of Commons Select Committee on 'arts and their connexion with manufactures' was appointed, a pivotal moment in British design reform, education, and indeed in articulating the relationship between artistic and industrial pursuits. It set out 'to inquire into the best means of extending a knowledge of the Arts and of the Principles of Design among the People (especially the Manufacturing Population) of the Country', as well as into the 'Constitution, Management and Effects of the Institutions connected with the Arts'. Art at the 1835/6 Select Committee encompassed both skilled labour in the production of fancy goods and the 'fine arts' of painting and sculpture. 'Art workmen' were defined as those engaged in the silk trade, ribbon manufacture, pottery, interior decor, and furniture.[17] The Select Committee positioned fine art as distinct from, but on a continuum with, art-manufacture. Its report was based on the belief that improving British design would lead to superior art-manufacture, and a stronger economy; art and industry were bound together in aspirations for national progress – a national progress consistently discussed and judged against French art-manufacture.[18]

By the end of the nineteenth century, fine art, crafts, art-manufacture and industries were united in another significant, and characteristically nineteenth-century, discourse; they were all the subjects of newly articulated histories. Histories of plastering, the industrial revolution, sculpture, woman's work, pottery, Christian painting, and cotton making acknowledge the significance of their subjects, and position them as fully emerged, identifiable categories.[19] The prestigious and influential periodical *Quarterly Review* described Fanny Bury Palliser, author of a *History of lace* (1865) as the 'Gibbon of the Decline and Fall of Lace', situating lace history writing alongside the venerated historiographical tradition of ancient Roman history; craft and industry were thus becoming part of high culture, not inimical to it. Here, Lara Kriegel's chapter looks beyond the art–industry binary to trace a history and a historiography of nineteenth-century attempts to revive lace making, whose decline was attributed to factors much wider than simply the mechanisation of production.

Lace was traditionally connected with women, both as producers and consumers, and Kriegel's lace texts, written largely by and for women, attempt to foster a common sisterhood through craft across centuries, age groups, class and national borders. The gendered nature of nineteenth-century art-industrial relations has played a foundational role in rethinking their purported antipathy.[20] New nineteenth-century art-industrial crossovers such as ceramics and textiles provided skilled and creative work opportunities for lower- and middle- class women. As Kyriaki Hadjiafxendi and Patricia Zakresi suggest, the emergence of female craft practitioners brought domestic crafts traditionally associated with women into the public (and historically construed as male) marketplace, challenging and confusing the art–industry binary.[21] Kriegel shows that lace texts offer a new, female nineteenth-century articulation of handicraft. They demonstrate the complexity and possibilities of craft in the nineteenth century – artistic, economic, personal and nostalgic. And as Glenn Adamson has argued, 'craft' was a moving target, only gathering specific recognition and construction as something distinct in the nineteenth century through contemporary debate – and indeed the writing of practice specific histories.[22] It could operate as art or industry, and sometimes both.

Fine artists as much as craft practitioners rejected the supposed division between fine arts and crafts well into the nineteenth century. The unity of art and craft was stressed by witnesses in the 1835/6 Select Committee as diverse as the architect and archaeologist Charles Cockerell and the vice president of the London Mechanics Institute Charles Toplis; in articles in the design reforming press; by mid-century sculptors like John Bell and Alfred Stevens, and later nineteenth-century academic painters like Lawrence Alma Tadema.[23] They called upon classical and Renaissance precedents for a continuum of art and craft, regularly citing Michelangelo's dictum that 'I know but of one art'.[24] And they welded this idea of unity and connectedness across artistic media and practices to new modes of industrial production. After designating that stove-grates (or indeed 'any other article of direct utility, in which exist qualities of art-beauty') could be 'a work of Sculpture', John Bell went on to plead that 'If the higher grade of formative art (Sculpture), be neglected, it will be in vain to look for improvement in taste, or judicious progress in the lower workings of the same department among the manufacturing industries.'[25] Fine art was essential to industry because it taught a communicable, fixed standard of good taste, vital for the production of any object. But industry and mass production were essential to art, because they provided a means of disseminating taste to wider audiences.

Gabriel Williams's chapter explores the ramifications of this nineteenth-century vision of unity across arts, crafts and industrial production, and shows how ideas about creating and sustaining a 'national taste' accompanied the development of new art-industrial technologies. He looks at the anaglyptograph, one of several machines developed partly in tandem with banknote printing technologies and used to make mechanical engravings after historic coins and medals. This technology, and the debates surrounding it, brought together sculptors, medallists, engineers, engravers and print publishers, and fed into wider hopes that the forces of mechanical reproduction and currency circulation could be harnessed for the improvement of national taste. The chapter shows how the hopes for this technology nonetheless ran aground on vexed discussions about reconciling mechanical and 'artistic' engraving, foregrounding debates over the relationship between hand and machine, original and reproduction in conceptualising both art and industry.

From 1851 onwards, international exhibitions offered a distinctly nineteenth-century location for public taste amelioration, via the display and classification of both artistic and industrial objects. Their aims were overtly pro-art-industrial, and printed guides, catalogues and periodicals like the *Illustrated London News* and *Illustrated Exhibitor*, which proliferated to report on these exhibitions, depicted and described marble sculptures, iron stoves, stained glass windows and steam engines alongside each other, encouraging their readers to contemplate relations between such objects. The Great Exhibition of the Industry of all Nations of 1851 has been central to twentieth- and twenty-first-century evaluations of nineteenth-century history, and exhibitions have become important places for thinking about vision in relation to commerce in nineteenth-century culture.[26] But the idea that international exhibitions' pro-industrial foundations might suggest a wider nineteenth-century sympathy towards and engagement with industrial production has only recently been acknowledged.[27] In many cases art at international exhibitions has been written about independently of the industrial objects that surrounded it, and in a founding work on the study of world's fairs, Paul Greenhalgh decisively severed the two, arguing that the presence of the 'fine arts' at the Great Exhibition prevented it from becoming a 'mere' trade fair.[28] Here, Jasmine Allen's chapter explores exhibitions in Britain and France as complex sites for both distinguishing – and conflating – the relationship between art and industry. She shows how official classifications of stained glass as a distinct form of manufacture contrasted with the exhibitions' stated aims to show the continuities between art and industry. Media specificity and exhibitionary requirements were just one factor among many that in this instance confused both official taxonomies, and exhibition visitors.

By the late nineteenth century, 'artist' was a recognisable career option for men and some women, a commercially viable profession, with training schools, trade connections, a specialist art press, professional dealers, and global job opportunities – not exactly divorced from financial speculation or industry. Colin Trodd's chapter shows how some members of the Arts and Crafts Movement sought to redefine art, and the status of the artist, through the precedent of eighteenth-century visionary painter William Blake. The Arts and Crafts conceptualisation of Blake's work (traced partly through Ruskin's idea of the grotesque) posited certain conflicts between art and industry, but also proposed resolutions to those conflicts in a reconfiguration of both terms. In this sense at least, Arts and Crafts theorists echoed the earlier concerns of the Select Committee on arts and manufactures and the less 'radical' and more 'pro-industrial' design reformers. These two broad theoretical perspectives may be seen, that is, not as inexorably opposed camps but as different points on a continuous spectrum of dialogue about making art and industry more mutually informative. Rethinking art and industry may also be a means to reevaluate the variety and nuance of the Arts and Crafts 'movement'.

Art and new technologies

The relationship between cultural production and the emergence and rapid development of new technologies is fertile territory for the investigation of the intersection between art and industry as it was figured and reconfigured in the nineteenth century. A particularly productive line of enquiry in the existing literature on the subject has been the paradigm shift caused by the invention of different forms of photographic image making.[29] Instead of focussing on the implications of photography, this volume interrogates less widely considered forms of technology with specific implications for the production and reproduction of art and design. Some of these forms share elements of the discourse generated by early photography, particularly the question of agency and the autogenic image or object, explored here by Nicole Garrod-Bush in her consideration of the kaleidoscope as a mechanical pattern-making apparatus, in turn appropriated as a decorative device in the paintings of William Holman Hunt and Dante Gabriel Rossetti.

There were two interrelated benefits to outsourcing the creative and physical labour of design and manufacture to mechanical or autogenic apparatus: matters of artistic judgment that had previously been subject to the vicissitudes of individual taste could be interpreted as objective and infinitely repeatable, and through mechanisation, the design process could enter the same realm of efficiency and standardisation populated by industrialised manufacture, promising a streamlined unity of input and output. As Siegfried Giedion noted in his historical analysis of mechanisation, 'the hand can be trained to a degree of automatic facility. But one power is denied it: to remain unvaryingly active'.[30] Despite the capacity of mechanised technologies to diminish the status and remuneration of the worker through the deskilling of their labour, Giedion characterised mechanisation as essentially neutral and entirely dependent on human agency. He recognised the creative potential for the designer, able to 'realize his every caprice, reasonable or absurd'.[31] This volume engages with examples of the creative appropriation of new technologies and the ways in which the historically and culturally embedded traditions of practices such as ornamental design, technical drawing and printmaking were both retained and transformed by the inventions that brought the spheres of art and industry into productive dialogue. In her chapter on the practice and status of engineers and draughtsmen, Frances Robertson identifies the intersectional figure of the 'visual technician' and reveals the ways in which the profession of technical drawing traversed the shifting terrain of art and industry in the second half of the nineteenth century.

Encounters between existing and emerging modes were sometimes engineered but more often haphazard, leading to unexpected collaborations and hybrid forms. Tom Gretton analyses the complex networks of authorship embedded in the illustrations produced for the *Graphic* and *Illustrated London News*, tracking the implications of the move away from the wood-block and towards photomechanical line-block printing. The chapter goes on to demonstrate how an industrialised mode of mass image production appropriated the pictorial traditions of Western art, but also furnished new claims to a form of collective artistic authorship in continuum with those traditions. Similarly, Graeme Gooday and Abigail Harrison Moore discuss the domestication of electric lighting as an example of an emerging technology made familiar (and therefore safe) through Arts and Crafts design. While many design reformers perceived that mechanised or industrialised production could endanger artistic manufacture, they also promoted new technologies of reproduction, such as Cheverton's sculpture reducing machine (see front cover). Although mechanically manufactured, the miniature sculptures in Parian-ware porcelain that it produced were held to be a means by which the threat posed by mechanisation to artistic manufacture might be reduced, since they widened the franchise of 'good taste' amongst new audiences and markets.[32]

The chapters in Part II share the approach articulated in Raphael Samuel's influential essay, 'Workshop of the world: steam power and hand technology in mid-Victorian Britain' (1977). Through his revisionist interpretation of the relationship between mechanisation and hand technologies, Samuel emphasised the diversity of industrial production and scrutinised 'the machinery question'. He presents mechanisation as a complex, discontinuous and uneven process, in which hand labour and craft skill were essential to, and coexistent with, new mechanised modes of manufacture. Technology is not conceived here as monolithic or deterministic, nor synonymous with mindless reproduction as it was for Herbert Read writing *Art and industry: the principles of industrial design* in 1934. Rather, for the examples in this volume, exemplified by Cheverton's sculpture reducing machine, it provided new modes of engagement with the world of art.

Resituating design reform and art and design education

Design reform refers to a diverse set of ideas, usually regarded as being current in Britain from the 1830s to 1860s, concerned with improving design and manufacture in order to bolster the economy. Nineteenth-century debates over design reform in particular suggest the permeable boundaries between the artist, designer, artisan, and operative, and it is perhaps not surprising that design reform has been the focus of the few existing discussions that move beyond an art–industry polarity.[33] Education was integral to the project of design reform, pursued through the combined mechanisms of the school and the museum in international, metropolitan and regional iterations. From mid-century onwards the sum of these activities was synonymous with South Kensington and the afterlife of the Great Exhibition, which came to represent a centralised and prescriptive set of cultural practices and governmental policies. The relationship between 'fine art' and 'art-manufacture', and more broadly between art and industry was a matter of particular concern for design reformers, although they were far from unanimous when it came to the degrees to which they were related, and the impact each had on the other.[34] For a long time, historians have explained design reforms as purely economically motivated.[35] More recently, design and art historians have argued that reformers were also concerned with the moral and social implications of the improvement of public taste.[36] Design reform was certainly a pro-capitalist and in many ways pro-industrial undertaking. But for its proponents, economic improvement was inextricably bound up with social, moral and aesthetic amelioration.

Chapters in Part III 'resituate' design reform and art education by placing them in different spatial contexts as well as among different disciplines, workers, practices and media beyond the prototypical South Kensington Schools and Museum. They discuss technical art schools, the Calcutta International Exhibition, the Alhambra, the Crystal Palace at Sydenham, sculpture as collaborative practice, Indian textile workers, and Italian marble cutters. This section of the book suggests that the design reform project cannot be properly understood by analysing official central government policy (Henry Cole *et al.*) or goings-on at South Kensington alone. Its chapters purposefully address other sides of the design reform and art education coins, considering the fraught, contingent and covert dialogues between this supposed 'centre' and wider geographical and industrial contexts.

Following Catherine Hall and Sonya Rose's discussions of the domestication and absorption of imperial goods and ideas in Britain, imperial encounters cannot but permeate *all* the chapters in a volume which deals with nineteenth-century manufacturing.[37] Indeed, as Chitralekha Zutshi has argued, 'the idea of the modern industrial product was itself clearly shaped by Victorian Britain's encounter with global commodities such as Kashmiri shawls and their indigenous imitations'. Shawls, for example, became 'modern industrial products' by being circulated, replicated and remade in new industrial contexts – but all with an eye to the design credentials and good taste of the original.[38] British ambitions to spread design reform and art education in colonial India, as well as nineteenth-century British encounters with Indian material culture 'at home' have been the subject of considerable research, and our claim to be 'resituating' design reform here does not rest exclusively on the chapters' consideration of this particular location.[39] The aspects of Indian visual culture and artisan practice analysed here by Renate Dohmen and Natasha Eaton offer different perspectives on design reform and emphasise the ways in which the power dynamics of colonial contexts might reshape the art-industrial relationship. They also extend the chronological framework of design reforming rhetoric, showing how it was co-opted into colonial schools of art and design well into the 1880s, and how it was repositioned alongside (rather than in opposition to) Arts and Crafts practices.

In addition to their overt art-industrial rhetoric, international exhibitions were preeminent nineteenth-century sites for displaying and creating the nation through its technological and artistic produce, and for encountering other nations' wares. International exhibitions did not operate on any set programmatic basis, and each in itself was far from a coherent entity. But the connection to design reform – to notions that industry and artistic endeavour could productively work together to enhance the production of goods, the training of artisans, and a populace's taste – was clear throughout nineteenth-century exhibitions across the globe. Dohmen's chapter on the only international exhibition to take place in India, held in Calcutta from 1883–34, makes clear the fundamental significance of an exhibition's location to the evaluation of its overall success, and more specifically to its articulation of the relationship between art and industry.

Contemporaries viewed international exhibitions as markers of progress and modernity. These attributes took on added significance in the colonial context; they were the purported benefits that Britain would bring to its subject colony India. But to British design reformers, the modernity signified by the idea of an international exhibition stood in tension with the objects of Indian art-manufacture that the exhibition housed, which they romanticised as pre-industrial craft objects, made by pre-industrial peoples. Although design reformers championed artistic associations with new technologies 'at home' (and indeed even in the reproduction of versions of Indian goods), these British modes of production were held to be a threat to Indian artisans, whose produce and practice was regarded as static, and traditional, definitively not modern. Anxieties about imperial governance were woven together with fears that industry would destroy 'traditional' art practices.[40] A new perspective on this paradoxical celebration and denigration of Indian artisan labour as ideally pre-industrial is provided by Eaton's examination of design reforming ideas about colour in relation to Indian art-manufacture. Colonial administrators attempted to define precise laws of colour, but the messy, ungovernable practices and practitioners of fabric dyeing troubled any such centrally diffused message. Eaton's study of colour as subaltern resituates design reform as something more complex than solely a successful tool of imperial governance or a means of social control.

The relationship between foreign and domestic design traditions is also the subject of Lara Eggleton's chapter. Eggleton looks outside (but alongside) British imperial governance to examine two distinct nineteenth-century understandings of the ornament of the Alhambra in Spain, through the reproductions of the Alhambra at another all too rarely acknowledged site of design reforming endeavour, the Crystal Palace post-1851, removed to Sydenham and reopened in 1854. The chapter offers a geographical relocation of design reform, but, perhaps more significantly, re-examines the Alhambra-related undertakings of one of design reform's keenest proponents, Owen Jones, in relation to the writings of John Ruskin, usually characterised as one of its most vehement critics. Analysed from the perspective of nineteenth-century art-industrial debates, throughout this section design reform appears in different forms, across and between cultures, and with a broad range of adherents and practitioners.

For the advocates of design reform, a centralised system of design education promised to be the means through which a productive and disciplined symbiosis of art and industry could be established and maintained, not just in Britain but across the Empire. Once Richard Redgrave and his South Kensington colleagues had established the National Course of Instruction as a universal curriculum in 1852, it seemed logical to extend the systematic and codified approach to control the education of the colonies. Natasha Eaton addresses the implications of this imposition in her chapter on the agency of colour in India, drawing out the ways in which this attempt to standardise taste and production were resisted and subverted. The resituating of art and design education is both figurative and geographical, confronting on one hand the legacy of the literature on art and design education predominantly published in the 1960s and 1970s that positioned Morris and Ruskin as the heroic and prescient figures who rescued design education from industry, and on the other, challenging the perception that regional and international activities were merely peripheral to dominant South Kensington narrative.[41] In her chapter on the career trajectories of the alumni of the South London Technical School of Art in the last quarter of the nineteenth century and into the opening two decades of the twentieth, Ann Compton considers the possibilities and the limitations produced by established networks of labour. By following a cohort of sculptors, those intersectional figures whose work and status had oscillated between art and industry for centuries, we witness the renegotiation and redefinition of craft and collaboration and in a sense, the fulfilment of the great promise of design reform.

Conclusion

The relationships between art and industry are perhaps more obvious in media which, through methods and materials, occupy a more self-evidently uncertain status – stained glass, sculpture, or photography, for example. *Art versus industry?*, however, emphasises the importance of art-industrial relations for painting on canvas as much as lacemaking, and the questions it addresses will, we hope, be as important to art historians as to historians of science and technology. The close case studies here testify to the array of diverse materials, practices, practitioners and locations that participated in forging the complex relations between art and industry in nineteenth-century British culture: from stained glass to plaster, sculpture machines to fabric dyers, engineers to lacemakers and print makers, Italian marble quarries to Indian jails, International Exhibitions in London, Paris and Calcutta, to domestic decor in Sussex. Many engage with John Ruskin and

William Morris, providing a more nuanced vision of these legendarily anti-industrialists' attitudes towards art-manufacture. Others focus on increasingly well-known figures in nineteenth-century design reform, such as Owen Jones and Henry Cole, resituating their endeavours alongside Ruskin and Morris. Together, the chapters present an intricate picture of the vexed relations between art and industry in the nineteenth century. Most importantly, they show that there *was* a relationship between art and industry in the nineteenth century, not simply a disavowal as has so often been presumed.

Notes

1 A version of the exhibition was conceived in 2008 for a project at Palais de Tokyo in Paris called *D'une révolution à l'autre* (From one revolution to another). After leaving Manchester, the exhibition was restaged in Nottingham, Coventry and Newcastle in 2014.
2 www.southbankcentre.co.uk/find/hayward-gallery-and-visual-arts/hayward-touring/future/jeremy-deller-curates-all-that-is-solid-melts-into-air (accessed 4 February 2015).
3 Ruskin, *Lectures on art*, pp. 94–5.
4 For an essential evaluation of the nineteenth-century creation of the 'myth' of the Industrial Revolution as a 'historical thing-in-itself' and of the precursors to Toynbee, see Coleman, *Myth, history, and the industrial revolution*, pp. 1–42.
5 Kristeller, *Renaissance thought and the arts*, pp. 163–227; Shiner, *The invention of art*. On the emergence of craft in relation to the changing valences of art and industry, see Cardoso, 'Craft versus design'.
6 See Gretton, '"Art is cheaper and goes lower in France"'.
7 Robinson, *Catalogue of a collection of works of decorative art*, p. 4.
8 De Marchi, 'Introduction'.
9 See Miller, 'Consumption as the vanguard of history', pp. 25–7.
10 See especially Hart, *Arts and crafts objects*.
11 Barringer, *Men at work*, p. 12.
12 Engels, *The condition of the working class*, p. 37.
13 For further discussion see Berg, 'Useful knowledge'.
14 These ideas were discussed by figures as diverse as Thomas Carlyle, Friedrich Engels, and Alfred Toynbee. See Coleman, *Myth, history and the industrial revolution.*
15 See Taylor and Wolff, *The Victorians since 1901*.
16 Peters Corbett and Perry, 'Introduction'; Barlow, 'Fear and loathing of the academic'.
17 *Report from the Select Committee on arts and their connexion with manufactures*, p. iii.
18 Gretton, '"Art is cheaper and goes lower in France"'.
19 Some examples include Marryat, *Collections towards a history of pottery*; Bremner (ed.) *Great industries*; Butterfield, *A complete history of the cotton trade*. On histories of plastering, see Compton's chapter 10 in this volume.
20 See, for example, Barringer, *Men at work*; Elliot and Helland, *Women artists and the decorative arts*.
21 Hadjiafxendi and Zakresi, 'Introduction: artistry and industry', pp. 8–9.
22 Adamson, 'Introduction', pp. 2–3.
23 *Report from the Select Committee on arts and their connexion with manufactures*, 110–11, 123 (1836), 104, 116; Taylor, 'The mutual interests of artists and manufacturers'; '"High art" and ornamental art', *Journal of Design and Manufacture*; Bell,

British sculpture; Alma-Tadema, 'Art in its relation to industry'.
24 Bell, *British sculpture*, p. 10. See further Nichols, *Greece and Rome at the Crystal Palace*, pp. 133–6; Irwin, 'Art versus design', 228–30.
25 Bell, *British sculpture*, pp. 10–11.
26 On the Great Exhibition's role in history writing, see Purbrick, 'Introduction'. On art, vision and commerce, Teukolsky, 'This sublime museum', pp. 84–100; Di Bello, '"Multiplying statues by machinery"'.
27 Thomas Richards' influential 1990 account of the Great Exhibition as the origins of commodity culture has to some extent re-written and disregarded the significance of the exhibition as a space of pro-industrial culture. See, however, Bizup, *Manufacturing culture*, pp. 147–76; Kriegel, *Grand designs*, pp. 86–159.
28 Greenhalgh, *Ephemeral vistas*, p. 198.
29 On the relationship between photography, painting, sculpture, industry and technology in the nineteenth century, see Roberts, *Art history through the camera's lens*; Hamber, *'A higher branch of the art'*; Haworth-Booth, *Photography: an independent art*; and Edwards, *The making of English photography*.
30 Giedion, *Mechanization takes command*, p. 47.
31 *Ibid.*, p. 346.
32 Atterbury, *The parian phenomenon*.
33 See, for example, Bizup, *Manufacturing culture*; Kriegel, *Grand designs*; Rifkin, 'Success disavowed'.
34 For an overview, see Lubbock, *The tyranny of taste*, pp. 248–70.
35 See especially Bell, *The schools of design*. Romans, 'Living in the past', 270–7 provides a useful historiography.
36 Lubbock, *Tyranny of taste*, p. xiii; p. 248; Romans, 'A question of "taste"', pp. 42–3.
37 Hall and Rose, 'Introduction'.
38 Zutshi, '"Designed for eternity"', 421.
39 See, among others, Dutta, *The bureaucracy of beauty*; Mathur, *India by design*; Mitter, *Art and nationalism*.
40 Zutshi, '"Designed for eternity"', 434–5. Dewan, 'The body at work', pp. 118–34 provides a rich examination of how these anxieties coalesced around the figure of the 'native craftsman'.
41 Bell, *The schools of design* and Macdonald, *The history and philosophy of art education* represent two traditional accounts of the history of art and design education in Britain. For more recent revisionist scholarship, see Romans 'Living in the past', 270–7, Romans 'A question of "'taste"'', pp. 41–53 and Quinn, 'The political economic necessity of the art school 1835–52', pp. 62–70.

Bibliography

Adamson, G. 'Introduction', in G. Adamson (ed.) *The craft reader* (Oxford, 2010), pp. 1–5
Alma-Tadema, L. 'Art in its relation to industry', *Magazine of Art* (January 1893), 8–10
Atterbury, P. (ed.) *The parian phenomenon: a survey of Victorian parian porcelain statuary & busts* (Shepton Beauchamp, 1989)
Barlow, P. 'Fear and loathing of the academic, or just what is it that makes the avant-garde so different, so appealing?', in R. Cardoso Denis and C. Trodd (eds.) *Art and the academy in the nineteenth century* (New Brunswick, 2000), pp. 15–32
Barringer, T. *Men at work: art and labour in Victorian Britain* (New Haven, 2005)
Bell, J. *British sculpture: in connection with the department of science and art* (London, 1858)
Bell, Q. *The schools of design* (London, 1963)

Berg, M. 'Useful knowledge, "industrial enlightenment", and the place of India', *Journal of Global History*, 8:1 (2013), 117–41
Bizup, J. *Manufacturing culture: vindications of early Victorian industry* (Virginia, 2003)
Bremner, D. (ed.) *Great industries of Great Britain* (London, 1877–80)
Butterfield, J. *A complete history of the cotton trade, including also that of the silk, calico-painting, and hat manufactories with remarks on their progress in Bolton, Bury, Stockport, Blackburn, and Wigan, to which is added an account of the chief mart of these goods, the town of Manchester* (Manchester, 1823)
Cardoso, R. 'Craft versus design: moving beyond a tired dichotomy', in G. Adamson (ed.) *The craft reader* (Oxford, 2010), pp. 321–32
Coleman, D. C. *Myth, history, and the industrial revolution* (London, 1992)
Deller, J. *All that is solid melts into air* (London, 2013)
De Marchi, N. 'Introduction', in N. De Marchi and C. D. W. Goodwin (eds.) *Economic engagements with art* (Durham, NC, 1999), pp. 1–30
Dewan, D. 'The body at work: colonial art education and the figure of the "native craftsman"', in S. Sen and J. Mills (eds.) *Confronting the body: the politics of physicality in colonial and post-colonial India* (London, 2004), pp. 118–34
Di Bello, P. '"Multiplying statues by machinery": stereoscopic photographs of sculptures at the 1862 International Exhibition', *History of Photography*, 37:4 (2013), 412–20
Dutta, A. *The bureaucracy of beauty: design in the age of its global reproducibility* (New York and London, 2007)
Edwards, S. *The making of English photography: allegories* (Pennsylvania, 2006)
Elliott, B. and J. Helland, *Women artists and the decorative arts* (Burlington, 2002)
Engels, F. *The condition of the working class in England, from personal observation and authentic sources* (London, 1969)
Giedion, S. *Mechanization takes command: a contribution to anonymous history* (New York, 1948)
Greenhalgh, P. *Ephemeral vistas: the Expositions Universelles, Great Exhibitions and World's Fairs, 1851–1939* (Manchester, 1988)
Gretton, T. '"Art is cheaper and goes lower in France." The language of the Parliamentary Select Committee on the Arts and Principles of Design of 1835–1836', in A. Hemingway and W. Vaughan (eds.) *Art in bourgeois society, 1790–1850* (Cambridge, 1998), pp. 84–100
Hadjiafxendi, K. and P. Zakreski, 'Introduction: artistry and industry – the process of female professionalisation', in K. Hadjiafxendi and P. Zakresi (eds.) *Crafting the woman professional in the long nineteenth century: artistry and industry in Britain* (Burlington, 2013), pp. 1–22
Hall, C. and S. Rose, 'Introduction: being at home with the empire', in C. Hall and S. Rose (eds.) *At home with the empire: metropolitan culture and the imperial world* (Cambridge, 2006), pp. 1–31
Hamber, A. J. *'A higher branch of the art': photographing the fine arts in England, 1839–1880* (Amsterdam, 1996)
Hart, I. *Arts and crafts objects* (Manchester, 2010)
Haworth-Booth, M. *Photography: an independent art: photographs from the Victoria and Albert Museum 1839–1996* (London, 1997)
Hemingway, A. and W. Vaughan (eds.) *Art in bourgeois society, 1790–1850* (Cambridge, 1998)
'"High art" and ornamental art', *Journal of Design and Manufacture*, 4:24 (1851), 161–4
Irwin, D. 'Art versus design: the debate 1760–1860', *Journal of Design History*, 4:4 (1991), 219–32
Kriegel, L. *Grand designs: labor, empire, and the museum in Victorian culture* (Durham, NC, 2007)

Kristeller, P. O. *Renaissance thought and the arts: collected essays* (Princeton, 1990)
Lubbock, J. *The tyranny of taste: the politics of architecture and design in Britain 1550–1960* (New Haven and London, 1995)
Macdonald, S. *The history and philosophy of art education* (London, 1970)
Marryat, J. *Collections towards a history of pottery and porcelain in the fifteenth, sixteenth, seventeenth and eighteenth centuries* (London, 1850)
Mathur, S. *India by design: colonial history and cultural display* (Berkeley, 2007)
Miller, D. 'Consumption as the vanguard of history: a polemic by way of an introduction', in D. Miller (ed.) *Acknowledging consumption* (London, 1995), pp. 1–52
Mitter, P. *Art and nationalism in colonial India 1850–1922: occidental orientations* (Cambridge, 1994)
Nichols, K. *Greece and Rome at the Crystal Palace: classical sculpture and modern Britain, 1854–1936* (Oxford, 2015)
Peters Corbett, D. and L. Perry, 'Introduction', in D. Peters Corbett and L. Perry (eds.) *English art 1860–1914. Modern artists and identity* (New Brunswick, 2001), pp. 1–12
Purbrick, L. 'Introduction', in L. Purbrick (ed.) *The Great Exhibition of 1851: new interdisciplinary essays* (Manchester, 2001), pp. 1–25
Quinn, M. 'The political economic necessity of the art school 1835–52', *International Journal of Art and Design Education*, 30:1 (2011), 62–70
Read, H. *Art and industry: the principles of industrial design* (London, 1934)
Report from the Select Committee on arts and their connexion with manufactures, House of Commons command paper 568 (1836)
Richards, T. *The commodity culture of Victorian England: advertising and spectacle 1851–1914* (Stanford, 1990)
Rifkin, A. 'Success disavowed: the schools of design in mid-nineteenth century Britain (An allegory)', *Journal of Design History*, 1:2 (1988), 89–102
Roberts, H. E. (ed.) *Art history through the camera's lens* (New York, 1995)
Robinson, J. C. *Catalogue of a collection of works of decorative art: being a selection from the museum at Marlborough House, circulated for exhibition in provincial schools of art* (London, 1855)
Romans, M. 'Living in the past: some revisionist thoughts on the historiography of art and design education', *International Journal of Art and Design Education*, 23:3 (2004), 270–7
Romans, M. 'A question of "taste": re-examining the rationale for the introduction of public art and design education to Britain in the early nineteenth century', in M. Romans (ed.) *Histories of art and design education* (Bristol, 2005), pp. 41–53
Ruskin, J. *Lectures on art: delivered before the University of Oxford in Hilary term, 1870* (New York, 1872)
Samuel, R. 'Workshop of the world: steam power and hand technology in mid-Victorian Britain', *History Workshop*, 3 (1977), 6–72
Shiner, L. E. *The invention of art: a cultural history* (Chicago, 2001)
Taylor, M. and M. Wolff, *The Victorians since 1901: histories, representations and revisions* (Manchester, 2004)
Taylor, W. C. 'The mutual interests of artists and manufacturers', *Art-Union* (1 March 1848), 69
Teukolsky, R. 'This sublime museum: looking at art at the Great Exhibition', in J. Buzard, J. W. Childers and E. Gillooly (eds.) *Victorian prism: refractions of the Crystal Palace* (Charlottesville, 2007), pp. 84–100
Wiener, M. J. *English culture and the decline of the industrial spirit* (Cambridge and New York, 1981)
Williams, R. *Culture and society, 1780–1950* (London, 1958)
Wood, P. 'Between god and the saucepan: some aspects of art education in England

from the mid-nineteenth century', in C. Stephens (ed.) *The history of British art: 1870–now* (3 volumes, London, 2008), pp. 164–87

Zutshi, C. '"Designed for eternity": Kashmiri shawls, empire, and cultures of production and consumption in mid-Victorian Britain', *Journal of British Studies*, 48:2 (2009), 420–40

PART I

The art–industry divide: nineteenth-century representations

2

Lace, ladies and labours lost: the meanings of handicraft in Victorian and Edwardian Britain

Lara Kriegel

John Ruskin never delivered the address that he had written for the occasion of the 1873 prize ceremony at the Mansfield Art Night Class. A note on the published version states, 'The address was written ... but not delivered by me. In my absence – I forget from what cause, but inevitable – the Duke of St. Albans honoured me by reading it to the meeting.' This was probably just as well, for the Victorian sage of art and industry had little that was complimentary to say when it came to the matter of awarding prizes to students at night schools. Indeed, the recipients might have felt themselves unduly chastened by his address. For Ruskin, there was great danger in prizes, which were given for diligence, and not talent. Inherently detrimental, such awards risked promoting hubris where humility should be cultivated. They could plant the seed of delusion in 'empty little eggshells of heads'. Awards for studiousness could be mistaken as endorsements of genius, a perilous condition according to Ruskin, who had intended to leave the assembled audience at Mansfield with the inconvenient truth that 'there is not one in a million of you who can be great at *any* thing'. The true prize, according to Ruskin, came in the fusion of humility and admiration, and in the admixture of industriousness and taste. Such marriages were evident when a man truly appreciated art and when a boy honestly emulated nature. And with this middle path came consolation. 'You must neither think your work the best ever done by man', Ruskin had planned to tell his audience, 'nor, on the other hand, think that the tongs and poker can do better.'[1]

If the aspiring art students were to find any consolation in Ruskin's address, it was located in his conviction about the superiority of the artful hand over the toilsome machine. 'While I plead with you for a true humility in rivalship with others', Ruskin had intended to beseech the students, 'I plead with you also for a just pride in what you can honestly do yourself.'

To illustrate this point, Ruskin looked to the lace trade, which had undergone mechanisation, most notably in nearby Nottingham, at the turn of the nineteenth century. The proliferation of new wares notwithstanding, there remained, Ruskin averred, a true and visible 'distinction' between the mechanised and the handmade object. If the former was distinguished by its ubiquity and cheapness, the latter was notable for its rarity and expense. It testified to the 'ability of its maker', envisioned by a designer with a 'pretty fancy' and wrought by a maker with 'fine fingers'. And while few could achieve the beauty of rare lace in their designs, all could aspire by learning to draw. In that effort, Ruskin concluded, lay the ultimate prize – honest labour that fostered 'kindness, modesty, and industry'.[2]

I begin with Ruskin's aborted address to the Mansfield School for two reasons. On the one hand, the text is exemplary of his general thinking. It is an attempt at a class-specific iteration of the quintessentially Ruskinian epithet, 'Life without industry is guilt; industry without art is brutality.' Proffered originally in one of his 1870 lectures at the University of Oxford, this quote has been circulated endlessly in our own age of viral reproduction, and well before too. The words indicate a presumably clear separation between the spheres of 'art' and 'industry', while suggesting, simultaneously, that the former might, in manifold forms, be a salve upon the latter. On the other hand, Ruskin's lecture is unusual within his corpus. Namely, it is rare for its engagement with the 'gossamer' subject of lace.[3] In his writings, Ruskin referred from time to time to lace; it was never, however, a topic that he would take up systematically. It appeared sporadically, instead, more often than not as the exemplar of excessive luxury on the part of wealthy women who might better spend their money in dressing the multitudes rather than ornamenting themselves, and who might better direct their energies to employing the many rather than contracting with the few. Lace was ultimately incidental rather than central in Ruskin's corpus. It was ornamental and not essential. If it inhabited the superfluous frills of clothing, it also resided at the 'imagined fringes' of aesthetic discourse, to use the words of literary critic Elaine Freedgood.[4]

Freedgood offered this formulation in a probing article that examined the plethora of handmade lace and texts produced about it in the later nineteenth century. In these annals, she located the emergence of 'filaments of a feminist version of political economy' that called into question shibboleths about modernising mechanisation. Texts about lace echoed, in 'bits and pieces', the better-known writings by Karl Marx, John Ruskin, and William Morris. Collectively, these thinkers had critiqued the iniquities and flaws within the nineteenth century's capitalist regime of machine production. According to Freedgood, a lesser-known subset of writings on lace to emerge concomitantly participated in a related project. Written primarily by women, these works valorised the trade in hand lace, made both by the needle and the bobbin. In the face of the mechanising industry, which had taken off at the beginning of the nineteenth century, they sought to uphold an ideal of 'utopian commodity consumption' evident in the cultivation of handicraft. Like the texts that described it, handmade lace was, by and large, the product of women. As the authors of lace books argued, it was a craft that had the potential to create a cross-class sisterhood in the face of strife, so connecting the poor rural maker to the urban patroness. By offering such an understanding, writings on lace unsettled a narrative that celebrated the unrelenting march of mechanisation. Even as they upended such a story, however, such accounts participated in a sort of mystification. Romantic and fanciful, writings on lace engaged in a particular variety of commodity fetishism as they celebrated the virtues of handicraft. They tended to marshal fiction's rosy rural labourers who toiled outdoors, rather than the trade's wizened, cold workers who struggled to survive.[5] Such concerns were not confined to manuals alone. Talia Schaffer has expanded upon this understanding as she has located a preoccupation with crafts of all sorts at the centre of Victorian novels, which are, in her reading, expressive of ambivalences about an industrial age.[6]

Heterogeneous and even contradictory, the lace texts, like writings on craft more generally, offer up a rich and provocative archive for understanding the gendered dynamics of hand production as it persisted and expanded in the face of industrialisation and commodification. They exemplify the creation of an essentially feminine discursive space around handicraft. This essay engages with the handicraft of lace as a way of working outside of the ossified dichotomy of high art versus mechanised industry that has characterised our understandings of design history during the Victorian and Edwardian ages. While indebted to Freedgood's penetrating readings about lace and Schaffer's expansive consideration of craft, I place lace books in a broader intellectual, institutional and social context. Certainly, the lace books allowed for a critique of political economy. But even more significantly, the lace books were just one vehicle through which women entered the largely male project of nineteenth-century design reform – a project that variably involved Henry Cole and his circle, Ruskin and his acolytes, as well as William Morris and the Arts and Crafts Movement.[7] During the later nineteenth century, a range of notable ladies sought to kindle appreciation for handicrafts such as lace. Their campaign involved a canny use of the growing exhibitionary apparatus of world's fairs, museums and galleries that developed in the nineteenth century, in London and elsewhere. Like lace itself, which adorned the peripheries of clothing, those ladies who sought to revive and restore the trade worked often at the edges of these august institutions. They included lace exhibits in world's fairs and international exhibitions, beginning in 1851; they loaned their own collections to the South Kensington Museum for display; and they used the spaces of the West End, devoted to show and to retail alike, to feature past and present efforts at lacemaking. But they also created distinctive institutions, namely schools, devoted to resuscitation and rescue, as they participated in the crafts revival that took off in rural England in the 1880s, and even earlier in Ireland, where the origins of the domestic lace trade were entwined with the Great Famine of the 1840s.[8] Efforts to promote these home industries would culminate during the years leading up to World War I, when crafts assumed centre stage at events such as the *Daily Mail* Exhibition of English Irish Lace, held to great fanfare at London's Royal Horticultural Hall in March 1908.[9]

Although Ruskin understood lace as a peripheral concern within a broader discussion of art and industry, the many lectures, reports, exhibition catalogues and souvenir booklets produced in the wake of these efforts indicate otherwise. By showing as much, this essay builds upon the arguments of Freedgood, who understood the later nineteenth century's archive on lace as a critique of political economy. At the same time, it broadens our understandings of the valences of handicraft reform in the long nineteenth century. As it sought to revive a trade long connected with women, this endeavour also offered particularly feminine visions of history and nationhood. The annals of lace not only united women across classes, but also bound them through epochs and ages, and across seas and oceans, too. In the end, narratives about the English and Irish crafts of lace reveal a distinctly feminine world of rescue and revival, agency and alienation, and labour and loss. For the Victorians, then, the lace revival offered opportunities for a range of actors, including women, to engage actively and creatively with a changing economic, political and cultural landscape. The archive that their efforts created allows us to move our discussions of design reform beyond the dichotomy of art versus industry and into uncharted registers. As the following pages will show, the handicraft revival did not only involve questions of aesthetics and economy, or even of nation and history, but ultimately, of affect and memory, too.

The decline and fall of lace

The story told of and by handmade lace in the nineteenth century is a story of decline. This was the case regardless of whether the lace was stitched by the needle or woven with the bobbin. Local industries in the East Midlands and Devonshire languished in both quantity and quality in the face of the mechanising trade, and especially after 1808, when John Heathcoat introduced his bobbin net frame.[10] The trend towards decline had begun in the two prior centuries, particularly in the wake of the successive waves of revolution – whether Puritan, French, or American – that had the cumulative effects of curtailing longstanding aristocratic habits of wearing lace. The narrative of decline is not only a story of revolution and mechanisation, however. Chroniclers attributed the trade's troubles to a number of other factors as well. They lamented the rise of middlemen and small dealers with little knowledge of the trade and less interest in the welfare of workers. They bemoaned the 'rage for cheap lace' so evident among the popular classes and the affinity for foreign goods so widespread in the upper reaches of society.[11] They also noted the vulnerabilities posed by the removal of trade barriers during the nineteenth century and by the decline of the United States market during the American Civil War. Finally, they waxed nostalgic over the 'gradual dwindling away' of traditional lace schools, which had taught the trade to rural children, and girls especially, beginning at the tender age of six or seven. Granted, there was a certain level of romance in these notices of the decline of what one writer called a 'cramping, bleaching, poverty-stricken' endeavour, where youngsters performed unrelenting work in cold environs under the disciplining rule of the rod.[12] Together, the Workshops Act of 1867 and the Education Act of 1870 took these young lasses out of the trade, with the result being that, 'as the older lace-workers in each area died off, there were few or none to replace them'.[13]

Yet the narrative of the trade in the Victorian and Edwardian ages is also punctuated by successive efforts at craft revival, particularly, though not solely, on the part of women worthies. During the early nineteenth century Queen Adelaide would become a stalwart steward of the lace trade, helping to revivify the Devonshire manufacture by introducing Maltese styles.[14] None other than Queen Victoria would give the trade a decisive boost, by donning a gown featuring Honiton lace sprigs for her 1840 wedding to Prince Albert. Indeed, the links between royal weddings and lace have endured, not only through the nineteenth century, but up to the present day. In 2011 Kate Middleton wore a dress with a Carrickmacross lace bodice, which featured designs emblematic of the four nations of England, Scotland, Ireland and Wales – respectively, the rose, the thistle, the shamrock and the daffodil. The dress was made at the Royal School of Art Needlework, in a manner that recalls Victorian duty and devotion. Working at Hampton Court Palace, the dressmakers replaced their needles every three hours and allegedly washed their hands every thirty minutes.[15]

At any rate, those who stepped in to defend the trade against degradation and degeneration during the latter half of the nineteenth century extended far outside of the royal ranks. For instance, Mrs Treadwin, an Exeter designer and entrepreneur, ran a lace shop whose designs won prizes at international exhibitions, notably, those of 1851 and 1862. Others used the space of international exhibitions to promote the craft at mid-century as well. And, increasingly, groups of well-meaning ladies looked to London's South Kensington Museum, where they sponsored a loan exhibition of antique laces intended to bring attention to the longstanding craft and its present day producers, in 1873. The show would provide the inspiration for travelling exhibitions in provincial towns including Nottingham, the cradle of mechanised industry, and Liverpool, a hub of transatlantic trade.[16] During the 1870s, the craft of lace and its promoters found an especially well situated advocate in Alan Summerly Cole, son of South Kensington Museum founder and Victorian reformer extraordinaire, Henry Cole. Working in the long shadow of his father, Cole carved out his own expertise, and his own calling, as the nation's foremost expert on lace. Not only did he seek to collect the finest specimens of handmade lace for the South Kensington Museum; he also travelled to the centres of the handmade trade, where he worked towards aesthetic and economic improvement alike, as he sought to upgrade the stock of patterns and to record the history of lace.[17]

As the century wore on, and as rural England faced the realities of depopulation, more systematic efforts to salvage the trade took root in the contexts of the craft revival movement. Working in London and in the countryside, 'public-spirited ladies' sought to forestall its 'degeneration'.[18] In the 1880s and 1890s, women such as Miss Dryden aimed to revive the craft of lace through a range of practices, forming associations, purchasing the handiwork of their poorer sisters and even selling these products to their friends. In these efforts, they relied upon London connections, whether to the worlds of fashion, retail, display or the press. For example, during the last decade of the century, as Victoria's reign drew to a close, the Home Arts and Industries Exhibitions, held in the Royal Albert Hall, became a regular event on the calendar of London exhibitions. Articles in such journals as the *Pall Mall Magazine* worked too to strengthen the trade, bringing in orders even from the Russian nobility.[19] While the primary agents of the lace revival were philanthropic women, even as august a figure as John Ruskin would take part in these efforts, bringing to the Lake District in 1883 an Italian pattern that would come, eventually, to be known as 'Ruskin Lace'.

It was in the context of these ebbs and flows that the lace books discussed by Elaine Freedgood appeared in print. Some were devoted expressly to chronicling the history of the trade, while others sought, in increasingly methodical manners, to disseminate patterns.[20] By far the most influential was the magisterial *History of Lace*, published originally in 1865 and written by Mrs Fanny Bury Palliser, who was called by one reviewer the 'Gibbon of the decline and fall of lace'.[21] Like the eighteenth-century historian of the *Decline and fall of the Roman Empire*, Mrs Bury Palliser would achieve acclaim for her labours in chronicling the trade. She was, in truth, just one of many writers to find inspiration for publication – and, arguably, an impetus to scholarship – in the annals of 'the most poetic of all textile tissues'.[22] Together, she and other women writers took up the task of gathering 'the loose threads of its history'.[23] It was a common conceit in their writings on lace, and on other crafts too, to begin with the wish that it could come to voice, and thereby tell the tale of its history and manufacture. 'If only lace could speak', effused many an author, 'how infinitely more interesting it would be to us.' The well-known designer and philanthropist Mrs Treadwin recognised lace's capacity as text as she declared, 'Old lace occupies in the minds of most refined people a position akin, if not equal to, old pictures, prints, and books. It speaks of the work and the life of past ages'.[24] In making such gestures, writers on lace invoked a common conceit of speaking things that pervaded nineteenth-century writings on craft, both domestic and foreign. As such, they would employ material objects as portals for meditations on particular productive geographies, labour practices and emotional economies.

Written by, about, or for women, the texts produced during the course of the revival envisioned a sisterhood in lace. Mythical, religious and historical, lace connoted the universal feminine.[25] It was 'prized by every woman'. Across nations, and across epochs, lace was 'interwoven with life's comedies and tragedies'.[26] Women were, literally and figuratively, bound by the craft. A fabric that punctuated the life cycle, lace reminded writers of the 'most interesting and important sacraments and solemnizations'.[27] It 'enveloped the infant at the baptismal font, veiled the bride at the altar, and enshrouded the dead in many countries'. It enjoyed singular status as the 'only ornament that is always suitable and becoming from infancy to old age'.[28] And lace was equally universal as a form of employment and occupation. It was 'a blessing to the old and the delight of the young'.[29] Lace provided funds for the elderly lady, restoration for the 'nervous delicate woman' and recreation for the crippled child or invalid.[30]

While they paid heed to lace's universalising capacities, its chroniclers also sought to uncover the origins of the craft. Though of relatively recent vintage, no consensus existed, with 'Spain, Italy, Belgium, France, and Germany' all making claims to be the birthplace.[31] It was even possible that lace came from the East. Ultimately, its beginnings seemed to be 'wrapped in mist'.[32] One chronicler attributed its start to an angel who had come down from heaven to dry the tears of a poor maiden who had no hopes of marrying. The angel provided the maiden with a lace pillow, and hence, with an ability to earn her own dowry.[33] Another fanciful narrative similarly located lace's origin with a lovesick Venetian girl, who imitated the token of coral given to her by a sailor by twining together small threads. More reliable, but still hovering, as one commentator noted, on the 'borderland between history and legend' was the story of Barbara Uttmann, a Nuremberg lady credited with introducing pillow lace into the mountain regions of Germany.[34] The wife of a wealthy miner, Uttmann had learnt the art of lace from a Brabant refugee. Eager to assist the handy girls of the Hartz Mountains on her arrival there, she introduced pillow lace into a workshop, so inspiring the spread of the trade throughout Germany. Her tombstone, and the many histories that commemorated her life, remembered her as the 'Benefactress of the Hartz Mountains' and the patroness of the lace trade.[35]

Uttmann was an appealing figure for women like Mrs Bury Palliser, who found worthy predecessors in the 'kindly disposed' ladies whose acts of 'benevolence' had enabled peasant women to make a living and so to supply the fashionable centres of Europe with ornament. Mary de Medici garnered credit for bringing the lace trade from Venice into France.[36] During the sixteenth century, Catherine of Aragon introduced lace to Bedfordshire, Buckinghamshire and Northamptonshire. Legend had it that Catherine bade her ladies in waiting to burn their own lace so that they could give work to poor women.[37] Queen Elizabeth, the sister of Emperor Charles V and Wife of Christian II, brought the trade to Denmark.[38] This sort of fertilisation continued throughout the nineteenth century, when fashionable ladies and royals obtained scraps of old lace as souvenirs as they travelled the European continent.[39] By the later nineteenth century, lace had become a transnational form of missionary charity, with English ladies teaching lace making in China, Japan, Ceylon, Brazil, Chile and, of course, India, to Christian converts.[40]

Ultimately, then, the history of lace provided one materialisation of the movement of ideas, goods and peoples throughout modern history. As one commentator noted, it was 'unceasingly tossed up and down in the gusts and storms of political passion and religious revolution'.[41] Many writers noted lace's imbrications with the history of religion, entwined as it was with the vicissitudes of Catholicism and Protestantism alike. On the continent, in Great Britain, and in Ireland too, convents had allowed the craft to flourish. Writers on lace habitually imagined nuns toiling from devotion, their craft a labour of love.[42] Their demise tended to threaten the livelihood of the craft.[43] Reversals for Protestantism too affected the progress of the trade.[44] Along with other crafts, lace making travelled out of Italy into Spain and Flanders.[45] It was from the Low Countries that lace subsequently made its way to Devonshire, when Protestants sought asylum on Albion's 'peaceful shores' in the sixteenth century.[46] Similarly, French émigrés – themselves influenced by the Italian trade – would buttress the Buckinghamshire trade in the eighteenth century.[47] Assessing these movements after the turn of the twentieth century, one critic explained that it was no mistake to consider English lace as fundamentally 'Italian in character'.[48] And it was these sorts of 'cosmopolitan' characteristics that would lead Alan Summerly Cole to ask, 'For after all what is nationality in art?'[49]

A long history of lace smuggling across borders only made this question all the more pressing. Beginning in the seventeenth century, puritanical sentiment and mercantilist policy had together informed edicts prohibiting the entry of the lace of Flanders, France, Spain and Italy into England. This stringency would wane in the eighteenth century, only to spike once again during the French Revolution and the Napoleonic era. The inability to procure suitable imitations in England gave rise to a ripe enterprise of smuggling. Inventive means of carrying contraband abounded. Hollowed-out loaves of bread, ships' buoys and Turks' turbans held smuggled lace, as did 'books, bottles, babies, false-bottomed boxes, and umbrellas'.[50] Ladies themselves got in on the act, as one celebrated instance of dinner party diplomacy so well indicated. Desirous of smuggling a Brussels veil into the country, the wife of a Member of Parliament notably enlisted the services of a bachelor gentleman, who had the treasure sewed into his waistcoat.[51] And in a most sensational incident, a bulk of Flanders lace replaced the body of a deceased clergyman crossing the channel to England.[52] In the face of these transgressions, the 'lynx eyed officers' of the Customs House acted harshly, burning and seizing foreign goods found in England's ports. They habitually searched carriages travelling through fashionable London, where they did not hesitate to cut mittens made of foreign black lace, presumably from Spain, directly off ladies' hands. And sailors paid for the crime with their lives. But, by the Victorian age, treasures of value filled the 'most obscure corners' of the nation, with Venice point gracing attic beds, Flanders guipure ornamenting cottage window curtains, and Alençon point dressing the most prosaic of dolls.[53] Such artefacts offered material traces of a particularly feminine history of movement. Indeed, 'like gold, silver, and precious stones', lace had travelled the world over.[54]

But as the century came to a close, and the Home Industries movement gained steam, it was to the national and local, rather than to the international and cosmopolitan valences of lace that attention turned. Such a focus resonated with a larger interest in folk cultures across Britain and Europe, motivated, variably, by the rise of popular nationalism, the trend of rural depopulation, and a growth in racial consciousness. Oftentimes, these preoccupations gave rise to an appreciation for rural handicraft as a material embodiment of a longstanding English race. Reformers who sought to protect the lace trade aimed to do nothing less than to preserve a disappearing way of life and with it, a vanishing tribe. The perorations of one aficionado are typical on this score. Waxing lyrical of the 'very small and dainty hands' of Northamptonshire's women, this writer remarked, 'they are certainly an artistic race', as an 'extreme fondness for flowers and appreciation of pretty scenery made evident'.[55] This turn to the ethnographic was embodied, too, in a fascination with the folk customs of the lacemakers, whether their popular songs, their 'Cattern Day' celebrations, or their collections of wooden bobbins, which offered an evocative antidote to the alienating machinery of the factory. Decorated by the workers themselves, bobbins often bore the names of potential lovers or deceased relatives. Routinely, these nostalgic pursuits led later Victorian and Edwardian commentators to turn their attention to elderly women – septuagenarians, octogenarians, and even nonagenarians – who were the only living conduits to the craft traditions of the past. It was, they argued, of the utmost importance to preserve the trade whose disappearance would mean 'irreparable loss' for these elderly women, as they strived to eke out a living and stave off boredom. In pursuit of this point, advocates waxed lyrical about the few remaining lacemakers who had made Victoria's wedding dress.[56] They also recalled the stories of other elderly women, including one whose mother had worked on a dress worn at the wedding of the Princess of Wales. Though the toil was demanding, the money earned for this special occasion allowed the family to buy 'a pony and a trap, the first they ever had'. Oftentimes, such nostalgic vignettes had the effect of obfuscating the gruelling conditions in the trade. But this was not always the case, for narratives of a bygone world could also recall past hardships, rendering sepia-toned sketches of 'old women' who still remembered the tears shed as young workers over long hours, punitive canings and 'burnt gooseberry pies'.[57]

Such manoeuvres were common in musings on continental lace, too. A superannuated nun of ninety represented the last trace of the lace trade in Venice.[58] At the turn of the century, old women languishing in hospices in Belgium told stories of the lace of bygone days. The revival of the lace trade overseas was also associated with old women. In the face of the fishermen's distress wrought by severe winters, a woman of seventy years of age, Cecelia Scarpariola, reinvigorated the trade in Burano lace, teaching it initially to eight girls. By 1897, over 400 workers supplemented the incomes of their families.[59] Mainstream efforts at design reform that sought to marry art and industry and so to uplift young male artisans may have operated on a broader scale. Yet, as these instances indicate, handicraft offered opportunities for revival, rescue and resuscitation among aging rural women, who often inhabited the fringes of society.

Hope for Ireland

Similar accounts abounded in Ireland, where narratives of loss and nostalgia would predominate in the nineteenth century. This commonality notwithstanding, Ireland boasted a distinct trajectory of design reform, and of lace rescue, too. Even more than in England, the lace trade was always linked to 'poverty, famine, and fashion'.[60] There, alongside crochet lace, four varieties of real lace – Carrickmacross, Limerick, Kenmare, and Youghal – took root. Efforts to kindle these trades were of relatively recent vintage, dating at the earliest to the eighteenth century, when the largess of philanthropic ladies invigorated the craft. Notably, Lady Arabella Denny taught children in a Dublin workhouse to make bone lace in the eighteenth century. Lace retained its associations with poverty and rescue into the nineteenth century. But in Ireland, the rise of the needle and crochet trades would become particularly associated with the great Famine of the 1840s. In fact, in the years between 1849 and 1859, the arts of the needle and crochet brought Irish women £15 million. Of this, £5 million would go to restoring their homeland, and nearly £10 million to enabling emigration – whether to England, the United States or the Antipodes.

Among those who responded to the exigencies of the famine were women worthies, including Miss Jane Clarke, a designer and entrepreneur, who worked through convents and art schools across Ireland to improve the lace trade and with it, the lot of the nation's poor.[61] Like their counterparts in England, these enterprising ladies sought opportunities to display the wares of the Emerald Isle to the fashionable world, most particularly in London, whether in Regent Street shops or in special exhibitions. Irish lace attracted considerable attention at the Great Exhibition of 1851, when journalists who surveyed it declared, just a few years after the potato blight, that there was, indeed, 'hope' for the Emerald Isle.[62] It showed equally well in 1862. However, by the early 1880s, decline in the short-lived trade was just as evident, if not more so, than in England. In an effort at revival, Irish Lace thus took centre stage at a dedicated show held in 1883 at the Mansion House in London.[63]

While efforts toward amelioration were largely of an amateur nature in Ireland, the lacemakers were fortunate to count as patrons the Irish Work Society and the Ladies' Industrial Society, which sought to find markets for Irish lace among London's elite. Moreover, at the behest of Irish Members of Parliament, Alan Summerly Cole too set to work to revive the Irish lace trade, making annual tours to the Isle, publishing investigative reports, and even giving lectures illuminated by magic lantern slides.[64] Though Cole found much to admire in the 'skill' of Ireland's poor women and children, he habitually bemoaned the 'stereotyped and poor design' that plagued the craft.[65] When he assessed the Irish handmade trade at the fin-de-siècle, Cole joined other contemporaries in offering a thoroughgoing critique of the relationship between national industry and cosmopolitan taste. Drawing upon a common refrain, he longed for guidance on the part of the fashionable world in London.[66] If a stylistic lag proved difficult in England, it was endemic in Ireland, where the rural locations of the convents, art schools and homes that manufactured lace made it especially difficult 'to keep up with the requirements of fashion'. The remoteness of the manufacture led to stylistic 'stagnation'. In Ireland, outdated 'shapes and ornaments' 'crystallized' as part of an unchanging design repertoire. Oftentimes, the tendency of consumers to seize on to national commonplaces posed the problem. When they bought Irish lace, for instance, many metropolitan consumers became prey to a 'sentimental desire for what is rather detrimentally called a "national production"'. Without reason, it seemed, an 'evanescent and uncertain fancy' for something 'quaint and original' overtook their better judgment. Otherwise savvy consumers thus succumbed to desires for primitive harps and clovers, dragging the national stock of designs down with them in the process. Indeed, such desires have had enduring staying power as the gown worn by Kate Middleton attests. As a salve, Cole and his comrades longed for 'a regulated supply of well-drawn and composed patterns' –

or perhaps, a storehouse of photographs – which was sure to elevate art and commerce alike. Only by forsaking national commonplaces, they held, would Ireland see the 'steady and continuous advances' that would bring lace and the lacemakers into a 'really prosperous state'.[67]

The lace revival in Ireland shared a good deal with its English counterpart. Both endeavours sought, ultimately, to reconcile philanthropic efforts with market demands; similarly, both aimed to deploy local talent in the service of cosmopolitan taste. And in England and in Ireland alike, humble lacemakers took centre stage in didactic middlebrow fiction that sought to exhort the virtues of humility and duty in the face of penury and want to a female reading public. In sentimental tales, English lacemakers exemplified Christian virtue. There was, for instance, the story of Mary Ann, a young lacemaker who personified diligent toil, familial duty and constant worship.[68] On her deathbed, she expressed a wish that young children would attend Sunday school. Similarly, the poor and lame lacemaker, Alice Mayfield, was an exemplar of humility, duty and charity to those more fortunate.[69]

The annals of sentimental fiction in Ireland offered up similar characters, but on the Emerald Isle these protagonists came to the fore in accounts of the Potato Famine. It was, according to several chroniclers, the potato blight that had occasioned the genesis of Irish point and Irish crochet. In the face of this great evil, ladies like Mrs Charles Meredith sought to teach the craft to their poorer countrywomen in schools and convents. By so doing, they hoped to awaken the dormant talents of the nation's women, who seemed, like their English and continental counterparts, to have a natural proclivity for craft. An erstwhile philanthropist, Mrs Meredith, would later make her name as an authoress, as she chronicled the crusade in crochet, which she called a 'war against misery in which every woman's hand in the land was engaged.' In an 1865 compilation of stories, she commemorated the 'delicate touch of the peeress' and the 'rough fingers of the peasant' Mrs Meredith's tales wove together observations on social economy, histories of the lace trade, and fictional character sketches. One told the story of the Fitzwalter sisters, two genteel ladies from Kildaire who founded a lace school in the darkest days of the famine in order to help the local peasantry and to save their own family's estate. Another recounted the tale of the orphaned Ellen Harrington, a gifted lacemaker who eventually found her way from the blighted Irish coast to the United States, where she married her beloved husband, Tom Neligan. Aspiring to the grand historical stage, Mrs Meredith noted that 'the story of this action [was] as touching and as beautiful as anything that the history of nations presents'.[70] Yet this greatness was poignant for its fleeting nature. Once the exigencies of the famine had faded, this patriotic marriage of female ingenuity and feminine duty would lamentably pass away.

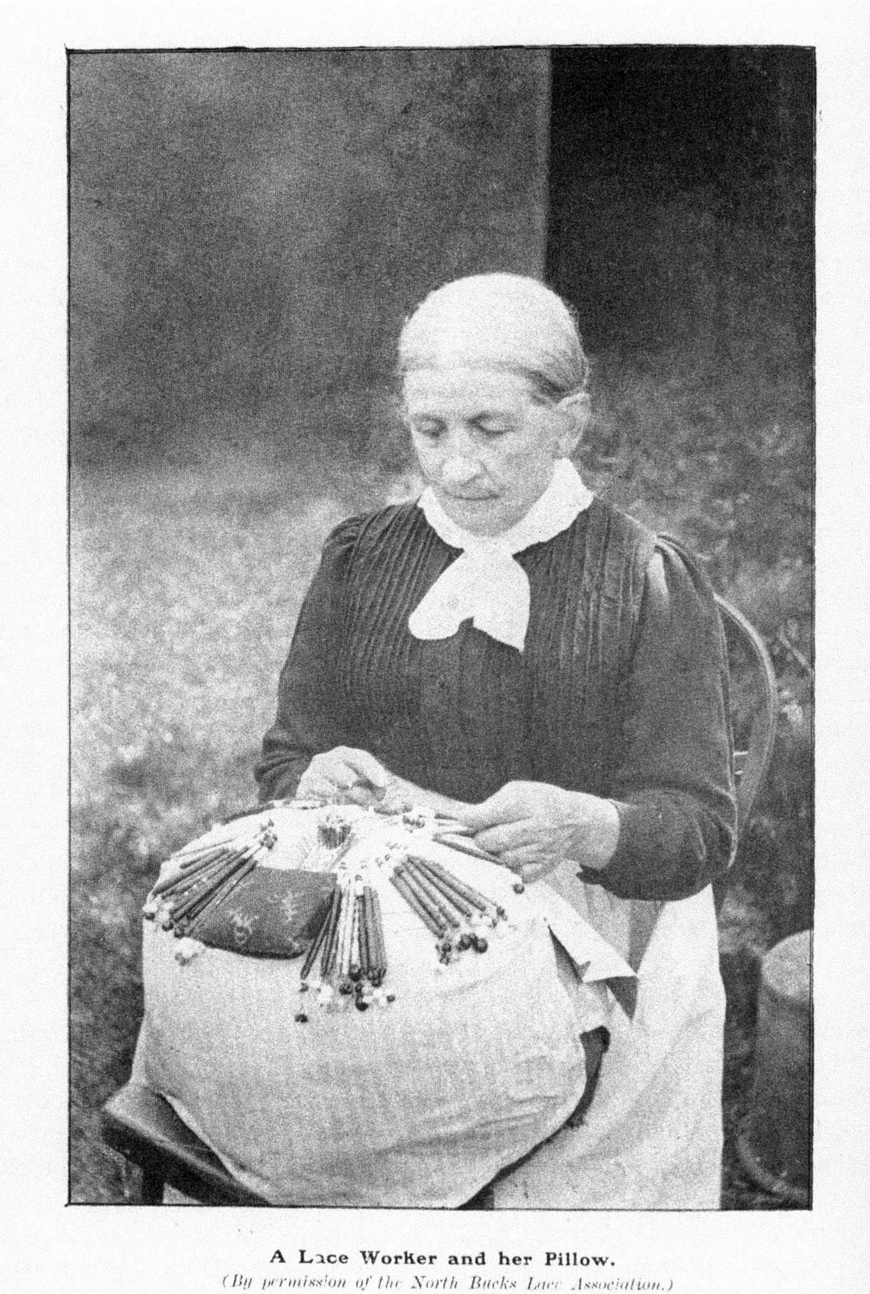

The work of craft in the age of photographic reproduction. Photograph of an elderly lacemaker at the Daily Mail exhibition of British and Irish lace, 1908. (© Victoria and Albert Museum, London.) **2.1**

Looking forward, looking backward

These English and Irish strands of craft production and aesthetic reform would come together in the early twentieth century, and most notably in the year 1908. As Deborah Ryan has noted, that year marked the 'pinnacle' of Edwardian public spectacle. The era, she and others have argued, was characterised by the arrival of 'distinctive forms of public display', and notably by a new 'mass culture' that coalesced in motion pictures, historical pageants and department stores.[71] If, as Ryan notes, Edwardian shows departed from later conceptions of alienated spectacle in their emphasis on lived and embodied experience, they also differed, in technological repertoire, tone and scale, from what had come before. By and large, the shows of 1908 gestured forward rather than backward. The most notable of these were the Franco-British Exhibition, the *Daily Mail* Ideal Home Exhibition, and the Summer Olympics, all held at the White City.

That said, there were also more modest exhibitions at the Royal Horticultural Hall, of tobacco, postage stamps and, of course, lace. Held in March of this new Exhibition year, which would vie for significance with 1851, the lace exhibition used past practices of display as it foregrounded the contemporary wares of English countrywomen and Irish peasant lasses. In line with the ethnographic turn that investigations into the craft had taken, it showcased the quaint bobbins used by lacemakers too. These displays were flanked by the contributions from lady amateurs, who were eager to get in on the show, as the steady stream of letters that they sent to the *Daily Mail* in the wake of the event's announcement attests.[72] So great was the excitement, in fact, that the newspaper declared the Exhibition as the harbinger of a 'new era of cottage industry', one that was certain to safeguard the trades of Devonshire, Buckinghamshire, Bedfordshire and Ireland in the face of continental competition – a particularly dire circumstance, to be sure, in the context of escalating diplomatic tensions.[73]

If nothing else, it was certainly a new era of travel, to exhibitions and elsewhere. Critics noted that new modes of travel were making rural crafts, and the countryside in general, ever more accessible. Taken together, the railway and that more recent innovation, the 'motor car', had 'reopened' isolated villages and hamlets 'to the outside world'.[74] Even as it embraced the mechanisms of modernity, however, the *Catalogue* and the Exhibition that it covered looked squarely to the past. Figure 2.1, a photograph of an elderly craftswoman provides a case in point. As the prevailing form of ethnographic documentation, it gestures squarely to the future. Yet it also recalls a bygone era as it features the figure of an elderly lacemaker, an exemplar of a dying breed, a fading age, and the mournful spectre of craft.

Perhaps we might consider the photograph a tribute to the end of an era. By the turn of the century, not only was the lacemaker a representative of a dying breed. The trappings of the Victorian world of aesthetic reform – the encyclopaedic shows, didactic museums and moralising lectures – had also become artefacts of a bygone age. John Ruskin and Henry Cole, the leading lights of aesthetic education and design reform, had exited the stage. The efforts of Cole and Ruskin have not wanted for scholarly attention. In large part, analyses of their contributions have sought to understand the relationship between art and industry in the nineteenth century. The concomitant efforts to rescue and revive handicrafts such as lace have received more limited attention. As I have shown in this essay, we find a different set of goals and vocabularies, of audiences and actors, and even of tones and emotions, when we look to the space of craft as exemplified in Victorian lace books, schools and exhibitions. Here, we see a distinctly female sphere of reform, concerned with the capacities of craft for rescue and revival, both artistic and economic. To express these goals, writers and reformers often looked to a real and mythological past. In these feminised regions of history, they found access to vivid stories and economic critiques. They also gained access to an affective register of handicraft that occupied the zones between art and industry. As they dwelt there, they conjured, through the registers of sentimentality and nostalgia, a realm on the fringes of society, one whose edges were fraying as it quietly passed away.

Notes

1 Ruskin, *The two paths*, pp. 134–40, esp. pp. 137, 139. Original emphasis.
2 *Ibid.*, pp. 138–40.
3 'Mrs Bury Palliser's history of lace', 166.
4 Freedgood, '"Fine fingers"'.
5 *Ibid.* See also Freedgood, *The ideas in things.* For one image of rusticity, see 'The Belgian lace-makers', 320–3.
6 Schaffer, *Novel craft.*
7 See, e.g., Kriegel, *Grand designs*; Cohen, *Household Gods.*
8 Spenceley, 'The lace associations'.
9 On the role of women in arts and crafts, and in design education more generally, see Anscombe, *A woman's touch*; Attfield and Kirkham (eds.) *A view from the interior*; Callen, *Women artists of the Arts and Crafts Movement*; Chalmers, *Women in the nineteenth-century art world*; Elliott and Helland, *Women artists and the decorative arts.*_
10 Baily, *Catalogue of the Daily Mail exhibition*, pp. 30–1; Palliser, *History of lace*, pp. 449–50.
11 Palliser, *History of lace*, pp. 409–11; Channer and Roberts, *Lace-making in the Midlands*.
12 Wilson, *Olney and the lace makers*, p. 62; Channer and Roberts, *Lace-making in the Midlands.*
13 Wardle, *Victorian lace*, pp. 133–6, esp. p. 136; Baily, *Catalogue of the Daily Mail exhibition*, pp. 30–1; Palliser, *History of lace*, pp. 409–11; 449–50; Cole, *Cantor lectures on the art of lace making*, p. 10.
14 Treadwin, *Antique point and Honiton lace.*
15 Alexander, H., 'Kate Middleton Wedding Dress is Sarah Burton for Alexander McQueen', *Telegraph*, 29 April 2011, http://fashion.telegraph.co.uk/article/

TMG8477689/Kate-Middleton-wedding-dress-is-Sarah-Burton-for-Alexander-McQueen.html (accessed 20 May 2014).
16 *Catalogue of the special loan exhibition of decorative art needlework*. See also *Catalogue of Lady Brassey's loan collection*.
17 Isemonger, 'Lace as a modern industry'.
18 Mincoff and Marriage, *Pillow lace*, p. 1.
19 Channer and Roberts, *Lace-making in the Midlands*, pp. 43; 57; 60.
20 Milroy, *Home lace-making*.
21 'Mrs Bury Palliser's history of lace', 166.
22 Lefébure, *Embroidery and lace*, p. vi.
23 Treadwin, *Antique point and Honiton lace*, p. 39.
24 Moody, *Devon pillow lace*, p. 3.
25 Lefébure, *Embroidery and lace*.
26 Goldenberg, *Lace: its origin and history*, p. iv; Cole, *Ancient needlepoint and pillow lace*.
27 Mrs Treadwin, *Antique point and Honiton lace*.
28 Palliser, *A descriptive catalogue*; Tebbs, *The art of bobbin lace*.
29 Channer and Roberts, *Lace-making in the Midlands*, p. 79.
30 Milroy, *Home lace making*, p. ix.
31 Goldenberg, *Lace: its origin and history*, p. 1.
32 Mincoff and Marriage, *Pillow lace*, pp. 9–10; 12.
33 Henderson, *The Madras educational exhibition*, p. 10.
34 Mincoff and Marriage, *Pillow lace*, pp. 9–10.
35 Palliser, *A descriptive catalogue*; Palliser, *History of lace*, p. 361.
36 'A day at the Nottingham lace manufactories', *Penny Magazine*, 117.
37 Palliser, *History of lace*, p. 376.
38 Palliser, *A descriptive catalogue*, p. 44.
39 Palliser, *History of lace*, p. 370.
40 Moody, *Devon pillow lace*, p. 94; Henderson, *The Madras educational exhibition*; Palliser, *History of lace*, p. 108.
41 'Mrs Bury Palliser's history of lace', 166.
42 Treadwin, *Antique point and Honiton lace*, p. 1.
43 Channer and Roberts, *Lace-making in the Midlands*, p. 19.
44 Moody, *Devon pillow lace*.
45 Cole, *Ancient needlepoint and pillow lace*, p. 5.
46 Palliser, *A descriptive catalogue*, pp. 57–8.
47 Palliser, *History of lace*, pp. 382; 399; 405.
48 Moody, *Devon pillow lace*, pp. 9; 13–14.
49 Cole, *Cantor lectures on the arts of tapestry-making and embroidery*, pp. 1–2.
50 Palliser, *History of lace*, p. 359.
51 'Mrs Bury Palliser's history of lace'.
52 Palliser, *History of lace*, pp. 362–3.
53 Palliser, *Notes on the history of lace*, p. 4.
54 *The Queen lace book*.
55 Channer and Roberts, *Lace-making in the Midlands*.
56 Moody, *Devon pillow lace*, chapter 5.
57 Channer and Roberts, *Lace-making in the Midlands*, p. 29.
58 Cole, *Report on Northampton, Bucks, and Beds lacemaking*.
59 Palliser, *A descriptive catalogue*, p. 61.
60 Helland, '"Caprices of fashion"', 195; see also Helland, *British and Irish home arts and industries*.
61 Palliser, *A descriptive catalogue*, p. 61.

62 'Ireland's contributions to the world's fair', *Cassell's Illustrated Exhibitor*, 142.
63 See Archive of Art and Design, Blythe House, London, BR/B14/068, Press Cuttings, April 1882–June 1883. On Irish reform in particular, see Linda Ballard, 'Irish lace: tradition or commodity?'
64 Cole, *Irish lace*.
65 Cole, *A Renascence of the Irish art of lace making*.
66 Cole, *Two lectures on the art of lace making*, p. 3.
67 Cole, *Report upon his visits to Irish lace-making and embroidery schools*, pp. 17–18. See also *Daily Mail Catalogue*, p. 14; Cole, *Two lectures on the art of lace making*, p. 19; Cole, *Renascence of the Irish art of lacemaking*, pp. ix; vi–vii.
68 Mary Ann C-, *A letter to a Bible class*.
69 Watson, *The happy lacemaker*.
70 Meredith, *The lacemakers*, pp. x–xi, 1, 52.
71 Ryan, 'Spectacle, the public, and the crowd', pp. 44–5.
72 'Lace Exhibition', *Daily Mail* (4 February 1908), p. 8; 'The Lace Exhibition' *Daily Mail* (3 February 1908), p. 6.
73 C. E., 'Cottage Industry's New Era', *Daily Mail* (31 January 1908), p. 3.
74 Moody, *Devon pillow lace*, p. 92.

Bibliography

Anscombe, I. *A woman's touch* (New York, 1984)

Archive of Art and Design, Blythe House, London, BR/B14/068, Press Cuttings, April 1882–June 1883

Attfield, J. and P. Kirkham (eds.) *A view from the interior: feminism, women, and design* (London, 1989)

Baily, T. J. H. *Catalogue of the Daily Mail exhibition of British and Irish lace* (London, 1908)

Ballard, L. 'Irish lace: tradition or commodity?', *Folk Life*, 31 (1992), 43–56

'The Belgian lace-makers', *Household Words*, 1 (1850), 320–3

C-, Mary Ann. *A letter to a Bible class, or a voice from the grave, of a humble Lacemaker* (London, 1849)

Callen, A. *Women artists of the Arts and Crafts Movement* (New York, 1979)

Catalogue of Lady Brassey's loan collection of ancient and modern lace (Hastings, 1882)

Catalogue of the special loan exhibition of decorative art needlework made before 1800, held in 1873 (London, 1874)

Chalmers, F. G. *Women in the nineteenth-century art world* (Westport, 1998)

Channer, C. C. and M. E. Roberts, *Lace-making in the Midlands: past and present* (London, 1900)

Cohen, D. *Household gods: the British and their possessions* (New Haven, 2006)

Cole, A. S. *Ancient needlepoint and pillow lace, with notes on the history of lacemaking and descriptions of thirty examples* (London, 1874)

Cole, A. S. *Cantor lectures on the art of lace making delivered before the Society of Arts* (London, 1881)

Cole, A. S. *Two lectures on the art of lace making* (Dublin, 1884)

Cole, A. S. *Cantor lectures on the arts of tapestry-making and embroidery* (London, 1886)

Cole, A. S. *A renascence of the Irish art of lace making* (London, 1888)

Cole, A. S. *Irish lace: report by Mr. Alan S Cole on his visit to lacemaking centres* (London, 1889)

Cole, A. S. *Report on Northampton, Bucks, and Beds lacemaking* (London, 1892)

Cole, A. S. *Report upon his visits to Irish lace-making and embroidery schools in 1897* (London, 1897)

'A day at the Nottingham lace manufactories', *Penny Magazine*, 12:705 (1843), 113–20
Earnshaw, P. *Victorian Lace* (London, 1968)
Elliott, B. and J. Helland, *Women artists and the decorative arts* (Burlington, 2002)
Freedgood, E. '"Fine fingers": Victorian handmade lace and utopian consumption', *Victorian Studies*, 45:4 (2003), 625–37
Freedgood, E. *The ideas in things: fugitive meaning and the Victorian novel* (Chicago, 2006)
Goldenberg, S. L. *Lace: its origin and history* (New York, 1904)
Helland, J. *British and Irish home arts and industries, 1880–1914: marketing craft, making fashion* (Dublin, 2007)
Helland, J. '"Caprices of fashion": handmade lace in Ireland, 1883–1907', *Textile History*, 39:2 (2008), 193–222
Henderson, A. E. *The Madras educational exhibition, 1907: a paper on woolwork, needlework, and lacework* (Madras, 1907)
'Ireland's contributions to the world's fair', *Cassell's Illustrated Exhibitor*, 9 (2 August 1851), 142
Isemonger, Miss. 'Lace as a modern industry', *Journal of the Royal Society of Arts*, 58 (29 May 1908), 702–17
Kriegel, L. *Grand designs: labor, empire and the museum in Victorian culture* (Durham, 2007)
Lefébure, E. *Embroidery and lace; their manufacture and history from the remotest antiquity to the present day*, trans. A. S. Cole (London, 1888)
Meredith, L. A. *The lacemakers: sketches of Irish character with some account of the effort to establish lacemaking in Ireland* (London, 1865)
Milroy, M. E. W. *Home lace-making* (London, 1906)
Mincoff, E. and M. S. Marriage, *Pillow lace: a practical handbook* (London, 1907)
Moody, A. P. *Devon pillow lace: its history and how to make it* (London, 1907)
'Mrs Bury Palliser's history of lace', *Quarterly Review*, 128:249 (1868), 166–88
Palliser, F. B. *A history of lace* (London 1869)
Palliser, F. B. *Notes on the history of lace* (London, 1872)
Palliser, F. B. *A descriptive catalogue of the lace in the South Kensington Museum* (London, 1873)
The Queen lace book: a historical and descriptive account of the hand-made antique laces of all countries (London, 1874)
Ruskin, J. *The two paths: being lectures on art, and its application to design and manufacture* (New York, 1889)
Ryan, D. 'Spectacle, the public, and the crowd: pageants and exhibitions in 1908', in M. O'Neill and M. Hatt (eds.) *The Edwardian sense: art, design, and performance in Britain, 1901–1910* (New Haven, 2010), pp. 43–72
Schaffer, T. *Novel craft: Victorian domestic handicraft and nineteenth-century fiction* (New York, 2011)
Spenceley, G. 'The lace associations: philanthropic movements to preserve the production of hand-made lace in late Victorian and Edwardian England', *Victorian Studies*, 78 (June 1973), 433–52
Tebbs, L. *The art of bobbin lace* (London, 1907)
Treadwin, C. E. *Antique point and Honiton lace* (London, 1873)
Wardle, P. *Victorian lace* (London, 1968)
Watson, K. *The happy lacemaker, and other tales* (Edinburgh, 1870)
Wilson, E. *Olney and the lace makers* (London, 1864)

3

Art, accuracy and the anaglyptograph: a debate about the mechanical translation of sculptures

Gabriel Williams

In 1836, the Parliamentary Select Committee on the British Museum sat to discuss whether the British government should patronise a new machine that replaced the hands and eyes of engravers. The anaglyptograph (to use the name of its British variant) translated the contours of low relief sculptures into lines on flat printing plates. It was a short-lived technology, and just one of many new processes for reproducing art developed in the second quarter of the nineteenth century. In its technical operation, the anaglyptograph was closely related to better-documented devices for creating three-dimensional copies of sculptures, such as pointing machines, powered carving lathes and sculpture reducing machines.[1] In its function of translating three-dimensional objects into two-dimensional images and linking sculptural and graphic media, however, it perhaps more closely prefigured photography, which swiftly followed it.

While presaging photography, anaglyptography also speaks directly to issues of mechanical reproduction that have exercised modern historians of both photography and graphic media. Examining photography in relation to pre-existing means of visual reproduction like engraving, various scholars have noted that photography enforced or emphasised a perceived contrast between the informative and aesthetic aspects of visual representation – between its own apparent 'transparency' and the less trustworthy artifice of hand-wrought illustrations.[2] In *Techniques of the observer* (1992), Jonathan Crary contends that the capacity of photographic media to reproduce artworks, and to be reproduced themselves, helped re-order practices of observation, verification and art appreciation in the later nineteenth century. Crary suggests that this effect paralleled the circulation of currency, in giving the visual appearance of things 'unprecedented mobility and exchangeability, abstracted from any founding site or referent'.[3] John Tagg has also forwarded the analogy between photography and money. The evidential or ideological 'truth' value of a photograph, Tagg suggests, may be contrasted with its aesthetic value, just as the monetary or exchange value of a coin in circulation and use contrasts with its function in a museum or numismatic collection.[4] In a crude sense, this is a distinction between an object's function as something looked *through* for the sake of other things, and as something looked *at* in its own right.

In the case of the anaglyptograph and its challenge to hand engraving, the connection between visual reproduction and currency is more than a scholarly analogy. On one hand, the technology sprang directly from and was imbricated with the production of real money. On the other, it was primarily used to reproduce historic coins and medals for numismatic publications, taking what were already established currencies for dating historic events or artistic styles, and offering more transparent, fungible paper substitutes for them. Period discussions of the anaglyptograph as a tool for antiquarian research, meanwhile, were implicated in wider debates about how the mechanical reproduction and circulation of art might benefit the trade in British manufactures. Bringing these contexts to bear on period discussions on anaglyptography, this chapter outlines ways in which nineteenth-century observers felt the 'currency' of mechanical reproduction to complement or conflict with art and artistic authorship – both that of the sculptors whose work the machine reproduced and the engravers it claimed to supersede. These discussions reveal the multiple investments that different kinds of artist retained in mechanical reproduction during this period, and also how, as a result, distinctions between informational and aesthetic currency – between looking *through* and looking *at* – could still be extremely confused and conflicted.

'Currencies of art'

The 'anaglyptograph' and rival machines worked by tracing the raised contours of a medal, coin or relief sculpture with a needle, and translating this needle's motion to that of an etching point, creating a two-dimensional array of extremely fine lines on a printing plate. Where the traced sculpture was flat, the etched lines would remain straight and parallel. When the tracer hit relieved contours, the etching point would swerve to one side in proportion to the magnitude of the relief, resulting in a set of curved, bunched lines that suggested convex forms with one side in shadow (see figure 3.1).

The development of such machines was bound up with currency production and those who produced currency. A machine to make prints of medallions was reportedly first developed by a Philadelphian die sinker in 1817.[5] Related machines were already used to rule perfectly parallel lines or waves onto printing plates or to engrave designs on watches.[6] In the following decade, 'medallic engraving' machines were introduced

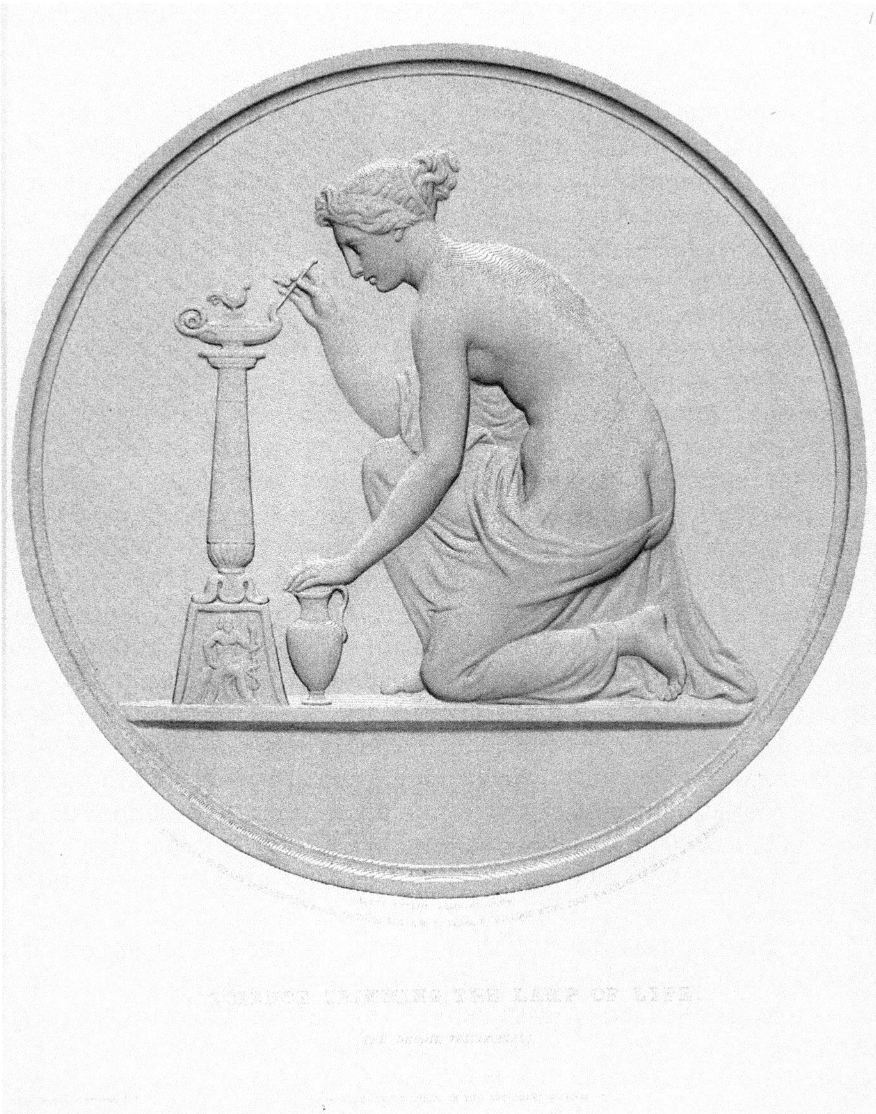

Alfred Robert Freebairn after William Wyon, 'Science trimming the lamp of life (the Brodie testimonial)', 1846. Engraving using Bate's patent anaglyptograph. (Reproduction by kind permission of the Syndics of Cambridge University Library.) 3.1

and developed in London for the purpose of engraving banknote designs.[7] Across the Atlantic, Joseph Saxton, a Pennsylvanian engineer who made machines for the US Mint, refined the technology.[8] In 1833 the chief engraver to the Bank of England had a new machine built to depict medals for the *Keepsake*, a gift-book published by the prominent illustrative engraver Charles Heath (1785–1848), who also did security engraving for banknotes.[9] This new, more 'accurate' machine was the 'anaglyptograph', patented by the optician and mathematical instruments maker John Bate.

Bate did little with his innovation until 1836, when he was provoked into competition with the French engineer Achille Collas. Collas had developed an equivalent machine in parallel with Bate since 1830, and in 1832 sold his patent to a company of artists called Lachevardiere & Co.[10] Collas exhibited machine engravings at the Salon in 1833 and the company were thereafter sponsored by the French state to publish *Trésor de numismatique et de glyptique*, a collection of mechanical engravings after historic medals, coins, intaglios, seals and relief sculptures, the first of which were marbles from the Parthenon and Bassae.[11] On 1 June 1836, the Fleet Street publisher Charles Tilt petitioned the British Parliament to sponsor a British version of *Trésor de numismatique* to be produced by Lachevardiere & Co. This would be a History of Great Britain told though 3,200 mechanical engravings of medals in the British Museum, printed over five years in eighty numbers, each number costing at 5s 6d (for around forty engravings spread over five plates) and sold by subscription to collectors and learned societies across Europe.[12] The work, Tilt claimed, was 'greatly wanted' by students of history and art, but was too ambitious to finance without the safeguard of government patronage.[13] In response, the ongoing 1836 Select Committee on the management of the British Museum called various expert witnesses and interested parties to assess the petition's merits, including Vincent Nolte of Lachevardiere & Co., Edward Hawkins (the Museum's keeper of antiquities), William Wyon (the medallist and chief engraver to the Royal Mint), Benedetto Pistrucci (the chief medallist to the Royal Mint and fierce rival of Wyon), the sculptors Francis Chantrey and John Henning and the artist-engineer William Brokedon.

The petition was timely. For one thing, it coincided with the first meetings to establish the Numismatic Society of London, and corresponded with pre-existing plans by Hawkins (who later became that society's president) to write a medallic history of Great Britain.[14] Moreover, Tilt made the petition just as the 1835–36 Select Committee on arts and manufactures was hearing evidence that framed the kind of publication he was proposing as a means to improve the artistic quality and competitiveness of British manufactures.[15] Prior to Tilt's petition, several influential members of Britain's art establishment had told this committee about how the Prussian government, for example, had elevated Prussia's manufactures and architecture through its liberal patronage and dissemination of copper engravings after historic ornament and sculpture.[16] William Wyon, meanwhile, gave the committee a similar argument for reproducing real coins and medals. He claimed that in ancient Greece and Rome, in England under the Commonwealth and Stuart governments, and in France under Bonaparte, coins and medals had furnished effective platforms for spreading taste and the general love of art.[17] The British state could reproduce this effect, Wyon argued, by commissioning more medals and commemorative coins, or decorating the copper coinage with the best modern or antique designs.[18] The demand for special coins, 'for purposes of curiosity or for purposes of circulation', would justify their expense and sustain their value.[19] The use of coins for trade, in turn, would circulate examples of art and stimulate 'a great demand for art among die engravers'.[20] The fortunes of the nation's art would thus be interwoven with those of its currency, and the spread of taste with the flow of wealth and manufactures.

In the same week that the British Museum Select Committee first sat to discuss Tilt's petition, the Select Committee on arts and manufactures heard from the engineers Edward Cowper and Benjamin Cheverton how printed reproductions and three-dimensional manufactures reciprocally promoted each other. Cowper, an inventor of steam printing machines, explained how publications like *Penny Magazine* had conveyed examples of old and new art to the doorsteps of manufacturers, workmen and the general population.[21] Manufacturers only had to re-apply such designs to existing articles to create new decorative wares and new markets. Growing markets for artistic manufactures had meanwhile fuelled the demand for more engravings to inform the customers of those markets. This function of engravings in sustaining their own circulation and that of other wares led Cowper and his examiner, William Ewart, to explicitly represent graphic reproduction as coinage: 'In fact, may not this diffusion of taste through the press be called the paper currency of art? – Yes, it is indeed the paper currency of art, and always represents sterling value.'[22]

Predictably, Cowper and Cheverton together emphasised the stimulus that this synergy between two- and three-dimensional reproductions had received from mechanisation. Cowper's own steam-powered printing machine had enabled cheap image circulation. Meanwhile, Cheverton's sculpture reducing machine, which he demonstrated to the committee with a miniature ivory version of Chantrey's bust of Robert Peel, also made art cheaper by copying sculptural designs in new scales and materials.[23] Engineers of such mechanisms had in turn been aided by what the committee dubbed 'the paper circulation of knowledge' in titles like *Penny Magazine* and *Mechanics' Magazine*. They also noticed that Pistrucci was currently developing a machine for replicating dies, which 'would be of great value to the national coinage'.[24]

In response to such testimonies, the Select Committee on arts and manufactures ultimately recommended that the state fund the two-dimensional and three-dimensional reproduction of sculpture, concluding that the superiority of Prussian and French design was largely owing to the greater 'extension of art throughout the mass of society abroad'.[25] The deliberations of this committee would have provided an advantageous backdrop for selling the medal engravings project to the parallel British

Museum Select Committee. In technical terms, Collas's engraving machine represented a bridge between the sculpture reproduction technologies of Cheverton and Pistucci and Cowper's printing machine. In theory, therefore, the machine might fully mechanise the transfer of a design from a medallist's die to the printed page, and promise another fruitful link between the kinds of three-dimensional and two-dimensional 'currencies of art' that Wyon and Cowper respectively advocated in coins and prints. This is more or less how those with a vested interest in the medal engravings project presented it to the British Museum Select Committee. Wyon extended his opinions about real medals and coins to their depictions, claiming that 'an extended circulation of engravings from medals' would similarly stimulate the medallists' art.[26] Tilt and Hawkins (the latter of whom expected to write the text for Tilt's publication) highlighted how the French, Danish and Austrian governments had opened up their national medal collections with engravings publications, principal among them *Trésor de numismatique*.[27] Wyon, Tilt and Hawkins meanwhile all claimed that the mechanical engravings would benefit not only numismatists and historians but also artists and art appreciators, and generate new markets for prints and sculpture.[28]

Accuracy and reproduction: machine versus hand

Witnesses to the British Museum Select Committee all agreed on the advantages of mechanising the process of engraving coins and medals. There were two main pre-existing methods of numismatic illustration – simple outline wood engravings and more luxurious copperplate engravings in line and stipple – and machine engravings combined the different benefits of both. Though machine engravings were inferior to the best copperplate engravings in generating aesthetic effects or capturing minute details,[29] they were said to cost a fraction of the price to produce.[30] Moreover, the actual engraving process was said to require little time or artistic skill, even if skilled labour was still needed to cast models for the machine to trace and to finish the plates.[31] Meanwhile, though they remained more expensive than simple 'outline' engravings, they made a far greater aesthetic appeal to artists and general public. They would therefore bridge markets for numismatic reference and visual pleasure, whereas the cheaper engravings, Tilt argued, 'would be bought only by the antiquary, or some few scientific men'.[32]

Besides its compromise between economics and aesthetics, the machine was said to possess an absolute and inherent advantage over all kinds of engraving by hand. This was its non-human predictability and dependability as a medium for comparing and evaluating the medals it depicted, either as historical artefacts or works of sculpture. As Hawkins said, 'one of the excellencies of the mechanical process is, that it does not give anything but what is upon the medal; it may not give a full and entire representation of all that is there, but the defect is one of deficiency, not of inaccuracy, or rather not a misrepresentation'.[33] Chantrey, meanwhile, declared that they had 'much more uniform fidelity, expression and likeness, than could be given by hand'.[34]

The replacement of engravers' handwork with a predictable machine was motivated by the idea of making prints more transparent to the realities of sculptures they depicted. Wyon and Brokedon, for example, admired the way the machine provided 'a more faithful and accurate representation as to the metallic appearance of the medal'.[35] In one respect, this particular feature could have been thought to capture a particular coalescence or sympathy between the media of engraving and medallic sculpture, both of which were based on carving metal. On the other hand, it represented a way of preserving the sculptor's artwork from the artwork of the hand engraver. The problem with hand engravers, Brokedon argued, was that the more skilful they were, the more they were tempted to re-create the human subject of the medal, substituting their own medium for the medallist's: 'they do not represent a metallic surface; a print is in fact only a conventional resemblance of a face in black and white, and line engravers have a conventional mode of touching by dots and crosses, so as to represent the texture of the flesh'.[36]

Two engravings by Alfred Robert Freebairn (who worked with John Bate and whose engravings the witnesses referred to in this context) illustrate Brokedon's point. Figure 3.2 is by hand, and 3.3 done using Bate's 'anaglyptograph', both after a cameo bust of Athena that was elsewhere engraved as the emblem of both the Athenaeum club and the *Art-Journal*. The shadows are cast from more or less the same angle in both cases, although a more full, 'fleshy', even flushed, appearance may be seen in figure 3.2's face, as the result of various artistic procedures off bounds to the machine: firstly, because variations in width between the machine's lines were tied to variations in the medal's physical relief, the machine was limited to a comparatively narrow and inflexible range of tone within each engraving. Secondly, it was more or less unable to alternate the orientation and solidity of its lines across the medal. Such alteration in the hand engraving enabled Freebairn both to distinguish Minerva's face from its ground (as if the engraving might just as easily represent a three-dimensional head in abstract space as the protuberance from a flat medallion), while using contrasts in modelling to suggest contrasts between differently textured substances such as skin, metal and hair. Particularly effective is the contrast between the uniform horizontal lines of the background and the diagonal, wavy lines across the cheek that undulate in both direction and darkness to give an organic swell to the face. It is possible Freebairn executed the uniform background lines with a ruling machine. If so, the contrast between the straight lines and human flesh becomes a

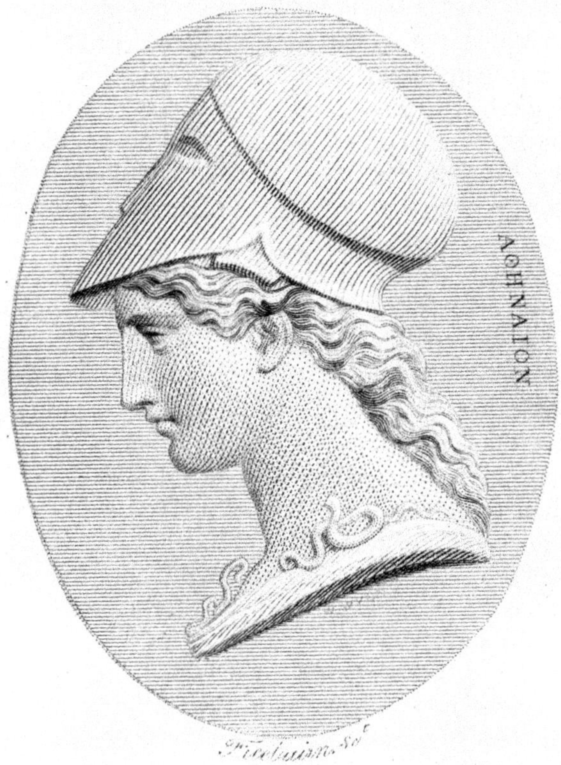

3.2 Alfred Robert Freebairn, Medal of Athena, detail of proof illustration to Hall (ed.), *The book of gems*, 1836–38(?). Engraving, 244 x 201 mm (detail). (©The Trustees of the British Museum. All rights reserved.)

meta-pictorial one, the delicacy of Athena's cheek registering that of the engraver's hand and burin, against the hardness of a machine's etching needle.

The preference for the machine's consistent, metallic representations over more individuated or 'fleshy' hand engravings did not, however, reflect a self-evident distinction between transparent accuracy and superimposed caprice, so much as a selective idea about what it meant to imitate sculptural art and what aspects of it needed imitating. The extent to which hand engravings could be said to approach or depart from the sculptural medium they depicted was contingent upon available comparisons. By comparison with Freebairn's hand engravings after paintings, for example, his many hand engravings after sculpture iterate the sculpted nature of the figures depicted by delimiting textural contrasts and including pedestals, fictive niches or the rims of medals.[37] In this context, the stippled modelling of the figures often evokes an ambiguous realm between stone

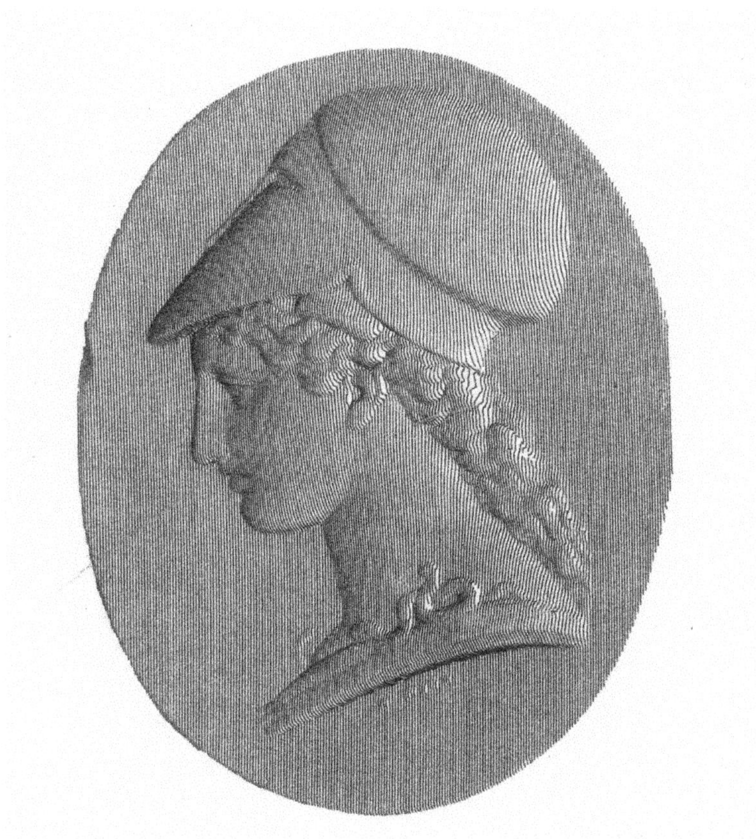

Alfred Robert Freebairn, Medal of Athena, detail of proof illustration to an unidentified publication, c.1833–46. Engraving using Bate's patent anaglyptograph, 220 x 290 mm (detail). (©The Trustees of the British Museum. All rights reserved.) 3.3

and skin. This was entirely appropriate to some influential theories about sculptural aesthetics. Charles Eastlake, for example, counselled that the sculptor's ultimate goal was to make the spectator forget the distinction between their marble or metal medium and living flesh, by modulating textural contrasts and forsaking the trivial simulation of cold, hard, inanimate surfaces.[38] The monotonous metallic quality of mechanical engravings more or less prohibited such ties between inked paper, sculpture and sculptural subject, despite their ability to trace shapes. Whether the 'conventions' (to use Brokedon's term) of the line engraver were more of an imposition than those of the machine depended on one's approach to the sculptures it traced: Despite Hawkins's claim it could not produce 'misrepresentations', Pistrucci hastened to tell the committee that the metallic veneer it standardly gave was quite inappropriate to his own cameos and gems, many of which involved luxurious colours and surface qualities.[39]

Accuracy and reproduction: machine versus machine

Contrasts between alternative, more or less faithful, appropriate or artistic modes of representing sculpture were not just found between hand and machine. As this section shows, they were redeployed in response to the sudden comparison between the productions of competing machines. The second sitting of the British Museum Select Committee was entirely absorbed by a challenge to the petition on behalf of John Bate, whose machine was said to eliminate systematic 'distortions' in engravings by the Collas machine. At points of high relief in the medal, the parallel lines in these engravings were said to bunch further than they should towards one side of the print, which compressed the linear dimensions across this half of each medal's face and caused the points of relief to warp that way. Wyon demonstrated this by comparing engravings by both machines after a single medal of Napoleon and Marie Louise. Copies of

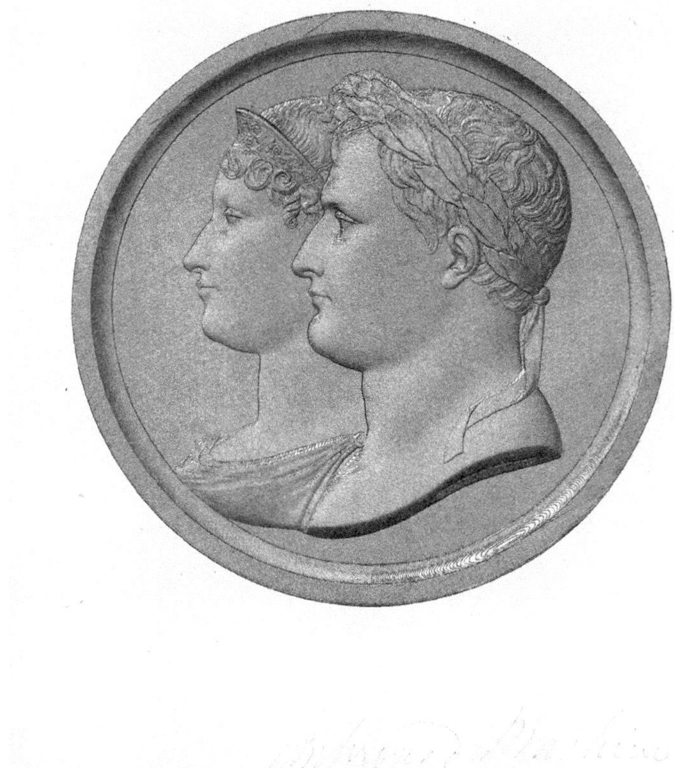

3.4 John Bate, Medal of Napoleon I and Marie Louise, c. 1833–36. Engraving using Bate's patent anaglyptograph, inscribed 'Improved Machine', 232 x 180 mm. (©The Trustees of the British Museum. All rights reserved.)

the prints used for this demonstration bear out his observations: whereas the medal's upstanding rim and adjacent hollow form concentric circles in the Bate machine engraving (see figure 3.4), in the Collas machine engraving (see figure 3.5) the rim contracts and the hollow expands on the left side. Horizontal proportions of the faces to the left are correspondingly shortened, as Wyon showed by using compasses to measure 'from the corner of the eye to the greatest projection of the frontal sinus' in Napoleon's head, and finding this shorter than in both Bate's engraving and the original medal.[40] 'For my own eye', Wyon said of a similar discrepancy in an engraving after his own John Soane medal, 'I do not require compasses, it is sufficiently obvious, but on measuring the great disproportion between the medal and the engraving, it becomes apparent.'[41] The sculptor Henning, who bore a grudge against Nolte and Collas for printing un-credited engravings after his reconstructions of the Parthenon frieze

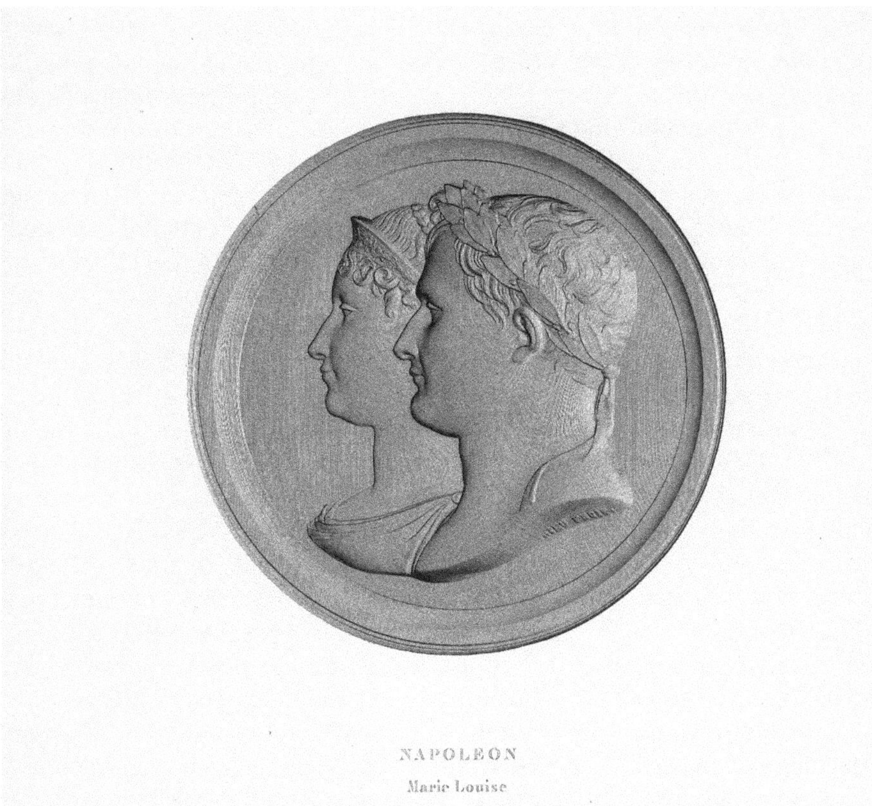

3.5 Rittner & Goupil, Medal of Napoleon I and Marie Louise, illustration to Delaroche *et al.*, *Trésor de numsimatique*, 1839. Engraving using Achille Collas's medal engraving machine, 355 x 255 mm. (©The Trustees of the British Museum. All rights reserved.)

in *Trésor de numismatique*, went further, testifying to the 'monstrosity of the distortion' Collas's engravings produced in sculpted faces.[42] John Bate underscored the point by publishing engravings after gems and cone shapes, which he claimed were executed using Collas's process, and which warped violently.[43]

The most influential evidence of the distortion, however, was a geometrical 'proof' supplied by Brokedon.[44] Brokedon's proof was an elaborate abstraction, fabricated without direct knowledge of Collas's machine, although the way it characterised the engravings' accuracy remains significant.[45] It did so in terms of orthographic projection, that is, the transcription of those two-dimensional proportions of a depicted object that stood parallel to an engraving's 'picture plane'.[46] According to Brokedon, Collas's machine traced cross sections of a medal's relief perpendicular to its flat face (and to the hypothetical picture plane), and depicted the relief by effectively just laying these sections flat across the picture plane. This necessarily warped the medal's orthographic dimensions in proportion to the perpendicular height of the relief. Bate's machine, however, traced oblique cross sections of the medal's relief at forty-five degrees to its face. These cross sections traced a displacement parallel to the medal's face that was always equal to their height perpendicular to that face, meaning that the latter component of the cross-section could be laid flat and still match its 'orthographic' components. The relief traced in Bate's lines was shallower, the lines less bulging and bunched, and the shadows less voluptuous, but they would catch a third dimension in the net of two, without warping the latter. Bate delightedly seized on Brokedon's 'proof' as an *a priori* rubber stamp of supremacy, asserting that the correctness of his machine and the distortions of Collas's were no more refutable than a problem in Euclid.[47]

The partisans of Collas's machine responded to the attacks on its accuracy by emphasising its greater artistic or aesthetic credentials. Nolte marshalled sympathetic witnesses such as Pistrucci for another hearing and continued the battle through the publications of Tilt. He accused Brokedon and Wyon of having spearheaded a 'hostile league' of British artists and thrusting Bate's device forward from obscurity at a moment's notice to stop a French company receiving the British Museum commission.[48] Wyon and Brokedon had already admitted that Lachevardiere & Co.'s less 'accurate' engravings surpassed Bate's in their 'brilliancy of impression', owing partly to skilled finishers and a committee of artists who decided on which direction the machine should engrave lines and throw shadows across each medal.[49] Nolte amplified these points, insisting that they had deliberately relinquished orthographic accuracy for dynamic relief and shadows, having also found that 'the hand of a skilful engraver was far more useful, and could be more intelligently applied than the operation of a diagonal tracer in the manner in which it was explained the machine of Mr. Bate was made to move'.[50] Their goal, Nolte argued, had been to realise so-called 'perspective' views of medals, as if they were held up to the light or looked at askance.

Nolte and his supporters did not simply defend 'artistry' against 'accuracy', however, but also questioned Brokedon's 'orthographic' standard of accuracy and asserted the alternative and higher truth-claims of artistic imitation in its stead. Pistrucci argued that the machines produced two incompatible modes of likeness – the French giving 'a correct idea of the work, but in a perspective view, or what I may call more appropriately fore-shortening ... in *chiaroscuro*, and with much effect'; the English one giving an image which was 'straight' but 'flat and hard, with little or no effect'.[51] As a translation of relief sculpture, Pistrucci argued, the so-called 'distortions' of the French machine had as much right to be called 'accurate' or 'correct' as the English. A friendly journalist in the *Athenaeum* seconded this idea of 'artistic' correctness, writing:

> the best representation of any subject, as a work of art, is the one which shall convey the most faithful and pleasing impression of its general effect; that, as the said representation is judged of by a pair of eyes, and not a pair of compasses, there are cases wherein the latter may *prove* a mathematical incorrectness, which the former will not acknowledge, and which, therefore, in no respect, impairs the merit of the copy.[52]

In a subsequent defence, Nolte equated these distinctions between 'faithful' and 'mathematical' copies, or 'eyes' and 'compasses', to further distinctions between initial impressions and prolonged studies, and between 'general effects' and particular relationships.[53] He noted how portraitists could transcribe proportions piecemeal, but thereby imperil the likeness of a final *ensemble* – a point made by Joshua Reynolds and reiterated in the engraver John Burnet's *An essay on the education of the eye* around the time Nolte penned this defence.[54] Nolte had thus taken familiar academic arguments that contrasted 'mechanical' copying with 'imitation' in the fine arts of easel painting and sculpture, and re-applied them to a process that was genuinely mechanical and explicitly reproductive. In response, Bate pilloried Nolte as a 'voluntary errorist', trying 'to prove that wrong is preferable to right'.[55]

In arguing for the existence or value of different forms of reproductive truth, the protagonists linked them to alternate perceptual capacities or forms of visual training based upon different trades. Chantrey and Wyon both cited their visual skills as artists to defend and criticise the Collas engravings respectively. Based on their pronouncements, however, their sculptural eyes were somewhat differently tuned: Chantrey said of the alleged 'distortion' in Collas's engravings, 'I should never have observed it; I look at medals as an artist, not as an antiquarian'.[56] Wyon, meanwhile, claimed that it was patently obvious enough to his naked eye (partly perhaps because he had sculpted many of the examples), even if he had to use compasses to demonstrate it to others.[57] Nolte, in turn, juxtaposed the pedantic technical analysis of the artists Wyon, Brokedon and Henning with more immediate, 'ocular' judgments from the sculptors Chantrey, Henry Weekes and Edward William Wyon (William Wyon's cousin and chief engraver of the Seals).[58] He also contrasted the 'geometric eye' of John Doubleday, a caster of medals at the British Museum who had also verified the 'distortions', with 'the eye of the public at large, and for collectors of medals', for whom their 'perspective views' were intended.[59] In doing so, Nolte rehearsed a set of conventional hierarchical distinctions between different artistic trades or practices: between sculptors 'proper' and reproductive casters or carvers, and between the more 'visual' act of conceiving or evaluating compositions and the labour of measuring or executing them. In tandem with the *Athenaeum*'s above-quoted contrast between pairs of eyes and compasses, he wrote:

> 'The slight, almost imperceptible deviation,' to use the words of Sir Francis Chantrey, cannot be perceived unless the original is forced under the eye of the spectator, to lend its aid to a mathematical demonstration, which answers to no purpose than that of satisfying a few punctilious medallists, who, in their zeal for geometric accuracy, entirely overlook the circumstance, that the eyes of the public are not like theirs, accustomed to the use of microscopic glasses and governed by compasses.[60]

Nolte continued by contrasting the medallists's eye for medals with those of the 'most eminent men in arts and sciences on the Continent' who subscribed to *Trésor de numismatique*, ironically deploying the idea of aesthetic 'effect' to undermine the professional judgment of artists.

The claims of aesthetic fidelity made on behalf of artists, machine operatives and engravers at Lachevardiere & Co. may have been a somewhat strained attempt at product differentiation, but they were not entirely rhetorical. Collas machine engravings in the British Museum evidence perhaps the closest approximation that was available, within the tight limitations of machine engraving, of the purposive use of line variation and graphic effects seen in hand engravings like Freebairn's Athena gem. As Brokedon had observed, the Collas machine engravings generally direct lines against the profiles of busts on medals, throwing these into shadow. This may have been done primarily to diminish the appearance of warping on facial features, by compressing them against the profile rather than stretching them out laterally or vertically, but in some examples it also resulted in a voluptuous accentuation of hair and hairpieces on the back of the head.[61] Meanwhile, it seems that line direction was more freely used in conjunction with the more varied compositions on the reverses of medals, with horizontal lines highlighting the tops of heads or evoking atmospheric perspective,[62] and vertical lines accentuating rows of soldiers or the fenestration of buildings, for example.[63] Sometimes the

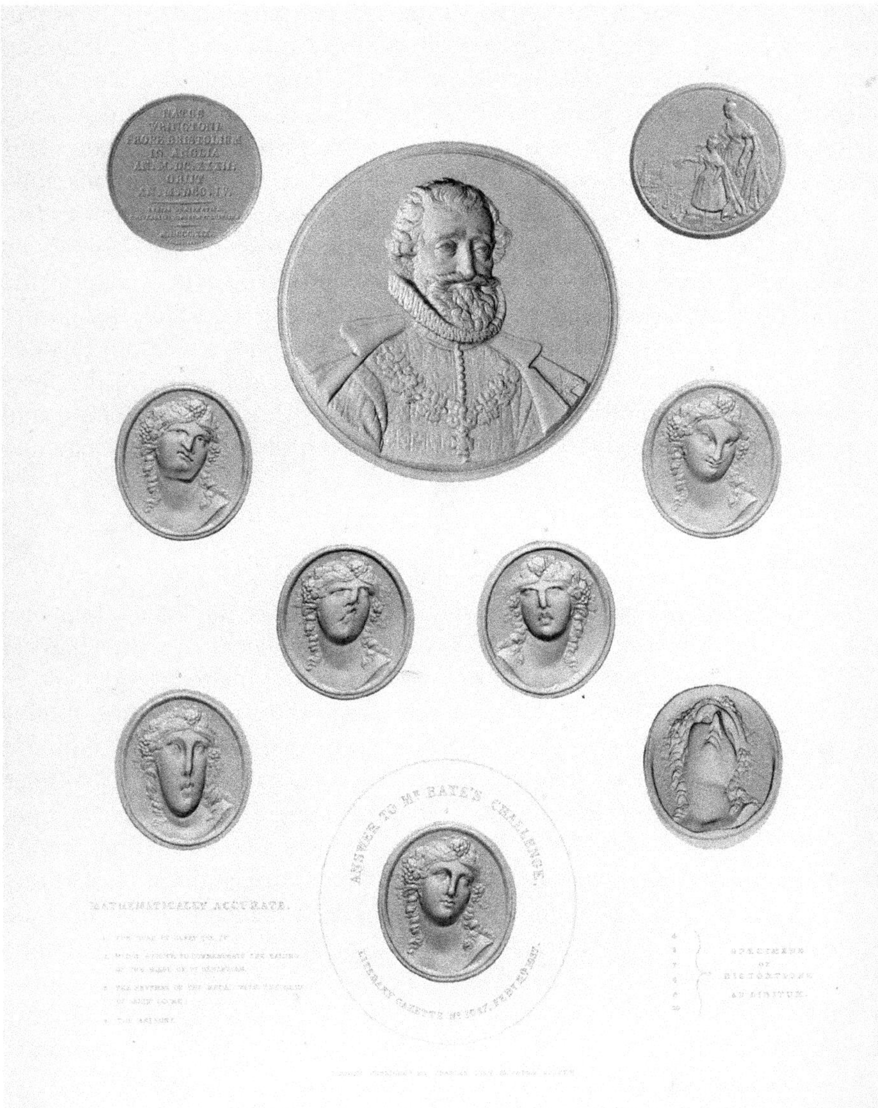

'Answer to Mr. Bate's Challenge', illustration to Nolte, 'Memorial of Facts' in *The authors of England*, 1838. Engraving using Achille Collas's medal engraving machine. (Reproduction by kind permission of the Syndics of Cambridge University Library.) 3.6

straight parallel lines are cross-hatched in selected areas to provide more tonal contrast within the medal.[64] Variation in the gauge of lines set for different medals also significantly affects the perception of materiality, with closely packed lines tending to give a comparatively 'fleshy' look, and widely spaced lines a more bright, metallic one. Such variations re-invest mechanical engravings with a degree of specificity to the medal and its subject, foreground the printmaker's craft as the gatekeeper of the sculptor's, and assert a fine but important distinction between accurate and uniform reproductions. Lachevardiere & Co.'s alternative combination of mechanics and artistry was most explicitly asserted in a print published to counter the accusations of distortion from Brokedon and Bate. This plate (see figure 3.6), Nolte declared, showed that the Collas machine could not only produce straight designs without a forty-five degree tracer, but could also 'embrace a variety of known and unknown combinations of which Mr. Bate has not even dreamt, nor probably ever will'.[65] At the bottom was a 'straight' engraving of the Ariadne gem that Bate had earlier engraved in a warped fashion to caricature the Collas machine. Besides this, however, was a less straight but more potent response, in the form of several other Ariadnes pulling faces at him, snorting, stretching and reversing to demonstrate the consummate subordination of the machine to its supervisors' will.

Conclusion

Amid the acrimonious contest between two machines, the British Museum put its medallic history of Britain on ice, and after a decade or so mechanical relief engraving or 'anaglytography' gradually disappeared. Nonetheless, the anaglyptograph was a crucial stepping-stone to more lasting modes of art reproduction. Lachevardiere & Co.'s efforts to produce two-dimensional reproductions of statuary laid the immediate ground for similar experiments with daguerreotypes.[66] This presaged an enduring syncopation of photographs and casts to which various scholars have attributed the globalisation, de-contextualisation and standardisation of encounters with art, as well as the foundations of modern art history.[67] Meanwhile, shortly after the anaglyptograph debate, Collas developed his more famous machine for reducing three-dimensional statues and went into business with the sculptor-founder Barbedienne, as he had done with Nolte.[68] Collas's reducing machine and its equivalents were central to a great expansion in the market for reproductive statuettes from the 1840s onwards.[69]

Owing to the heterogeneous involvement of artists in the reproduction of art, the nuanced debate about mechanics and translation that attached to the anaglyptograph were rehearsed in relation to other technologies of the period. Collas and Barbedienne, as Meredith Shedd has detailed, promoted their statuettes as especially faithful copies of canonical statues, but also argued that the acts of reduction, re-assembly and re-touching they required made them original artworks, in order to assert copyright over them.[70] Ironically, this echoed complaints which John Henning made about Lachevardiere & Co. pirating his cast reductions of the Parthenon frieze in *Trésor de numismatique*, on account of the artistic labour he had invested in reconstructing, rather than simply replicating, the work of

Phidias.[71] Such concerns, further fermented by photography, intersected with reproductive engravers' long march for artistic status in Britain against the public opinion, as the engraver John Burnet put it to the Select Committee on arts and manufactures, that they were only 'a set of ingenious mechanics'.[72] For Burnet and others, this question of artistry in reproduction was a consistent touchstone for comparing British and French attitudes or approaches towards art, mechanics and industry. During the Great Exhibition, for example, the illustrator and numismatist Henry Noel Humphreys, who produced various books on coins using hand engravings and lithographs, contrasted the way artistry was stifled and conventionalised by mechanical reproduction in Britain whilst in France it was propagated conscientiously:

> Our continental neighbours ... have rather developed artistic feeling, aided, certainly, by the subdivision of labour in production, but never losing sight of a good original design as the all-important thing, the more or less cheap reproduction of which was deemed of less consequence than the excellent manner in which the artistic idea was preserved in the process of multiplication. Even in the partial adoption of machinery they have not so much sought cheapness as a more excellent and unfailing mode of reproduction, in some cases, than hand labour.[73]

While Humphrey's point related to textile production as much as sculptural or 'fine art' reproductions, balancing the use of mechanics to reproduce and circulate art with the need for artistic reproduction was an ongoing concern of design reform debates in general from the Select Committee on arts and manufactures onward.

The anaglyptograph debate is a useful window on how mechanical imaging and dissemination was imagined to help or hinder art, prior to the invention of photography or its ultimate triumph over reproductive engraving. On one hand, the variety of media and art practices the anaglyptograph brought into dialogue – intaglio plate engraving, die engraving, relief sculpting and mechanical engineering being the principal ones – reminds us that the question of whether mechanisation and standardisation conflicted with pre-existing hand-art varied entirely according to the art form one was interested in. Mechanical reproduction *per se* did not just reproduce or replace art; at least for a time, it mediated between the arts of reproduction and arts that were reproduced. It has been often noted that photography and photomechanical printing ultimately promoted the history of sculpture and painting, precisely as they devalued the currency of prior artworks that reproduced paintings and sculptures. William Ivins, for example, narrated the progressive development and circulation of photographic imagery as an unstoppable solvent eating its way through the heterogeneous layers of handwork, arbitrary convention and artistic pretension which characterised nineteenth-century graphic media and impeded the flow of visual information.[74] Scholars since Ivins have contested this alignment of the hand engraving–photography divide with a distinction between artificial and transparent mediation,[75] and have also emphasised ways in which early photography did not undercut so much as promote hand engraving.[76] Certainly, photography presented a new and powerful visual contrast 'between the creative approximation and the mechanical counterfeit ... between hand and machine as reproductive instruments', as Trevor Fawcett puts it.[77] But this is not to say that the truth claims of hand-wrought artistic representation and mechanical record were always felt to be inexorably distinct or economically irreconcilable, at least to begin with.[78] As we have seen, anaglyptography may have trumped hand engraving for the British Museum commission (though the expense of traditional copperplate engravings ruled them out anyway), but even then, the exigencies of competition prompted the re-investment of aesthetics and artistic authorship in the use of machinery. Attempts to quantify and evaluate the respective British and French 'currencies' of sculptural reproduction became almost absurdly fine-toothed, but they did not for that reason all point in the same direction.

Notes

1 On such machinery, see: Bogart, 'In art the ends just don't always justify the means'; Droth, 'The ethics of making'; Fawcett, 'Plane surfaces and solid bodies'; Shedd, 'A mania for statuettes'; Sobieszek, 'Sculpture as the sum of its profiles'; Taylor, 'Sculpture, science and society'.

2 See Ivins, *Prints and visual communication*, pp. 94–134. See also Crary, *Techniques of the observer*, pp. 20–2; Fawcett, 'Graphic versus photographic'.

3 Crary, *Techniques of the observer*, p. 14.

4 Tagg, 'The currency of the photograph', 120.

5 Spencer's medal engraving machine (article untitled), *Mechanics' Magazine, and Journal of the Mechanics' Institute*, 206–7; 'Engraving in relief', 204–5; 'Medallic engraving', 706–7.

6 *Ibid.*, 706; Wakeman, *Victorian book illustration*, pp. 28–32.

7 *Mechanics' Magazine, and Journal of the Mechanics' Institute*, 206–7.

8 'Medallic engraving', *Athenaeum*, 706.

9 *Ibid.*, *Report from the Select Committee on British Museum*, p. 483; Heath, 'Heath family'.

10 *Ibid.*

11 Delaroche *et al*, *Trésor de numismatique*.

12 *Report from the Select Committee on British Museum*, pp. 463–4.

13 *Ibid.*, pp. 464–7.

14 Blackburn, 'Edward Hawkins'; Royal Numismatic Society, 'History of the society, part 1'.

15 See Ashwin (ed.) *Art education*, pp. 8–25; Kriegel, *Grand designs*, pp. 19–51.

16 *Report from the Select Committee on arts and their connexion with manufactures*, part 1, p. 9 and part 2, pp. 31–5. On the publications in question, see Irwin, 'Neo-classical design', 296.

17 *Report from the Select Committee on arts and their connexion with manufactures*, part 1, pp. 134–8. On Napoleon I's patronage of medals, see M. Jones, *The art of the medal* (London: 1979), pp. 100–5.

18 *Report from the Select Committee on arts and their connexion with manufactures*, part 1, pp. 134–8.
19 *Ibid.*
20 *Ibid.*
21 *Report from the Select Committee on arts and their connexion with manufactures*, part 2, pp. 49–54.
22 *Ibid.*, p. 50.
23 *Ibid.*, p. 55.
24 *Ibid.*, p. 55.
25 *Ibid.*, p. iv.
26 *Ibid.*, p. 485.
27 *Ibid.*, pp. 464–73.
28 *Ibid.*, pp. 468, 470 and 485 respectively.
29 *Ibid.*, pp. 477–83.
30 *Ibid.*, pp. 464–70.
31 *Ibid.*
32 *Ibid.*, p. 465.
33 *Ibid.*, p. 470.
34 *Ibid.*, p. 469.
35 *Ibid.*, pp. 483, 488.
36 *Ibid.*, p. 488.
37 See, for example, Freebairn's engravings for Hall (ed.) *The book of gems*. For comparable engravings, see Hervey, *Illustrations of modern sculpture* and Hall, *The gallery of modern sculpture*.
38 Eastlake, 'The same subject', pp. 31–44. These principles persisted as the official rationale for decisions by the sculpture jury at the 1851 Great Exhibition: Waagen, 'Class XXX. Supplementary report', p. 692.
39 *Report from the Select Committee on British Museum*, p. 498.
40 *Ibid.*, p. 485.
41 *Ibid.*, p. 484.
42 *Ibid.*, p. 493.
43 See 'Coin illustrations', and 'Fine arts: medallic engraving', 93–4.
44 *Report from the Select Committee on British Museum*, pp. 485–90. Brokedon's proof was reprinted in 'Engraving medals by machinery', 336–9 and 'Fine arts: medallic engraving', 90–6.
45 The complicated workings of a similar machine by Asa Spencer are illustrated in Spencer's medal engraving machine (article untitled), *Mechanics' Magazine, and Journal of the Mechanics' Institute*, 206–7.
46 On the contemporary significance of orthographic projection to machine-building, machine operation and visual education, see Denis, 'An industrial vision' and Purbrick, 'Machines and the mechanism of representation', pp. 97–118, and Frances Robertson's chapter 7 in this volume.
47 'Fine arts: medallic engraving', 90.
48 Nolte, 'Memorial of facts', pp. 4–6.
49 *Report from the Select Committee on British Museum*, pp. 485. 488–9.
50 *Ibid.*, p. 495.
51 *Ibid.*, pp. 497–8.
52 Medallic engraving', *Athenaeum*, 706.
53 Nolte, 'Memorial of facts', p. 9.
54 Burnet, *An essay on the education of the eye*, p. 18. Reynolds, 'Discourse fourteen', *Discourses*, pp. 221, 227–8.
55 'Fine arts: medallic engraving', 89–90.

56 *Report from the Select Committee on British Museum*, pp. 468–9.
57 *Ibid.*, p. 484.
58 Nolte, 'Memorial of facts, pp. 5–9.
59 *Ibid.*, p. 6; *Report from the Select Committee on British Museum*, p. 495.
60 Nolte, 'Memorial of facts', p. 9.
61 See the engraving of a medallion of George I: British Museum number 1870, 0514.2255.
62 See the engraving after the obverse of a medal of Catherine the Great: British Museum number 1870,0514.2270.
63 See the engraving after a medal of Elizaveta Petrovna: British Museum number 1870,0514.2271.
64 See the engraving after a medal of Christ by Dannecker: British Museum number 1870,0514.2291.
65 Nolte, 'Memorial of facts', p. 9.
66 Fehlmann, 'Under the light of Helios', 165; Fawcett, 'Plane surfaces and solid bodies', p. 63.
67 Fehlmann, 'Under the light of Helios', 161–70; Fawcett, 'Plane surfaces and solid bodies', pp. 59–81.
68 Shedd, 'A mania for statuettes', 38.
69 See Caso, 'Serial Sculpture', 4–10.
70 Shedd, 'A mania for statuettes', 41–4.
71 'Engraving medals by machinery', 340–2.
72 *Report from the Select Committee on arts and their connexion with manufactures*, part 2, p. 79; p. ix.
73 Humphreys, *Ten centuries of art*, pp. 111–12.
74 Ivins, *Prints and visual communication*, pp. 94–108, 113–34. See also Crary, *Techniques of the observer*, pp. 20–2.
75 Haskins, *The* Art-Journal *and fine art publishing*, pp. 18, 191–3; Codell, 'The aura of mechanical reproduction', 6–7.
76 Fawcett, 'Graphic versus photographic', 185–95; G. Beegan, 'The mechanization of the image'.
77 Fawcett, 'Graphic versus photographic', 192; Codell, 'The aura of mechanical reproduction', 6–9.
78 See Tom Gretton's chapter 8 in this volume.

Bibliography

Ashwin, C. (ed.) *Art education: documents and policies 1768–1975* (London, 1975)

Beegan, G. 'The mechanization of the image: facsimile, photography, and fragmentation in nineteenth-century wood engraving', *Journal of Design History*, 8:4 (1995), 257–74

Blackburn, M. A. S. 'Edward Hawkins', www.oxforddnb.com, accessed 11 February 2014

Bogart, M. 'In art the ends just don't always justify the means', *Smithsonian*, 10:3 (June 1979), 104–10

Burnet, J. *An essay on the education of the eye, with reference to painting* (London, 1837)

Caso, Jacques de. 'Serial sculpture in nineteenth-century France', in Jeanne L. Wasserman (ed.) *Metamorphoses in nineteenth-century sculpture* (Cambridge, MA, 1975), pp. 1–13

Codell, J. 'The aura of mechanical reproduction: Victorian art and the press', *Victorian Periodicals Review*, 24:1 (Spring 1991), 4–10

'Coin illustrations', *Literary Gazette: A Weekly Journal of Literature, Science, and the Fine Arts*, 1042 (7 January 1837)

Crary, J. *Techniques of the observer: on vision and modernity in the nineteenth century* (Cambridge, MA and London, 1992)

Delaroche, P. H. Dupont and C. Lenormant (eds.) *Trésor de numismatique et de glyptique* (Paris, 1834)

Denis, R. C. 'An industrial vision: technical drawing in mid-Victorian Britain', in L. Purbrick (ed.) *The Great Exhibition of 1851: new interdisciplinary essays* (Manchester, 2001), pp. 53–78

Droth, M. 'The ethics of making: craft and English sculptural aesthetics c. 1851–1900', *Journal of Design History*, 17 (2004), 221–35

Eastlake, C. L. 'The same subject considered with reference to the nature and various styles of the formative arts; by the secretary', *Third report of the commissioners on the fine arts* (London, 1844)

'Engraving in relief', *Mechanics' Magazine, and Journal of the Mechanics' Institute*. 5:4 (April 1835), 204–5

'Engraving medals by machinery', *Mechanics' Magazine, Museum, Register, Journal, and Gazette*, 26:704 (4 February 1837), 332–42

Fawcett, T. 'Graphic versus photographic in nineteenth-century reproduction', *Art History*, 9:2 (1986) 184–212

Fawcett, T. Plane surfaces and solid bodies: reproducing three-dimensional art in the nineteenth century', in H. Roberts (ed.) *Art history through the camera's lens* (London, 1995), pp. 59–85

Fehlmann, M. 'Under the light of Helios: early photography and the Parthenon sculptures', *Sculpture Journal*, 15:2 (2006) 161–72

'Fine arts: medallic engraving', *Literary Gazette: A Weekly Journal of Literature, Science, and the Fine Arts*, 1047 (11 February, 1837), 89–95

Haskins, K. *The* Art-Journal *and fine art publishing in Victorian England, 1850–1880* (Farnham, Surrey, 2012)

Heath, J. 'Heath family', www.oxforddnb.com, accessed 11 February 2014

Humphreys, H. N. *Ten centuries of art: its progress in Europe from the IXth to the XIXth century* (London, 1852)

Irwin, D. 'Neo-classical design: industry plunders antiquity', *Apollo*, 97 (1972), 288–97

Ivins, W. M. *Prints and visual communication* (Cambridge, MA and London, 1969)

Jones, M. *The art of the medal* (London, 1979)

Hall, S. C. (ed.) *The book of gems* (3 volumes, London, 1848–53)

Hall, S. C. *The gallery of modern sculpture* (London, 1854)

Hervey, T. K. *Illustrations of modern sculpture: a series of engravings, with descriptive prose and illustrative poetry* (London, 1832)

Kriegel, L. *Grand designs: labor, empire, and the museum in Victorian culture* (London, 2007)

'Medallic engraving', *Athenaeum*, 466 (1 October 1836), 706–7

Nolte, V. 'Memorial of facts connected with the history of medallic engraving, and the process of M. Collas', in H. F. Chorley, *The authors of England. A series of medallion portraits of modern literary characters, engraved from the works of British artists, by Achille Collas, with illustrative notices by Henry F. Chorley* (London, 1838), appendix pp. 1–12

Purbrick, L. 'Machines and the mechanism of representation: the display of design in mid-nineteenth-century Britain' (PhD dissertation, University of Sussex, 1994)

Report from the Select Committee on British Museum, House of Commons command paper 440 (1836)

Report from the Select Committee on arts and their connexion with manufactures, House of Commons command paper 568 (1836)

Reynolds, J. *Discourses on Art* (New York, 1961)

Royal Numismatic Society. 'History of the society, part 1: 1836–1874', http://numismatics.org.uk/about-the-society/history-of-the-society/part-1/, accessed 10 October 2014

Shedd, M. 'A mania for statuettes: Achille Collas and other pioneers in the mechanical reproduction of sculpture', *Gazette des Beaux-Arts*, 120 (1992), 36–48

Sobieszek, R. A. 'Sculpture as the sum of its profiles: François Willème and photosculpture in France, 1859–1868', *Art Bulletin*, 62:4 (1980), 617–30

Spencer's medal engraving machine (article untitled), *Mechanics' Magazine, and Journal of the Mechanics' Institute* 1:4 (April 1833), 206–7

Tagg, J. 'The currency of the photograph', in V. Burgin (ed.) *Thinking photography* (London, 1982)

Taylor, S. 'Sculpture, science and society: the "inventive Yankee stonecutter" and the growth of mechanization in the fine arts statuary of nineteenth-century America' (MA dissertation, University of Delaware, 1994)

Waagen, G. 'Class XXX. Supplementary report', in *Exhibition of the works of industry of all nations, 1851: Reports by the juries on the subjects in the thirty classes into which the exhibition was divided* (London, 1852)

Wakeman, G. *Victorian book illustration: the technical revolution* (Newton Abbot, 1973)

4

'Why are the painted windows in the industrial department?' The classification of stained glass at the London and Paris International Exhibitions, 1851–1900

Jasmine Allen

In the second half of the nineteenth century, stained glass was simultaneously perceived as an applied art, art-manufacture, craft, decorative art, industrial art, manufactured product and commodity. This chapter considers how these perceptions informed, and were shaped by, the official classification and critical commentaries of stained glass at the International Exhibitions, or *Expositions Universelles*, held in London and Paris between 1851 and 1900. At these events stained glass panels and windows were exhibited *en masse* to an international public. The exhibitions also provided opportunities for artists, architects, critics and the public to discuss the status of stained glass and its role in nineteenth-century society.

This chapter demonstrates how exhibition classification schemes categorised stained glass as a manufacture rather than a fine art, revealing contemporary attitudes towards the medium that have had a lasting effect on our categorisation and interpretation of stained glass today. It shows how the iconography of some stained glass exhibits and their displays contradicted, refuted and exposed inconsistencies in the classification schemes. Finally, it suggests that the division of labour within nineteenth-century stained glass studios may have contributed to a classification problem.

Stained glass taxonomies, 1851–1900

Exhibition classification systems attempted to organise a vast collection of exhibits into comprehensible sections. The schemes reflect an era preoccupied with taxonomies and ordering the world and its contents: naturally, scientifically, philosophically and commercially. Almost all exhibition classification schemes were derivatives of the hierarchical system used at the Great Exhibition of 1851 in London, which divided exhibits into thirty

Table 4.1 Classifications for stained glass at selected International Exhibitions, 1851–1900

Exhibition	*Department*	*Group*	*Class*	*Sub-class*	*Jury Award Class*
1851 London Great Exhibition of the Works of Industry of All Nations	Manufactures		XXIV Glass.	A. Window Glass. B. Painted and Ornamented Window Glass.	XXX Fine Arts.
1855 Paris Exposition Universelle	Manufactures		XXVIII Industries de la céramique et de la verrerie.	A: Verre à vitres et à glaces. B. Objets de céramique et de verrière ayant spécialement une valeur artistique.	
1862 London International Exhibition	Manufactures		XXXIV Glass, for decorative, and household purposes.	A. Stained Glass and Glass Used in Buildings and Decoration. B. Glass for Household Use and Fancy Purposes.	
1867 Paris Exposition Universelle	Manufactures	III Meubles et autres objets destines à l'habitation.	XVI Cristaux, verrière du luxe et vitraux.		
1873 Vienna Weltausstellung 1873 Wien	Fine Arts	Group XXIII Art Applied to Religion.	Decoration of Churches (wall decoration, stained glass, glass painting, &c.).		
1876 Philadelphia Centennial Exhibition	Dept. IV Fine Arts	Classes 450–459: Decoration with Ceramic and Vitreous Materials, Mosaics and Inlaid Work.	Class 453 Stained Glass.		Group XXVII Plastic and Graphic Art.
1878 Paris Exposition Universelle	Manufactures	III Mobilier et accessoires	Class XIX Cristaux, verrerie et vitraux.	VIII Vitraux peints.	
1889 Paris Exposition Universelle	Manufactures	Group III Mobilier et accessoires	Class XIX Cristaux, verrerie et vitraux.		
1900 Paris Exposition Universelle	Manufactures	Group XII Décoration et mobilier des edifices publics et des habitations.	Class LXVII Vitraux.		

Table compiled by the author.

classes within four categories demonstrating the progressive stages of the manufacturing process: raw materials, machinery, manufactures and the fine arts.

The systematic and scientific classification of objects served the purpose of constructing and disseminating knowledge. In *London Labour and the London Poor* (published serially in 1840s and as three volumes in 1851), journalist and social reformer Henry Mayhew declared, 'of all scientific processes, the classification of the various phenomena ... is perhaps the most important; indeed, ... without distinguishing between one object and another, there can be no knowledge, nor, indeed, any perception'.[1] After the Great Exhibition of 1851, Cambridge philosopher William Whewell advocated a universal classification scheme and standardised units of measurement that created a 'settled and common' language amongst the manufacturer, man of science, artisan and merchant.[2] This was important in raising the standards of national production to compete in a global marketplace, reminding us of the economic objectives of the exhibitions.

At subsequent exhibitions, classification schemes gradually became more complex, with the addition of new sections and sub-sections to reflect novel technologies and shifts in scientific or philosophical perception, especially concerning the autonomy of individual products and groups of people.[3] By 1900 the comprehensive classification system at the Paris *Exposition Universelle* consisted of eighteen subject groups subdivided into a further 121 classes and ranked by their importance to mankind, from education and fine arts to colonisation and military objects. This was a remarkable change from the industrial classification system of 1851, reflecting developments in the valuation and appreciation of art, as well as the political agendas of nation states and imperial rulers.

Yet the endless revisions and additions made to classification schemes between 1851 and 1900 also highlighted the philosophical problems of taxonomy; as cultural and literary scholar Isobel Armstrong has articulated in *Victorian Glassworlds* (2008), the 'anarchic, exponential multiplication of classification actually defeats ordering principles'.[4] In spite of the fact that International Exhibitions aimed to unite art and industry, classification schemes continually separated manufactured industrial products and the fine arts.

Stained glass at the International Exhibitions was subject to three distinct levels of classification: firstly, as a fine art or manufacture; secondly, according to its material structure (glass) and production techniques (kiln-fired); and, thirdly, according to its practical application (decorative, domestic, ecclesiastical). At almost all of the Exhibitions held in London and Paris between 1851 and 1900, stained glass was classed as a manufacture rather than a fine art (see table 4.1). Consequently, the stained glass exhibits were critically discussed in articles on glass materials and industries rather than fine art reviews, and a browse through the official exhibition catalogues finds stained and painted glass windows amongst an extensive collection of ceramic and vitreous products in classes dedicated to 'Glass', 'Glass and pottery' or 'Crystal and window glass'.

At the Great Exhibition of 1851, the stained glass exhibits formed part of Class XXIV, the 'Glass' manufactures, sub-divided into 'A. Window glass', and 'B. Painted and ornamental window glass' which included stained glass. Subsequent exhibitions followed this format and categorised stained glass with other glass manufactures. The first Paris *Exposition Universelle*, held in 1855, assigned stained glass to Class XVIII, 'Glass and Pottery' (Industries de la céramique et de la verrerie), a group of mineral-based manufactures which require firing in a kiln. Stained glass was admitted into two sub-sections of this class which highlighted its dual architectural and decorative function: A. 'Verre à vitres et à glaces' ('Window glass and mirror glass'), and B. 'Objets de céramique et de verrière ayant spécialement une valeur artistique' ('Ceramic and glass manufactures, having especially an artistic value').

By the time of the London International Exhibition of 1862 many more classes had been created to incorporate growing branches of industry. Yet stained glass was again classed as a manufacture in a group devoted to general glassware, Class XXXIV, within subdivision A. 'Stained glass and glass used in buildings and decoration'. The further subsections within this classification demonstrate that multiple categories for stained glass existed according to its intended symbolic or functional use and level of painted decoration: (i) 'Window glass, including sheet glass, crown glass, and coloured sheet glass', (ii) 'Painted and other kinds of ornamented window glass' and (iii) 'Stained and painted windows for ecclesiastical decoration'.

In 1867, at the second Paris *Exposition Universelle*, stained glass remained classed with glass manufactures in Class XVI, 'Cristaux, verrièrre du luxe et vitraux' ('Crystals, luxury glass and stained glass') within Group III, a section devoted to 'Meubles et autres objets destinés à l'habitation' ('Furniture and other articles intended for human habitation'). Similarly at the following Paris Expositions of 1878 and 1889, stained glass was categorised with all industries for which glass was the object or base material, in Class XIX, 'Cristaux, verrerie et vitraux' ('Crystal, glassware and stained glass'), within Group III, 'Mobilier et accessoires' ('Furniture and fixtures'). This class included drinking glasses of crystal and cut glass; plated and mounted crystal; table glass; common glass and bottles; window and mirror glass; cast, enamelled, crackled, frosted and tempered glass; glass for optical purposes; ornamental glass; and stained glass. The inclusion of stained glass amongst this wealth of glass products caused Édouard Didron, stained glass artist and nephew of French archaeologist Adolphe Napoléon Didron, to remark, 'il est véritablement trop défectueux de réunir les vitraux peints aux diverses industries du verre' ('it is truly too defective to combine stained glass with various glass industries').[5] As we shall see, this statement reflected Didron's opinions that stained glass was a unique art form with particular display requirements.

At the *fin-de-siècle* Paris Exposition of 1900, for the first time at an Exhibition held in Europe, stained glass received a full class of its own: Class LXVII, 'Vitraux', within Group XII, 'Décoration et mobilier des edifices publics et des habitations' ('Decoration and furnishing of public buildings and homes'), incorporating both religious and secular glass. Yet despite this new separate class, stained glass remained categorised as a 'manufacture'. For almost fifty years then, stained glass windows were categorised as manufactured products and grouped with other vitreous and ceramic objects of mineral composition that required kiln firing.

One exception to this developing pattern of classification was the series of London International Exhibitions scheduled to take place annually throughout the 1870s but which only occurred from 1871 until 1874, having been discontinued as a result of large deficits.[6] These exhibitions were international, but not universal; the exhibition of manufactured exhibits varied from year to year, with each focusing on a particular group of items, for example: pottery and porcelain, or cotton and woollen worsted. A special exhibition of glass manufactures, including 'stained glass used in buildings', scheduled for 1878 never took place, yet stained glass was exhibited each year under the 'Fine Art' category in a class devoted to 'paintings of all kinds in oil and water-colours, distemper, wax, or enamel; on glass, porcelain, or mosaics, &c.'[7] Thus at this series of Exhibitions, stained glass was 'officially' classed as a manufacture, but admitted and displayed as a fine art.

Although these exhibitions were deemed a failure by contemporaries and have been relatively ignored by scholars since, the inclusion of stained glass within the 'Fine Art' category was a significant moment, which influenced the classification of stained glass as a fine art beyond the European centres of London and Paris. Both the Vienna *Weltausstellung* of 1873 and the Philadelphia Centennial of 1876 also categorised stained glass as a fine art (see table 4.1). The fleeting recognition of stained glass as a 'Fine Art' at these exhibitions may reflect the increasing regard given to decorative arts by the emerging Arts and Crafts Movement. However, at later exhibitions in Paris throughout the century (1878, 1889 and 1900), as well as Glasgow (1888) and Chicago (1893), stained glass remained categorised as a manufacture.

To complicate matters, stained glass was exhibited under multiple categories at individual exhibitions and judged in additional classes. For instance, at the Great Exhibition of 1851, stained glass was classed as a 'glass manufacture', but the Fine Arts jury awarded medals for stained glass. These examples draw attention to the 'incongruities' and 'impossibilities' of nineteenth-century classification systems.[8] Stained glass could be construed as both a 'manufacture' and a 'fine art', even though official classification systems necessitated that it was categorised as either one *or* the other.

Counter-classifications: innovative architectural displays

When it came to displaying stained glass, attempts to arrange exhibits by material classification and national provenance generally yielded to the practical requirements of stained glass, as an architectural art that requires transmitted light. For example, at the Great Exhibition, the stained glass exhibits were separated from the glass products on the ground floor and displayed in a first-floor gallery along the outer wall of the north side of the Crystal Palace, where natural light could be transmitted from behind (see figure 4.1).

During the Paris Expositions French artists engaged with and constructed taxonomies for themselves, explicitly and implicitly, by participating in key discussions over the symbolic and literal placing of stained glass at these Expositions.[9] At the 1855 Paris *Exposition Universelle*, the decision to display stained glass in the *Palais de l'Industrie*, rather than the *Palais des Beaux-Arts* caused French glass painter Alfred Gérente to write to the General Commissioner of the *Exposition des Beaux-Arts* on 15 March 1855:

> j'ai été fort surprise lorsque vos employés, ayant pour mission de recevoir les depots des artistes, m'ont declare que les vitraux ne pouvaient être considérés comme œuvres d'art et devaient être exposés au palais de l'Industrie.[10]
>
> (I was very surprised when your employees, in charge of receiving the goods of artists, declared to me that the stained glass windows could not be regarded as works of art and were to be exhibited at the Palace of Industry.)

Despite the agreement of architect and committee-member Jean-Baptiste Lassus, who wrote in the margins of this letter that 'la peinture sur verre ne doit pas être reléguée à l'exposition des produits industriels' ('painting on glass should not be relegated to the exhibition of industrial products'),[11] Gérente received a reply from the General Commissioner two weeks later asking him to come to the *Palais des Beaux-Arts* to withdraw his case of stained glass. Across the Channel, this decision was also contested. A writer for *The Ecclesiologist*, journal of the Cambridge Camden Society (known as The Ecclesiological Society from 1845), questioned 'why are the painted windows in the industrial department?'[12]

Although stained glass windows were restricted to the *Palais de l'Industrie*,[13] some designs and full-scale cartoons for stained glass were displayed in the *Palais des Beaux-Arts* alongside grand history paintings. A room devoted to the neoclassical paintings of French artist Jean-Auguste-Dominique Ingres featured cartoons for windows in the Chapel of Saint

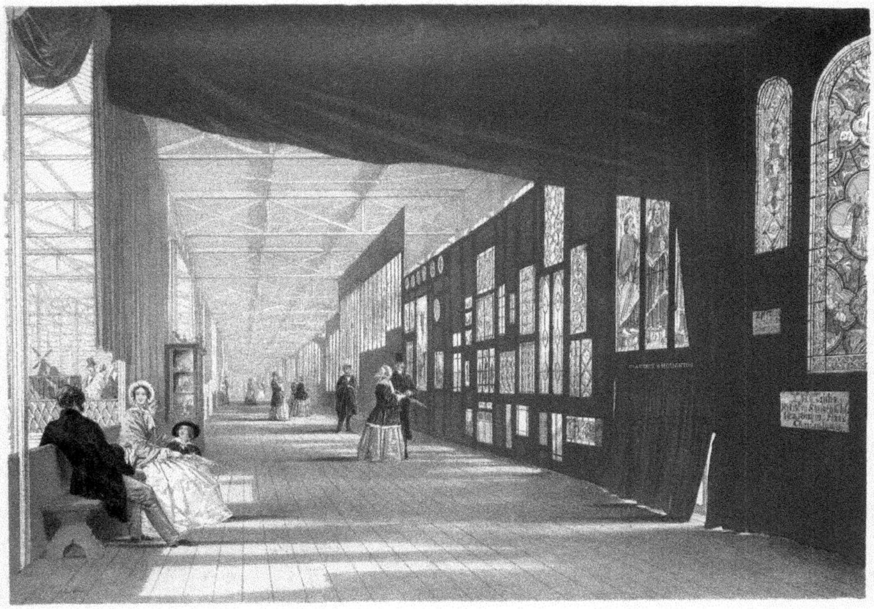

4.1 The Stained Glass Gallery, Great Exhibition, Hyde Park, London, 1851. Joseph Nash et al., 1852. Chromolithograph. (© University of Exeter Special Collections.)

Ferdinand, Neuilly (1842–43), and the Royal Chapel at Dreux (1843–44), both prestigious buildings with royal connections.[14] Ingres' cartoons had been adapted by gothic revival architect Eugène Emmanuel Viollet-le-Duc, and transformed into stained glass by the French Royal manufactory at Sèvres. Yet the presence of the cartoons in the fine art displays reflected a prejudice towards painting and drawing over the functional architectural and decorative arts.

From the outset, French stained glass exhibitors found ways of defying classification schemes and elevating the status of the medium through their own displays. After his successful participation at the Great Exhibition, glass painter Charles-Laurent Maréchal returned to France eager to ensure that the first Paris *Exposition Universelle* presented a favourable display of French stained glass.[15] Maréchal wrote a letter to Prosper Mérimée, member of the Imperial Commission for the Beaux-Arts, proposing that a building with a special gallery to house the stained glass exhibits should be erected at the forthcoming Exposition.[16] Although Maréchal's request was not granted, he was honoured with a significant commission from Louis-Napoléon Bonaparte (Emperor Napoléon III) to design two large stained glass windows to fill the *tympana* at either end of the *Palais de l'Industrie*, erected along the *Champs-Elysées* for the 1855 Exposition. This was the first major stained glass commission for an International Exhibition building, and marked a new and emphatically modern application of the medium, which elevated its status as a monumental architectural decoration. The lunette windows were composed of multiple rectangular panes of white (clear) glass painted with washy vitreous enamel pigments in the pictorial style. Although the windows were destroyed when the *Palais de l'Industrie* was demolished between 1897 and 1899, surviving descriptions and photographs reveal their iconographic importance.[17]

Maréchal's lunette windows, each of which filled a space 42m in diameter, celebrated the *Exposition Universelle* and served as visual propaganda for the newly established French Republic and Napoléon III's regime, following the French Revolution of 1848 and during the Crimean War. The windows contained large groups of allegorical figures in which France and England were, both ideologically and physically, depicted at the centre on the basis of their imperial and industrial prowess. The first window, *La France conviant les nations à l'Exposition Universelle* (*France inviting all nations to the Exposition*), depicted an allegorical figure of France seated on a throne accompanied by the figures of 'Art', holding a lyre, and 'Science', with a celestial sphere, seated at her feet. 'Art' turned towards the 'East', whose 'primitive' industries were represented by a seated shepherd, a trio of upright women carrying an Indian shawl, a Chinese vase, precious stones and weapons of Arabia, the latter suggesting the historic characteristic of war compared to the enlightened European trade. 'Science' turned towards the 'West', whose 'modern' industries were represented by a seated blacksmith at work, a trio of upright women carrying a steam engine, an electric telegraph and a power loom.

In the second window, *L'équité préside à l'accroissement des échanges* (*Equity governing the increased exchanges amongst nations*), the figure of Equity was depicted seated on a throne carrying a balance (see figure 4.2). In this composition, 'Art' was shown giving a pediment of the Parthenon inscribed 'The beautiful one!' to 'Science', who, in turn, presented 'Art' with a formula of the German mathematician Leibniz, inscribed 'Truth'. The mutual exchange of these objects and ideas demonstrated the role of the International Exhibitions in bringing together nations, encouraging international artistic and industrial exchange, and examining progress. Each nation's attribute, as represented in the first window, was redistributed in the second window. So that, in *L'équité préside à l'accroissement des échanges*, the Indian shawl was carried by England, who rested one hand on the Chinese vase. In return, India received the steam engine. China looked with curiosity at the dial of the electric telegraph, the shepherd raised a horn of plenty overflowing with the manufactured products of Europe. France oversaw Arabia receiving the power loom, and received a scarf and weapons from Algeria. Italy, wrapped in seersucker (a popular material used for clothing in warm climates), revealed a pile of thread ending in the dial carried by China. The blacksmith seized a horn of plenty containing fruits and raw materials from the East. This exchange of

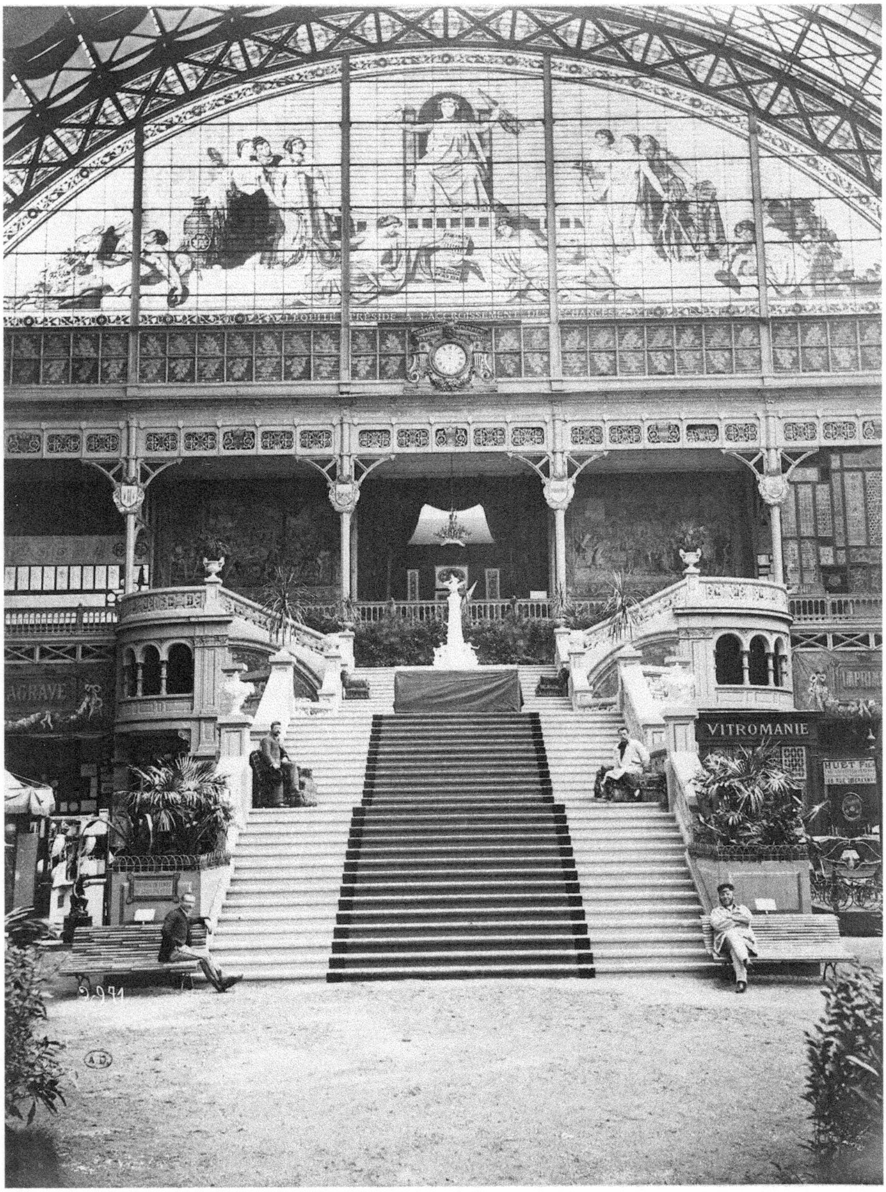

Photograph of the Palais de l'Industrie, Paris, late-nineteenth century, showing Charles-Laurent Maréchal's 1854-55 stained glass window, *Equity governing the increased exchanges amongst nations*, installed for the 1855 Exposition Universelle. (©Bibliothèque des Arts décoratifs, Paris, Collection Maciet.) **4.2**

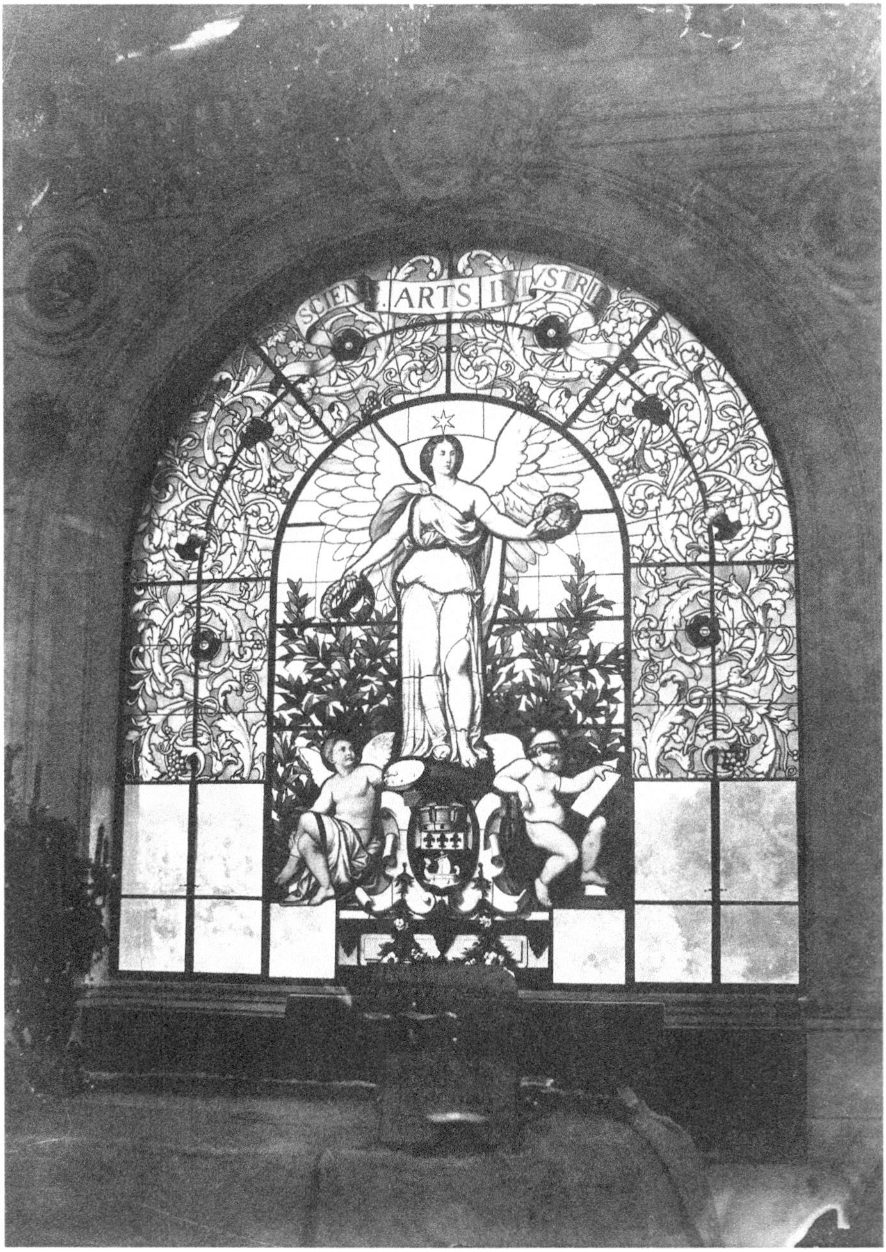

4.3 Photograph of Charles-Laurent Maréchal, *La Science, l'Art et l'Industrie*, 1854–55, window decorating the façade of the Palais de l'Industrie, built for the Exposition Universelle, 1855, Paris. (© RMN-Grand Palais [domaine de Compiègne] / René-Gabriel Ojéda.)

natural resources and industrial products demonstrated the classification schemes' division into raw materials and manufactures, and the exhibitions' role in stimulating world trade and commerce.

A smaller allegorical stained glass window dedicated to *la Science, l'Art et l'Industrie*, also executed in Maréchal's studio, adorned the triumphal-arch shaped entrance to the *Palais de l'Industrie* from the *Avenue des Champs-Élysées* (see figure 4.3).[18] This window stood as a prominent reminder of the unifying aims of the Expositions Universelles. France was depicted as a heroic, winged figure with a star halo holding a victory wreath in each hand, ready to crown the allegorical figures of 'Art' and 'Industry', seated at her feet leaning on the shield of the city of Paris.

The windows decorating the *Palais de l'Industrie* should be considered in relation to an extensive architectural decorative scheme, which celebrated art and industry in equal measure. The stained glass decoration made visual parallels with sculpture, another artistic medium that resisted categorisation and could be found throughout both the *Palais de l'Industrie* and *Palais des Beaux-Arts*. Maréchal's windows followed the triangular composition of the sculptural group on the summit of the triumphal arch by Élias Robert, depicting *France crowning Art and Industry*. Robert's sculpture, which today lies in the Parc de Saint-Cloud, depicts France with her arms outstretched, accompanied on her right by 'Industry' wielding a hammer, and, on her left, by 'Art' clutching a canvas. Directly beneath this sculptural group a frieze depicted supplicants in classical drapery presenting gifts of art, agriculture and industry to a bust of Napoléon III. The *Palais de l'Industrie*'s decorative scheme enforced the idea that Exhibitions celebrated the unification of art and industry, even though exhibition displays and classification schemes attempted to divide exhibits into these two categories.

At the London International Exhibition of 1862 stained glass exhibits were found in spaces devoted to both fine art and industry. One display placed stained glass in the central south gallery and refreshment rooms adjacent to the sculpture and picture galleries, while another installed large windows in the transepts of the Exhibition building as architectural decoration, directly above the entrance to the Machinery annexe (see figure 4.4). Such displays contradicted the official classification schemes based on materials and manufacturing processes.

At later Exhibitions, many French exhibitors erected private pavilions or chapels in which to show their stained glass exhibits. One of the most innovative examples of such a display was the full-sized, yellow-brick chapel erected by Charles Lévêque, a glass painter from Beauvais, in the French section of the large park surrounding the main elliptical exhibition building at the 1867 *Exposition Universelle* in Paris. Visitors were charged 50 centimes entrance fee to enter this Chapel, which contained stained glass windows of predominantly ecclesiastical subjects by nine French glass painters, alongside other church furnishings.[19]

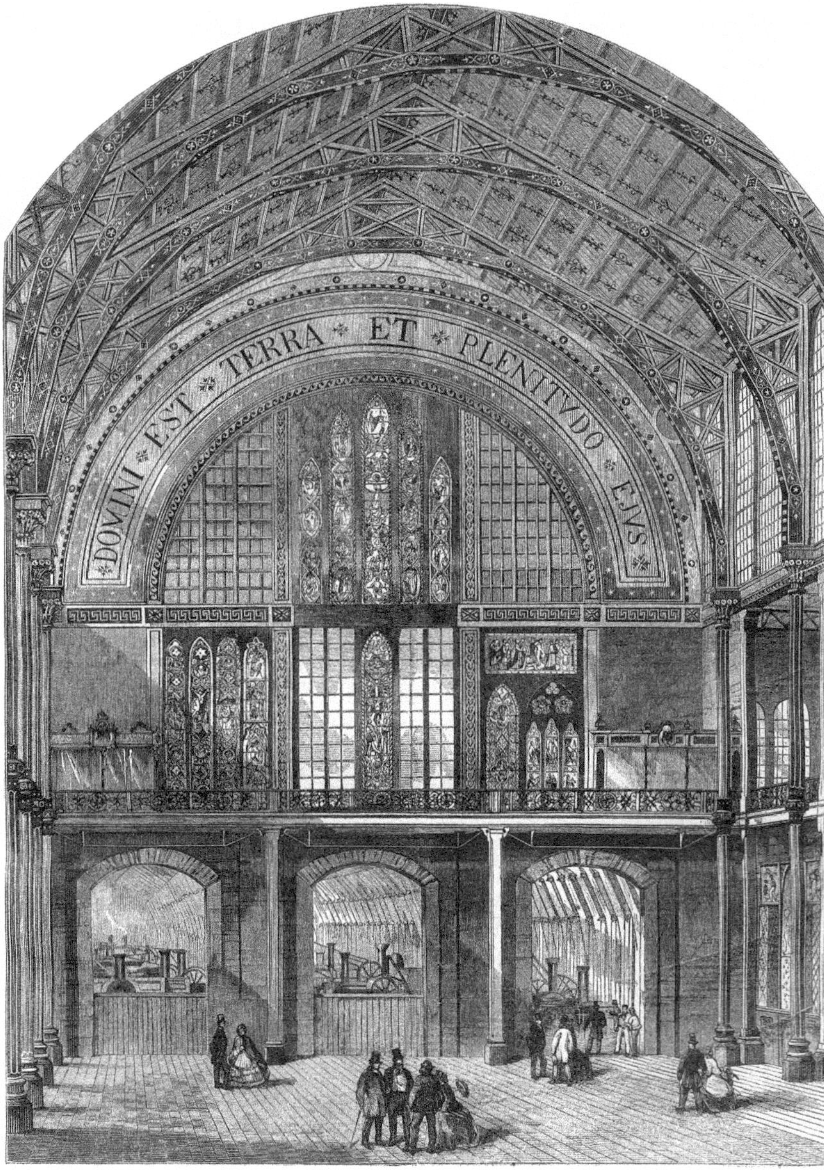

OPENING OF THE INTERNATIONAL EXHIBITION: ENTRANCE TO THE WESTERN ANNEXE.—SEE PAGE 478.

4.4 Engraving showing the stained glass exhibits installed in the North-West transept, 1862, International Exhibition Building, South Kensington, London. (© Mary Evans Picture Library.)

In 1876, meanwhile, Didron, a member of the Committee of Admission and Installation for Class XIX of the 1878 Paris Exposition, requested that the stained glass exhibits should be displayed in a special gallery, with well-lit bays of a sufficient size, in a wing of the *Palais du Champ-de-Mars* for the 1878 Exposition.[20] In order to level the competition between glass painters, Didron proposed that exhibitors should not be allowed to erect their own independent pavilion – a practice that had become popular at the previous 1867 Exposition. Although the Committee agreed to Didron's proposal, on the condition that the glass painters paid for the construction, the project was abandoned in 1877. Some dissatisfied glass painters refused to exhibit. The Corporation des artistes peintres-verriers de France sent a petition to the Ministère de l'Agriculture, Commerce et d'Industrie requesting that stained glass be categorised and displayed with the fine arts, but by this time the classification scheme had already been published and could not be altered.[21] Consequently, some glass painters continued to display in private pavilions where they could ensure their exhibits would be seen in good conditions. When the exhibition opened, Nicolas Lorin and Charles François Champigneulle showed their stained glass exhibits in private pavilions erected on the periphery of the *Palais du Champ-de-Mars*.

At the following Paris Exposition in 1889, glass painters remained exasperated at the poor classification and provision for the display of stained glass, most of which was displayed in the vast iron and glass *Galerie des Machines*. In his jury report, Champigneulle exclaimed that 'Quatre Expositions décennales sont déjà passés et l'erreur du premier jour subsiste. Il est temps qu'elle cesse enfin, et qu'on rende au vitrail sa vraie place!' ('Four decennial expositions have already passed and the error of the first day remains. It is time that this ceases at last, and that one gives stained glass its true place!')[22] The Exhibition commissioners' disregard of the special display requirements of stained glass had taken its toll on the glass painters, as Léon Appert reported, 'Les peintres verriers semblent se désintéresser de plus en plus des expositions où leurs œuvres sont placés généralement dans de mauvaises conditions d'éclairage, d'élévation et surtout de classification' ('the glass painters seem to be more and more uninterested in exhibitions where their works are generally placed in bad conditions of lighting, elevation and above all classification').[23] Champigneulle called for the General Commissioner to ensure stained glass would have a unique class of its own, an allocated building and individual jury at the 1900 Paris Exposition.

Champigneulle's request was finally granted at this *fin-de-siècle* exhibition, even if stained glass remained categorised as a manufacture rather than a fine art. In an attempt to unite the two, some French glass painters exhibited stained glass windows adjacent to their original designs. For instance, one of Henri Carot's windows, *Au Buffet* (1891) intended for the Hôtel de Ville, Paris, was displayed next to Albert Besnard's full-scale cartoon.[24] Léon Daumont-Tournel, Parisian glass painter and author of the jury report, embraced this collaborative display. He wrote:

> L'artiste n'avait pas craint que le verrier pût trahir son oeuvre. L'examen comparatif du carton et du vitrail présentait un grand intérêt: on avait le sentiment que la collaboration ainsi entendue était féconde, que chacun apportait sa part de talent àol'oeuvre commune.[25]
>
> (The artist did not fear that the glassmaker could betray his work. Comparative examination of the cartoon and the stained glass was of great interest: it was felt that a collaboration like this was fertile, that each brought his share of talent to the shared work.)

Thus, in such a combined display, the work of designer and glass manufacturer could be recognised equally, and both contributors were acknowledged by name.

Labour and commerce

The art of stained glass is central to the debate about the role of human labour in nineteenth-century industrial society. In the twentieth century, the writings of both Walter Benjamin and Nikolas Pevsner suggested that industrial art was characterised by mass-production.[26] Art critic Herbert Read and his peers similarly associated nineteenth-century stained glass with mass-production.[27] In his 1959 publication *Stained glass: history, technology and practice*, stained glass artist E. Liddall Armitage remarked 'The larger [nineteenth-century] firms developed a streamlined process of production that might have served as a prototype for a twentieth-century car factory'.[28] Stained glass windows were, to an extent mass-produced in this period; large studios repeated designs and reused cartoons with little variation.[29] Yet if we are to gain a better understanding of what industrial production meant in relation to stained glass during the nineteenth century, we need to examine the discourse surrounding the displays of stained glass at the International Exhibitions.

As a medium produced by divided artistic and industrial labour, stained glass refuted rigid classification schemes based on the progressive stages of the manufacturing process, exposing problems and inconsistencies with exhibition taxonomies that divided art and industry. Stained glass was not alone in this problem. Alison Yarrington has drawn attention to the fact that nineteenth-century sculpture was similarly 'unstable, both distinguished and uneasy in its role as high art and industrial product'.[30] The then-recent invention of photography also confounded classification, as Steve Edwards has demonstrated.[31] As George Wallis, Superintendent of the British and Colonial manufactures at the 1855 *Exposition Universelle* professed, 'It's almost impossible to draw the line at which Industrial Art ends and Fine Art *par excellence* begins'.[32] In his capacity as Jury Reporter for the stained glass exhibited at the 1867 Paris Exposition, French glassmaker George

Bontemps similarly conceded: 'Il est assez difficile, en effet, de tracer une limite rigoureuse entre les productions qui sont du domaine de l'art et celles qui appartiennent à l'industrie' ('It is quite difficult, in effect, to draw a rigorous line between those productions in the realm of art and those which belong to industry').[33] But how did one make this distinction? One of the ways this differentiation was articulated was through studio practice. A paper read to the Oxford Architectural Society on 11 March 1858 by Gothic Revival architect Charles Buckeridge, entitled 'The production of modern stained glass windows' (of which an extract was printed in *The Ecclesiologist*), addressed the main issues:

> with a few exceptions, our stained glass windows are turned out of establishments the owners of which have no more artistic skill than a linendraper; these men turn art into a trade, and deal with it in much the same spirit as a greengrocer deals in vegetables. 'Is the production of stained glass windows an art or a manufacture?' Some call it one, some the other, and others split the difference and call it an 'art-manufacture,' – a very ambiguous term this, which generally means that manufacture has more to do with it than art.[34]

Buckeridge recognised that stained glass was commonly perceived and treated as a manufacture, despite its artistic characteristics.

Bontemps' review of the stained glass exhibited at the 1867 Exposition declared that if we must distinguish between industrial art and fine art, then a work of art must be executed by the artist's hand.[35] But in the nineteenth century, there were many people involved in the production of a stained glass window, including the chemist, glassblower, designer, cartoonist, glass cutter, painter, workman responsible for firing the glass, and the glazier to lead and install the window. The language used by nineteenth-century critics demonstrates an awareness of this divided labour. An anonymous writer for *The Illustrated Exhibitor* of the 1851 Great Exhibition noted, 'great as is the difference between a first sketch and a finished painting, or between the clay and the marble, it is still more difficult to pronounce how a very showy cartoon will turn out in actual execution in glass'.[36] In an article published in the *Art Journal* (1887), decorative artist Lewis Foreman Day, who had begun his career in stained glass as a designer for Lavers & Barraud and then Clayton & Bell, before becoming a freelance designer in 1869, declared that 'the translation of the artist's design by another and almost inevitably lesser artist, must be to the detriment of Art, if to the profit of the manufacturer'.[37]

According to Didron, the division of labour and collaborative production of stained glass was the main reason for its classification as a manufacture at the International Exhibitions. In his report on stained glass at the 1867 Paris Exposition, he declared:

> L'egalement la qualité d'oeuvres d'art àrces produits qui lui semblent tomber dans le domaine de l'industrie. Pourquoi? La cause en est bien simple, en apparence du moins: c'est que le vitrail ne sort pas, achevé de pied en cap,

> des mains de l'artiste, et que celui-ci doit s'adjoindre des collaborateurs ayant chacun une spécialité.[38]

> (The administration also denies the quality of these products as works of art, which may seem to fall into the domain of industry. Why? The reason is simple, in appearance at least; that the stained glass window does not leave, complete from head to toe, the hands of the artist, and that it must enlist the services of collaborators, each with a speciality.)

Such emphasis on the hands of an individual artist did not accurately reflect artistic labour in nineteenth-century stained glass studios. Large studios employed in-house designers as well as freelance designers, with varying knowledge and understanding of the properties and material conditions of stained glass. When signatures, marks and monograms are found on nineteenth-century stained glass panels, they tend to belong to the stained glass studio where the window was made rather than the individual designer or glass painter.[39] Similarly, most stained glass panels were catalogued and exhibited at the International Exhibitions under a studio name, for example Hardman & Co., or Powell & Sons, thus associating the medium with commercial businesses rather than individual artists.

An Arts and Crafts ethos was firmly in place by 1889, when stained glass artist Hugh Arthur Kennedy wrote, 'I am convinced that the comparative indifference of the public to-day to glass-work indirectly results from the improper division of labour in its execution', and emphasised that the 'artist' should be present at every stage in the production of a stained glass window.[40] Thus, the mechanical copyist, employed to work from stock cartoons or catalogues of another's stained glass designs and transfer them to glass, was set up in opposition to the independent artist-designer who designed and made (or at least supervised the execution of) his own windows. Although unrepresentative of the complex and varied roles and production methods of stained glass, this binary position sparked a prolonged debate over the status of stained glass, inciting responses from critics, exhibitors and stained glass artists throughout the International Exhibitions.

In his review of stained glass exhibits at the 1878 *Exposition Universelle*, Didron introduced another element to the debate – the effects of public taste, or fashion for stained glass upon the supply and demand for stained glass. He wrote,

> Si la peinture sur verre est un art, sa mise en œuvre est un partie industrielle: il n'en a pas fallu d'avantage pour la faire verser dans une ornière commerciale, qui a étée commerciale, qe par les besoins factices d'une consommation excessive .... Grâce àeune concurrence que, d'ailleurs, le goût particulier des clients ordinaires a trop encouragée, la peinture sur verre cesse, dans bien des cas, d'être un art véritable pour devenir une industrie condamnée à produire beaucoup, rapidement et àrbon marché.[41]

> (If glass painting is an art, its implementation is in part industrial: nothing more was needed to let her fall into a commercial rut, which was prepared by the false needs of an excessive consumption ... Due to competition, moreover, the particular taste of regular customers has been too much encouraged, painting on glass stops, in many cases, being a truthful art and becomes an industry condemned to produce much, quickly and cheaply.)

According to Didron, the increased demand for stained glass during this period inevitably led to mass production and commercial competition, and hindered development. Yet competition and commerce were primary motives for exhibitors to display their stained glass at International Exhibitions.

Conclusion

As a medium dependent upon both artistic design and skilled execution, stained glass exposed the limitations of exhibition classifications based on the binary division of manufactured products and the fine arts. Many exhibitors protested against its continual classification as a manufacture, and some went a step further in raising the medium's status by forming their own innovative displays.

The division of labour involved in the production of stained glass further complicated its status.[42] Nineteenth-century stained glass production relied upon the collaborative labour of many individuals with varying degrees of artistic and technical input. Despite recognition by Exhibition critics that a stained glass artist 'must be a good glass manufacturer, and a skilful designer', stained glass studios and exhibition catalogues invariably advertised the artistic skill of their designers, leaving anonymous the glass painter, cutter, glazier and other individuals involved in making a stained glass window.[43]

At the International Exhibitions stained glass was categorised and ordered according to nineteenth-century concepts of artistic labour, revealing contemporary attitudes towards the medium's status and significance. These classifications played an important role in shaping public understanding of the medium in this period, and triggered debates over its artistic status. This influence has extended to our classification and interpretation of the medium today. For example, at the Victoria and Albert Museum in London, a legacy of the Great Exhibition of 1851, stained and painted glass remains categorised according to its mineral composition and kiln-manufacture in the 'Ceramics and Glass' Department, following precedents set by the International Exhibitions.

By considering how Exhibition classification schemes, displays and critical commentaries on stained glass developed perceptions of the medium in the second half of the nineteenth century, we can gain new perspectives on the history of stained glass production. At the same time, we learn about the ways in which stained glass, and stained glass practitioners, complicated debates about art and industry.

Notes

1 Mayhew, *London labour and the London poor*, vol. 3, p. 452.
2 Whewell, 'On the general bearing of the Great Exhibition', p. 25.
3 Allwood, 'International exhibitions and the classification of their exhibits', 450–1.
4 Armstrong, *Victorian glassworlds*, p. 192.
5 Didron, 'Section II. Vitraux', p. 4.
6 Findling and Pelle, *Historical dictionary of world's fairs*, pp. 44–7.
7 Cole, *A special report*, p. 39.
8 Whewell, 'On the general bearing of the Great Exhibition', p. 20.
9 Luneau, 'Les peintres verriers dans les expositions universelles', pp. 244–57.
10 Pillet, 'La plume et l'épée', 53.
11 *Ibid.*, 54.
12 'The Paris Exhibition of 1855', 265–6.
13 The stained glass exhibits were displayed in the four pavilions located by the staircases at each corner of the building. Wallis, 'The artistic, industrial, and commercial results', p. xv.
14 Trapp, 'The Universal Exhibition of 1855', p. 305; Mainardi, *Art and politics of the Second Empire*, p. 51, n. 8.
15 Maréchal & Guynon were awarded a Prize Medal at the Great Exhibition. Winston, 'Awards and notices – glass paintings', pp. 686, 702.
16 For a transcript of this letter, see Pillet, 'La plume et l'épée', 53.
17 This building was replaced by the *Petit Palais* and *Grand Palais*, built for the 1900 Exposition Universelle. De Finance and Hervier (eds.) *Un patrimoine de lumière 1830–2000.*
18 'The Palais de l'Industrie', 409.
19 Gautier, *Les curiosités de l'Exposition de 1867*, p. 31.
20 Hardouin-Fugier, 'Le vitrail Français en 1878', 207–14.
21 L. G., 'Les peintres-verriers aux Expositions', 82.
22 Champigneulle, 'Classe 19', p. 182.
23 Appert and Henrivaux, 'La verrerie à l'Exposition Universelle de 1889', p. 372.
24 David, 'Les vitraux de l'Hôtel de Ville de Paris', p. 298.
25 Daumont-Tournel, 'Classe 67 – Vitraux', p. 56.
26 In his essay, 'Design and industry through the ages', first published in *The Journal of Royal Society of Arts*, 92 (1948), Pevsner identified industry as 'the production of identical objects in large numbers'. Pevsner, *Studies in art, architecture and design*, vol. 2, p. 11.
27 Read, *English stained glass*; Baker, *English stained glass.*
28 Armitage, *Stained glass*, p. 64.
29 Most stained glass studios had 10–30 employees, although larger studios such as Maréchal and Champigneulle employed 100 to 125 people. Hardouin-Fugier, 'Le vitrail Français en 1878', 211.
30 Yarrington, '"Made in Italy"', p. 86.
31 Edwards, 'Photography, allegory, and labor', pp. 39–40. When photography was categorised as a 'philosophical instrument' and displayed in the machinery section at the Great Exhibition, some photographers boycotted the exhibition in protest. In 1862 photography was categorised as 'machinery'.
32 Wallis, 'The artistic, industrial, and commercial results', iii.

33 Bontemps and Bœswillwald, 'Groupe III. Classes 14 à 26. Section II. Vitraux', p. 88.
34 'Mr Buckeridge on modern stained glass', 119.
35 Bontemps inferred that a stained glass cartoon, designed by an 'artist', was a work of art, but a stained glass window, produced by a small team of skilled glaziers, was an industrial production. Bontemps and Bœswillwald, 'Groupe III. Classes 14 à 26. Section II. Vitraux', p. 88.
36 Cassell & Co., *The illustrated exhibitor*, p. 380.
37 Day, 'Victorian progress in applied design', 194.
38 Didron, *Les vitraux à l'Exposition Universelle de 1867*, pp. 3–4.
39 In 1887 E. G. Howard suggested that signatures of both the designer and glass painter should be included on windows. Howard, 'Ancient and modern painted glass', pp. 808–9.
40 Kennedy, 'An art not generally understood', 63.
41 Didron, 'Section II. Vitraux', p. 87.
42 Holiday, *Stained glass as an art*, pp. 110–11.
43 *Dickinson's Comprehensive Pictures*, Vol. II, text accompanying Plate XIII.

Bibliography

Allwood, J. 'International Exhibitions and the classification of their exhibits', *Journal of the Royal Society for the Encouragement of Arts, Manufactures and Commerce*, 128:5287 (1980), 450–5

Appert L. and J. Henrivaux, 'La verrerie à l'Exposition Universelle de 1889', *Arts Industriels. Revue technique de l'Exposition Universelle 1889* (Paris, 1890), pp. 353–446

Armitage, E. L. *Stained glass: history, technology and practice* (London, 1959)

Armstrong, I. *Victorian glassworlds: glass culture and the imagination 1830–1880* (Oxford, 2008)

Baker, J. *English stained glass* (London, 1960)

Bontemps, G. and Bœswillwald, E. 'Groupe III. Classes 14 à 26. Section II. Vitraux', in *Rapports du jury international publiés sous la direction de M. Michel Chevalier*, 6 Vols (Paris, 1868), pp. 88–97

Cassell, J. & Co. *The illustrated exhibitor, a tribute to the world's industrial jubilee; comprising sketches, by pen and pencil of the principal objects in the Great Exhibition of the Industry of All Nations, 1851* (London, 1851)

Champigneulle, C. 'Classe 19. Cristaux, verrerie et vitraux. Part II. Vitraux', in A. Picard (ed.) *Exposition Universelle Internationale de 1889 à Paris. Rapports du jury international publiés sous la direction de M. Alfred Picard. Groupe III: mobilier et accessoires, classes 17 à 29* (Paris, 1891), pp. 175–83

Cole, H. *A special report on the annual international exhibits of years 1871, 1872, 1873 and 1874* (London, 1878–79)

Cormack, P. *Arts and crafts stained glass* (London, 2015)

Daumont-Tournel, L. 'Classe 67 – Vitraux', in *Rapports du Jury International de l'Exposition Universelle de 1900* (Paris, 1902), pp. 27–75

David, V. 'Les vitraux de l'Hôtel de Ville de Paris', in M. Clément (ed.) *Monumental: revue scientifique et technique des monuments historiques. Dossier vitrail, semestriel 1* (Paris, 2004), pp. 38–47

Day, L. F. 'Victorian progress in applied design', *Art-Journal* (June 1887), 185–202.

De Finance, L. and D. Hervier (eds.) *Un patrimoine de lumière 1830–2000: verrières des Hauts-de-Seine, Seine-Saint-Denis, Val-de-Marne* (Paris, 2003)

Dickinson's comprehensive pictures of the Great Exhibition of 1851. From the originals painted for H. R. H. Prince Albert by Messrs. Nash, Haghe, and Roberts, R. A. (London, 1854)

Didron, É. *Les vitraux à l'Exposition Universelle de 1867* (Paris, 1868)
Didron, É. 'Section II. Vitraux', in É. Didron and L. Clémandot (eds.) *Exposition Universelle internationale de 1878 à Paris. Groupe III – Classe 19. Rapport sur les cristaux, la verrerie et les vitraux* (Paris, 1880), pp. 51–88
Edwards, S. 'Photography, allegory, and labor', *Art-Journal*, 55:2 (1996), 38–44
Findling, J. E. and K. D. Pelle (eds.) *Historical dictionary of world's fairs and expositions, 1851–1988* (New York and London, 1990)
Gautier, H. *Les curiosités de l'Exposition de 1867* (Paris, 1867)
Hardouin-Fugier, É. 'Le vitrail Français en 1878. L'Exposition Universelle et l'enquête du ministère de l'industrie', *Bulletin de la Societie d'Histoire de l'Art Français* (1990), 207–14
Holiday, H. *Stained glass as an art* (London; New York, 1896)
Howard, E. G. 'Ancient and modern painted glass', *National Review*, 9:54 (1887), 793–810
Kennedy, H. A. 'An art not generally understood', *Contemporary Review* (1889), 427–42
L. G. 'Les peintres-verriers aux Expositions', *La chronique des arts et de la curiosité: supplement à la Gazette des Beaux-Arts*, 9 (3 March 1877), 82
Luneau, J.-F. 'Les peintres verriers dans les expositions universelles: histoire d'un désamour', in A-L. Carré, M. S. Corcy, C. Demeulenaere-Douyère and L. Hilaire-Pérez (eds.) *Les Expositions Universelles en France au XIXe siècle. Techniques. Publics. Patrimoines* (Paris, 2012), pp. 244–57
Mainardi, P. *Art and politics of the Second Empire: the Universal Expositions of 1855 and 1867* (New Haven; London, 1987)
Mayhew, H. *London labour and the London poor: the condition and earnings of those that will work, cannot work, and will not work* (vol. 3, London, 1861)
'Mr Buckeridge on modern stained glass', *Ecclesiologist*, 16 (1858), 119–20
Pevsner, N. *Studies in art, architecture and design: Victorian and after* (vol. 2, London, 1968)
Pillet, É. 'La plume et l'épée. Le capitane de Montluisant chroniquer de l'Exposition Universelle de 1855', *Documents d'histoire Parisienne*, 8 (2007), 51–70
Read, H. *English stained glass* (London and New York, 1926)
'The Palais de l'Industrie', *Critic* (15 August 1855), 409
'The Paris exhibition of 1855', *Ecclesiologist*, 8 (October 1855), 263–99
Trapp, F. A. 'The Universal Exhibition of 1855', *The Burlington Magazine; French art in the later nineteenth century*, 107:747 (1965), 300–5
Wallis, G. 'The artistic, industrial, and commercial results of the Universal Exposition of 1855', *Art-Journal* (January 1855), i–xx
Whewell, W. 'On the general bearing of the Great Exhibition on the progress of art and science', in *Lectures on the results of the Great Exhibition of 1851* (London, 1852–53), pp. 1–34
Winston, C. 'Awards and notices – glass paintings', in *Jury reports IV: Classes XXVIII–XXX* (London, 1852), pp. 533–5; 680–707
Yarrington, A. '"Made in Italy": sculpture and the staging of national identities at the International Exhibition of 1862', in M. Pfister and R. Hertel (eds.) *Performing national identity: Anglo-Italian cultural transactions* (Amsterdam; New York, 2008), pp. 75–99

5

William Blake, the Arts and Crafts Movement and the mythography of manufacture

Colin Trodd

> Fine Art must always be produced by the subtlest of all machines, which is the human hand. No machine yet contrived, or hereafter contrivable, will ever equal the machinery of the human fingers.[1]

Does William Blake live in the future? Does he belong in a universal world of unstoppable creativity where all production systems are married with aesthetic principles? Should he be seen as an engine of change who proclaims that all art exists to affirm the reality of shared sensuousness? Many late Victorian commentators convinced themselves that these claims were plausible, although they used different hypotheses to support their arguments and conclusions. For one group, Blake was both consummate craftsman and prophet of cultural revolution; for another group, he represented a condition of reckless joy and dynamic experimentation; for a third group, he incarnated the values of play, hospitality and fellowship; for yet another group, he perfected the idea that art represented the public authority of the imagination. Under the influence of these schools of thought, many people came to believe that Blake's work was a paradigm of participation and altruism, a way of understanding, and then overcoming, the life-orders behind existing social systems and social relations.[2]

To a surprising extent, there are few detailed studies on Blake's critical afterlife in the visual arts. This essay, which offers an overview of the matters noted above, concentrates on the interpretative schema that allowed commentators to put forward the view that the future belonged to the artist-as-manufacturer; that authentic manufacture was one of the key elements in the aesthetic ideal of society; and that Blake's art accelerated progress towards this truth. In essence, this is an essay less about Blake himself than about how he is remembered within the Victorian cultural imagination.

Let us begin with a more familiar reading. W. B Yeats and E. J. Ellis, trailblazers in late Victorian Blake studies, posited Blake as an idiosyncratic figure weaving a new mythos from the strands of the Perennial Tradition, a mythic collective of mystical thinkers and artists. Their Blake, forever on the threshold of realising the supreme logic of the magical universe, is pushed back into the diurnal world because he cannot escape from the rationality of mainstream metaphysics, its addiction to planning, sequencing and development. A thinker trapped by the mechanisms of thought, Blake wants to live in the elusive world of occult vision, the ideal human society, but his art is oriented to a realm that is fundamentally limited, that forecloses the deeper questions of the Perennial Philosophy (esoteric spirituality) from being answered.[3]

Other commentators saw things rather differently. Walter Crane and C. R. Ashbee, leading designer-theorists, did not belong in Yeats's conceptual and linguistic universe; and their vocabulary differs, significantly, from that of their esoterically minded contemporaries. As explained by them, Blake prophesied the emergence of a New Life, a perfected spiritual state where subjects would achieve self-unity through the union of manual and intellectual labour. Their Blake was even more magical and therapeutical than the star-like figure imagined by Yeats, Ellis and their neo-Rosicrucian chums: he represented the restlessness of the creative spirit; he demonstrated the triumph of dynamism over mechanism; and he incarnated the mind of humankind. Equally, their Blake, who belonged to a community of creative manufacturers, saw brotherhood as activism, not a secret order of elect spirits united in the concept of occult knowledge.[4]

These, then, were some of the conditions in which the artists, designers and thinkers of the Arts and Crafts Movement imagined how Blake belonged to them. Unlike the Yeatsian Blake, who wants to transform everything into inwardness, Crane and Ashbee discover an inspirational leader who equates art with transformation of consciousness and the social order. Although there are important exceptions to this view, the Arts and Crafts Blake was, on the whole, a prophet of social cooperation: he wanted to change the world by arguing that the dynamism of inner life found its greatest expression in the world of free manufacture, the ideal state of creativity, where humanised value opposed itself to the cult of competition, the quantification of labour and systems of life-management. It was around these issues that commentators came to believe that Blake, in his fusion of art and work, had found a way of making spirit sensuous: his life was in harmony with the vibrating universe, a universe in a continual state of renewal, a universe which knew nothing of profit, capitalist utility or industrial society (figure 5.1).

As will be seen, this interest in a catalytic Blake, who combined technical, ethical and aesthetic activity to become an ideal cultural being, was part of a bigger story about the nature and efficacy of mechanism

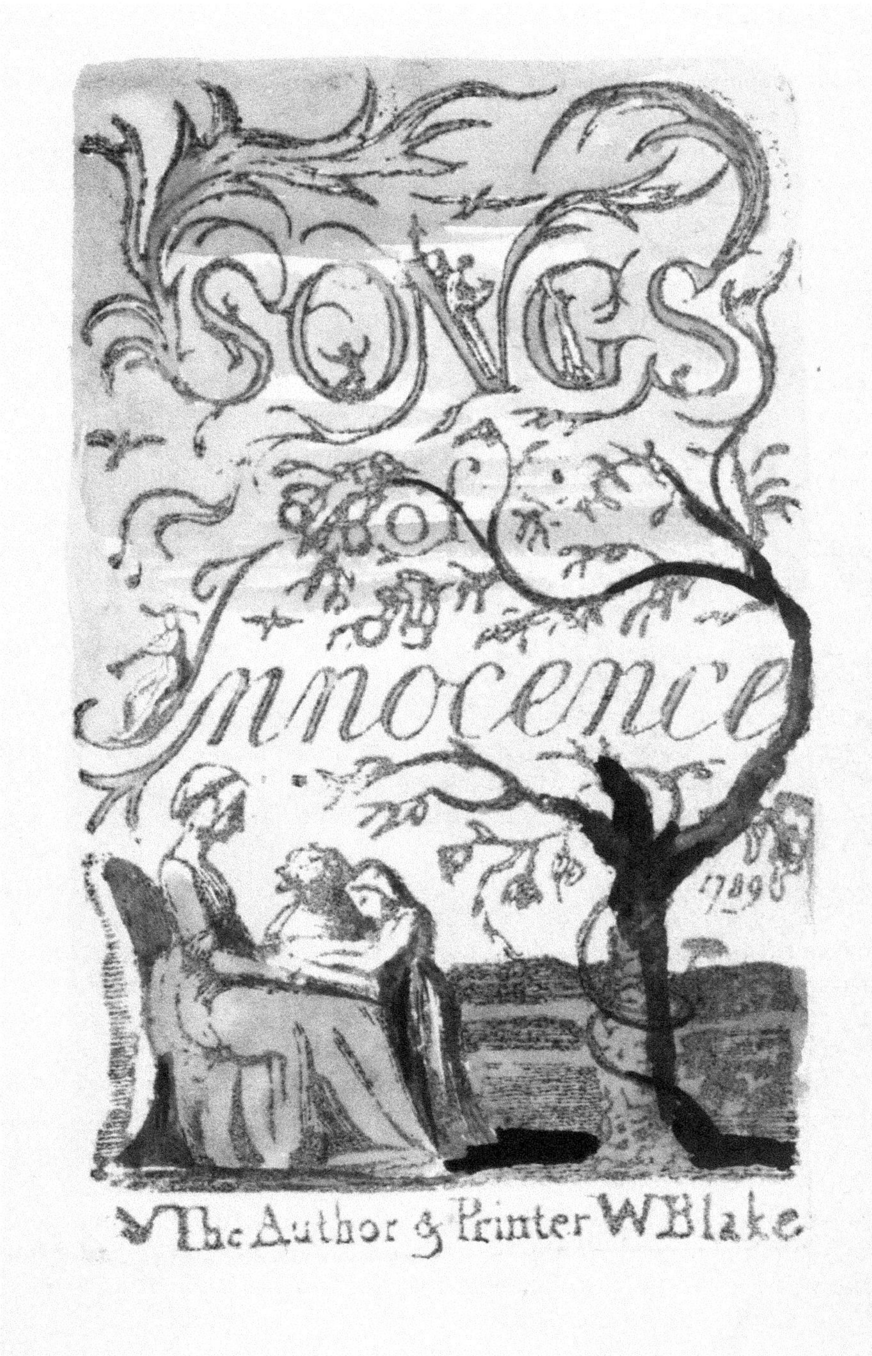

William Blake, *The songs of innocence*, plate 2, 1789. Relief etching, 120 x 74 mm. The Lessing J. Rosenwald Collection, Rare Book & Special Collections Division, Library of Congress. (Courtesy of Library of Congress, Washington DC.) **5.1**

and manufacture. Mechanism, the measure of human performance, would be seen as evidence that art was being incorporated into a bureaucratic world of commands and observations; manufacture, by contrast, would be used to point to an ethical schema, a condition of knowledge, experience and value derived from intuitive life rather than institutional regulation or analytical science. The defining characteristic of this discourse is the vision of contemporary industrial life, a vision where production means no more than reproduction – and where reproduction implies a condition of servile labour.[5]

It is not difficult to link these concerns to a more general argument within the Arts and Crafts Movement. For instance, at the first meeting of the National Association for the Advancement of Art and its Application to Industry in 1888, Walter Crane, the president of this organisation, stated that 'the problem before us in the matter of art and industry' is to find the means to transform 'our artists into craftsmen, and our craftsmen into artists'.[6] He agreed with William Morris, C. R. Ashbee, J. D. Sedding and T. J. Cobden-Sanderson, all of whom believed that the mechanisation of inner life could be resisted by a process of integrated production at the centre of which was the independent manufacturer of handmade objects.[7]

There is a general analogy to be drawn between this dynamic of production and the dynamic visible in discourse concerning the critical potential of cultural labour. In 1881 William Morris stated that any call for cultural renewal had to start by recognising that this was a 'time of barbarism', an era which reduced the workman to 'the slave to a machine.' He half-imagined the birth of 'the new art', but feared that all change was blocked by something 'alive and devouring ... a river of fire'. 'New art' meant the condition of creative independence in which all workers would derive pleasure from labour; 'river of fire' meant a social system based on class division, industrial capitalism and the multiplication of wants within a market economy. Morris ended on a suitably apocalyptic note: 'one must turn to hope', he said, 'and only in one direction do I see it – on the Road to Revolution: everything else is gone'.[8]

In December 1887 C. R. Ashbee went to see Morris to discuss the formation of a new guild, but Morris was more interested in exploring ideas of political resistance. Ashbee attempted to capture this struggle to imagine the experience of hope by depicting Morris as 'a great soul rushing through space with a halo of glory around him, but this consuming, tormenting and goading him on' (figure 5.2).[9] In all this, he associated Morris with the fiery qualities of Blake's Los, the subject of surging creativity, the heroic artist-craftsman whose labour incarnates struggle. Morris, like Los, is simultaneously alienated from social experience and the embodiment of revolutionary energy; his raw power is derived from his vertiginous vision of things.[10] At war with the world of normative commands, Ashbee's dazzling creator seems to embody the visualisation of

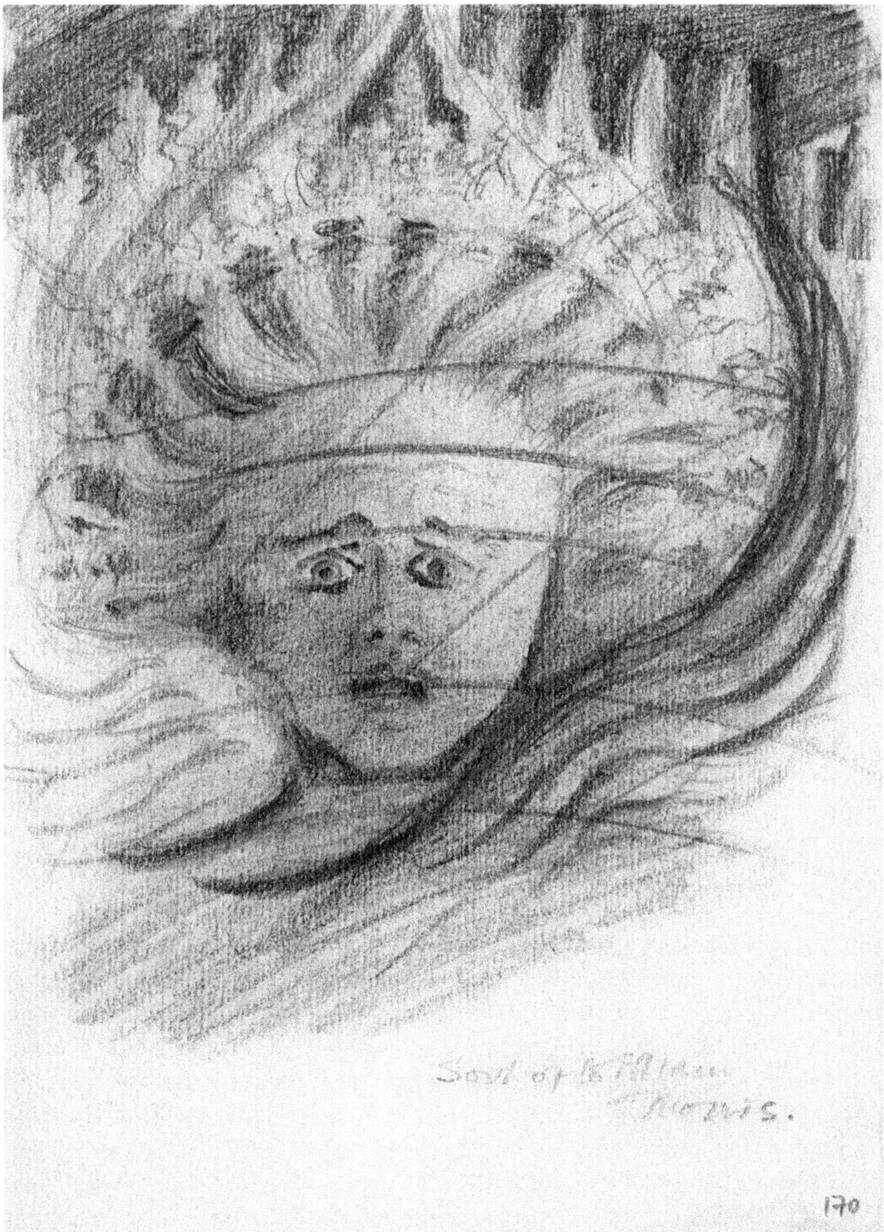

C. R. Ashbee, *The soul of William Morris*, 1887. Pencil drawing with chalk, 120 x 90 mm. **5.2**
(© King's College Library, Cambridge University.)

sensory experience *and* a condition of psychic trauma. Here the sensuous life of the subject brings with it both exhilaration and despair. Morris is at once Blakean form and phosphorescent consciousness, an expression of imaginative animism and sign of anguish or pain. The immediate impetus for this division – between a creationist world of social enjoyment, and a commercialist world of material abundance – can be traced to Ruskin.

Like Morris and Ashbee, Ruskin found a Kraken-like monster stalking the universe of labour. Despite their obvious political differences, all three of them noted the consolidation of capitalism in modern social life. Almost everything of importance in Ruskin's social criticism depends on his model of work, a vision of creativity, expression, agency and manufacture that coloured subsequent perceptions of the nature of craft, industry and design.[11]

It will not be realistic here to deal in any responsible way with Ruskin's voluminous writings on labour and its values, but by focusing on his theory of the grotesque it is possible to characterise the nature of his influence on later models of art, design and manufacture. I do so in order to argue that Ruskin's model of the noble grotesque – where art is triumphant and redemptive because it is rooted in the physicality of labour and critical limitation – shaped Blake's articulation within the Arts and Crafts Movement. There is much that could be said about these matters, but at this stage it should be noted that the Blake imagined by leading members of the Art Workers' Guild (founded in 1884), the Arts and Crafts Exhibiting Society (founded in 1887), and the Guild of Handicraft (founded in 1888) supported Ruskin's assertion that 'to banish imperfection is to destroy expression ... to paralyse vitality'.[12]

Ruskin argues that the grotesque escapes from academic art, where mastery is equated with the performance of skill and the uniformity of faithful resemblance. If the grotesque does more than represent information about the world, then this arises from the belief that one of the main functions of art is to get the viewer to reflect on the activity of visual attention itself. As he sees it, the grotesque is a weapon in the war against standardisation; it arises from the desire to live existence as a multiple process composed as separate parts. Unsurprisingly, he equates the academic view of the beautiful with the tendency of normalised artistic perception to misrepresent a value beyond itself. In opposition, he advances the view that the grotesque is the apprehension and appreciation of the 'irregular and accidental contemplation of terrible things, or evil in general ... [It is the] confusion of the imagination by the presence of truths which it cannot wholly grasp'.[13]

That is to say, the grotesque, as protean image of life, remodels Burke's materialistic reading of the sublime.[14] According to Ruskin, the fantastical and fearful symbolism of the grotesque is an expression of sublime vision reconnected with its spiritual roots. This point runs throughout *Modern*

Painters and *The Stones of Venice*, both of which are concerned with the relationship between seeing and knowing. Burke, as is well known, saw the sublime as a form of power; Ruskin, by contrast, identifies the grotesque as unstable fullness of energy, a willingness to display human identity as something unsettled and disturbed by its desire for full knowledge and authority. Grotesque art is the labour of a vision that recognises *and* embodies human limitation. In effect, Ruskin detaches the grotesque from the tradition of monstrosity; as he sees it, the grotesque is the *incarnation of failure*. From this viewpoint, the grotesque derives its power from acknowledging that struggle with confusion – conceptual, physical and formal – is the true purpose of art making.[15]

None of this explains adequately how Ruskin came to use the grotesque as a way of opposing commercialistic and monopolistic forms of culture. We need to dig deeper. On one level, Ruskin finds in the grotesque a symbolic language which records competing processes of visualisation. In contrast to academic art theory, where representation is equated with logical unities, Ruskin's theory of the grotesque celebrates the exuberance, variety and vitality of the natural world. This colours his treatment of Classical, Gothic and Renaissance cultures, as he argues that medieval artists and craftsmen incorporated human limitation into their forms and designs. The difference between Medieval and Classical-Renaissance modes of perception is conceptualised in terms of the morality of seeing, as is seen in his famous account of two griffins (figure 5.3) in *Modern Painters*:

> The difference is, that the Lombard workman did really see a griffin in his imagination, and carved it from the life, meaning to declare to all ages that he had verily seen with his immortal eyes such a griffin as that; but the classical workman never saw a griffin at all nor anything else; but put the whole thing together by line and rule.[16]

Ruskin actually insists that without true work there is no proper understanding of the aesthetic dimension. This thought runs throughout his writings: in 'noble' art the object is never distinct from the bodily presence of the maker; in 'ignoble' art the object is an abstraction from life. Thus, the Medieval griffin is organic form; the Classical-Renaissance griffin reveals the deadly influence of abstraction, of mechanisation. The Medieval griffin is autographic art: it preserves the individual vitality of experience in the active life of the craftsman; the Classical-Renaissance griffin is simulated art: it repeats a generic formula. On one side, the ontology of the imagination: notice how Ruskin claims the Lombard craftsmen sees the griffin 'in his imagination' and 'carved it from the life.' On the other side, occluded vision: notice how Ruskin associates the classical craftsman with order, homogenisation and control – his is a bureaucratic vision of life and art.

In making his griffin, then, the medieval craftsman conveys his visceral, sensory response to work itself. Work is sacramental because it manufactures the visual experience of the craftsman. In essence, Ruskin's vision of medievalism is an image of art as public craft and ethical value. The medieval grotesque is at once critical vision, physical process and practical activity; the medieval craftsman knows perception is spontaneous and active. This is part of a much larger argument, outlined in 'The Nature of Gothic', where Ruskin claims that the medieval guild preserved the integrity of imagination and manufacture. By contrast, the classical world was self-adoring: it recognised nothing beyond its own programmatic nature. The former was altruistic, the latter was narcissistic; the former incarnated ideal manhood, the latter embodied pure thraldom.[17]

As is well known, Ruskin's aesthetic exalts experience, in particular the experience of pleasure derived from free labour. This model impacts on his reading of the relationship between culture and mechanisation. He championed the roughness and irregularity of certain forms and called attention to what he termed their rudeness and redundancy. These traits were marks of integrity, evidence that the creator confessed to personal imperfection and acknowledged the imperfection of his subject. Imperfection implied variation, and both had practical and epistemological value. On the one hand, imperfection meant the creative union of labour and play, delight in craft activity that recognised the limitation of mental work and human power. On the other hand, imperfection signalled a kind of spiritual well-being, an understanding of the transformative nature of the imagination. At a key point in 'The Nature of Gothic', we are informed

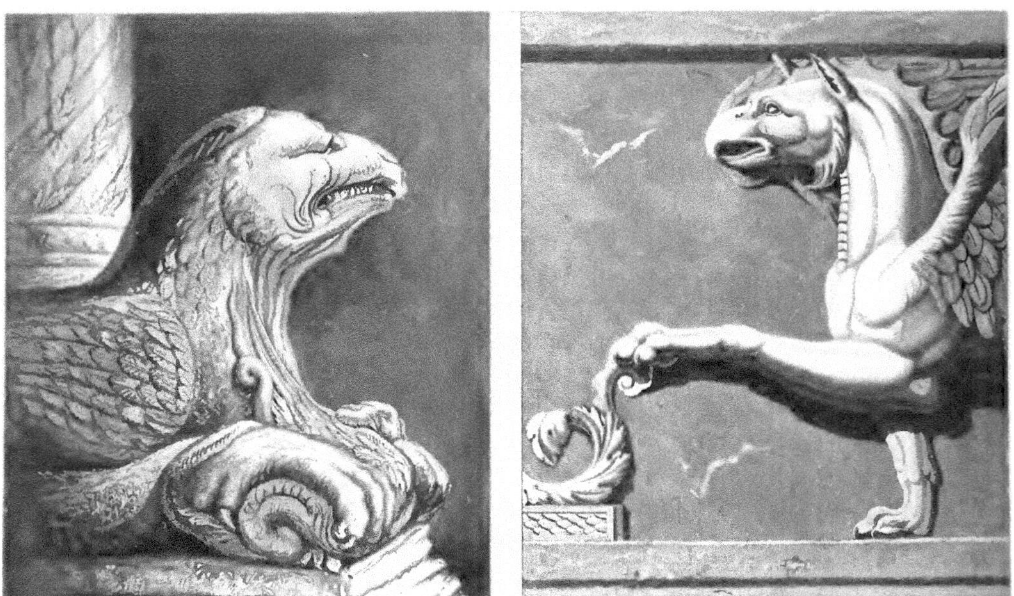

5.3 R. P. Cuff after John Ruskin, 'True and false Griffins: medieval and classical', 1856. Lithograph after drawing. (Author's collection.)

that the 'vital principle is not love of *Knowledge* but love of *Change*'.[18] Gothic art was infinitely greater than Greek art because incompletion was the final synthesis of all its attributes. Unsurprisingly, Ruskin deplored Victorian industrial design on the grounds that it was no more than the manufacture of sameness, the creation of a system devoted to the cult of similitude and uniformity.

In complete contrast to the standardised world of industrial products, the noble grotesque is a brotherhood of the imagination, a condition where 'delightfulness consist[s] *in those very imperfections* which mark it for work done in times of rest. It is not its own merit so much as the enjoyment of him who produced it, which is the source of the spectator's pleasure.' Where the noble grotesque struggles to marry the dynamism of inner life to the experience of the object of art, the ignoble grotesque is no more than 'manufactured terribleness ... measured by line and rule, and dependent on legal shapes of feature.'[19]

Despite this standpoint, it should be conceded that technology is not the origin of Ruskin's woe. For instance, it could be argued that his theory of art adapts the classical notion of *techne*, the poetic revelation of truth in work, to Christian metaphysics, which finds solace in the subject of mutability and failure. Correlative with this preoccupation is the idea that the modern world exists in a mesmerised state, where 'mechanism' controls manufacture through the principle of intermeasurability, the organisation of an object or a process – or a set of labourers – into programmed units.[20] In the hands of Ruskin, the term modern manufacture generates a false language; it is a product of a defective and dishonest system because it distrusts the idea of variable materials and mentalities, the diversity inherent in creation. Modern manufacture is a localised case of a broader process of social and industrial rationalisation. And so it comes to be the task of the critic, in Ruskin's view, to reveal that the operational logic of this system requires that men are '[d]ivided into mere segments of men – broken into small fragments and crumbs of life'.[21]

The trajectory of modern life is described as a process where a culture of handmade grotesque forms gives way to a condition of technological fetishism, something Ruskin finds more dispiriting than the slave economy incarnated in Greek art:

> We have much studied and much perfected, of late, the great civilized invention of the division of labour; only we give it a false name. It is not, truly speaking, the labour that is divided; but the men: – Divided into mere segments of men – broken into small fragments and crumbs of life; so that all the little piece of intelligence that is left in a man is not enough to make a pin, or a nail, but exhausts itself in making the point of a pin, or the head of a nail.[22]

In this modern world, shaped by the idea of beauty advanced in the Greco-academic-mechanical model, people 'esteem smooth minuteness above shattered majesty'. Yet, as he notes in 'The Nature of Gothic', 'Men were not intended to work with the accuracy of tools, to be precise and perfect in all their actions. If you will have that precision out of them, and make their fingers measure degrees like cog-wheels, and their arms strike curves like compasses, you must unhumanize them'.[23] Here, as elsewhere, Ruskin's tirade is directed at the programmatic nature of modern culture, which, he argues, separates producer and viewer from the language of human value and social understanding. We could sum all this up, I want to suggest, by saying that modern manufacture, equally absolutist in design, production and application, is alienated from the truth incarnated in the noble grotesque: true work – true vision – is acceptance of the imperfection of human life.

It is possible to engage with these matters from a number of points and from a number of angles. But we need a critical focus. Therefore, the remainder of this essay examines how the root terms in Ruskin's discourse – 'inner life', 'invention', 'expression' and 'manufacture' – became the preferred terms of discussion when late Victorian designers and craftworkers engaged with Blake's artistic productions. A key issue here is the conceptualisation of the quality of the experience of labour and its relationship to imaginative life. To this end, it is important to note how Ruskin's critique of the cult of perfection coloured Arts and Crafts readings of Blake, where he exists as a creator of a dynamic artworld opposed to notions of standardisation and mass-production.[24]

Most important for our purposes, is understanding why members of the Arts and Crafts Movement used Ruskin to explain Blake's designs and their production processes. The answer lies in how individual designers reimagined the relationship between Ruskin's critical methodology and his value system. That is, the Blake of the Arts and Crafts Movement is taken to incarnate the Ruskinian aesthetic, which emphasised the pleasurable, creative aspects of work as a means of self-realisation. As we will see, Blake became the perfect vehicle for describing the shared sensuous ground Ruskin imagined in *The Stones of Venice*, where the manufacture of art arises from the synthesis of labour, play and the imagination.

Before we turn to this subject, however, a brief overview of Ruskin's torturous engagement with Blake is necessary. Like earlier commentators, such as Allan Cunningham, Ruskin applauds Blake's tenacity and vitality, but there is little of the flashing sympathy we find in his reading of Turner. Blake, he affirms, 'was sincere, but full of wild creeds and somewhat diseased in brain ... The impression that his drawings once made is fast and justly fading away, though they are not without noble merit ... [Apart from the] ... majestic series of designs from the book of Job ... [he produced] nothing for his life's work but coarsely iridescent sketches of enigmatic dreams.'[25]

This is Ruskin's settled view of the matter: Blake's art may be rich in material energy, but this is at the expense of unified consciousness; and so, Blake's vision remains alienated from life because he is a victim of a bio-chemical condition. Just as we must reject the 'warped power' of Blake's designs, so we must note that he was unable to perceive a unity external to himself.[26] This judgment – where Blake fails to distinguish between mental images and the objects of the external world – would be repeated by many commentators throughout the second half of the nineteenth century.[27] Ruskin's Blake burns brightly – in colour he is greater than Rembrandt – but his art is really no more than a kind of juvenile phosphorescence. It is tempting to say that Ruskin found it hard, if not impossible, to relate the Blake cult, which bubbled up from the 1850s, with a model of intellectually serious criticism. It would be left to others to socialise and canonise Blake, to transform him into a public figure, to make him part of national life.[28]

All the same, Alexander Gilchrist and the Rossetti brothers announced that Ruskin's theories of imperfection and penetrative imaginative sympathy were embodied in *The Songs of Innocence and of Experience*, *The Book of Thel* and other examples of Blake's 'composite art' of word and image (figure 5.4). In these serial designs they found the joyous expression of undivided labour, satisfying hand-craftsmanship, and the marriage of mental and physical joy. What distinguishes this Blake from earlier critical models is his identification as a social figure: his first allegiance is to the world of universal experience; his artlife is a vision of the marriage of invention and collaboration; his aesthetic detaches manufacture from the idea of competition; and his genius is the transformation of imaginative life into dynamic designs. In essence, this was to adapt Ruskin's theory of the noble grotesque, the living force of the hand in the energy of the image or object, to make Blake the great master-manufacturer of a magical universe where the observer finds imaginative representations of living phenomena.

Nothing better symbolises this argument, where Blake controls the dynamism of inner life through the experience of work, than Gilchrist's landmark *Life of William Blake* (1863). Gilchrist, a supporter of the Romantic aesthetic as championed by Ruskin and Carlyle, focused on Blake's creative and critical faculties. These sentiments are accompanied by lavish praise of key designs by Blake. As explained by Gilchrist, Blake's images should be understood as incarnations of spontaneity, demonstrations of the free play of imagination. The designs to *The Marriage of Heaven and Hell* are 'highly finished':

> Blake had worked upon them so much, and illuminated them so richly, that even the letterpress seems as if done by hand. The ever-fluctuating colour, the spectral pigmies rolling, flying, leaping among the letters; the ripe bloom of quiet corners, the living light and bursts of flame, the spires and tongues of fire vibrating with the full prism, make the page seem to move and quiver within its boundaries, and you lay the book down tenderly, as if you had been handling something sentient.[29]

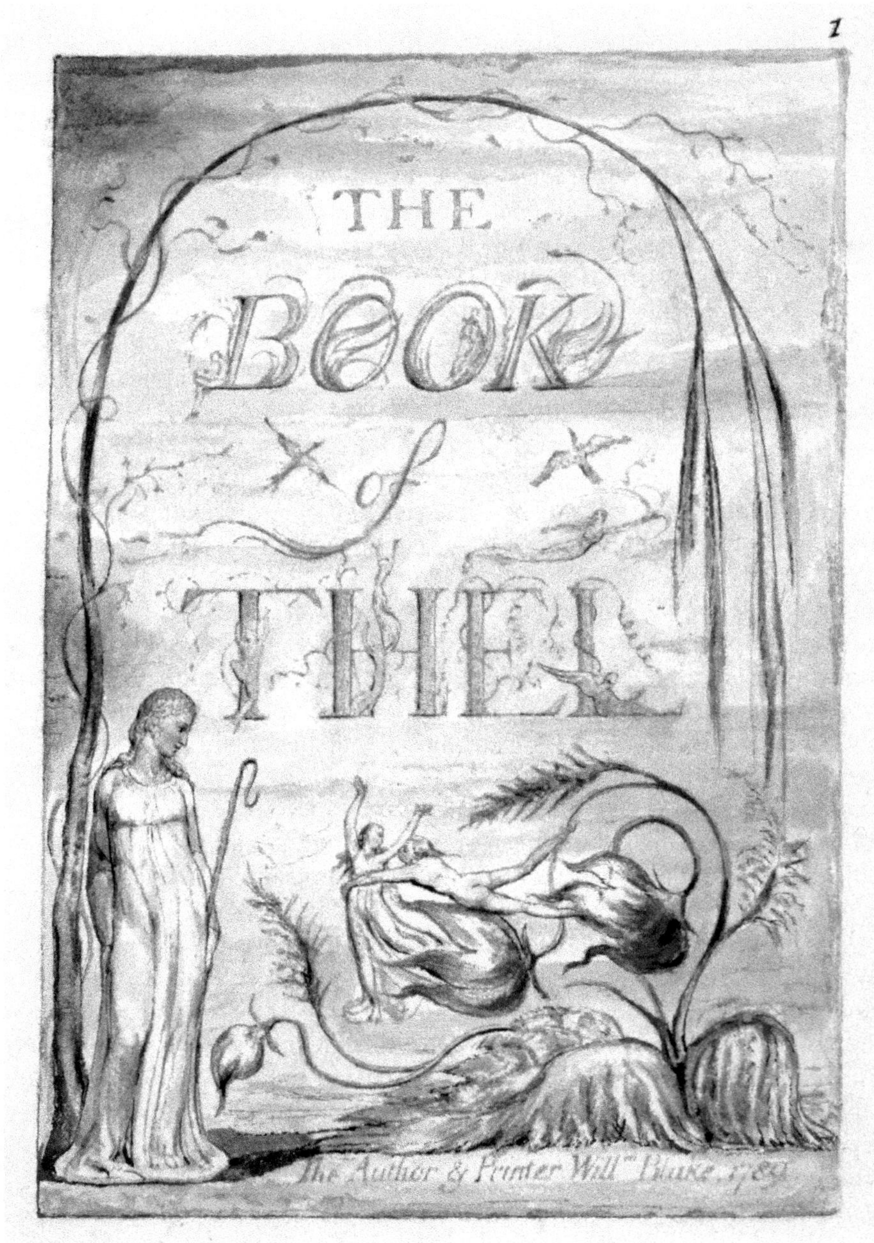

5.4 William Blake, *The book of Thel*, plate 1, 1789. Relief etching, 155 x 107 mm. The Lessing J. Rosenwald Collection, Rare Book & Special Collections Division, Library of Congress. (Courtesy of Library of Congress, Washington DC.)

Blake's creative thinking – his entire mental framework – came from his desire to picture the irrepressible wealth of the outside world, to imagine the fullness of experience in terms of the constructive power of perception. Gilchrist's vision of Blake's art as the energy of life runs in parallel with Ruskin's reading of the noble grotesque, which confirms a universal consciousness beyond the personal self. Blake's grotesque aesthetic acts as counterpoint to mechanism, which Gilchrist and Ruskin identified as the enemy of creative life. This argument, that the human subject is more than another object in the material world, was derived from Carlyle, Gilchrist's great hero.[30] Carlyle's writings, shadowed by cumulatively pessimistic anxieties, circle around the state, function and nature of consciousness within modernity:

> Were we required to characterise this age of ours by any single epithet, we should be tempted to call it, not an Heroical, Devotional, Philosophic Age, but above all others, the Mechanical Age. Nothing is now done directly, or by hand; all is rule and calculated contrivance ... Not the external and physical alone is now managed by machinery, but the internal and spiritual also. Here nothing follows its spontaneous course, nothing is left be accomplished by old natural methods.[31]

The closing lines, which morph into a lament about the phenomenological nature of the mechanism of modernity, recall Blake's famous vision of mind-forged manacles, the imposition of repressive order on all aspects of existence.

Gilchrist's Blake is at once intensely individualised and an expression of a whole way of life. Blake's existence, in his view, is a blueprint for rethinking the nature of creativity and social relationships in contemporary society. It is here, also, that Gilchrist departed from accounts of the liberating potential of the commercialised art world, as, like Carlyle, he identifies academies as instruments or machines of commerce, symbols of the advance of mechanism and the retreat of dynamic or organic manufacture.[32]

Running alongside this interpretation, Gilchrist draws attention to Blake's understanding of the sociology of capitalism and the organisation of social life. To this end, he imagines Blake's images declaring war on 'garniture', the stuff through which art becomes cheap experience and home decoration.[33] In Gilchrist's view, Blake's composite art depicts a 'luminous', 'radiant' and 'ever-fluctuating' world of 'prismatic colour', 'which has the lustre of jewels'.[34] Throughout the *Life*, Gilchrist argues that Blake converts the book into a Ruskinian work of art, by integrating different skills – writing, designing, editing, setting, printing, publishing and marketing. In essence, Gilchrist's Blake outlines the ideal of the Arts and Crafts Movement: he is the consummate creator of sensory qualities and material effects, the master-craftsman whose patterned surfaces should be read as human pictures, images of the reality of aesthetic perception as perfected in the union of hand, heart and mind.

Conceived in these terms Blake becomes important for two reasons. First, it is asserted that he was a master of self-realisation on the grounds that he controlled all aspects of the system in which his works were made. Here manufacture is coeval with perception and mind: it confirms that art, as vision, should be distinguished from the notion of technical accomplishment. Second, it is claimed that Blake's art-life demonstrated the centrality of the aesthetic imagination, but not as something detached from the world of practical life.

These matters – where Blake is at once priest, craftsman and activist – encouraged those involved in the Arts and Crafts Movement to understand perceptual and cultural reform. From this viewpoint, the Blakean aesthetic is understood in terms of creation, craftsmanship and community – care for work, life and humanity. That is, Blake's achievement is to point to a world of undivided being held together by Ruskinian values set against the norms of modern industrial production.

These ideas were vitally important to C. R. Ashbee, Edward Carpenter, Moncure Conway, Walter Crane, Alexander Fisher, W. R. Lethaby, W. J. Linton, Dante Gabriel Rossetti, William Michael Rossetti, William Bell Scott, Frederic Shields, James Smetham, and Phoebe Traquir, all of whom equated Blake with a vision of human wholeness, the unity of social and creative life.[35] Some of these figures saw Blake living in the aesthetic state of sensual freedom, others found a noble Ruskinian artist, an authentic manufacturer, who symbolised a new cultural world where the workshop would be ethically superior to the fine art studio and the sphere of the industrial arts.

Other characteristics, especially Ruskin's distinction between stagnation and energy, sameness and variation, conformity and independence, and industrial production and craft manufacture, could be located in Blake's critical writings. In Blake's idiosyncratic account of the cult of the Old Masters, where masterliness is little more than the manufacture of signs of painterly value, we discover Ruskin's critique of the impersonality of much post-Renaissance art. Nor should it be forgotten that Blake's many maledictions deployed the rhetoric of mechanism and monopoly, the seizure of art by the market, and the transformation of artist into businessman or merchant, to explain systems of cultural production and taste. For instance, his enemies become authorised to dictate the standards of the art world because they 'turn that which is Soul & Life into a Mill or Machine'. Predicting the language of Ruskin and Carlyle, Blake berates those, like Rembrandt and Rubens, who 'cause that every thing in art shall become a Machine'.[36] 'But a Machine is not a Man nor a work of Art[.] [I]t is destructive of Humanity & of Art.'[37] Here, as elsewhere, art is pressed out of shape by material instruments and ideological representations; as agents and addicts of utility and logical process, the compacted forms known as 'Rembrandt' and 'Rubens' uphold system-rationality, the identification of the modern art world in terms of the rational management of resources, the quantification of human performance. These formulations, where artist and art world become mechanised through the iteration of repeatable materiality, predict Ruskin's argument that the study of cultural life includes society and institutions – and the complex forms by which they communicate.

Blake's model of art, arising from the need for ethical-aesthetic unity, attracted a number of Ruskin-inspired critics, including William Michael Rossetti, who framed Blake in terms of the struggle of labour to maintain ownership of its own cognitive and cultural environments: 'He was ... incessantly and indefatigably laborious, patiently toiling on ... turning only from one occupation to another as a relief. Often he would write away at a poem in brief intervals, almost without discontinuing his spell of engraving.' And so, 'a child-like simplicity of personal character, free from self-interest, and ignorant or careless of any policy of self control, though habitually guided and regulated by noble emotions and a resolute loyalty to duty – these are the main lines which we trace throughout the entire career of Blake.' Such qualities make him 'so peculiarly loveable and admirable as a man, and invests his works ... with so delightful a charm'.[38] Again and again in Rossetti's essay, Blake is a vehicle of an overarching view of culture in which the aesthetic life of work makes human consciousness purposeful. Rossetti's Ruskinian Blake, irresistibly fascinating, has mastered the most difficult of arts: the art of enjoying life *through* labour.

Other Ruskinian commentators preferred to promote Blake on the basis that, in the separation of handmade crafts from industrial products, Blake localised the creative potential of manufacture in the recursive freedom of the hand. Crane and Ashbee, leading designers and theorists in the Arts and Crafts Movement, are important exponents of this view, where the prophetic Blake, transcending all division, promotes culture by humanising labour. Their full-impact Blake stimulates new forms of expression and opposes the values fostered by liberal utilitarianism. According to Crane, Blake is 'distinct, and stands alone ... in him seemed to awake something of the spirit of the old illuminator ... He became his own calligrapher, illuminator and miniaturist.' Thus, his 'hand-coloured drawings, the borderings and devices to his own poems, will always be things by themselves'. Crane's Blake represents the victory of dynamic vision over mechanical form: 'the early years of the nineteenth century were illuminated by the name and work of William Blake, whose fresh inspiration and clearness of inner vision', combined with 'poetic feeling and social aspiration both in verse and design', resulted in 'books engraved and printed by himself which remain the remarkable monument of his neglected genius'.[39] Once again, Blake fuses labour and joy because he controls every aspect of the production process.

Crane and Ashbee adhere to Ruskinian dicta by seeing Blake as a prodigy of physical endurance and aesthetic intelligence. Inner vision, at

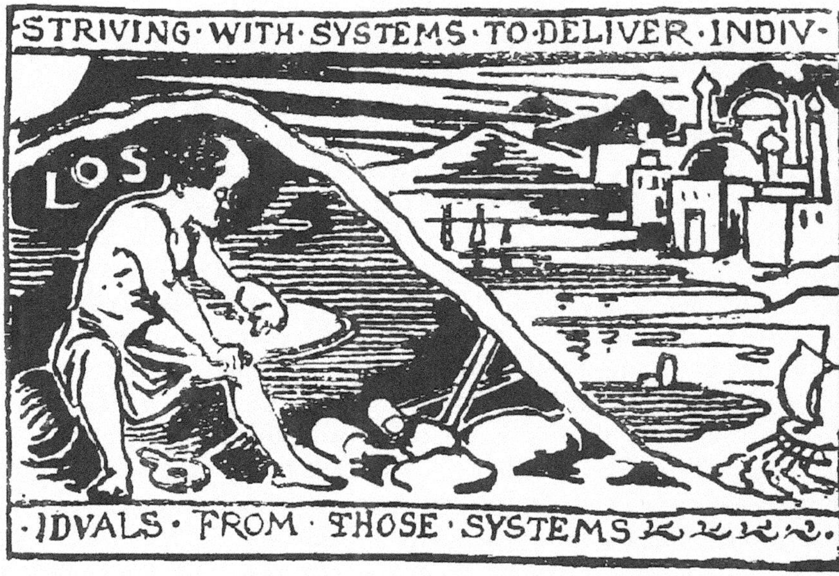

5.5 C. R. Ashbee, 'Striving with systems to deliver individuals from those systems', 1890. Printed design, 90 x 70 mm. (Author's collection.)

once the truth of human life and the origin of the manufacturing process, is the natural source of work. This is why Blake is so important to the Arts and Crafts Movement. Just as he defends work as an expression of concrete human obligation, so he connects the romantic critique of industrialism and the socialist critique of capitalism. Although isolated from his own society, he is, by his morality of work and action, delivered from all notions of cultural isolation by his system of manufacture and so incorporated into the greater spiritual community of creative producers. This leads Ashbee to declare that, in imagining Golgonooza, his sacred city of artistic and spiritual unity, Blake had prophesied the utopian space of Socialism (figure 5.5).[40]

Closely tied to this reading is the proposal that the creator is at once exceptional and normal, a cultural god-king and communal craftsman, folkic idol and hero of hardship. This vision is developed and enhanced in Arts and Crafts discourses where Blake fuses the qualities of the handicraftsman with the virtues of the radical worker: he is the medium by which a vision of the *value* of work becomes an immediate *experience* of work.[41] Such a theme – where Blake articulates human society as something other than the conflict or tension of egos, and where aesthetic production engenders human freedom – comes to the fore in Ashbee's *Socialism and politics* (1906) and *Transactions of The Guild and School of Handicrafts* (1890), which includes this revealing passage on his guild:

> The next three years will try its final success as a movement, test its methods of government, and prove whether it should have done something to establish even a portion of that Sacred City of Art, which Los, the God of Time, in Blake's Jerusalem, sought to build; but if its object ... shall at the end of that period have found fulfilment and justification, The Guild and School of Handicraft will have contributed its mite towards establishing a healthier system on which to build the labour of the English Workman.[42]

The above conditions alone, however, are sufficient for Ashbee to believe that Blake encapsulates artistic individualism, 'where the whole power of creation depends on [the] freedom to create'.[43] At the centre of this criticism is the idea that the creative producer, who initiates his own means of production, is a true manufacturer on the grounds that he presents his work independently of commerce and patronage alike. What disturbs Ashbee and other members of the Arts and Crafts Movement is that industrial society treats the manufacturer as someone who exists in a space dominated by financing capitalists (dealers, bankers, monopolists and 'middlemen').[44] This explains Ashbee's fascination with Blake, whom he associated with confirmation of human individuality, triumph of dynamism over mechanism, the marriage of art and industry in a non-industrial version of value. In short, Blake signalled a condition where the individual controlled all stages in the production of the artwork. With Blake, then, Ashbee found the one historical subject who embodied his definition of Socialism: 'Socialism is a faith whose objective is the betterment of society, which objective it is sought to arrive at through a more equitable distribution, based upon a more collective production of wealth, and the sanction for which rests upon scientific, historic and ethical principles.'[45]

The abiding impression left by the various claims made by members of the Arts and Crafts Movement is that Blake *belonged* to them. A second and related reorientation is seeing Blake as the means by which the idea of manufacture is untethered from ideas of mechanism and processes of industrialisation. The Ruskinian Blake makes art inventive by humanising each and every stage of the production process.[46] It is clear that these two loci of debate – cultural value and material production – which coloured the reception of Blake in the second half of the nineteenth century, should be understood holistically. This essay has argued that it is difficult to avoid the conclusion that Ruskin's broader critical concerns – sensory awareness, aesthetic perception, cultural autonomy and social solidarity – became the means by which Blake was assigned perpetual authority within the Arts and Crafts Movement. Blake converged with Ruskin for two overlapping reasons. First, to confront him was to discover a world where art is at odds with measures of economic use value and mass production; and second, he was imagined as a cultural Petri dish, within which could be cultured the perfect artist-craftsman of the future. In both cases, he stands for aesthetic wholeness as opposed to mechanical unity, the integrity of organic form over formal organisation, and the victory of the handicraftsman over the division of the labour.

In conclusion, the development of Blake criticism allowed members of the Arts and Crafts Movement to at once continue and enrich Ruskinian discourse, where art criticism is social criticism. Blake, as engineered within the Arts and Crafts Movement, addresses material and aesthetic differences between industrial products and handmade crafts. It is clear from this literature that Blake functioned as a heuristic device that permitted certain frameworks of interpretation. Although Ruskin's Blake was an uncooperative purveyor of broken vision, a victim of monomania, the Ruskinian Blake of the Arts and Crafts Movement belonged to their terminological systems, to their community of interpretation, and to their vision of the world as activity, process and manufacture. In one sense, then, Blake's entanglements with Ruskinian discourse produced the scaffold of theory that enabled him to become modern, to become canonical. In the final reckoning, Ruskin's writings on culture provide an important context for approaching the Blake we know today, where he is figured as the source of absolute self-creation, the creator of an artworld of handmade things opposed to notions of work as training, standardisation, mass-production and social programming. Moreover, the arc of Ruskin's argument prefigures the nature of contemporary Blake criticism, where Blake is seen to celebrate work in terms of variation and difference rather than quantification or standardisation.

Notes

1 Ruskin, 'The unity of art', 1859, in Cook and Wedderburn (eds.) *The works of John Ruskin*, vol. 26, pp. 293–318.
2 For a fuller discussion of these matters, see Trodd, *Visions*, pp. 13–86, 140–229.
3 Ellis and Yeats, *The works of William Blake*, vol. 1, pp. 270–9.
4 These ideas are examined by Trodd, *Visions*, pp. 162–3, 203–5.
5 For a fuller description of these discourses and practices within the Arts and Crafts Movement, see Crawford, *C. R. Ashbee* and Stansky, *Redesigning the world*.
6 Crane, 'Presidential Address to the Applied Art Section', pp. 212, 216.
7 See, especially, Ashbee, *Socialism and politics*; Cobden-Sanderson, *Art and life*; Morris, 'The prospects of architecture', pp. 135–50; Sedding, *Art and handicraft*.
8 Morris, 'The prospects of architecture', pp. 140, 149. He adds, at p. 140, 'that fire is the hurry of life bred by the gradual perfection of competitive commerce which we, the English middle classes, when we had won our political liberty, set ourselves to further with an energy, an eagerness, a single-heartedness that has no parallel in history'.
9 The Ashbee Journals, Kings College Library, Cambridge, 4. December 1887.
10 Ashbee's engagement with Blake is examined by Crawford, *C. R. Ashbee*, pp. 222–7.
11 Ruskin's ideas are crystalised in 'The unity of art' and 'Modern manufacture and design', in Cook and Wedderburn (eds.) *The works of John Ruskin*, vol. 26, pp. 293–318, 319–45.
12 Cook and Wedderburn (eds.) *The works of John Ruskin*, vol. 10, pp. 203–4.
13 *Ibid.*, vol. 5, pp. 130–1.

14 Burke, *A philosophical enquiry into the origin of our ideas of the sublime and beautiful.*
15 For background on these matters, see Trodd, Barlow and Amigoni, 'Introduction' in Trodd, Barlow and Amigoni (eds.) *Victorian culture*, pp. 1–20.
16 Cook and Wedderburn (eds.) *The works of John Ruskin*, vol. 5, pp. 146–7.
17 For more on this matter, see Hartley, "'Griffinism, grace and all", in Trodd, Barlow and Amigoni (eds.) *Victorian culture*, pp. 81–96.
18 Cook and Wedderburn (eds.) *The works of John Ruskin*, vol. 10, p. 214 (emphasis in original).
19 *Ibid.*, vol. 11, pp. 158, 168, 176 (emphasis in original).
20 Here I borrow and adapt Eaves's penetrating description of Blake's attitude to the ideas of mechanism and automation: see Eaves, 'Blake and the artistic machine', pp. 903–27.
21 Cook and Wedderburn (eds.) *The works of John Ruskin*, vol. 10, p. 196.
22 *Ibid.*, p. 196.
23 *Ibid.*, p. 192.
24 The best introductions to these matters are Stansky, *Redesigning the world*, pp. 12–68; and Thompson, *William Morris*, pp. 243–330.
25 Cook and Wedderburn (eds.) *The works of John Ruskin*, vol. 5, p. 323; vol. 22, pp. 138, 470. It should be noted that Ruskin scholars have had very little to say about Ruskin's understanding of Blake. For instance, this topic is completely marginalised in Hewison (ed.) *Ruskin's Artists*, the standard work in the field.
26 For more on this matter, see Trodd, *Visions*, pp. 36–7.
27 For an overview of anti-Blake discourse, see Trodd, *Visions*, pp. 106–50.
28 For an account of Ruskin's attitude to Blake, see *Ibid.*, pp. 34–6, 96–7, 171–3, 257–8.
29 Gilchrist, *The life of William Blake*, vol. 1, p. 88.
30 The Gilchrist–Carlyle connection is examined by Dorfman, *Blake in the nineteenth century*, pp. 65–76; Trodd, *Visions*, pp. 49–50; and Viscomi, 'Blake after Blake', p. 214.
31 Carlyle, 'Signs of the times', pp. 441–2. He developed these views in 'Characteristics', *Edinburgh Review*, 1831, although here manufacture is equated with mechanism rather than dynamism and vitality.
32 Guido Reni and the Carracci, the great heroes of academic discourse, are dismissed as 'the gods of the servile crowd'. See Gilchrist, *The life of William Blake*, p. 10.
33 This topic is addressed by Trodd, *Visions*, pp. 13–26.
34 Gilchrist, *The life of William Blake*, pp. 371–3.
35 For a detailed examination of this literature, see Trodd, *Visions*, pp. 140–229.
36 Blake, 'A descriptive catalogue of pictures' [1809], in Erdman (ed.) *The complete poetry and prose of William Blake*, p. 547.
37 Blake, 'Public address' [1809], *Ibid.*, pp. 575–6.
38 Rossetti, 'Prefatory memoir', pp. xxx, lxvi, lxix, lxx–lxxi.
39 Crane, *The decorative illustration of books*, pp. 110–11.
40 Ashbee, *Socialism*, p. 10.
41 See the discussion of this topic in Trodd, *Visions*, pp. 161–2, 388–91.
42 Ashbee, *Transactions*, pp. 30–1.
43 Ashbee, *Socialism*, p. 7.
44 *Ibid.*, pp. 17–18.
45 *Ibid.*, p. 4.
46 It should be noted that Ruskin wanted Victorian industrialists to see themselves as manufacturer-artists, in the manner of Wedgewood, rather than 'merchants': '[Y]ou must remember always that your business, as manufacturers, is to form the market, as much as to supply it.' Cook and Wedderburn (eds.) *The works of John Ruskin*, vol. 16, pp. 343–4.

Bibliography

Ashbee, C. R. *Transactions of The Guild and School of Handicrafts* (London, 1890)
Ashbee, C. R. *Socialism and politics: a study in the readjustment of the values of life* (London, 1906)
Blake, W. 'Public address' [1809], in David V. Erdman (ed.) *The complete poetry and prose of William Blake* (New York, 1988), pp. 571–82
Burke, E. *A philosophical enquiry into the origin of our ideas of the sublime and beautiful* (London, 1757)
Carlyle, T. 'Signs of the times', *Edinburgh Review*, 49 (June 1829), 349–59
Cobden-Sanderson, T. J. *Art and life, and the building and decoration of cities* (London, 1897)
Cook, E. T. and A. Wedderburn (eds.) *The works of John Ruskin* (39 volumes, London, 1903–12)
Crane, W. 'Presidential address to the Applied Art Section', in *Transactions of the National Association for the Advancement of Art and its Application to Industry* (London, 1888)
Crane, W. *The decorative illustration of books* (London, 1896)
Crawford, A. *C. R. Ashbee: architect, designer and romantic socialist* (New Haven and London, 1985)
Dorfman, D. *Blake in the nineteenth century* (New Haven and London, 1969)
Eaves, M. 'Blake and the artistic machine: an essay in decorum and technology', *PLMA*, 92 (1977), 903–27
Ellis, E. J. and W. B. Yeats. *The works of William Blake: poetic, symbolic and critical* (2 volumes, London, 1893)
Erdman, D. V. (ed.) *The complete poetry and prose of William Blake* (New York, 1988)
Gilchrist, A. *The life of William Blake* (2 volumes, London, 1863 and 1880)
Hartley, L. '"Griffinism, grace and all": the riddle of the grotesque in John Ruskin's *Modern Painters*', in Colin Trodd, Paul Barlow and David Amigoni (eds.) *Victorian culture and the idea of the grotesque* (Aldershot, 1999), pp. 81–96
Hewison, R. (ed.) *Ruskin's artists* (Aldershot, 2000)
Morris, W. 'The prospects of architecture' [1881], in May Morris (ed.) *Collected works* (vol. 22, London, 1914), pp. 135–50
Rossetti, W. M. 'Prefatory memoir', in William Michael Rossetti (ed.) *The poetical works of William Blake, lyrical and miscellaneous* (London, 1874)
Sedding, J. D. *Art and handicraft* (London, Kegan Paul, 1892)
Smetham, J. 'Gilchrist's life of William Blake', *London Quarterly Review*, 31 (June 1869), 265–71
Stansky, P. *Redesigning the world* (Princeton, 1985)
Thompson, E. P. *William Morris: romantic to revolutionary* [1955] (London, 1976)
Trodd, C. *Visions of Blake: William Blake in the art world 1830–1930*. (Liverpool, 2012)
Trodd, C., P. Barlow and D. Amigoni (eds.) *Victorian culture and the idea of the grotesque* (Aldershot, 1999)
Viscomi, J. 'Blake after Blake: a nation discovers genius', in Steve Clark and David Worrall (eds.) *Blake, nation and empire* (Basingstoke, 2006), pp. 214–50

PART II

Art and new technologies

6

Repetition, virtuality and mechanical pattern: the significance of the kaleidoscope for the 'fine and useful arts'

Nicole Garrod-Bush

The kaleidoscope is one of the few items of nineteenth-century optical technology still in popular use to the present day. Its simple and self-contained design means it requires no additional equipment to function and can be operated almost immediately by anyone, regardless of their technical expertise. It is often, then, seen as a frivolous toy for making pleasing patterns or a whimsical commodity item. Yet for its original nineteenth-century users, the kaleidoscope was a much more complex and important technological device which had a significance beyond that of play. Its inventor, Sir David Brewster (1781–1868), was a prominent mathematician and natural scientist who regularly contributed to leading scientific journals; he specialised in optics and made important advances to understandings of light polarisation, visual dimensional perception and retinal afterimages.[1] His invention of the kaleidoscope in 1815 was a result of this research, and although certainly used as a gadget for visual entertainment, it originated as a functional instrument of scientific and industrial value that had a wide application. It could produce, quickly and cheaply, a vast number of mechanically designed patterns, marking it for some commentators (such as Ruskin, as I discuss below) as a tool for the industrial production of design which required little or no artistic input or imaginative endeavour. Indeed, its inventor repeatedly emphasised its use as a labour-saving device, aligning it to discourses of industrial manufacture and commodity production.

This chapter positions the kaleidoscope as a creative tool, used across what Brewster called the 'fine and useful arts'. Users of the device had full control over which items were used to create patterns, could choose the arrangement and ratio of colours to be displayed, and were able to manipulate the speed at which the kaleidoscope's reflecting mirrors operated, thus effecting particular types of symmetrical pattern. As Brewster claimed, to use the kaleidoscope relied upon and imparted a large degree of imaginative flexibility and artistic control, and in this way can be seen as an artistic aid rather than an unimaginative instrument. This chapter explores the language of its promotion as a tool to aid in the efficient production of mechanically designed patterns which, although technologically produced, relied upon a clear imaginative vision which was driven by the individual designer. Further, it argues that the kaleidoscope functioned as a stylistic influence on the visual art and design of two Pre-Raphaelite painters. In considering its use across the decorative and fine arts I re-evaluate the significance and value of the kaleidoscope in terms of its applicability to industry or art and for its contemporary users through a new analysis of Brewster's 1858 treatise on his device. This popular publication, reissued three times across the century, aims to educate readers in the mathematical and scientific operation of the kaleidoscope, instructs in how to productively combine the device with other optical technologies, and makes clear the value of its instantaneous pattern-creation to artists, sculptors, print-makers and stone masons. By assessing Brewster's writings on the function and importance of his invention to the fine and useful arts, this chapter demonstrates the relevance of the kaleidoscope to contemporary debates on economic and aesthetic worth, and the relation of the imagination to mechanical precision and replication, extending our understanding of this simple nineteenth-century optical technology beyond rudimentary conceptions of its use as an amusing toy or fashionable gadget.

Brewster's *Treatise* and the popularity of the kaleidoscope

Alongside his publication of scientific work Brewster wrote a number of popular treatises on visual perception. His 1832 work *Letters on natural magic* – a wide-ranging study which centres on physiology, anatomy and the body's vulnerability to sensory manipulation – attempts, as Verity Hunt explains, to inculcate 'a transition from superstition to an educated wonder' by redefining particular fears and superstitions 'as illusions of sense, via scientific description and explanation'.[2] His commitment to popularising contemporary science for a public audience was marked by a keen interest in the operation and function of optical instruments. In 1849, he adapted Charles Wheatstone's mirror stereoscope (an instrument which gave the visual perception of a three-dimensional photograph) into the less cumbersome lenticular stereoscope, making the device newly 'mobile and convenient' for its domestic users, as Sheenagh Pietrobruno points out.[3] Three months after its display in 1851 at London's Great Exhibition, reports suggested that a quarter of a million stereoscopic images had been sold in England and France.[4] The popularity of Brewster's device was supported by his publication of *The stereoscope: its history, theory, and construction* (1856) which detailed the scientific understanding of binocular vision and gave an account of the use to which the device could be put in the service of architecture, engineering, natural history, education and amusement. Recent scholarship has focused on the applicability of the stereoscope to art and sculpture, concentrating especially on its mechanical mass-reproduction of a three-dimensional photographic copy, yet little attention has been paid to the similar multifunctionality of the kaleidoscope as an instrument of art and industry.[5] Brewster's earlier invention and its accompanying treatise had also set out the ways in which a simple optical technology could be of value to the decorative and fine arts, collapsing strict distinctions between mechanised labour and artistic craft, repetition and creativity, and replication and authenticity.

While undertaking research on the polarisation of light, Brewster found that planes of mirrored glass inclined at a certain angle simultaneously created and exhibited a symmetrical arrangement of colours and shapes reflected around a centre. Seeking to recreate this mechanical pattern-work, Brewster designed a simple instrument consisting of an outer tube containing specifically inclined mirrors with an aperture for the eye at one end and a glass cell at the other, in which coloured beads and other such objects could permanently be fixed. When the tube and the cell were rotated against each other, the mirrors multiplied the reflections into a symmetrical image able to be put in motion by the hand of the viewer, thereby displaying a successive series of circular patterns. The device began manufacture in 1817 but was quickly copied and a number of crude versions began to appear for sale. However, Brewster was still able to keenly delight in the popularity of this pirated version. In a letter to his wife, he writes that: 'You can form no conception of the effect which the instrument excited in London; all that you have heard falls infinitely short of the reality. No book and no instrument in the memory of man ever produced such a singular effect. They are exhibited publicly on the streets for a penny ... and thousands of poor people make their bread by making and selling them.'[6] An article in the *Journal of Science and the Arts* on the history of the kaleidoscope corroborates this level of popular appeal: 'A universal mania for the instrument seized all classes, and from the lowest to the highest, from the most ignorant to the most learned, every person not only felt, but expressed the feeling, that a new pleasure had been added to their existence'.[7] We notice here the almost viral appeal of the kaleidoscope: both Brewster's account and the *Journal*'s article reference the wide uptake of the device and the speed with which its popularity 'seized' its users, who were gripped by enthusiasm for its visual effect.

However, Brewster's central concern about the numerous copied devices was that they were not constructed with adequate mathematical precision, and in offering an inferior spectacle could not demonstrate how the kaleidoscope might be used as an artist's tool. To counter this, he composed *A treatise on the kaleidoscope* (1819) with the purpose of

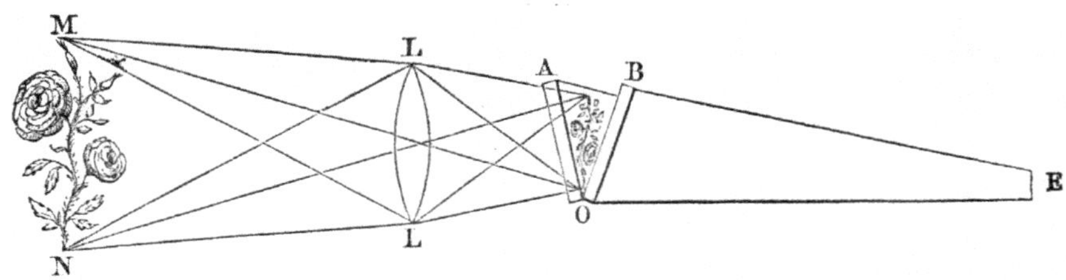

6.1 The kaleidoscope utilizing a telescope lens, 1858. (© Bill Bryson Library, Durham University, UK.)

'explaining, in as popular manner as I could, the principles and construction of the Kaleidoscope; ... of pointing out the various methods of using it as an instrument of recreation; and of instructing the artist how to employ it'.[8] The *Treatise* was revised and republished in 1858 (and reissued in 1870) as *The kaleidoscope: its history, theory, and construction, with its application to the fine and useful arts*, evidencing the continued popularity of the device at mid-century.[9] Its generous employment of diagrams and illustrations articulates a desire to educate, in language accessible to the general reader, the scientific and mechanical principles involved in its operation (a model his treatise on the stereoscope would later follow).

The treatise describes two types of kaleidoscope: the simple and compound. Using the former, small miscellaneous items such as bits of glass, beads or lace are placed into the fixed cell and in rotating this against the tube's angled mirrors a symmetrical pattern of reflecting, moving forms would be produced. It is this configuration of the kaleidoscope with which we are most familiar, and which tends to be reproduced and sold to the present day. However, it was possible to extend its visual range: by adding a telescopic lens in place of a fixed cell, the compound kaleidoscope could view any external objects, paintings, sculptures or buildings and create a kaleidoscopic pattern from these structures (figure 6.1). Brewster termed this adaptation the 'tele-kaleidoscope'.[10] It became possible to make patterns from objects placed at any distance from the lens, thereby 'extend[ing] indefinitely the use and application of the instrument'.[11] It is this development which allowed Brewster to assert its use not just as an item of play or 'rational amusement' but as a valuable tool applicable to artistic practice: 'Without such an extension of its power, the Kaleidoscope might only be regarded as an instrument of amusement; but when it is made to embrace objects of all magnitudes, and at all distances, it takes its place as a general philosophical instrument, and becomes of the greatest use in the fine, as well as the useful arts'.[12]

Virtual design and mechanisms of efficiency

The kaleidoscope's operation of inverting and reflecting an image to create a structured design made it a valuable tool for the swift creation of perfectly symmetrical patterns – an element which Brewster writes was essential to beautiful works of art: 'If we examine the various objects of art which have exercised the skill and ingenuity of man, we shall find that they derive all their beauty from the symmetry of their form, and that one work of art excels another in proportion as it exhibits a more perfect development of this principle of beauty'.[13] That the device simultaneously made and displayed in its viewfinder a changeable visual field of harmonious symmetrical forms encouraged Brewster to situate his invention as a tool of artistic productivity: beautiful design could be mechanically manufactured. His revised treatise extended this value by instructing how each design could be copied, thus conserving each transient arrangement for further use. This was effected by combining the device with other optical instruments such as the camera, microscope or projecting magic lantern. The ability to capture a design photographically meant that, as Brewster advises, 'the most complex figures can be almost instantaneously transferred to paper, or the plated copper, and hundreds of designs offered to the choice of the artist who is to employ them'.[14] Brewster lectured on this process and exhibited kaleidoscopic photographs at the St Andrews Literary and Philosophical Society in the same year, as Martin Kemp explains.[15] Its display could also be projected, enabling the spectacle to be enlarged and viewed by an audience; there is evidence for this practice from the 1860s at London's Royal Polytechnic Institution, through to the 1890s.[16] In projecting and collecting copies of kaleidoscopic views, a catalogue of designs could be made and its shifting, transitory spectacle refigured as a system of constant mechanical creativity.

A further aspect which could benefit those tasked with the creation of symmetrical design was the kaleidoscope's ability to present a virtual image of a finished creation: a partially completed design could be mirrored to give an indication of the symmetrical whole, or a motif might be repeated to give a sense of the overall pattern. Further, when used in conjunction with a magic lantern, the projected display could show a large-scale rendering of 'the final effect of the design' and offer a virtual visual prediction of the finished piece.[17] Brewster lists particular areas of design to which the kaleidoscope might contribute, the first of which is architectural ornamentation. Giving the example of decorative stonework, he instructs that once the first elements of the design are carved, the kaleidoscope's lens should be trained upon the stone and, 'by varying the inclination of the reflectors, an immense variety of the most beautiful designs will be exhibited, in the finest relief, and as perfect as if they had been carved out of stone by the most skilful workman'. Utilising the kaleidoscope in this way allowed the artist to see a visual impression of the whole carving without having to complete the entire design. This is illustrated with an example of a symmetrical carving of a lion's head with leaf motif. Brewster writes that 'If one half of the leaf is an inverted image of the other half, it is necessary to only carve one half of it, and place the reflectors at an angle [enabling] the whole leaf to be multiplied. [The artist can] then examine what will be its final effect'. The kaleidoscope operates as 'a most important auxiliary' in its ability to render a virtual visual prediction, offering the artist flexibility to alter his design during the process of composition.[18]

Next, Brewster considers the value of the kaleidoscope to painters and to designers of textile products, asserting that the device's key appeal here is its ability to perform the 'double task' of showing line *and* colour arrangements: 'while it creates the outline, it at the same time fills it up with colour; and by representing the effect of the two in a state of combination, it enables the artist to judge of the harmony of his tints, as well as of the proportion of his forms'.[19] Using the example of carpet design, sample material arranged on a flat surface could be reflected and inverted by the kaleidoscope's mirrors, enabling the designer to judge the overall effect produced, and make adjustments to the predominance or juxtaposition of particular colours. Brewster explains, 'The artist thus has it in his power, not only to produce any kind of outline that he chooses, but *regulate* the masses of colour by which it is to be filled up'.[20] Again, the kaleidoscope operates as a tool for visualising a virtual completed design whose formal arrangement of colour could be easily and quickly altered without the potential costs to labour incurred if the final design had to be amended.

Central to Brewster's claim that his instrument provided a 'high degree of utility' to those arts 'in which the creation of symmetrical ornaments forms a necessary part' was the idea of its efficiencies in time and labour. His treatise promoted the kaleidoscope for its ability to quickly generate a catalogue of kaleidoscopic designs: it produces, as Brewster writes, 'hundreds of designs' which could be 'offered to the artist who is to employ them'.[21] The *Literary Gazette* went even further, proclaiming that 'When the instrument is thus applied, an infinity of patterns are created, and the artist can select such as he considers most suitable to his work'.[22] Although controlled by the hand of the user and composed of preselected elements, the kaleidoscope's designs were the result of mechanical chance, meaning it could generate new patterns faster and more consistently than the human imagination (and indeed the human hand). On one hand, keen to emphasise the beauty and artistry of kaleidoscopic patterns, Brewster's treatise did not draw back from promoting the device's mechanical operation or from directly comparing this to the productivity of the craft practitioner: its 'unexampled rapidity … will create, in a single hour, what a thousand artists could not invent in the course of a year', Brewster writes. In using the kaleidoscope, increased economic productivity could be achieved. It offered a 'regular supply' of desired items 'at a cheaper rate' and 'in a more perfect state'.[23] Artistic production is here riveted to an economic model of efficient labour as the instabilities and inconsistencies of human imagination and craft are set aside to make way for the steady supply of machine-manufactured design.

It was precisely these claims that John Ruskin responded to in an 1859 lecture, a year after the publication of Brewster's revised treatise. Speaking on the importance of interpretive sketching as a way to express the fundamental aspects of an object or landscape, he pronounced that this practice 'gets the student quit at once of the notion of formal symmetry'.[24] The spontaneity of a sketch, Ruskin argued, confers the characteristics of the artist's subject and encourages thoughtful and engaged design, whereas: 'If you learn only to draw a leaf well, you are taught in some of our schools to turn it the other way, opposite to itself; and the two leaves set opposite ways are called a 'design': and thus it is supposed possible to produce ornamentation, though you have no more brains than a looking-glass or a kaleidoscope has'.[25] Although dismissive, Ruskin's timely reference to kaleidoscopic mirroring further engaged the device in debates about the mechanical augmentation of artistic work and the relation of imaginative labour to economic values of industrial productivity. Responding to Brewster's example of using the kaleidoscope to create a stonework leaf motif, Ruskin derided the device as a tool of unimaginative mirroring, capable only of replication and lacking thoughtful creativity. However, as discussed above, it was Brewster's contention that instead of replacing imaginative endeavour, the kaleidoscope would augment artistic creation and pattern design. His treatise anticipates potential dismissals such as Ruskin's, and makes a continual effort to stress that the kaleidoscope would not supplant the artist; instead, his skilled operations 'may be facilitated and improved' and his labour 'abridged'.[26] In combining the discourses of artistic creation and industrial manufacture Brewster's treatise attempts to wed the imaginative work of creating an ornamental design to contemporary demands that production (of any category) be temporally and economically efficient.[27]

Mechanical reproduction, optical technologies and the fine arts

In *The exposition of 1851*, Charles Babbage makes a distinction between fine and decorative (what he terms 'industrial') arts, based on their reproducibility and economics of production. 'The characteristic of the fine arts', he writes, 'is, that each example is an individual – the production of individual taste, and executed by individual hands', making it necessarily 'costly', whereas of industrial arts 'each example is but one of a multitude, – generated according to the same law, by tools or machines ... Their produce is consequently cheap'.[28] Babbage uses the example of machine-manufactured lace and categorises it as an industrial art, yet in comparison the kaleidoscope sits uneasily between the two definitions. Considered against Babbage's definition of industrial arts, a kaleidoscopic

Deepest Red, . .	Blue and Green equally mixed.
Red, ...	Blue and Green, with most Blue, mixed.
Orange Red, . .	Blue mixed with much Indigo.
Orange, . . .	Blue and Indigo, the Indigo predominating.
Orange Yellow, .	Indigo unmixed.
Yellow, . . .	Violet and Indigo nearly in equal portions.
Greenish Yellow, .	Pale Violet.
Green, ...	Violet.
Greenish Blue, .	Violet and Red in equal portions.
Blue, ...	Orange Red, Red.
Indigo, ...	Orange Yellow.
Violet, ...	Green.

6.2 Brewster's table of harmonic colours, 1858. (© Bill Bryson Library, Durham University, UK.)

pattern was extremely cheap to produce, both in terms of material and labour: the device could be bought cheaply, its display was composed of very basic miscellaneous items such as cloth or glass beads, and it required minimal effort on the part of the user-viewer to operate. Following Babbage's language, each iteration was generated in accordance to the same law. Yet at the same time its display fits his definition of the fine arts: its unique designs were produced according to individual taste and executed individually each time by hand. For Brewster, the production of each kaleidoscopic pattern could not be separated from the generative hand of the artist, who was crucial to both the design of the pattern and its continual execution with each controlling twist of the mirrored tube against the lens.[29] Brewster's treatise frequently emphasises this 'individual' aspect of the kaleidoscope's visual production and the importance of imaginative design when selecting the colours of its display: he offers readers a table of harmonic colours to ensure the most aesthetically pleasing combinations are created (see Figure 6.2), aligning it with Babbage's description of fine arts.[30]

Babbage continues that in the display of 'new methods of surface printing for multiplying original designs', such as engraving, 'it would be very desirable to place before the eye of the spectator, the original forms from which the copies were derived'.[31] Here we find a further operational aspect which set the mechanical pattern-making of the kaleidoscope apart from other new technologies and processes for the production of copies. Engraving, photography, and the electrotype process for recreating sculpture, for example, were all able to produce replicas from an original artefact or image, whereas the kaleidoscope's visual display had no extant original. Its mirrors produced a unique design *based* on the view in front of its lens, not a simulation or exact imitation. In this way, the kaleidoscopic view was an abstraction of colour and line, but not an indexical copy in the way that photography was understood to be.[32]

Yet it shared a commonality with photography: its uneasy status as both a mechanical system for the mass-production of visual images and a highly interactive, hand-operated tool which required the imagination of the user to design the fundamental aspects of its patterning evokes the similarly difficult contemporary positioning of the new technology of the camera. An article in *The Critic* admitted to being 'in doubt whether to treat this [photography] as a contribution to Science or Art', and cautioned that while there is 'abundant evidence of the utility of the Calotype process to the traveller; ... to the naturalist; ... and to the world at large', its 'value to the artist' should not go unnoticed.[33] The photographer might have been using a technological process but a proficient artistic skill was still required in order to create a photographic image of high standard, a combination of artistry and mechanism commented upon in the *Spectator*'s review of William Henry Fox Talbot's *Pencil of nature* (1844): of Talbot's photographic renderings of sculpture taken from different distances and under different lighting conditions, the reviewer allows that such 'delicate gradations of light into shade produce an appearance of relief and rotundity, which attests to the superiority of the "pencil of nature" to that of art'.[34] Diane Waggoner notes the increase of various societies, groups and journals devoted to the expressive and artistic properties of photography after the Great Exhibition (the Society of the Arts in London held their first photography exhibition in 1852, and 1857 saw the inclusion of photography at the Manchester Art Treasurers Exhibition).[35] Such large events were, as Waggoner shows, integral to the development of a language for the discussion of photography as not only a technological process but a new artistic medium.

Although a much more modest device, the kaleidoscope held much in common with the positioning of and debate around the status of photography in relation to technological reproduction and artistic design, assisted in no small part by the language of Brewster's treatise and the potential uses he advocated for the instrument. Emphasising its labour-saving properties and mapping its mechanical productivity onto models of industrial efficiency, his publication simultaneously pronounced strongly upon the artistic merit of the kaleidoscope as a tool for the creation of 'splendid tints' which were 'the most beautiful in optics'.[36] Such views could only be crafted through the skilful and imaginative composition of palettes of 'harmonic colours' and 'fine forms', the combination of which 'communicates richness and variety' and gives a 'sensation of pleasure'.[37] The aesthetic potential of its display made it highly relevant to the fine arts, Brewster asserted, and in the final part of this chapter I want to consider a particular use of the kaleidoscope as a stylistic motif in work by two Pre-Raphaelite painters.

Kaleidoscopic motifs in Pre-Raphaelite art

The visual art of the Pre-Raphaelites has been associated with types of nineteenth-century optical technology, and particularly that of photography. Discussing the 'radical optical fidelity' of their style, Lindsay Smith cautions that 'Critics align conditions of photographic exactitude with microscopic detail in discussion of Pre-Raphaelite technique ... However, such references to microscopic clarity elide precisely those culturally specific relationships of Pre-Raphaelitism with innovative optical devices ... In short, critics, ironically, have sought analogues in the wrong instruments, in the microscope and the camera.'[38] Taking the stereoscope as such an overlooked 'innovative optical device', she persuasively demonstrates that both 'Pre-Raphaelitism and stereoscopy articulate a newly arousing depth of field' and makes the extended point that Pre-Raphaelite work often 're-inscribes the illusionism of depth' in order to subvert the monopoly of what she terms Romantic 'monoscopy'.[39] In particular, the use of perceptual dimensionality in John Everett Millais's *The woodsman's daughter* (1850–51) 'foregrounds both the position of a Victorian stereoscopically empowered beholder and the agency of depth of field'.[40] The interaction of viewer and subject which this implies, and Smith's reading of the painting's stylistic mimicry of an active perceptual experience – that of seeing three-dimensionally – extends our reading of the Pre-Raphaelites' engagement with contemporary developments in optics and visual technology. Yet beyond photography and its associated devices there is a further and little-appraised context in which we find Pre-Raphaelite work responding to and utilising the instruments of mid-Victorian perception: that of the kaleidoscope and its motif of reflected, repeating symmetry.

First, an undated watercolour by William Holman Hunt, entitled 'Kaleidoscope' (see figure 6.3), depicts an enlarged and vividly coloured kaleidoscopic view and offers intriguing evidence that the kaleidoscope was used by, and was of artistic interest to, fine art practitioners. Hunt's sketch records a background of hexagonal shapes overlaid with reflected shapes and colours which are repeated three times around an axis of kaleidoscopic reflection. John Gage considers the piece an exercise in 'searching for a rational principle of colour harmony as applied in pattern' and dates it from the period when Hunt was working on *The finding of the saviour in*

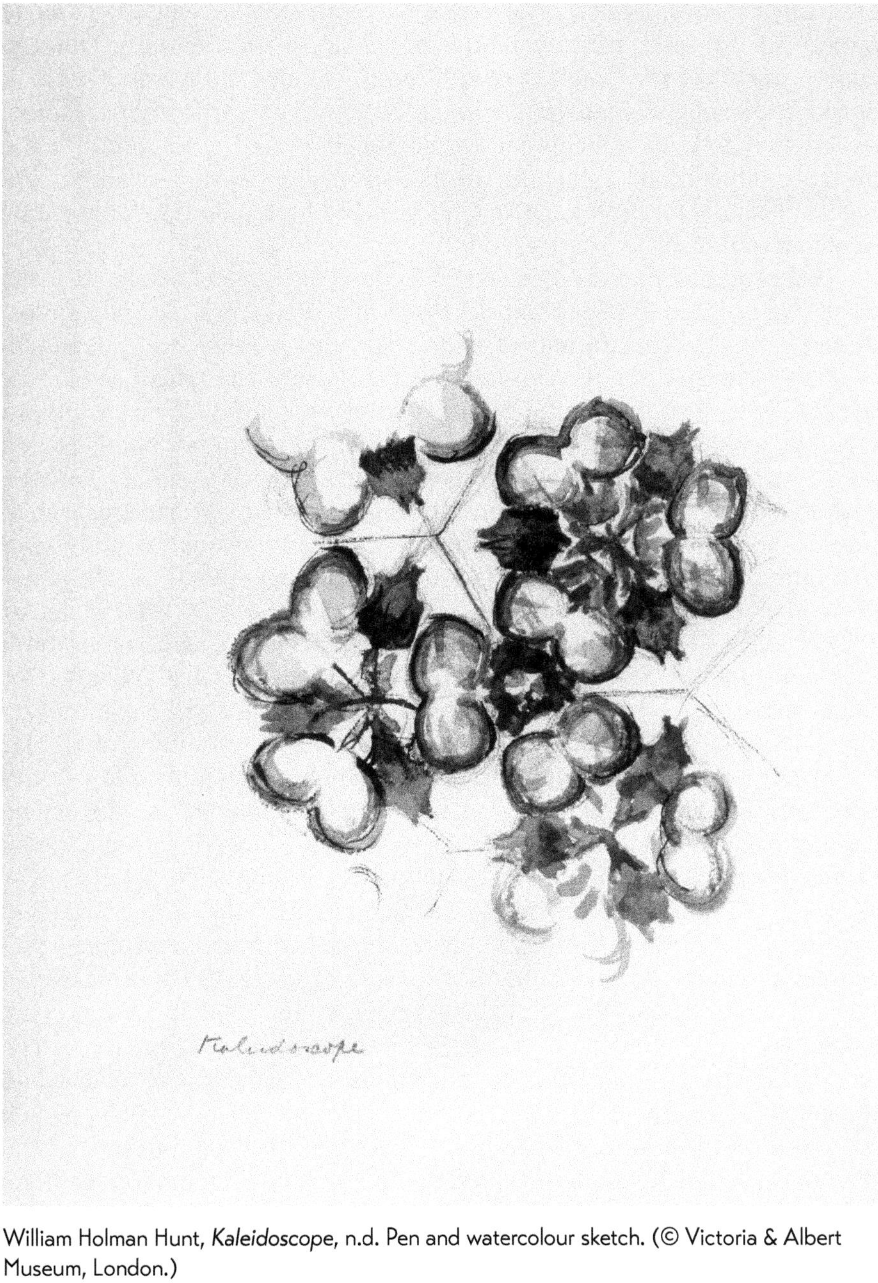

William Holman Hunt, *Kaleidoscope*, n.d. Pen and watercolour sketch. (© Victoria & Albert Museum, London.) **6.3**

the temple (1860), as both evidence a 'concern with repeated decorative patterns'.[41] No other representations of kaleidoscopic views are found in Hunt's work, yet this small (130 x 98 mm), detailed appraisal of a kaleidoscope's display demonstrates the utilisation of its particular perceptual experience as both a technique for composition and a resource for the sketch's subject, and evidences an interest in the device's function as a mechanical tool for producing symmetrical and harmonious arrangements of colour and form.

A second and previously unacknowledged example of a kaleidoscopic motif can be seen in Dante Gabriel Rossetti's 1865 work, *The blue bower* (figure 6.4), the background of which provides a remarkable depiction of the all-over patterning seen through the device. The female subject of the piece, dressed in sumptuous and vibrantly coloured fabrics, is placed centrally within a bower of trailing passion flowers with her hands placed on a Japanese koto. Behind her head, and occupying almost half the canvas, is a background composed of hexagonal blue tiles featuring a white prunus blossom motif. Art historians have pointed towards the mid-Victorian interest in Oriental design as providing the inspiration for the painting's distinctive background, and indeed Rossetti was a keen collector of such pieces.[42] Described by his brother, William Rossetti, as having a 'passion for blue china', he competed with James McNeill Whistler for the most extensive and striking collection.[43] The particular blue and white vine pattern of *The blue bower* originates from a type of Chinese ginger jar – Rossetti coined these 'hawthorn pots' – which recur in his mid-century paintings.[44] In the watercolour *Woman combing her hair* (1864), the female subject sits beside a white vase painted with a blue bird. However, Rossetti produced another version of this painting a year later (the same year as he painted *The blue bower*) under an identical title and added a second vase: a small hawthorn pot of vivid blue overlaid with the distinctive white prunus blossom motif. His later 1867 portrait of Mrs F. R. Leyland, *Monna Rosa*, features a large identical blue hawthorn pot containing pale pink roses. Yet the treatment of this Oriental ceramic pattern differs in *The blue bower* to Rossetti's other representations. Treuherz, Prettejohn, and Becker write that the design of its background is an 'invented form' which is 'based on the hawthorn pattern'.[45] Modifying this, I propose that the tiled background is less an invented geometric design stemming from the blossom motif but is instead an accurate rendering of a hawthorn pot as it would appear to a viewer looking at the object through the inclined, rotating mirrors of a kaleidoscope. Although a repetitious pattern, each iteration is turned at a slightly different angle and represents the continual twisting of the lens against the mirrors as the kaleidoscopic view steadily rotates to offer incremental variations of its pattern. Meanwhile, the tiles have a hard, lacquered sheen that contrasts with the sumptuousness of the sitter's curled hair and abundant dress. The defined folds of the green

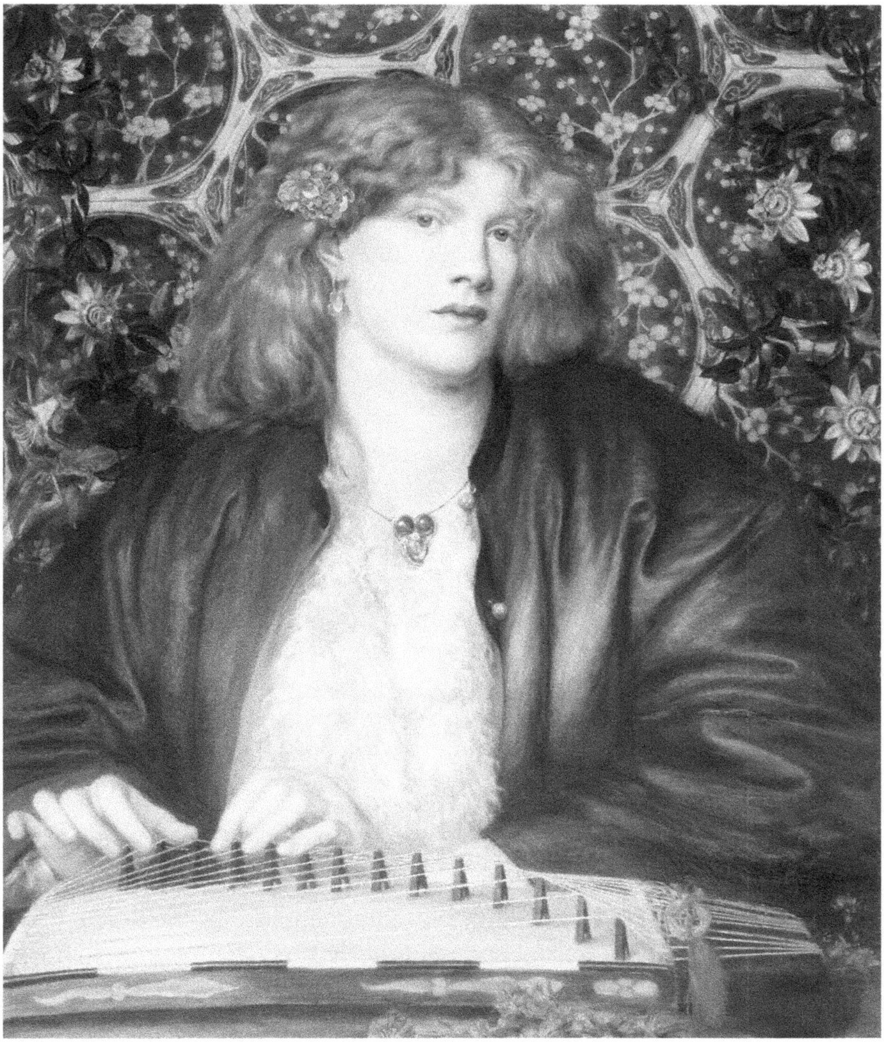

Dante Gabriel Rossetti, *The blue bower*, 1865. Oil on canvas. 840 x 709 mm. (With kind permission of The Henry Barber Trust © The Barber Institute of Fine Arts, University of Birmingham.) 6.4

garment imply a thickness and depth to the fabric that opposes the flatness of the tiles behind. This again produces a kaleidoscopic effect: looking through its lens, all sense of texture and depth would disappear, flattened into a visual environment controlled by and displayed upon smooth glass. Finally, the addition of thick white dividing lines calls particular attention to the kaleidoscopic style of Rossetti's geometric background. Their function on first glance is to signify a backdrop composed of segmented individual tiles, as opposed to wallpaper, for example. Within their hexagonal net, each corner where the tiles meet a smaller, thrice-reflected blue flourish is depicted. These white intersections represent the lines within the kaleidoscope's display formed by the boundary of each reflecting mirror. The patterned blue tiles turn and repeat around a reflective axis, as a kaleidoscopic pattern turns around fixed lines of reflection.

Paul Spencer-Longhurst comments that the tiles of Rossetti's painting 'correspond to no Oriental prototypes' but that 'Perhaps coincidentally, the effect produces star-like patterns'.[46] However, when we consider the popularity of Brewster's device at the mid-century and Hunt's sketch of a view down a kaleidoscope featuring identical hexagonal netting and a motif of thrice-reflected patterning, it is clear that Rossetti is deliberately combining the contemporary fashion for Chinese design with the operation and perceptual experience of looking through a kaleidoscope. Beyond coincidentally creating a geometrical star-like patterning, as Spencer-Longhurst claims, the systematically structured background productively contrasts with the central female subject and enables the painting to simultaneously exhibit states of inertia and mobility. Alongside the opposition between the tactile appeal of the sitter's garments and the background's glassy, kaleidoscopically flattened hawthorn pots, a further opposition is found in the stillness of the sitter and the implied motion of the tiled display. The model, Fanny Cornforth, holds the gaze of the observer captive while the hexagonal tiles behind evidence the slow rotation of a kaleidoscope, suggesting a continual movement off edges of the canvas and outwards in a steadily renewing pattern. The kaleidoscopic tiles speak back to the meaning of the painting's title: the bower proliferates around the sitter, creating an encasement, just as the viewer looking into a kaleidoscope finds their entire visual field overtaken by endlessly repeating symmetrical forms – a bower for the eye. Additionally, the steady circular hand-rotation of the kaleidoscope's display is picked out by the gentle arc of the koto's black bridges and the sitter's poised fingers indicate their readiness to manipulate the instrument's strings, allowing Rossetti to layer his painting with further instances of stillness and motion and the moment of potentiality between these two states. The blue tiles then, offer more than a vibrant and fashionable backdrop: their kaleidoscopic mirroring draws attention to the medium of the canvas as a flattening, mediating device, analogous to the kaleidoscope itself, but also offers a sense of mobility, animation and renewal, which we see echoed in the trailing passion flowers and in the dynamic potential of the unplucked strings.

Conclusion

The nineteenth-century kaleidoscope defies easy categorisation: at once promoted by its inventor for its use to the decorative *and* fine arts, its ability to make numerous mechanical patterns swiftly and cheaply associated it with the values of industrial production and models of labour-saving economy. Yet its operational model necessitated constant human intervention from the hand of the artist to design each individual arrangement of colour and form, and to control the speed and alignment of its rotating, symmetrical patterns. Although mechanical in operation, the kaleidoscopic view, therefore, fundamentally stems from a unique and imaginative act of creation. Further, its association with the body tempers its alignment with models of industrial production and unthinking replication (as Ruskin charges it) and instead connects it to the hand of the craft practitioner and the use of instruments to assist, not overtake, artistic composition. The device encourages us to fragment an oppositional understanding of artistic and industrial value and instead piece together a more holistic understanding of a visual culture which was able to simultaneously contain and draw on imagination and technology, the artistic and the mechanical, just as Rossetti's painting skilfully combines the tactile and the visual, repetition and creation, and suggests the aesthetic harmony of colour and music through the symmetrical patterning of mechanical kaleidoscopic reflection.

Notes

1 See Wade, *Brewster and Wheatstone on vision* for a survey of Brewster's writings on physiological optics and ocular instruments.
2 Hunt, 'Raising a modern ghost', paras 2–3.
3 Pietrobruno, 'The stereoscope and the miniature', p. 172.
4 Stafford and Terpak, *Devices of wonder*, p. 357. See also Plunkett's survey of the popularity of the stereoscope and its revival of interest in the twentieth century in 'Selling stereoscopy'.
5 See Di Bello's 'Editorial' for a good overview of these debates.
6 Letter dated 24 May 1818, quoted in Gordon, *The home life of Sir David Brewster*, p. 55.
7 'History of Sir David Brewster's kaleidoscope', *Journal of Science and the Arts*, 335.
8 Brewster, *A treatise on the kaleidoscope*, p. 8.
9 This resurgence of interest was likely encouraged by the exhibition of various other optical technologies at the Great Exhibition and in venues for the popular demonstration of practical science. See Chapter Three of Morus, *Frankenstein's children* and Plunkett, 'Transparencies, optical recreations and the invention of the screen' for a good overview.
10 Brewster, *The kaleidoscope*, p. 85.
11 *Ibid.*, p. 6.
12 *Ibid.*, p. 82.
13 *Ibid.*, p. 134.
14 *Ibid.*, p. 148.
15 This lecture took place 30 January 1858. See Kemp, '"Philosophy in sport" and the "sacred precincts"', p. 229.
16 A late nineteenth-century article in *Hobbies* titled 'An improved kaleidoscope' informed its readers that by utilising a light source and a kaleidoscope holder, the device's 'design may then be reflected on to a sheet of paper' to be viewed by 'a whole company of persons'. Reproduced in Herbert (ed.) *A history of pre-cinema*, pp. 239–40. Helen Groth records an earlier instance of the projected kaleidoscope

at the Royal Polytechnic Institution during a lecture given by Dr John Henry Pepper and advertised in the *Illustrated London News* on 31 March 1866. Groth, 'Kaleidoscopic vision and literary invention in an "age of things"', p. 235.

17 Brewster, *The kaleidoscope*, p. 137.
18 *Ibid.*, p. 140.
19 *Ibid.*, p. 141.
20 *Ibid.*, p. 146 (emphasis added).
21 *Ibid.*, p. 148.
22 'The kaleidoscope', p. 356.
23 Brewster, *The kaleidoscope*, pp. 135–6.
24 Cook and Wedderburn (eds.) *The works of John Ruskin*, vol. 16, p. 330.
25 *Ibid.*, p. 331.
26 Brewster, *The kaleidoscope*, pp. 135–6.
27 Lindsay Smith, writing on Brewster's treatise on the stereoscope, argues that the publication is important for the 'rhetoric of legitimacy' it lends the device as it 'forges for the discourse of optics new contextual relationships' between technological innovation, theories of perception, and debates about the production of art. See 'The elusive depth of field, pp. 87–9.
28 Babbage, *The exposition of 1851*, pp. 48–9.
29 *Ibid.*, p. 50.
30 Brewster, *The kaleidoscope*, pp. 71–2.
31 Babbage, *The exposition of 1851*, pp. 49, 53.
32 See Di Bello, 'Photography and sculpture', p. 20.
33 *The Critic*, 1:1 (15 August 1844), quoted in Schaff, *Out of the shadows*, p. 147.
34 *Spectator*, 17:838 (20 July 1844), 685, quoted *ibid*.
35 See Waggoner, 'Uncompromising truth', pp. 2–17.
36 Brewster, *The kaleidoscope*, p. 2.
37 *Ibid.*, pp. 158–60.
38 Smith, 'The elusive depth of field', pp. 84–5. Smith has in mind Alan Bowness's 'Introduction' to *The Pre-Raphaelites* (London, 1995).
39 *Ibid.*, pp. 84–5.
40 *Ibid.*, p. 92.
41 Gage, *George Field and his circle*, p. 65.
42 For an overview, see Pierson, *Collectors, collections, and museums*, p. 64.
43 Quoted in Merrill, *The peacock room*, p. 60.
44 Treuherz, Prettejohn and Becker, *Dante Gabriel Rossetti*, p. 234. Merrill points out that in 1867 Rossetti bought a pair of these pots (one remains, and is currently displayed at the National Trust property Cragside) which he described as 'sumptuous'. *The peacock room*, p. 170.
45 Treuherz, Prettejohn and Becker, *Dante Gabriel Rossetti*, p. 234.
46 Spencer-Longhurst, *The blue bower*, pp. 10–11.

Bibliography

Babbage, C. *The exposition of 1851, or, views of the industry, the science, and the government of England* (London, 2nd edn, 1851)

Brewster, D. *A treatise on the kaleidoscope* (Edinburgh, 1819)

Brewster, D. *The kaleidoscope: its history, theory, and construction, with its application to the fine and useful arts* (London, 1858)

Cook, E. T. and A. Wedderburn (eds.) *The works of John Ruskin* (39 volumes, London, 1903–12)

Di Bello, P. 'Editorial', *History of Photography*, 37:4 (2013), 385–8

Di Bello, P. 'Photography and sculpture: a light touch', in P. Di Bello and G. Koureas (eds.) *Art, history, and the senses: 1830 to the present* (Farnham, 2010), pp. 19–34

Gage, J. *George Field and his circle: from romanticism to the Pre-Raphaelite Brotherhood* (Cambridge, 1989)

Gordon, M. *The home life of Sir David Brewster* (Edinburgh, 3rd edn, 1881)

Groth, H. 'Kaleidoscopic vision and literary invention in an "age of things": David Brewster, *Don Juan*, and "a lady's kaleidoscope"', *English Literary History*, 74 (2007), 217–36

Herbert, S. (ed.) *A history of pre-cinema* (volume 1, London and New York, 2000)

'History of Sir David Brewster's kaleidoscope', *Journal of Science and the Arts*, 5:10 (1818), 324–35

Hunt, V. 'Raising a modern ghost: the magic lantern and the persistence of wonder in the Victorian education of the senses', *Romanticism and Victorianism on the Net*, 52 (2008), paras 1–18. www.erudit.org/revue/ravon/2008/v/n52/019806ar.html?lang=en; last accessed 27 January 2014

'The kaleidoscope', *Literary Gazette*, 71 (30 May 1818), 354–6

Kemp, M. '"Philosophy in sport" and the "sacred precincts": Sir David Brewster on the kaleidoscope and stereoscope', in B. Castel, J. Leith and A. Riley (eds.) *Muse and reason: the relation of arts and sciences 1650–1850* (Kingston, Ontario, 1994), pp. 203–32

Merrill, L. *The peacock room: a cultural biography* (New Haven and Washington, DC, 1998)

Morus, I. R. *Frankenstein's children: electricity, exhibition, and experiment in early-nineteenth-century London* (New Jersey, 1993)

Pierson, S. *Collectors, collections, and museums: the field of Chinese ceramics in Britain, 1560–1960* (Bern, 2007)

Pietrobruno, S. 'The stereoscope and the miniature', *Early Popular Visual Culture*, 9:3 (2011), 171–90

Plunkett, J. 'Transparencies, optical recreations and the invention of the screen', in S. Popple and V. Toulmin (eds.) *Visual delights II* (vol. 2, London, 2005), pp. 175–93

Plunkett, J. 'Selling stereoscopy, 1890–1915: penny arcades, automatic machines and American salesmen', *Early Popular Visual Culture*, 6:3 (2008), 239–55

Schaff, L. J. *Out of the shadows: Herschel, Talbot, and the invention of photography* (New Haven and London, 1992)

Smith, L. 'The elusive depth of field: stereoscopy and the Pre-Raphaelites', in Marcia Pointon (ed.) *Pre-Raphaelites re-viewed* (Manchester, 1989), pp. 83–99

Spencer-Longhurst, P. *The blue bower: Rossetti in the 1860s* (London, 2000)

Stafford, B. M. and F. Terpak, *Devices of wonder: from the world in a box to images on a screen* (Los Angeles, 2001)

Treuherz, J., E. Prettejohn and E. Becker, *Dante Gabriel Rossetti* (London, 2003)

Wade, N. *Brewster and Wheatstone on vision* (London, 1983)

Waggoner, D. 'Uncompromising truth: photography and Pre-Raphaelitism', in D. Waggoner with T. Barringer et. al. *The Pre-Raphaelite lens: British photography and painting, 1848–1875* (Farnham, 2010), pp. 2–18

7

'Mere adventurers in drawing': engineers and draughtsmen as visual technicians in nineteenth-century Britain

Frances Robertson

From Charles Babbage to Eugene Ferguson, many industrially minded writers have celebrated drawing as the non-verbal 'intellectual component of technology' coming from the 'mind's eye' of the engineer.[1] But while this formulation now implies a specialist skill limited to the workplace, in the nineteenth century mechanical drawing was promoted to a much broader public. By the time of the Great Exhibition of 1851 such drawings presented some of the most distinctive and widespread visual statements of the 'machine dreams' of this period, on display in exhibitions and in print.[2] The drawing practices of technical draughtsmen exploited key points of contact between art and industry; their training and aspirations as active practitioners can add to our understanding of the 'thick' lived experience of workers in the visual economy in the second half of the nineteenth century. This chapter shows how draughtsmen developed a command of different drawing languages through self education, then moves to examine working practices in the industrial city of Glasgow. Between 1850 and 1890 such draughtsmen negotiated the fragmentation and conflict of increasing specialisation in industrial occupations, while hoping to find new opportunities in training for graphic and design work.

By claiming autonomy in the workplace, draughtsmen asserted distinct skills that were at odds with those of the manly actors in the 'aristocracy of labour' of manual craft trades.[3] Instead, they were touchy, striving, autodidacts in a productive economy of arts, manufactures and commerce.[4] Technical workers, from elite ranks to the most humble, have been an awkward category in various accounts of 'class' in modern industrial societies, appearing to hold 'ambiguous and intermediate' status, acting as deputies for capital against broad labour interests.[5] Within the organisational structures of engineering itself, draughtsmen, like technicians in science and in art, have become invisible in comparison to their elite masters, the 'technicians of technicians' as it were.[6] Draughtsmen from Britain are particularly vulnerable in this respect: by contrast with the more regulated state-funded technical education systems in France and other European countries,[7] Britain's more *laissez-faire* approaches to training saw both employers and the state avoiding responsibility, so there are few official business or educational records that relate to this work, and because draughtsmen worked across genres it has been hard to talk about and categorise the hybrid meanings within technical draughtsmanship.[8]

Art and design historians have only given selective attention to this discourse, their views largely tinged with the shadow of John Ruskin and his campaigns to redirect the values of art and design education at the end of the nineteenth century. Those polemics poured scorn on the methods and aims of Government Schools of Design that held sway between 1837 and the 1880s; later commentaries on the history of art and design education have frequently dismissed those four decades of activity under the control of the Department of Science and Art as a faintly ludicrous episode dominated by a power-crazed Henry Cole.[9] This collective blindness does a disservice to the students, artists, designers and teachers of this period, both within these institutions and within the associated networks around them. Recent critical writing in art history has examined the 'coercive' force of mechanical drawing on passive workers,[10] while celebratory histories of design and technology, equally selective, often focus instead on the individual creativity of elite engineers.[11] I suggest an alternative approach that looks between these categories, at draughtsmen as active practitioners who modified both drawing practices and their working environments. This approach questions some invisible workings of the visual economy and shakes up the field of art and design history, where for varying reasons the average or mundane worker is rarely studied.[12]

This chapter argues that both artistic and technical manners were habitual to artisans, workers and jobbing designers working in manufactures. Draughtsmen sought out and used artistic and decorative modes loaded with cultural resonance. In the large organisations where draughtsmen were employed, art and industry were both insisted on to a high degree. Prestigious construction contracts displayed their cutting edge credentials through lavish visual demonstration both of scientific and technological invention, and of cultural heft. Whilst bearing in mind the fact that industrial development across Britain was extremely patchy, and that engineering itself had many localised cultures and values, this article will use examples taken from the developing visual economy in Glasgow in the period between 1850 and 1890.[13] Glasgow at this time was the self-styled second city of Imperial Britain, an industrial centre rich in local mineral resources of coal and iron, and with a flourishing shipbuilding trade that dominated the world market in the production of high-class passenger liners.[14]

Engineers, drawing, and training the self

In Britain, engineers and draughtsmen had eighteenth-century trade practices and nineteenth-century artisan self-help movements to provide models of drawing practice.[15] In training themselves, technicians copied widely, inhabiting and reproducing the motifs and manner of artistic, ornamental and practical styles of drawing. The ambition of artisans' visual expression is seen in exhibitions such as that of the Derby Mechanics' Institution in 1839, filled with copies of antique statues, paintings and architectural ornaments, alongside scientific instruments, models of machines and technical drawings.[16] A groundswell of self-education through reading and attendance at provincial academies from the late eighteenth century onwards fed into the ways in which artisans used the Government Schools of Design after 1839.[17] These all served a very similar social demographic of artisans, tradesmen, entrepreneurial and lower-middle-class workers. Training continued on the job, as we see from archive apprentice and employment contracts, surviving sketchbooks and drawings, and from autobiographical accounts.[18] Because there was no systematic approach to drawing and design education, artisans and engineers absorbed everything that might be useful. Comparable professional practitioners, architects and military officers, had similar strategies.[19]

At the beginning of the nineteenth century, when engineers were just starting to construct their professional status, working as a draughtsman was a highly desired means of advance.[20] Changes in the organisation of large companies from around 1850, however, meant that the word 'draughtsman' came to denote a more limited occupational category within the growing hierarchy of specialisations in engineering that we return to later in this chapter.[21] But at the beginning of the nineteenth century, young, aspiring draughtsmen filled their sketchbooks with a multitude of drawing styles and subjects, and with an eye always on the cultural status of their sources.[22] The manuscript book of William Creighton in the Boulton & Watt archive in Birmingham presents one extensive but not untypical example from the first decades of the nineteenth century. Creighton, who was an apprentice around 1793, became head of the Drawing Office in 1822.[23] During his training, around 1800, Creighton copied an astonishing range of printed images that included works of architectural history and theory, geographical and antiquarian exploration, cartography, astronomy, and landscape sketches to create drawn pages that are almost exact simulacra of the printed originals. Maps, taken from the atlas, were gridded up and delineated with the same unvarying and accurate lines of the steel engraved originals, while landscapes that at first glance appear as sketches from life, often turn out to be faithful copies of aquatint renderings of picturesque views from sources in print.[24]

Due to this eclectic self-education, draughtsmen developed a varied

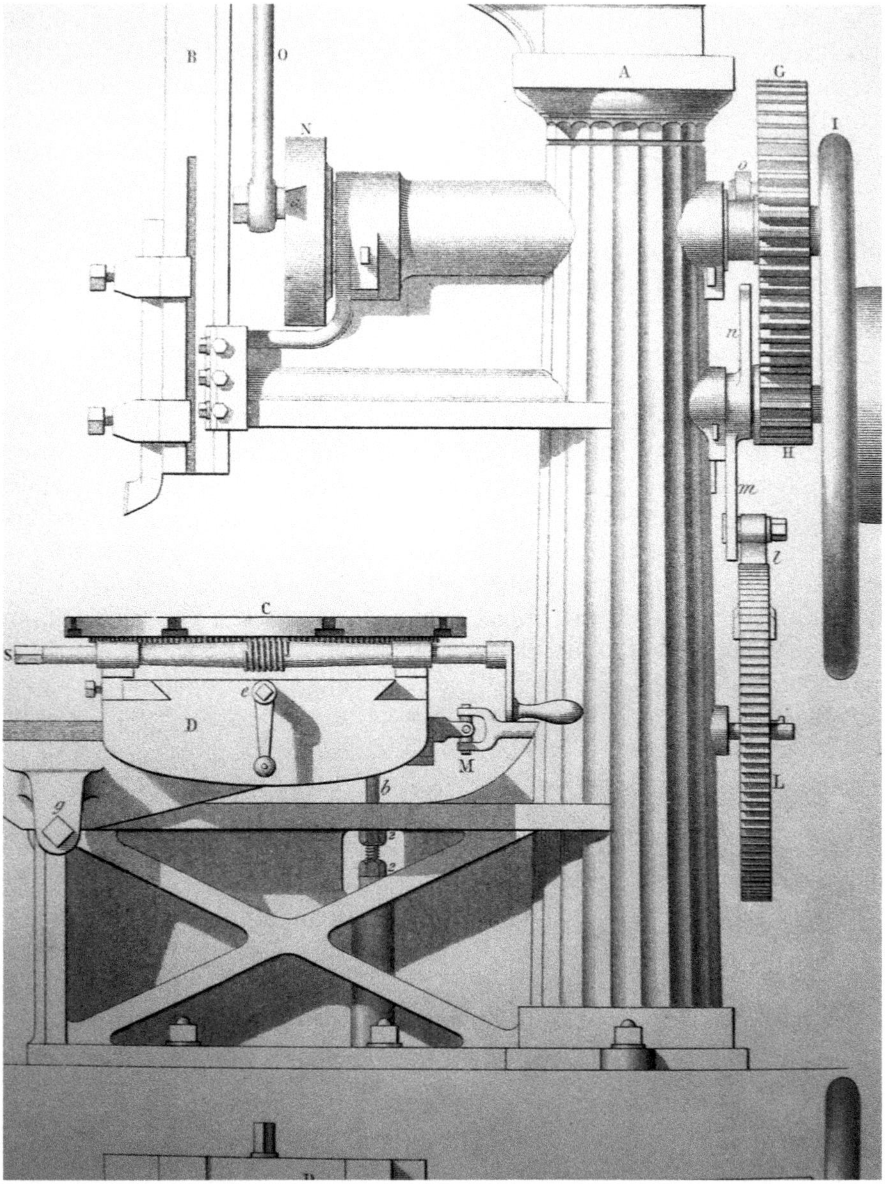

'Self acting slotting machine, Caird & Co. Greenock', in Scott, *The engineer and machinists assistant*, 1849. (Courtesy of the Institution of Mechanical Engineers library.) **7.1**

repertoire of drawing languages, mixing styles in a promiscuous way. Their distinctive graphic technique, using line predominantly, allowed draughtsmen to pillage different conventions and references to historical styles in a montage approach. Clean lines and formalised techniques of shadow blocking allowed many disparate conventions to sit together on the page and created a unified graphic statement, pulling in decorative historical detailing alongside structural and mechanical calculation. The example in figure 7.1 from the 1840s shows how the sparsity and graphic contrasts of technical illustrations allowed draughtsmen to take effects from different discourses of representation. This example, a slotting machine from *The engineer and machinist's assistant* (1849), used the conventions of orthographic projection, rendered in line and unmarked paper, alongside oblique cast-shadow projections in uniform blocks of tone, while a few selected forms in this image display further pictorial effects of tonally graded shadow. Normally these conventions would be used separately. Orthographic projection is a face-on style that offers a two-dimensional diagrammatic view of a single face of rectangular objects, presented in parallel with the picture plane. By contrast, the use of cast shadows, creating the illusion of light falling from the upper left hand corner, normally belong with architectural and topographic views that are generally fully three-dimensional through the use of oblique or pictorial perspective. The graphic style holds these discontinuities together, the medley of stylistic conventions complements an assembly of design languages and structural functions in the object depicted, in which a classical column has been welded in to other more overtly functional planes, cylinders, and gearing mechanisms. The teeth of the large cogs and the column's volutes, for example, appear almost to be cut from the same virtual stuff, a unity asserted through graphic integration on the page.

The 'morality of taste': drawing, education and the politics of industrial culture

The breadth and diversity of draughtsmen's visual training contradicts the caricatured and limited view of the kinds of visual and design knowledge available to manufacturing workers that is given by hostile critics and historians. John Ruskin famously feared that the drawing styles encountered by workers were all industry and no art, dreamt up and imposed from without by enemies of creativity such as Henry Cole, the civil servant who reorganised the former Government Schools of Design, and his associate William Dyce, author of *The drawing book of the Government School of Design* (1843).[25] To Ruskin, exercises in geometrical drawing were formulaic styles that denoted servitude and the horrors of industrialisation, part of the terrible machine seeking to teach students to 'make money by designing for manufacture', rather than his ideal of using drawing to foster worshipful observation of nature.[26]

Ruskin's doctrines shaped a new ethos of art school education at the end of the nineteenth century in Britain and North America, and still shape (or rather, distort) current histories, as we have inherited his fear that mechanical styles of drawing were a weapon for indoctrinating workers into an 'ideology of industrialisation'. So David Brett, for example, has argued that abstract supposedly 'ahistorical' geometrical drawing was intended to wipe out the past in order to train workers to accept the factory regime; here, the Government Schools of Design are presented as part of a conspiratorial programme to expand education to the docile masses in the service of positivist manufacturing and 'science-based technology'.[27] These Foucauldian arguments are familiar, but not entirely convincing. We are asked to believe in shadowy but all-powerful forces coercing passive workers, where the activity 'drawing' is given an agency, whilst the actual people who draw become hapless minions. But this simplified analysis leaves out the thoughts and experiences of the diverse groups of people who did these drawings, for even if bosses did aim to control the factory floor through drawing, the supposed control centre (the drawing or design office) was a gathering of educated ambitious employees whose aims both individually and collectively were to a great extent uncontrollable and opaque.

Instead of being dominated by drawings imposed on them from above, self-educated artisans and engineers used their varied pictorial skills in the struggle for status in competition with various groups in unpredictable ways. Many factory workers deliberately sought out drawing classes in their spare time to advance their ambitions to become decorative designers or industrial draughtsmen.[28] Industrial workers did not all become powerless because the unfamiliarity of mechanised factory operations demanded increased skills and initiative from workers in the first decades of the nineteenth century.[29] Schmeichen has argued that artisans, having consciously set out to acquire drawing and design ability through self-education, actually increased the demand for such skilled industrial labour in the 1830s and 1840s.[30] Drawing education was of course a hot topic at this time, not only amongst artisans but equally with manufacturers, frightened that alleged deficiencies in 'taste' amongst British designers and makers of export goods would damage export sales,[31] with consolidating artistic professions,[32] and ultimately with civil servants who formulated public policy.[33] These concerns were first given a very public airing during the Select Committee on arts and manufactures of 1835–36, set in motion by liberal politicians favourable to commercial interests. The Select Committee took the position that there was a dearth of drawing education amongst 'the manufacturing population', and its findings were used to support the establishment of the Government Schools of Design from 1837 onwards.[34]

Although questioners and witnesses in the Select Committee often claimed that British workmen had no knowledge of drawing, many statements give unwitting testimony to the contrary. John Jobson Smith described a seething world of unofficial drawing activity amongst the ornamental ironfounders of Sheffield, in which manufacturers constantly sought new ornaments, procuring them from self-taught designers or through getting draughtsmen to steal or copy new designs.[35] Other witnesses from the textile industries supported this view.[36] When witnesses and questioners stated that workers could not draw, what they really meant was not in an approved manner. The architect and designer J. B. Papworth attacked the 'debased' style of Rococo 'grotesque scrollwork' as perpetrated by 'designers and artists of very mediocre talents'.[37] Papworth's comment suggests that artisans and manufacturers in the 1830s continued the design procedures and Rococo embellishments of the late eighteenth century, maintaining their informal traditions of drawing training from that period, and for which they had a market.[38]

Even though the cultural debates associated with the establishment of state-funded art and design education in Britain are well known, their relation to the working practices of technical draughtsmen and decorative designers in industry has been less often considered. That complaint about 'debased' Rococo scrollwork shows us that the discourses of art and industry were not separate. Designing for machine production was not merely about the 'primitive or elementary geometrical figures' of mechanical action;[39] Papworth reminds us that insistent and elaborated surface decoration was another important aspect of designing for manufactures in the nineteenth century.[40] Publications read by artisans tell a similar story. The *Artizan* for example revelled in a striking and aggressive eclecticism, with articles on the morality of taste, on 'Modern art in Germany', the 'Construction of sewers' or 'Staircases in octagonal towers' in gleeful succession.[41] Throughout, the editors insisted on the unity of fine arts and mechanical arts embodied in the persons of their imaginary readers: 'It is with the *artizans* that art has ever originated: it was born in the workshops of Athens, and resuscitated in the workshops of Italy ... it will be in the workshop, we are confident, where the revival [of art] will take place'.[42]

The scope of draughtsmen's ambition indicated by the *Artizan* was grandiose but not completely unrealistic in this period of open competitions to decorate public buildings such as the new Houses of Parliament, part of a tide of construction rising across Britain and its Empire of ornate public buildings, whose surfaces and whose fittings, inside and out, were covered in insistent patterning in various historical styles, using repeated units that were made by industrial techniques in wood, ceramic, stone, iron or textiles.[43] Construction and decoration in prestigious projects like this depended on draughtsmen's plans for machine production.[44] To critics such as Ruskin this was repellent, a standardised 'expression of wanton expenditure and vulgar mathematics', but to us it is confirmation that draughtsmen combined art and industry, as normally understood, in their work.[45]

Glasgow, decorative manufactures, and drawing education

To engage with details of these interactions of art and industry in practice, this chapter now moves to Glasgow in the period 1850–1890, taking examples from two sites of production: the library of the Glasgow Government School of Design, and sketchbooks and drawings from the archives of the shipbuilding firm of Robert Napier & Sons. Glasgow workers were accustomed to seeking out education in drawing. The city saw the start of its Mechanics' Institution in 1823, one year earlier than the London Mechanics' Institution in 1824.[46] Glasgow artisans received a lot of attention from industrial tourists on the trail of James Watt or Robert Owen, with Charles Dupin, for example, promoter of worker education in France, admiring the 'sagacious workmen' that he encountered in the city.[47] By 1834, the Mechanics' Institution had well-established classes in mechanical and architectural drawing and was in correspondence with

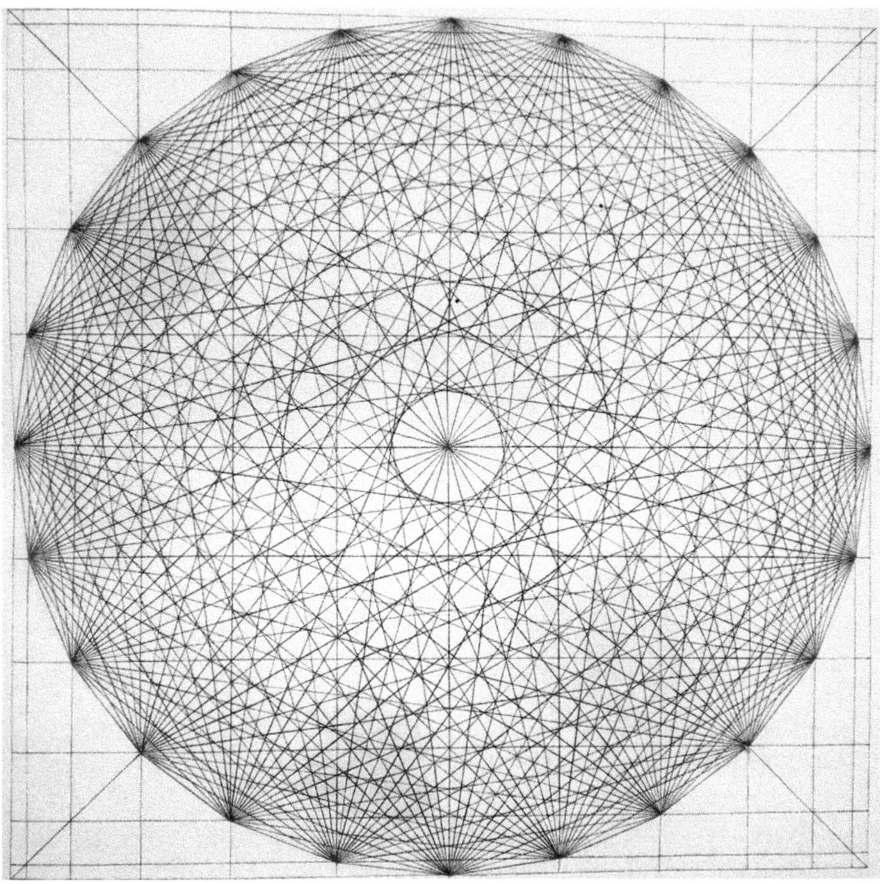

'Harmonic diagram', in Hay, *Proportion*, 1843. (Courtesy of Glasgow School of Art Library Special Collections.) **7.2**

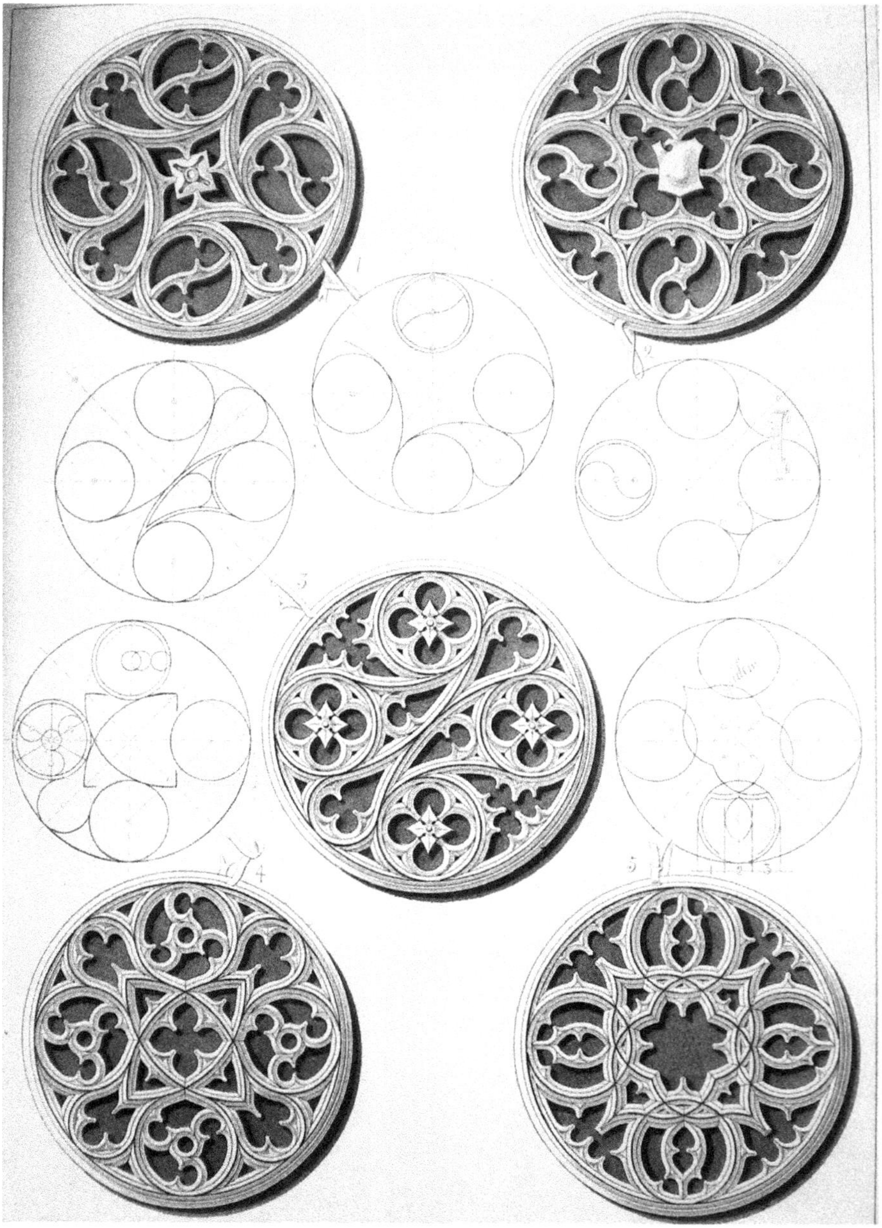

7.3 Designs for tracery panels, in Billings, *The infinity of geometric design exemplified*, 1849. (Courtesy of Glasgow School of Art Library Special Collections.)

other worker organisations about staging national exhibitions. By 1856 the Institution had to hire two teachers as demand for drawing classes continued to expand even with the competition from the newly founded Government School of Design in Glasgow from 1845.[48] Indeed, the School of Design offered very similar tuition, attracting similar constituencies of workers from backgrounds of skilled manual work, manufacturing, trade, or commercial business, who attended classes in the evening after finishing work.[49] Former students from both institutions sought work as draughtsmen, chief foremen or designers in various manufacturing industries. The library holdings of Glasgow School of Art allow us to see some of the working of this local world where art, design and manufacturing interpenetrated.

Geometrical design was not perceived here as stultifying, lacking in creative satisfaction, or in cultural resonance, despite claims to the contrary.[50] Geometrical drawing was a source of pride to many autodidact workers.[51] Contributors to the *Mechanics' Magazine* argued about geometry in combative and playful self-assertion, stating its value as a means of maintaining agency in their lives. Many publications eulogised the spiritual and cultural lineage of geometrical drawing and design, for example in David Ramsay Hay's *Proportion, or the geometric principle of beauty, analysed* (figure 7.2).[52] Hay developed geometric rules of visual beauty from Greek theories of harmony in music, dividing up his pictorial field into proportions such as thirds and fifths. His method gave rise to complex but controlled abstract patterns, similar to those generated by the Moorish decorators.[53] Hay, however, and despite the orientalist fashions of the time, emphasised instead his direct contact with the world and philosophy of the ancient Greeks and their grasp of the underlying richness of the cosmos. Abstract patterning like this, he argued, offered the 'geometric poetry of graphic art'.[54] Victorian geometrical mystics called on a rich range of references; the classical world of Euclid, Islamic 'saracenic' designs, and the gothic that appealed to technically minded investigators like Robert William Billings (Figure 7.3).[55] This synthesis of 'poetic' gothicised creativity and technical teaching had an influential outcome in the *Practical draughtsman's book of industrial design* (three editions, 1853–69) by the Glasgow author, journalist and engineer William Johnson.[56] Dedicated to the 'industrial reader', and with a gesture to Ruskin, Johnson described a divided world that could be united by the practical draughtsman who could bring together the 'dexterous hand and the thoughtful mind, the labourer who toils with sweated brow, and he who exerts the conceptions of the imaginative brain'.[57]

Art, industry, and luxury liners

Our final examples come from the shipbuilding firm of Robert Napier & Sons, from the Clyde. By the early 1850s this company dominated the fast-expanding marine engineering and shipbuilding industry in the West of Scotland, and was closely linked to research that fostered imperial sea power.[58] Large firms like Napier's were important sites of negotiation between art and industry, where scientific and industrial invention united

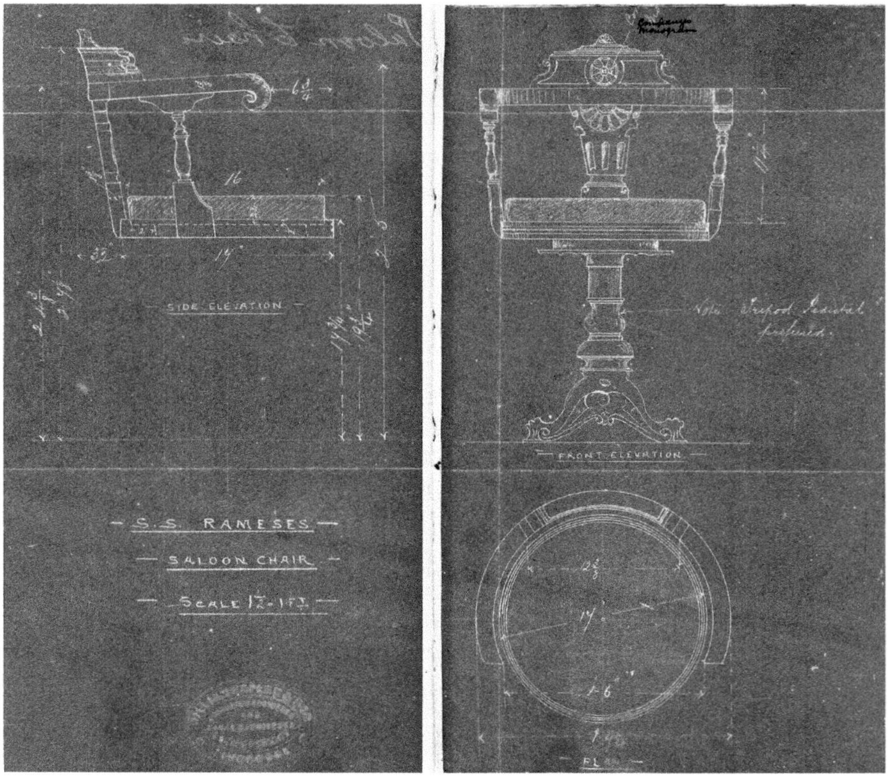

7.4 Double page spread from designer notebook, showing blueprint copy of design drawing of saloon chair for SS *Rameses*, late nineteenth century, Robert Napier & Sons Archive. (© CSG CIC Glasgow Museums Collection.)

with lavishly decorated products.[59] Capital-intensive single orders were floated as 'loss-leaders' throughout Napier's existence, elegant liners with elaborately florid machine-carved furnishings, stained glass, sanitary fittings, carpets; every contrivance of lush interior design.[60]

Robert Napier & Sons employed several chief draughtsmen such as William Denny, John Elder and David Kirkaldy, who later founded various engineering businesses.[61] Below them were ranks of lesser mortals with different kinds of status but all jostling for advancement. Surviving drawings by lower-ranking draughtsmen at Napier's gather together technical, scientific and decorative genres, in various mediums and styles, ranging from detailed pen and ink linear parts drawings, to more impressionistic and expressive sketches enhanced with watercolour.[62] Draughtsmen's day books juxtaposed mathematical tables against clippings from furniture catalogues, blueprints for machines against blueprints of saloon chairs (figure 7.4). Larger working drawings in the same archives also show decorative exterior ironwork and interior wall detailing with vestigial Corinthian columns and sub-rococo panelling (figure 7.5). These examples

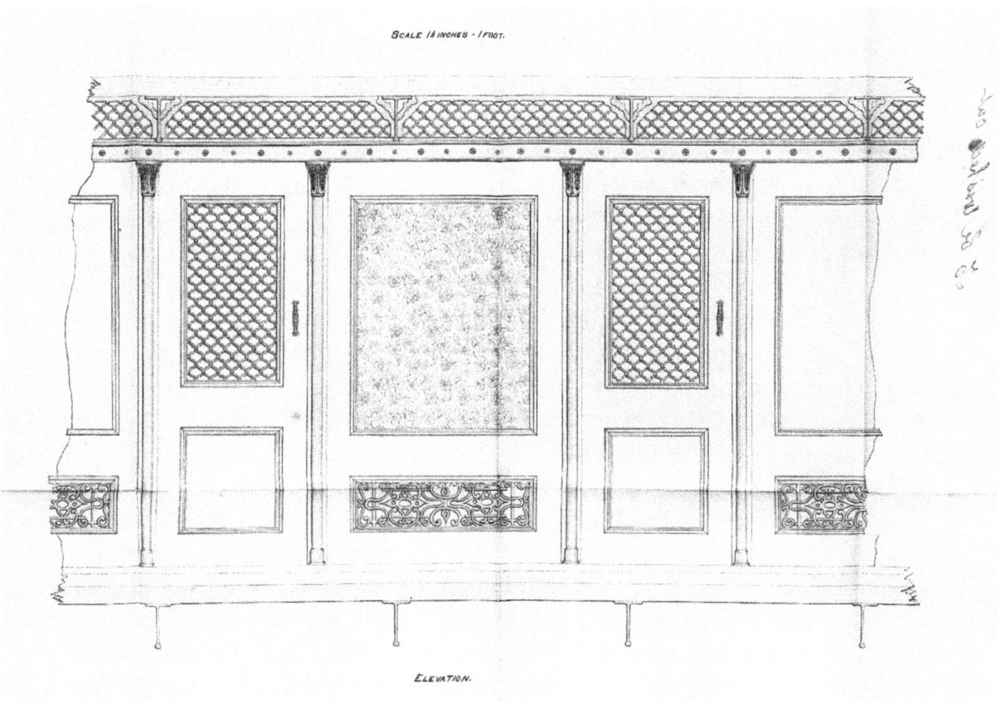

Design for cabin framing, Robert Napier & Sons Archive (© CSG CIC Glasgow Museums Collection.) 7.5

from Napier's firm confirm the range of draughtsman's work proclaimed in publications such as the *Mechanics' Magazine* or the *Artizan* and indicate a working tradition of decorative design that was not in accord with the taste of either Ruskin or his enemies, design reformers such as Owen Jones.[63] Evidently, earlier forms of eclectic autodidacticism still lingered; the polemics of design commentators, although well-known, do not necessarily tell us what was happening in day-to-day drawing and design practice.

'Mere adventurers in drawing': draughtsmen and the status of anonymous workers in design

Around mid-century, changes in the organisation of work in large companies meant that drawing offices expanded and developed their own hierarchies. Draughtsmen found their status was becoming contested and problematic. A bad-tempered correspondence in the *Engineer* journal on the subject of draughtsmen and their duties throughout 1859 began provocatively with the slighting statement that these 'servants' had simply to 'draw the various parts of machinery'.[64] There were various howls of protest following this, with some draughtsmen trying to assert their 'gentlemanly' status whilst others acknowledged their new 'proletarian' ranking.[65]

Elite engineers began to distance themselves from the drawing office rank and file, as we read in the memoirs of John Wigham Richardson (1837–1908), recalling with a shudder his first factory drawing office experience at a shipbuilding firm in the North of England in the late 1850s. To him this was a 'new world' where the respectable companions he was used to were replaced by 'an atmosphere of debauch from highest to lowest' with drunkenness everywhere amongst workers, and in the drawing office 'a continual chatter going on about amusements or sprees and much coarse practical joking, and just about as little work done as would pass muster'.[66] Even the trade journal the *Engineer* accused lower ranking draughtsmen of being 'mere adventurers in drawing' with 'gentlemanly pretensions' to artistic judgment.[67] Indeed, as draughtsmen lost caste, they suffered all the agonies of those who are losing status because fellow skilled technical workers also gave them the cold shoulder for being a standoffish snobbish crew.[68]

Drawing for the factory was a hybrid art. Many rancorous debates about drawing, art and industry came about not because cultural categories were clearly separated but because they were confused and confusing. Styles of technical drawing and illustration were so varied in technique, appearance and function, that applying standard terms to this genre would be misleading. Despite the Education Act (1870) and the Technical Instruction Act (1889) instruction remained chaotic and unsupported as employers continued to block worker education.[69] The unsystematic and informal character of British 'policy' at the very time when visual economies were increasing meant that draughtsmen invented forms and styles in opportunist ways at variance with any of the well-known commentaries on design that dominate accounts of the period.

Too many accounts of worker education and self-improvement, either from the nineteenth century or from more contemporary sources, express the kind of freezing hostility that Jonathan Rose described, in his study of autodidact readers, as the weapon of intellectuals trying to maintain a 'perilous social distinction' against those just snapping at their heels in the race for social advancement.[70] This has minimised the importance of anonymous designers and draughtsmen. But even though they are unknown, it does not follow that drawing was a vehicle for imparting an 'ideology of industrialisation', imposed centrally or from above, onto passive receptacles. Instead, draughtsmen and jobbing designers were actively constructing new forms of expression and negotiating new patterns of work, inviting further research into the networks of practice in these working lives before 1890. If they do not fit well with the emerging philosophies of art education in the late nineteenth century, neither do they resemble established 'working-class' stereotypes. Instead, the cultural expression of office draughtsmen echoes more with accounts of touchy, ill-fitting autodidact workers in the work of Patrick Joyce or

Jacques Rancière, and as part of the construction of ideas of the 'lower middle class' with its allegedly self-imposed 'isolation and loneliness'.[71]

Notes

1 Ferguson, 'The mind's eye', 827–36; Babbage, *On the economy of machinery and manufactures*, p. 262; Giedion, *Mechanization takes command*.
2 Sussman, 'Machine dreams', 197–204.
3 Gray, *The aristocracy of labour in nineteenth-century Britain, c. 1850–1900*; McClelland, 'Masculinity and the "representative artisan" in Britain, 1850–80', pp. 74–91; Johnston and McIvor, 'Dangerous work, hard men and broken bodies', 135–51.
4 McClelland, 'Time to work, time to live', pp. 180–209; Rancière, *The nights of labor*; Joyce, *Democratic subjects*.
5 Joyce (ed.) *Class*; Meikskins and Smith (eds.) *Engineering labour*, p. 235; Barley 'What we know (and mostly don't know) about technical work', pp. 376–403.
6 Shapin, 'The invisible technician', 554–63.
7 Cardwell, *The organisation of science in England*; Edmonson, *From mécanicien to ingénieur*; Day, *The école des arts et métiers and the rise of French industrial education*.
8 Cronin, *Technology, industrial conflict, and the development of technical education in nineteenth-century England*.
9 See for example the droll commentary of Frayling, 'The strange case of the Duke of Wellington's funeral car', pp. 132–3; also Macdonald, *The history and philosophy of art education*.
10 Brett, 'Drawing and the ideology of industrialization', 59–72; Denis, 'The educated eye and the industrial hand'; Purbrick, 'Ideologically technical', 275–93.
11 Booker, *A history of engineering drawing*; Baynes and Pugh, *The art of the engineer*; Fox, *The arts of industry in the age of enlightenment*.
12 Margolin, 'Design in history', 94–105.
13 Berg, *The machinery question and the making of political economy 1815–48*, pp. 22–4; Marsden 'Engineering science in Glasgow', 319–46; Harwood, 'Engineering education between science and practice', 53–79.
14 McClelland and Reid, 'Wood, iron and steel', pp. 151–84.
15 Puetz, 'Design instruction for artisans in eighteenth-century Britain', 217–39; Styles, 'Manufacturing, consumption and design in eighteenth-century England', pp. 527–54; Saumarez Smith, *The rise of design*, 118–33; Bird, 'The development of art and design education in the United Kingdom in the nineteenth century'; Denis, 'The educated eye and the industrial hand'; Schmeichen, 'Reconsidering the factory, art-labor, and the schools of design in nineteenth-century Britain', pp. 167–77; Romans, 'Political, economic, social and cultural determinants in the history of early to mid-century art and design education in Britain'; Robertson, 'Ruling the line'.
16 For Samuel Rayner's engraving of this event, see Fox, *The arts of industry in the age of enlightenment*, p. 457.
17 Brookes, 'The Trustees' Academy 1760–1801'; Bignamini, 'The "academy of art" in Britain', pp. 434–50; Turpin, *A school of art in Dublin since the eighteenth century*.
18 Clapham, *John Brunton's book*; Richardson, *Memoirs of John Wigham Richardson 1837–1908*.
19 Spiers, *Architectural drawing*; Jones, 'Aspects of relief portrayal on nineteenth-century British military maps', 19–33; Lever, 'Architects offices', pp. 59– 64; Thorne, 'Architects and engineers', pp. 53–8; Bermingham, *Learning to draw*.

20 Watson, *The civils*; Buchanan, *The engineers*.
21 Berg, *The machinery question and the making of political economy 1815–48*, p. 153.
22 See both the impoverished Daniel Gooch and more privileged Brunel in Platt, *The life and times of Daniel Gooch* and Buchanan, *Brunel*.
23 Tann, '"Two knights at pandemonium"', 47–72; Hunt and Jacob, 'The affective revolution in 1790s Britain', 491–521.
24 A striking example of Creighton's 'visual ventriloquism' can be seen in copies he made of plates from *A treatise on civil architecture* by William Chambers, just as pupils in architectural offices also used Chambers as a 'key text' during their training (see The Manuscript Book of William Creighton, Birmingham City Council Library, MS 117631 IIR 44, p. 463).
25 Bonython and Burton, *The great exhibitor*.
26 Cook and Wedderburn (eds.) *The works of John Ruskin*, vol. 15, p. 344.
27 Brett, 'Drawing and the ideology of industrialization', Denis, 'The educated eye and the industrial hand', and Purbrick, 'Ideologically technical' have all argued that technical drawing education was a key weapon used to instill an 'ideology of industrialisation'.
28 See in particular Schmeichen, 'Reconsidering the factory'.
29 This was the case in both Britain and France: Pollard, *The genesis of modern management*, pp. 101–3; Edmonson, *From mécanicien to ingénieur*, pp. 201–2.
30 Schmeichen, 'Reconsidering the factory', 167–77.
31 Rifkin, 'Success disavowed', 89–102.
32 Trodd, 'Culture, class, city', p. 33; Duncan *Civilizing rituals*; Hoock, *The King's artists*.
33 Minihan, *The nationalization of culture*; Green, *Education and state formation*.
34 Romans, 'Political, economic, social and cultural determinants in the history of early to mid-century art and design education in Britain'.
35 *Report from the Select Committee on arts and their connexion with manufacturers*, 27 July 1835, p. 11, and see also the career of Godfrey Sykes whose work linked Sheffield manufacturing with teaching in the South Kensington system in Barringer, *Men at work*.
36 Evidence of Benjamin Spalding, Thomas Field Gibson, Robert Harrison and Claude Guillotte in *Report from the Select Committee on arts and their connexion with manufactures*, 31 July 1835, p. 23; 3 August 1835, 27–8; 3 August 1835, p. 33; 14 August 1835, pp. 55–7.
37 *Ibid.*, 21 August 1835, p. 92; Cates, 'Papworth, John Buonarotti'.
38 See Puetz, 'Design instruction for artisans in eighteenth-century Britain'.
39 Nasmyth, 'Nasmyth on tools and machines', pp. 393–418; 394.
40 See Puetz, 'Design instruction for artisans in eighteenth-century Britain'.
41 See the *Mechanics' Magazine* founded 1823, *passim*, also the *Artizan* (1843), pp. 221–6; (1846) pp. 26, 29.
42 'The march of art', *Artizan* (1844), 218–20; on the relationship between ancient and modern artisans, see also Nichols, *Greece and Rome at the Crystal Palace*, chapter 4.
43 See calls for design tenders for woodcarving and stained glass, the *Artizan* (1843), 148; also Treuherz, *Victorian painting*, pp. 42–4; Willsdon, *Mural painting in Britain, 1840–1942*, p. 47.
44 Brett, *On decoration*, pp. 2–16.
45 Cook and Wedderburn (eds.) *The works of John Ruskin*, vol. 16, p. 283.
46 Hudson, *The history of adult education*, pp. 29–31; Tylecote, *The mechanics' institutes of Lancashire and Yorkshire before 1851*, pp. 3–4.
47 Dupin, *The commercial power of Great Britain*, vol. 2, p. 237; Bradley and Perrin, 'Charles Dupin's study visits to the British isles 1816–24', 47–68.
48 Fairfull-Smith 'Art and design education in Glasgow in the eighteenth and nineteenth

centuries', 9–16; Rawson, 'The Glasgow Government School of Design, 1845–53', Robertson, 'Ruling the line'.

49 The Glasgow School of Design Reports listed student occupations, and also 'father's occupation'.

50 See notes 10 and 27 above.

51 Richards, *Mathematical visions*, p. 1; p. 187; see also Howsam, Stray, Jenkins, Secord and Vaninskaya, 'What the Victorians learned', 262–85.

52 Hay, *Proportion, or the geometric principle of beauty, analysed*; this was one of the foundation titles in the Glasgow School of Design, gifted to GSA by Glasgow designer John T. Walker.

53 See for example Jones, *Plans, sections, elevations and details of the Alhambra*, and that foundation text of all Schools of Design, Jones, *The grammar of ornament*; see also Lara Eggleton's chapter 13 in this volume.

54 Hay, *Proportion, or the geometric principle of beauty, analysed*, p. 58.

55 For a contrast to Ruskin's more organic descriptions of craftsman-based medieval construction, see the functional, structural and engineering Gothic enthusiasms of the Cambridge men of science, such as Robert Willis, or Whewell, *Architectural notes of German churches*; Yanni, 'On nature and nomenclature', 204–21; Billings, *The infinity of geometric design exemplified*, list of engravings, n.p.

56 Johnson, *The practical draughtsman's book of industrial design*.

57 *Ibid.*, p. 196.

58 Moss, 'Napier, Robert'; Canfield, 'Robert Napier'; Smith and Wise, *Energy & empire*; Marsden and Smith, *Engineering empires*.

59 Accounts of interactions between art and industry in Glasgow often focus on the later more celebrated *art nouveau* 'Glasgow style' and its star designer Charles Rennie Mackintosh; see G. and C. Larner, *The Glasgow style*, pp. 14–19 or Kinchin, '"To knock fire out of men"', pp. 232–55.

60 Moss and Hume, *Workshop of the British Empire*, p. 91; p. 149.

61 *Ibid.*, pp. 87–8.

62 Robert Napier & Sons archive at Glasgow Museums Resources Centre (DC90), Glasgow City Council Museums Resource Centre.

63 Jones, *The grammar of ornament*.

64 *The Engineer* (21 January 1859), p. 45.

65 As one writer remarked, there was now 'One competent person to superintend, and half a dozen boys to make circles, curves and straight lines ... and when the boys become men and require the pay of men, they will be discharged, to look back with disgust upon a portion of the best part of their life ... their vacant places will be supplied by other boys, to serve awhile and share the same fate', *The Engineer* (18 February 1859), p. 119.

66 Richardson, *Memoirs of John Wigham Richardson 1837–1908*, pp. 71–87, 105; see also F. Robertson 'David Kirkaldy', pp. 125–32.

67 *The Engineer* (30 December 1859), p. 471.

68 *The foreman engineer and draughtsman* (1876), p. 19. This stereotype of the 'narrow-minded and snobbish' draughtsman was still going strong in the 1960s; see for example J. E. Mortimer *A history of the association of engineering and shipbuilding draughtsmen* (London, 1960), p. 6.

69 Cardwell, *The organisation of science in England*; Cronin, *Technology, industrial conflict, and the development of technical education in nineteenth-century England*, p. 3; p. 237. Employers' desires for complete independence blocked standardisation agreements on drawing until BS 308: 1927 'Engineering drawing office practice', 16 August 1927, cited in Booker, *A history of engineering drawing*, p. 175.

70 Rose, *The intellectual life of the British working classes*, pp. 393–4.

71 For Joyce, Rancière and associated writers, see notes 4 and 5 above. See also Crossick, *The lower middle classes in Britain 1870–1914*, p. 27; Bailey, 'White collars, gray lives?', 273–90.

Bibliography

Babbage, C. *On the economy of machinery and manufactures* (London, 1835)

Bailey, P. 'White collars, gray lives? The lower middle class revisited', *Journal of British Studies*, 38 (1999), 273–90

Barley, S. R. 'What we know (and mostly don't know) about technical work', in S. Ackroyd, R. Batt, P. Thompson and P. S. Tolbert (eds.) *The Oxford handbook of work and organisation* (Oxford, 2005), pp. 376–403

Barringer, T. *Men at work: art and labour in Victorian Britain* (New Haven and London, 2005)

Baynes, K. and F. Pugh, *The art of the engineer* (Guildford, 1981)

Berg, M. *The machinery question and the making of political economy 1815–48* (Cambridge, 1980)

Bermingham, A. *Learning to draw: studies in the cultural history of a polite and useful art* (New Haven and London, 2000)

Bignamini, I. 'The "academy of art" in Britain', in A. W. A. Boschloo, E. J. Hendrikse, L. C. Smit and G. J. van der Sman (eds.), *Academies of art between the Renaissance and Romanticism*, Leids Kunsthistorische Jaarboek (vols 5–6, The Hague, 1989), pp. 434–50

Billings, R. W. *The infinity of geometric design exemplified* (Edinburgh and London, 1849)

Bird, E. 'The development of art and design education in the United Kingdom in the nineteenth century' (PhD thesis, University of Loughborough, 1992)

Bonython, E. and A. Burton, *The great exhibitor: the life and work of Henry Cole* (London, 2003)

Booker, P. J. *A history of engineering drawing* (London, 1979)

Bradley, M. and F. Perrin, 'Charles Dupin's study visits to the British isles 1816–24', *Technology and Culture*, 32:1 (1991), 47–68

Brett, D. 'Drawing and the ideology of industrialization', *Design Issues*, 3:2 (1987), 59–72

Brett, D. *On decoration* (Cambridge, 1992)

Buchanan, R. A. *Brunel: the life and times of Isambard Kingdom Brunel* (London and New York, 1988)

Buchanan, R. A. *The engineers: a history of the engineering profession in Britain 1750–1914* (London, 1989)

Canfield, T. 'Robert Napier (1791–1876)', in P. Cross-Rudkin and M. Chrimes (eds.) *Biographical dictionary of civil engineers in Great Britain and Ireland, volume 2: 1830–1890* (London, 2008), pp. 565–7

Cardwell, D. S. L. *The organisation of science in England* (London, 1972)

Carline, R. *Draw they must: a history of the teaching and examining of art* (London, 1968)

Cates, A. 'Papworth, John Buonarotti (1775–1847)', rev. J. Elliott, *Oxford Dictionary of National Biography* (Oxford, 2004), online edition, January 2008, www.oxforddnb.com/view/article/21254, accessed 9 December 2012.

Clapham, J. H. *John Brunton's book: memories of John Brunton, engineer 1812–1899* (Cambridge, 1939)

Cook, E. T. and A. Wedderburn (eds.) *The works of John Ruskin* (39 volumes, London, 1903–12)

Cronin, B. *Technology, industrial conflict, and the development of technical education in nineteenth-century England* (Aldershot, 2001)

Crossick, G. *The lower middle classes in Britain 1870–1914* (London, 1977)

Day, C. R. *The école des arts et métiers and the rise of French industrial education* (Cambridge, MA, 1987)
Denis, R. C. 'The educated eye and the industrial hand: art and design instruction for the working classes in mid-Victorian Britain' (PhD dissertation, Courtauld Institute of Art, London, 1995)
Duncan, C. *Civilizing rituals: inside public art museums* (London, 1995)
Dupin, C. *The commercial power of Great Britain; exhibiting a complete view of the public works of this country* (vol. 2, London, 1825)
Dyce, W. *The drawing book of the Government School of Design* (London, Edinburgh, Glasgow and Dublin, 1842–3)
Edmonson, J. W. *From mécanicien to ingénieur: technical education and the machine building industry in nineteenth-century France* (New York and London, 1987)
Efland, A. D. *A history of art education: intellectual and social currents in the teaching of the visual arts* (New York and London, 1990)
Fairfull-Smith, G. 'Art and design education in Glasgow in the eighteenth and nineteenth centuries', Journal of the Scottish Society for Art History, 4 (1999), 9–16
Ferguson, E. S. 'The mind's eye: non-verbal thought in technology', *Science*, 197 (26 August 1977), 827–36
The foreman engineer and draughtsman (1876–84)
Fox, C. *The arts of industry in the age of enlightenment* (New Haven and London, 2009)
Frayling, C. 'The strange case of the Duke of Wellington's funeral car', in D. Walker (ed.) *The great engineers: the art of British engineers 1837–1987* (London, 1987), pp. 132–3
Giedion, S. *Mechanization takes command: a contribution to anonymous history* (New York, 1970)
Gray, R. *The aristocracy of labour in nineteenth-century Britain, c.1850–1900* (London, 1981)
Green, A. *Education and state formation: the rise of educational systems in England, France and the USA* (London, 1991)
Harwood, J. 'Engineering education between science and practice: rethinking the historiography', *History and Technology*, 22:1 (2006), 53–79
Hay, D. R. *Proportion, or the geometric principle of beauty, analysed* (Edinburgh, 1843)
Hoock, H. *The King's artists: the royal academy of arts and the politics of British culture 1760–1840* (Oxford, 2003)
Howsam, L., C. Stray, A. Jenkins, J.A. Secord and A. Vaninskaya, 'What the Victorians learned: perspectives on nineteenth-century school books', *Journal of Victorian Culture*, 12:2 (2007), 262–85
Hudson, J. W. *The history of adult education* (London, 1851)
Hunt, L. A. and M. C. Jacob, 'The affective revolution in 1790s Britain', *Eighteenth-century studies*, 34:4 (2001), 491–521
Johnson, W. *The practical draughtsman's book of industrial design: forming a complete course of mechanical, engineering, and architectural drawing translated from French of Armengaud, ainé, Professor of design at the Conservatoire Nationale des Arts et Metiers, and Armegaud jeune, and Amouroux civil engineers, rewritten and arranged with additional matter and plates, and contemporary references and examples* (London, 1853)
Johnston, R. and A. McIvor, 'Dangerous work, hard men and broken bodies: masculinity in the Clydeside heavy industries, c. 1930–1970', *Labour History Review*, 69:2 (2004), 135–51
Jones, O. *Plans, sections, elevations and details of the Alhambra* (London, 1836–45)
Jones, O. *The grammar of ornament* (London, 1868)
Jones, Y. 'Aspects of relief portrayal on nineteenth-century British military maps', *Cartographic Journal*, 11 (1974), 19–33

Joyce, P. *Democratic subjects: the self and the social in nineteenth-century England* (Cambridge, 1994)

Joyce, P. (ed.) *Class* (Oxford, 1995)

Kinchin, J. '"To knock fire out of men": forging modernity in Glasgow', in M. Hvattum and C. Hermansen (eds.) *Tracing modernity: manifestations of the modern in architecture and the city* (New York and London, 2004), pp. 232–55

Larner, G. and C. Larner. *The Glasgow style* (Edinburgh, 1979)

Lever, J. 'Architects offices', in G. Worsley (ed.) *Georgian architectural practice: papers given at the Georgian group symposium* (London, 1991), pp. 59– 64

Macdonald, S. *The history and philosophy of art education* (London, 1970)

Margolin, V. 'Design in history', *Design Issues*, 25:2 (2009), 94–105

Marsden, B. 'Engineering science in Glasgow: economy, efficiency and measurement as prime movers in the differentiation of a scientific discipline', *British Journal for the History of Science*, 25:3 (1992), 319–46

Marsden, B. and C. Smith, *Engineering empires: a cultural history of technology in nineteenth-century Britain* (Basingstoke, 2005)

McClelland, K. 'Time to work, time to live: some aspects of work and the re-formation of class in Britain, 1850–1880', in Patrick Joyce (ed.) *The historical meanings of work* (Cambridge, 1987), pp. 180–209

McClelland, K. 'Masculinity and the "representative artisan" in Britain, 1850–80', in M. Roper and J. Tosh (eds.) *Manful assertions: masculinities in Britain since 1800* (London, 1991), pp. 74–91

McClelland, K. and A. Reid, 'Wood, iron and steel: technology, labour and trade union organisation in the shipbuilding industry, 1840–1914', in R. Harrison and J. Zietlin (eds.) *Divisions of labour: skilled workers and technological change in nineteenth-century England* (Sussex, 1985), pp. 151–84

Meikskins, P. and C. Smith (eds.) *Engineering labour: technical workers in comparative perspective* (London, 1996)

Minihan, J. *The nationalization of culture* (London, 1977)

Mortimer, J. E. *A history of the association of engineering and shipbuilding draughtsmen* (London, 1960)

Moss, M. S. and J. R. Hume, *Workshop of the British Empire: engineering and shipbuilding in the West of Scotland* (London, 1977)

Moss, M. S. 'Napier, Robert (1791–1876)', *Oxford Dictionary of National Biography* (Oxford, 2004), www.oxforddnb.com/view/article/19769, accessed 6 June 2011

Nasmyth, J. 'Nasmyth on tools and machines', in R. Buchanan, *Practical essays on millwork* (London, 3rd edn, 1841) vol. 2

Nichols, K. *Greece and Rome at the Crystal Palace: classical sculpture and modern Britain, 1854–1936* (Oxford, 2015)

Platt, A. *The life and times of Daniel Gooch* (Gloucester, 1987)

Pollard, S. *The genesis of modern management* (London, 1965)

Puetz, A. 'Design instruction for artisans in eighteenth-century Britain', *Journal of design history*, 12:3 (1999), 217–39

Purbrick, L. 'Ideologically technical: illustration, automation and spinning cotton around the middle of the nineteenth century', *Journal of Design History*, 11 (1998), 275–93

Rancière, J. *The nights of labor: the workers' dream in nineteenth-century France*, trans. J. Drury, introduction by Donald Reid (Philadelphia, 1989)

Rawson, G. 'The Glasgow Government School of Design, 1845–53', *Journal of the Scottish Society for Art History* 4 (1999), 18–25

Report from the Select Committee on arts and their connexion with manufactures, House of Commons command paper 568 (1836)

Richards, J. *Mathematical visions: the pursuit of geometry in Victorian England* (San Diego, 1988)

Richardson, J. W. *Memoirs of John Wigham Richardson 1837–1908* (Glasgow, 1911)

Rifkin, A. 'Success disavowed: the schools of design in mid-nineteenth century Britain (an allegory)', *Journal of Design History*, 1:2 (1988), 89–102

Robertson, F. 'Ruling the line: learning to draw in the first age of mechanical reproduction' (PhD thesis, Glasgow School of Art, 2011)

Robertson, F. 'David Kirkaldy (1820–1897) and his museum of destruction: the visual dilemmas of an engineer as man of science', *Endeavour*, 37:10 (2013), 125–32

Romans, M. 'Political, economic, social and cultural determinants in the history of early to mid-century art and design education in Britain' (PhD thesis, University of Central England, 1998)

Rose, J. *The intellectual life of the British working classes* (New Haven and London, 2001)

Saumarez Smith, C. *The rise of design: design and the domestic interior in eighteenth century England* (London, 2000)

Schmeichen, J. A. 'Reconsidering the factory, art-labor, and the schools of design in nineteenth-century Britain', in D. P. Doordan (ed.) *Design history: an anthology* (Cambridge, MA, 1995), pp. 167–77

Scott, D. *The engineer and machinist's assistant* (Glasgow, 1849)

Shapin, S. 'The invisible technician', *American Scientist*, 77 (1989), 554–63

Smith, C. and W. N. Wise, *Energy & empire: a biographical study of Lord Kelvin* (Cambridge, 1989)

Spiers, R. P. *Architectural drawing* (London, 1887)

Styles, J. 'Manufacturing, consumption and design in eighteenth-century England', in John Brewer and Roy Porter (eds.) *Consumption and the world of goods* (London, 1993), pp. 527–54

Sussman, H. 'Machine dreams: the culture of technology', *Victorian Literature and Culture*, 28:1 (2000), 197–204

Tann, J. '"Two knights at pandemonium": a worm's eye view of Boulton, Watt & Co., c.1800–1820', *History of Technology*, 20 (1998), 47–72

Thorne, R. 'Architects and engineers', in G. Worsley (ed.) *Georgian architectural practice: papers given at the Georgian group symposium* (London, 1991), pp. 53–8

Treuherz, J. *Victorian painting* (London, 1993)

Trodd, C. 'Culture, class, city: the National Gallery, London and the spaces of education, 1822–57', in M. Pointon (ed.) *Art apart: art institutions and ideology across England and North America* (Manchester, 1994)

Turpin, J. *A school of art in Dublin since the eighteenth century: the history of the National College of Art and Design, Ireland* (Dublin, 1995)

Tylecote, M. *The mechanics' institutes of Lancashire and Yorkshire before 1851* (Manchester, 1957)

Watson, G. *The civils: the story of the institution of civil engineers* (London, 1988)

Whewell, W. *Architectural notes of German churches* (London, 1842)

Willsdon, C. A. P. *Mural painting in Britain, 1840–1942: image and meaning* (Oxford, 2000)

Yanni, C. 'On nature and nomenclature: William Whewell and the production of architectural knowledge in early Victorian Britain', *Architectural History* 40 (1997), 204–21

8

Industrialised graphic technologies in symbiosis with the world of art: the *Illustrated London News* and the *Graphic* c. 1870–c. 1890

Tom Gretton

The *Illustrated London News* (first published in 1842, hereafter *ILN*) and the *Graphic* (first published, also in London, in 1869) were aimed at, and also we may take it predominantly bought by or for, the rich and powerful in the United Kingdom and round the Anglophone world.[1] The *ILN* and the *Graphic* were made for exactly the same segment of society that was the target market for art and for discourses and institutional practices around art; that is not of itself significant; so were Purdey's shotguns.[2] However, art, as a subject matter, was a major resource for these magazines' editors as they worked from week to week to fill their pages with pictures. As a rough indication, over this period, between 10 and 20 per cent of the pictures in any given six-monthly volume of either of these magazines would have the fine arts, its institutions and its practitioners, in some form or other, as their subject matter.[3] Royalty, Empire, the work of the military and natural and man-made catastrophes also took large shares, but art was among the top handful of iconographical themes.

This chapter, however, frames the symbiosis between art and industry in such publications not as a topic in iconography but in rather different ways. It describes the technologies and divisions of labour of industrial print-making in these magazines, and then, in discussions of selected wood-engravings, considers first how pictorial modes from the artist's studio were put to work on the journalistic production line, and second, some of the ways in which these titles offered their reader-viewers pictures that made uncompromising claims to be original art-multiples. It focuses on these magazines in a period when the confident distinctions that we now make between art and illustration, or art and the informational products of graphic technologies, were not so firmly established as they have come to be since the domestication of the half-tone screen in the 1890s.

The 'public' for the images discussed here was well educated and well funded, already participating in the culture of art and both intensifying and extending their participation through the visual resource that magazines of the *ILN* genre offered.[4] The pictures produced for that public are best understood as an aspect of industrialised metropolitan high culture, just as much as the work of William Morris or George Eliot. In the wake of Adorno and Horkheimer, it is a commonplace to consider that an industrialised high culture is a contradiction in terms.[5] This essay was not, however, conceived in engagement with their pessimistic and gripping critique of the capitalist culture industries, but, following the call for papers of which this book is one outcome, as an attempt to think through some hegemonic cultural practices in a time and space which form a crucial moment in Martin Weiner's book *English culture and the decline of the industrial spirit 1850–1980* (1981), refusing the polarisation between culture and industry in terms of which his influential book makes its arguments. It seems to me that Weiner's pessimism about the anti-entrepreneurial effects of the UK's hegemonic classical/romantic high culture, and Adorno's pessimism about the deadly impact of capitalist modes of production on cultural difference and innovation are interesting mirror images of each other. At the risk of taking a Pollyanna position in rejecting forensic engagement with either of these serious and influential critiques, this essay shows that the antagonism they describe between 'culture' and 'industry' did not, in practice, exclude alternatives or third options. It demonstrates that the binaries on which these critiques both depend map poorly onto some salient features of the archive, and that the categorical distinction between easel-painting and its cognates and magazine illustration is impossible to sustain on the level of genre, of communicative competence, of pictorial ambition. It only survives on the level of commodity form.[6]

The period under discussion is framed by two events, one commercial, one technological. Starting in 1870 lets the argument range over two distinct titles, fighting for a share of a large, rich and agenda-setting market, since the *Graphic* was, at least until the First World War, the *ILN*'s major competitor, and its sustained success makes it possible to characterise a genre. The 'domestication' after 1890 of the half-tone enabled the reproduction without redrawing of photographic images, either those which come out of Kodaks or those made in a photographic studio from sketches or other works of art.[7] Closing the discussion in 1890 avoids having to cope with the impact of this technology, as it transformed the picture-making practices of these magazines, and the picture-consumption practices of their reader-viewers, particularly because it permitted much less obviously mediated access to the image worlds of already-existing art pictures, and of course to photographic images too.[8] It is much harder to observe and understand a half-tone screened image as a triumph of modern art-craft, skill and know-how than it is to understand it as a photograph. The half-tone screen seems to put the world of art at a stage prior to the world of reproductive technology, to make it inviolate, to make the mythic binaries on which both Adorno and Weiner feed seem natural. Before the half-tone came to supplant wood-engraving as the default technology for reproducing images, even in a genre that was using more and more line-blocks, the labour of making the magazine's pictures was understood, because it was so performed, as being shared between its commissioners, its originators, its artwork-producers and its printing-surface-makers: we will return to these four distinct forms of agency.[9]

During these twenty years three key technological changes affected this part of the capitalist culture industries. The first was the domestication around 1870 of photography onto wood-blocks, to provide the image that the wood-engraver turned into a relief surface: this transformed the balance of power and of representational initiative between the people who made the drawings and the people who made the printing matrices. The second came from the development of wood-pulp paper; a story of plunging raw-material costs, that brought about both a widening and a deepening of the market for expensive magazines. Before 1890 the hegemonic and totalising 'illustrated-magazine-of-record' status which the *ILN* had achieved, and which the *Graphic* managed to share, had remained relatively unshaken, not yet undermined by the authority of specialist titles in the worlds of sport, theatre, arts or country life: these titles increased their page numbers and their print-runs, incorporating increasing quantities of display advertising. The third major change came from the introduction of the photo-mechanical line-block. In the 1850s handicraft ways of producing a relief printing surface directly from a lithographic pen or chalk drawing on zinc had been developed.[10] In the 1870s techniques of producing acid-resistant photographic images of such drawings on zinc or copper plates were developed. These could then be etched in stages, in the same manner as hand-made lithographs had been processed since the 1850s; the resulting relief surfaces came to be called line-blocks in the Anglophone world. From the early 1870s in France, and from the late 1870s in England, line-blocks became a commonplace resource for the *ILN* genre.[11]

The half-tone screen was a development of the line-block's photo-etching process. It had been in slow experimental development since the early 1870s, both in Europe and the USA, but it only became a commonplace resource in the 1890s.[12] Even then the half-tone continued to be employed alongside wood-engraving and the line-block in these magazines, and for another generation it was used as much to reproduce photographs of wash and even pen drawings as to reproduce photographs of people, places and things. Before 1890 it did not provide a 'domesticated' alternative to the work of artists and other sketchers in the supplying of news or features pictures for the magazines.

In its Christmas number for 1882, the *Graphic* showed its readers how that issue had been compiled, produced and distributed. The four-page feature focused on the role of photo-etching and electrotyping in the making of the colour plates, on the specialised labour needed to print a special edition in colour, on the recently introduced folding machine, and on the logistics of distribution through the Anglophone world. In doing so it evoked the more general production process of a normal week's issue, with its demands for copy and for 'art', for a wide range of manufacturing skills, for motive power and for fixed and working capital. The magazine was at that date produced on three presses running in parallel, each carrying identical printing surfaces, entailing the 3D electrotype or stereotype copying of every image and block of type. The text says:

> counting artists, authors, papermakers, printers etc., we calculate that the *Graphic* employs about a thousand people, that the annual outlay is over one hundred and twenty thousand pounds, the weight of paper used a thousand tons ... the sheets of paper used by the *Graphic* in one year, if laid side by side, would reach just half round the world.[13]

It's good to have a sheets-of-paper-laid-around-the-world statistic, though, like Dorothy Parker, I would like to know whether they actually mean 'end to end'. The point it underlines is that the *Graphic* was a significant industrial undertaking, with a voracious appetite for paper, at that moment in the throes of the most significant industrial transformation since its invention, as wood-pulp came to supplant recycled textile fibres as the dominant paper-making material in the west.

In considering specifically the *ILN* and the *Graphic* I am looking at a small, but paradigmatic, part of the booming global newspaper and magazine industry. In some respects magazines in the *ILN* genre were 'normal' magazines: their makers needed to acquire copy, set type-matter, print pages, assemble them, distribute copies by deadlines, and, one way and another, get paid for their work. The specificity came with the fact that alongside texts, their producers had to acquire pictures, and process them in ways both like and unlike the processing that editors, typesetters and proofreaders gave to copy. In this period a picture in a magazine emerged from a sketch or a photograph, on the one hand, and from editorial decisions on the other. Is the magazine going to cover this story, run this feature? If the answer to that is 'yes', which of the range of available pictures will be used, and what shapes, and what sizes are those printed pictures going to be? Increasingly in the 1870s editors also had to decide how the 'artwork' developed from the sketch or the photograph was to be mediated: was it to be a wood-engraving or a line-block? How was its appearance going to be preserved or changed in the process of turning it from a wash or line drawing on paper, perhaps a slight sketch from a reporter or an amateur, perhaps a finished production commissioned from 'an actual professional artist', into a printing surface, a block of wood or metal carrying an image in relief that could be run through a press alongside type-matter? If a wood-engraving, was it to be a facsimile wood-engraving (mimicking the marks of a pen-drawing as closely as possible), or one which gave the image a 'house-style' (so that it looked 'like an *ILN* illustration'), or one sent to a specialist virtuoso wood-engraver, with a valued reputation for their own style and finish?

It seems to me that this list of decisions has considerably more impact on the pictures we see than equivalent editorial processes have on the copy we read, even though the comparison is one between apples and oranges. In both cases, the demands of producing the magazine each week, so that it continued to act both as a brand and as the guarantor of the knowledge and pleasure that it offered, entailed the position that authorship was always substantially collective, and the inscription of individual authoriality, when it happened, always a contingent and factitious representation of divided and collaborative labour. This point can be reinforced when we look at two distinct aspects of the production line in the 1870s and 1880s. The first is the process of turning the visual reporter's sketch, or the feature-artist's worked-up creation, or, with increasing frequency, a photograph of a person, an object or a scene, into artwork to be handed to the specialists who made the relief-printing surfaces. The second is the widening range of ways that 'artwork' could, especially in and after the 1880s, be turned into those printing surfaces.

Almost every sketch provided to the editors of magazines of the *ILN* genre would have to be redrawn and reinterpreted in-house before it could be made into a printing surface and be published; until the advent of the half-tone screen, every photograph likewise. This might usually entail re-scaling and re-proportioning, and unless the magazine had access to the negative, the making of a drawing from a photograph, but it would also routinely involve the clarifying of narratives, the pointing up of significant details, and very frequently the conflation of more than one sketch or photograph or other resource, such as pre-existent pictures from the British Museum print-room. The paradigmatic image in the *ILN* genre thus had a highly interventionist and engaged commissioner, and both an originator and a person who reworked and transmuted any 'original' into 'artwork'; the image that was going to be turned into a printing surface. In the vocabulary of the *Graphic* of 1882, this second group, the re-worker/artwork-producer group, were as integrally what they called 'our actual professional artists' as headline-grabbers such as Hall, Herkomer or Holl.[14] In 1882, typically, the artwork would still be wood-engraved, rather than being processed as a photomechanical line-block, the relief-printing technology that had been emerging over the previous decade. Wood engraving might be done in-house, but was, especially for 'features' as distinct from 'news' pictures, more likely to be sent out to a wood-engraving business.

In the 1850s artwork was either pasted down onto the box-wood block from which the relief-printing surface would be made, or, more likely, made as a copy-drawing on its surface. From the later 1860s wood-engraving firms in London, in Paris and all across the first world, had routinised the technique of printing a positive photograph onto the whitened surface of a block of box-wood. Photography onto the block had been one of the causes of a very important shift in the relations of interpretative power and autonomy between wood-engravers and those other agents in the originator-collective, the art editor, the sketch-makers, and the work-up artists.[15] Until then, the paradigmatic wood-engraving had been a facsimile reproduction of a line-drawing (which might itself be a re-drawing of a photographic image rather than of a correspondent's sketch). If instead of a finished line-drawing, the wood-engraver is given a photo-positive of a wash drawing, or a drawing combining wash and line, or as it may be a print from a *carte de visite* negative, to carve out, then the decisions about translating the contours and tones of the image into an analogical system of black-and-white lines and voids has to be left to the engraver. Facsimile wood-engraving accounted for a smaller and smaller proportion of wood engravings in this period, whereas modernised versions of the white-line wood-engraving that Thomas Bewick had developed in the 1780s took a larger and larger part. In 'white-line' wood engraving, the marks of the carving tool themselves carry information about edge, tone, texture and contour, rather than serving to remove areas of wood, leaving behind black lines or dots to carry that information.

In these years, in these magazines, editors, artists, artisans and process operatives collaborated as mutually dependent equals to produce each week's issue of the illustrated magazine. The way in which magazines of the *ILN* genre inscribed authorship in their pages and in the images they printed was in the circumstances complicated. In the UK the paradigmatic position was to ascribe authorship of newspaper articles to the journal: most articles were anonymous, and one can see how this text-world paradigm shaped the way that images were treated.[16] But the paradigm did not in fact fit very well: 'our actual professional artists' regularly did very much more than sub-editors ever did; wood engravers working with wash copy photographed onto the block also put their hand and their mark on what we see much more obviously than any typesetter did with the copy they turned into type-matter. Every image in a magazine of the *ILN* genre was the result of divided but collective labour, and artistic authorship, at once the apotheosis and the opposite of productive labour, was an elusive and slippery presence in its numbers. Sometimes artists' signatures, initials or monograms survive on the art-work; sometimes art-work-producers add theirs, sometimes wood-engraving or process-engraving businesses left their trademark-signatures there.[17] Sometimes sketch-providers or art-work producers are named in captions or other texts, the makers of

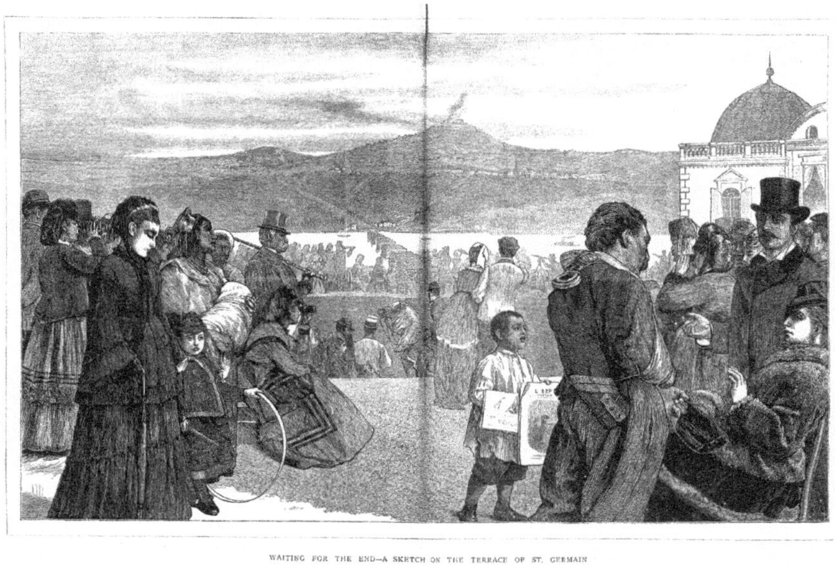

8.1 JDL (drawn by), anonymous artwork producer and anonymous wood engraver, 'Waiting for the end – a sketch on the terrace of St. Germain', *Graphic* (3 June 1871). Wood engraving, 302 x 502 mm. (Kensington and Chelsea Public Libraries.)

the matrices, never.[18] The information is unclear, inconsistent, partial and scattered: in the circumstances the agency of authorship, in as much as it is inscribed in these texts, is given above all to the magazine itself.

The second half of the chapter looks at some images from both titles; it discusses only wood-engravings in which the wood-engraver has worked from elaborated wash-drawings. The first three figures deal with representations of the Franco-Prussian war of 1870–71 and of the civil war that closely followed it, looking at the way the resources of easel painting were deployed in the service of news and topical features. The last three figures offer evidence that these magazines imagined themselves not merely to be harnessing art's resources, but also to be producing images with an authentic claim to be works of art, their status as industrially produced multiples notwithstanding.

This two-page spread from the *Graphic* of 3 June 1871, 'Waiting for the end', 1,516 square centimetres of wood-engraving labour, was published just after the fall of the Paris Commune: a week of burning and butchery had ended on 28 May (see figure 8.1). The picture represents *Versaillais* spectators of the final acts of the civil war on the terraced bank of the Seine at St Germain en Laye. Centrally, it points out that the press is an omnipresent part of modern existence, and that bereavement, disablement and displacement, as well as bloody cataclysm, are part of modernity's spectacle. The report exaggerates the height of Paris's

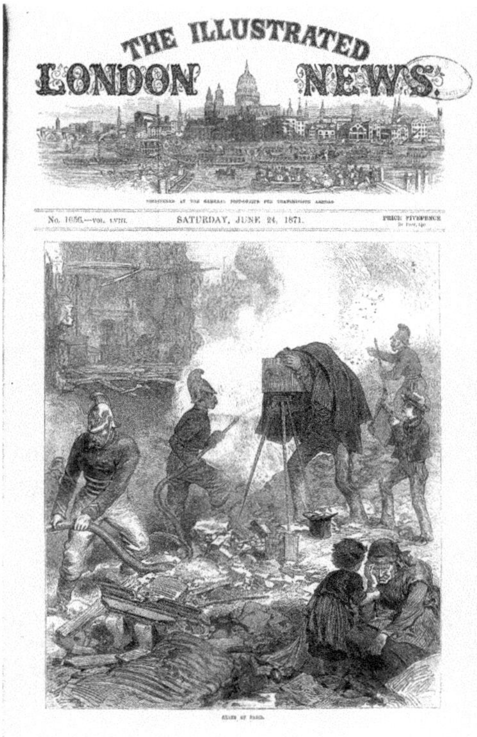

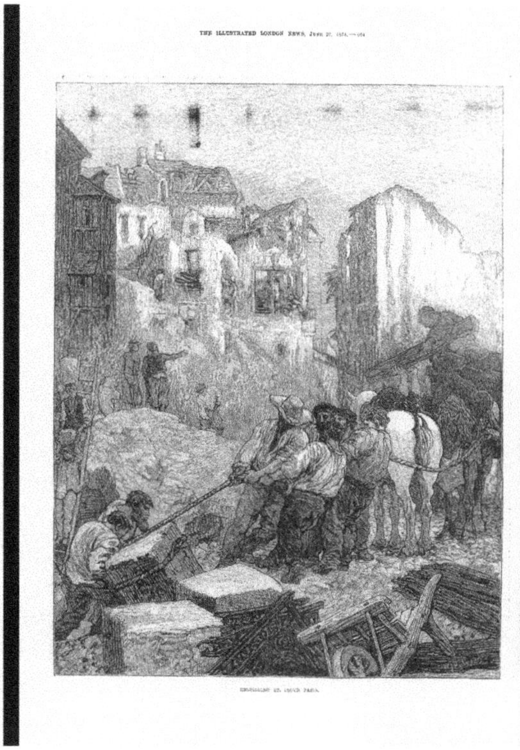

Anonymous artist, anonymous artwork producer and anonymous wood engraver, 'Ruins of Paris', *Illustrated London News* (24 June 1871). Wood engraving, 249 x 213 mm; and G. Régamey (drawn by), anonymous artwork producer and WJB (wood engraver), 'Rebuilding St. Cloud, Paris', *Illustrated London News* (27 June 1874). Wood engraving, 311 x 235 mm. (Kensington and Chelsea Public Libraries.) **8.2**

northern hills to increase the anecdotal legibility of what is otherwise an accurate topographical landscape, and fuses this mode of representation with contemporary genre conventions, and with the summarising and commemorative techniques of the history painting, to give the *Graphic*'s reader-viewers access both to the spectacle and to a range of resources for moralising commemorative reflection on the news. As a centrefold this picture has been singled out for our attention, but as a sample of the way news pictures were made by synthesising an *ad-hoc* range of the conventions of Western painting, so as to manage and reward a range of sorts of spectatorship, it is nothing special.

The routineness of such a deployment of art's resources is borne out by this pair of pictures (see figure 8.2). They are both from the *ILN*; one is a front-page picture, the other is given a whole inside page. They both present to British reader-viewers the destruction of lives and property around Paris as a result of the fighting of 1870–71. The 24 June 1871 front page 'Ruins of Paris' comes from an editorial artist probably on the basis of a sketch or two, perhaps on the basis of a verbal description, and like the *Graphic*'s centrefold, thematises both the work of representation and the centrality of the spectacle, here using a photographer, his apparatus and his assistant to make the points. The composition is put together much more like a subject painting than like a topographical photograph. It leads us from the dark foreground with its figure-group, via the serpentine hoses and gestures of the firemen to the photographer and his camera, from which crux it moves diagonally upwards to the left, past the fireman's haloed helmet to the gutted bourgeois interior. That interior is of course in representational cahoots with the scene of the homeless and hopeless pair in the right foreground, the poor old woman and the distressed young girl. It is a workaday picture, made to fill a slot and to meet a deadline; the point here is that the work it does is art work. The 27 June 1874 image 'Rebuilding St. Cloud, Paris' is by Guillaume Régamey, one of two artist-entrepreneur brothers who did a good deal of work for both French and English magazines of the *ILN* genre. It shows reconstruction in Saint Cloud, the town on Paris's western fringe where the war with Germany had been declared in July 1870, whose chateau had been burned down in an artillery exchange in October 1870, and which was a key location in the Parisian army's last failed attempt to break the siege in January 1871, a battle which led immediately to Bismarck's decision to start shelling Paris. This anniversary picture is thus a scene in which the everyday meets and touches a totalising narrative, occupying the territories of both the painting of modern life and of history. It is constructed using exactly the same representational and compositional tools as the 1871 front page, with its allegorical objects in the foreground, its interiors violently ripped open in the background, and a zig-zag up and back into the picture-space, to articulate action and narrative, encourage reflection and support commentary. The production deadline here will not have been so urgent; the commemorative status of the picture tending more to 'features' than to news; that may be one reason why the signatures both of Régamey and the wood-engraver are visible in the block.

Another pair from the range of images generated in London magazines by the Franco-Prussian war and the sieges of Paris shows just how deeply saturated in art practice and art history, just how close to the representational agenda of contemporary art the news-orientated image-making of these journals was, and just how well-equipped in those areas art-editors and 'actual professional artists' imagined their public to be (see figure 8.3). The two pictures in this opening of the *Graphic* from 3 December 1870 show, first, 'A reverie – Versailles' in which a German officer convalesces in the field hospital set up in the occupied Chateau of Versailles. He has fallen into that reverie reading French satirical magazines, each with their caricature of Napoleon III humiliated in defeat. In attendance is a nursing sister taking a nap; on the wall behind her is Jacques-Louis David's

'Napoleon crossing the Alps', its frame topped by a French eagle bearing an imperial crown. The picture's didactic agenda is perhaps overloaded and over-emphatic to our eyes, but the image is very well-educated both in terms of its composition (golden sections meet at the cigar) and in terms of its deployment of relevant iconographies, genres and intertextualities: nothing in its modes, ambitions or pictorial procedures would prevent it being a rather conservative salon painting. Of its companion in this opening, 'A friend in need', critics might say that like its figure-drawing, its X-logic composition is clunky, architectural forms playing too obviously against action and narrative, that it perhaps over-indicates the everyday at the expense of the transcendental, that the relationship between its human figures is unresolved, and that the carrier pigeon is stuck unconvincingly in space. They might note that the wood-engraving has not managed to communicate enough background detail for us to see that Paris is an actor in the scene. But this picture too occupies the same art-aspiration space as easel painting, in this case as vanguard easel painting. Its making undoubtedly predates that of Puvis de Chavannes' siege-of-Paris painting 'The Pigeon' (1871), and might just have been a

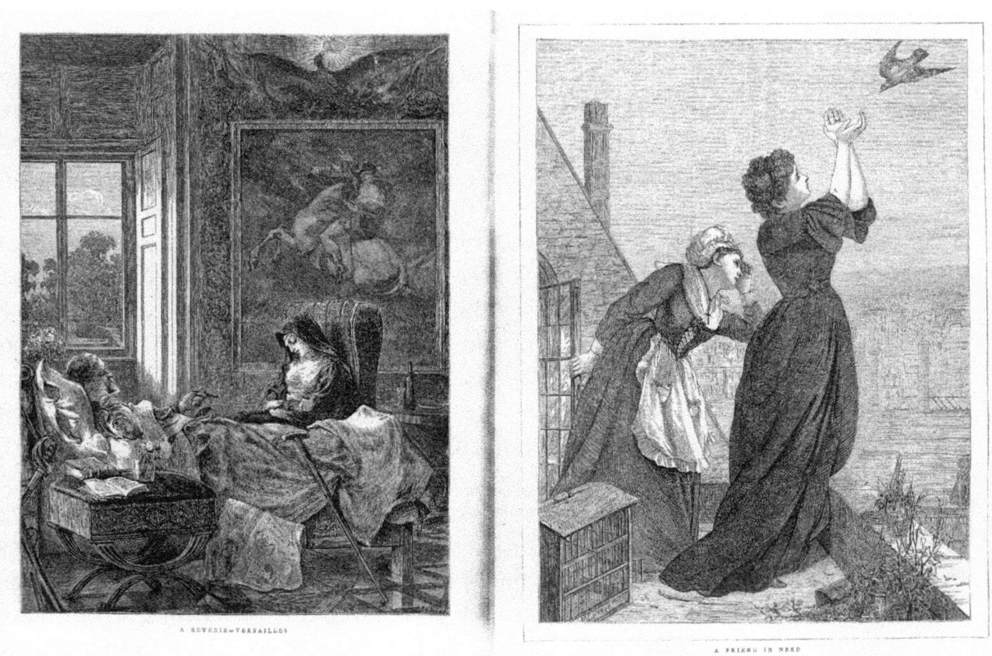

8.3 E. J. Gregory (drawn by), anonymous artwork producer and anonymous wood engraver, 'A reverie – Versailles', *Graphic* (3 December 1870). Wood engraving, 303 x 227 mm; and M. E. Freer (drawn by), anonymous artwork producer and anonymous wood engraver, 'A friend in need', *Graphic* (3 December 1870). Wood engraving, 306 x 228 mm. (Kensington and Chelsea Public Libraries.)

resource, both as model and as counter-model, for him.[19] The point here is that its industriality is no bar to its full participation in the field of contemporary art-picture-making.

The *Graphic* declared in its prospectus that it would be more ambitiously 'artistic' than the *ILN*, so we should not be surprised to see it mobilising the resources of 'art' in this way.[20] The *ILN* quickly responded by emulating the *Graphic* (as the Régamey print in figure 8.2 shows), so that by the mid-1870s it is hard to identify stylistic differences, as both of them give their reader-viewers elaborated and visually knowing pictures of the worlds of news and features.

In the siege of Paris scenes, in thousands of reports from palace or concert hall, boulevard, tourist mecca or imperial campaign, we can map the close dependence of this extraordinarily powerful and productive representational machine on art's ways of seeing and of making. No other relationship was possible: the world of journalistic picture-making was a fully integrated dimension of the world of art. But the relationship has more than this one powerful axis. In the remainder of the chapter I will look at one further intimacy between this mass-circulation industrially produced representational commodity form and the world of art – the way that these magazines projected at least some of the new editorial pictures they offered their reader-viewers as art, as well as being work.

E. F. Brewtnall (1846–1902) was one of the *Graphic*'s founding team of artists, and continued to work for magazines in the *ILN* genre to the end of the century. 'The artist and his critics', the front page of 29 April 1871, is not offered to the *Graphic*'s reader-viewers as a work of art with an existence outside the pages of the magazine, nor as having any relation to current events. All its iconography places the image in the world of art (see figure 8.4). We are clearly in an artist's studio, not only because of the easel, which carries a painting that we cannot see, but because of the accoutrements that fill the room's spaces – the suit of jousting armour, the Turkish shield, the fool's baton, the lay-figure. The way that the critics are represented, as three superannuated Graces pontificating about the unseen painting, puts us evidently in the orbit of the young, graceful, lounging, smoking artist, who is sure that he knows better than they the value of his labour, and who, by elbowing the edge of the picture space, puts himself both in the picture and in the magazine. He mediates between the picture that we can see and the one that we cannot, and as the latter's guarantor, raises our expectations of the former. The theme of the sclerotic critic was an old one in print culture. Here the particular charge of the picture is that it is, in all its pictorial rhetoric, not a differential comment from the world of printmaking about the precarious dependency of the easel-painting artist on idiosyncratic patronage, but instead an assertion of the independence of the modern artist from the object-orientated connoisseurship of the old school and its old men. Here, surely, though in no sense polemically, the industrialisation of picture-making is the future of art. There is no news value in this picture as there had been of the report of the convalescent ward in Versailles: the only available status for this image is that of art.

These status-switching efforts did not always produce results invulnerable to the reproach of kitsch. The *ILN* and the *Graphic* both developed practices that made it hard for reader-viewers to make clear distinctions between editorial imagery and the reproduction of current works of art. A pair of *ILN* images will make the point (see figure 8.5). These neatly convergent 'modern life' pictures of beauty out walking, one in a wintry pastoral scene and one in a chilly urban one, each fill a page of the *ILN* in the early months of 1889, and are both captioned in a way that shows they are images made for this publication. They converge in status and format and genre, but there are differences. 'The nearest way to church' (2 February 1889) generalises its English rural background, except that we know we are in a park (doubtless her father's), since the sapling is protected against the deer. We are invited to imagine soberly sexy prosperous femininity as irresistible, as indeed the nearest way to church. The gendering of the viewer is monolithic, the implied narrative, of the exchange of women between father/publisher and viewer/husband, obvious and closed (like much Victorian genre painting). 'A frosty morning' (2 March 1889) tells a story at once much more specific in its localisation, in a West-end square, and in its staffage with idle and industrious road-menders and their tools (including a trestle of which Escher would have been proud), and much more ambiguous in its message. Does the gendering of the viewer have to be male? If we are her male viewer, are we also her faithful sheep-dog? Is the dog actually hers, or, in the absence of a lead, is it a *flâneur* following her scent, and offering the viewer a different inscription? What is wrong with the man with the brush that he has not noticed her? Should we be transferring the epithet 'frosty' from the morning to the heroine? These ambiguities and this narrativity without narrative achieve an intention effect, make us refer back to the author if we want to find a stable meaning. But this is an editorial image in an occasional series of pictures of modern beauties, not a report from the world of art, as it might have been if it had reproduced a convergent painting, perhaps by Tissot or Clausen: the authoredness that the intention effect produces is the *ILN*'s.[21]

To conclude, I want to bring things back from the ways in which these magazines made claims about the artistic status of their pictures to the way that the *ILN* genre could articulate the three-cornered relationship between art, labour and the labour of representation, and back to the early years of the *Graphic*.

In 'An artist's dream in Pompeii' (11 January 1873, see figure 8.6) the protagonist, who is named neither through a signature on the image nor in the caption, falls asleep in Pompeii, his legs and his left elbow excluded

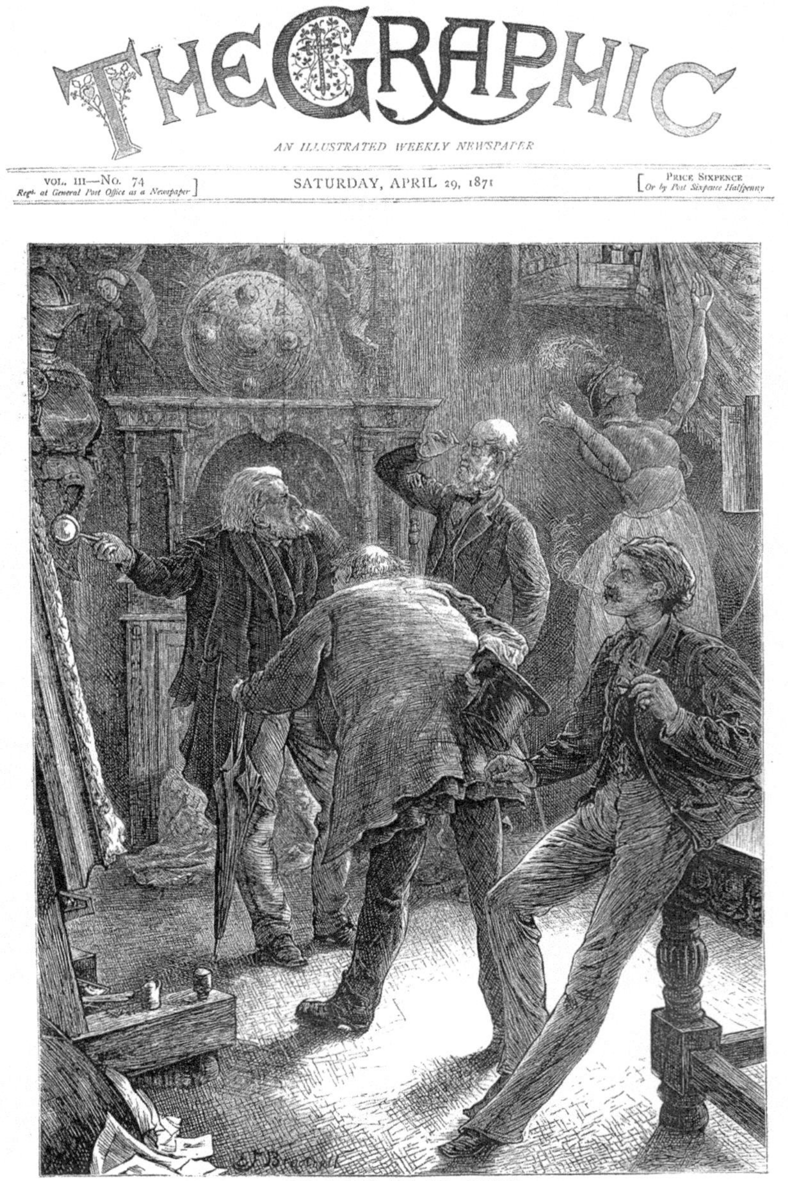

8.4 E. F. Brewtnall (signed in the block), anonymous artwork producer and anonymous wood engraver, 'The artist and his critics', *Graphic* (29 April 1871). Wood engraving, 288 x 225 mm. (Kensington and Chelsea Public Libraries.)

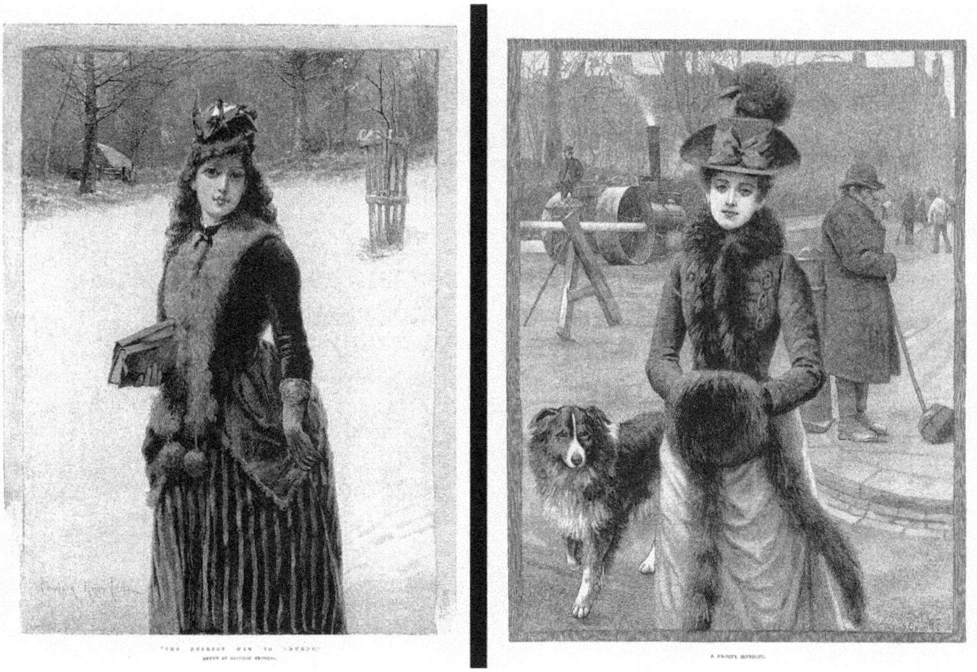

R. Taylor (wood engraver), '"The nearest way to church." Drawn by Davison Knowles', *Illustrated London News* (2 February 1889). Wood engraving, 316 x 239 mm; and S. Cowell (signed) and R. Taylor (wood engraver), 'A frosty morning', *Illustrated London News* (2 March 1889). Wood engraving, 305 x 231 mm. (Kensington and Chelsea Public Libraries.) **8.5**

from the picture-space, somewhat as in Brewtnall's work. A lizard darts onto his sketch-book, and another climbs the sun-struck stone block on which he rests, while behind him his reverie peoples the scene of labour in the food industry with Herculean bakers, a starveling stoker, and strong-but-comely slave girls toiling at millstones. This fantasy has been wood-engraved by Eugène Froment, whose tiny signature can be found in the space between the artist and the rock. Froment has represented the relationship between the actual professional artist and his reverie by producing the dream-scene in a greyer overall tonality, showing a stupendous control over the relief-engraved lines, even though we may judge him to have been over-anxious about defining outlines. We cannot know what convention for differentiating levels of the real was used in the art-work he reproduced, so we cannot know where that emphaticness originated: facsimile reproductions of Sydney Hall's sketches in other issues of the *Graphic* suggest that substantial work on this one had been done back in London. Froment and his editors could be confident that the big high-speed rotary presses of the *Graphic*, working from electrotypes rather than from the original box-wood surface, would be able to communicate the effect of his subtle skill.

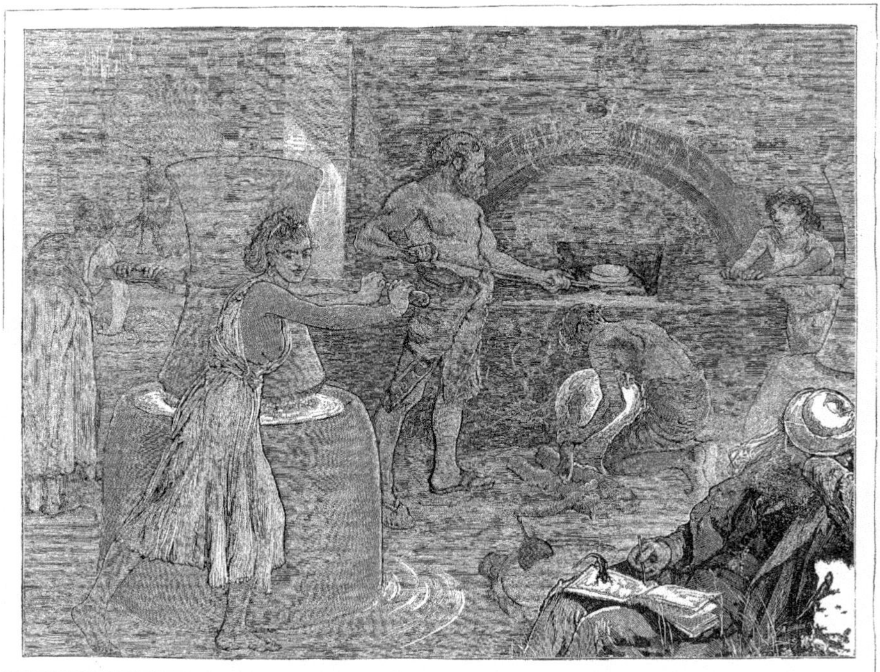

AN ARTIST'S DREAM IN POMPEII

8.6 Sydney Hall (sketch by), anonymous artwork producer and E. Froment (wood engraver), 'An artist's dream in Pompeii', *Graphic* (11 January 1873). Wood engraving, 229 x 300 mm. (Kensington and Chelsea Public Libraries.)

From a two-line text elsewhere in the issue, we know that the artist we see is the *Graphic*'s 'actual professional artist', Sydney Hall, taking a break in Pompeii after reporting an eruption of Vesuvius. Hall also supplies an unsigned text, of around 500 words, about his visit, describing his waking failure to get his imagination and his fund of classical and art-scene knowledge to connect with the evidence of his eyes. This text gives hints as to why the sketcher chose to place an artist as a framing device for the fantasy, at once anchoring it in and distancing it from the real.

One must wonder: is an artist's dream always-already a work of art, whatever its mediation? Or are we looking at a culture industry doing its ineluctable collective job, not even needing to be awake to do it? Here, surely, as throughout the flow of pictures I have discussed, we are in contradiction. In this representation the *Graphic* both makes and ironises the visual claim to be offering us art, and both makes and ironises the rhetorical claim that art turns its back on industry, except as exotic subject-matter. As regards the iconography of art and industry in this picture, it is easy to give it a Manichaean interpretation. Art falls asleep in the presence of labour and hierarchy and the daily grind, and dreams of the antique and the exotic, turns classical culture once again into a hegemonic modern 'middle-brow' value, and in doing so offers a fig-leaf to oppression. But there are not just two terms in the relationship which is here represented and performed, since in this construction of spectatorship, it is not 'the artist' but the editorial collective that is the representer. Art and its fantastic relation to its sources and values is the thing represented, though it is, as it has to be, represented through art, represented using the tools, the range of sorts of labour and skill that art has invented, disseminated, divided and made available to the industry.

As with many of the images I have discussed, I think this is a striking, successful and thought-provoking picture. But I can hear Willie Nelson in my head (singing in 1981, the year Wiener's book came out), telling me 'how it's exquisitely constructed yet mechanical and somehow slightly wrong'.[22] That may be true about Hall and Froment's recursive reverie; and if so it may be useful, in some discourses, to establish that truth. But in as much as such dismissive critiques are used to make categorical distinctions between 'art' and 'not-art', they miss the most important aspect of the picture-making work of the *ILN* genre. Mechanicalness is not either a necessary or a sufficient condition of wrongness, of expulsion from art's Eden. For the editorial collectives of these magazines, and for their publics, industry was not the other of art, but its constitutive and indispensable medium, and art was both the raw material and the product of this powerful and plethoric industry.

Notes

1 I thank Kate Nichols, Rebecca Wade and Gabriel Williams for convening the conference that prompted this essay, and all those who attended it, for providing such stimulating discussions. Thanks also to the people who discussed a version of this paper at the CAA in Chicago in 2014.

2 Purdey received their first royal warrant in 1868. On the *ILN*, Sinnema, *Dynamics of the pictured page* is authoritative. Brown, *Beyond the lines* is a groundbreaking study of a different part of the wood, focused on a magazine with a more demotic market niche.

3 All the evidence for this and other assertions in this piece is based on a survey of the *ILN* and the *Graphic* from first publication to 1910 (and *L'Illustration* and the *Monde illustré* from Paris), at five-yearly intervals (x0 and x5) using the January–June period from each year, surveying and (more arbitrarily) classifying all the editorial images from a six-number sample from that period. Page sizes in these magazines were roughly 400 x 300 mm; page numbers rose from typically twenty-four to typically thirty-two in the period; print-runs were then a closely guarded secret for both titles, but were probably typically between 50,000 and 100,000 for the *ILN*, and rather less than that for the *Graphic*; Christmas-number print-runs could reach half a million.

4 The distinction between 'public' and 'audience', the former as a construct in the mind of maker and critic, the latter as actual reader-viewers, follows T. J. Clark in *Image of the people*, p. 12.

5 In 'The culture industries' chapter of *The dialectic of enlightenment* (German versions cyclostyled 1944, revised and printed 1947, English translations 1972 and 2002), Adorno and Horkheimer (it seems to me most un-dialectically) argue ruthlessly that the capitalist culture industries are monopolistic and that all their products are self-same, all differences between market-niches or marketed contents superficial and illusory: middles between mass culture and art are excluded, sometimes it feels by definition.

6 For a discussion of the distinction between genre and commodity form in these magazines see Gretton, 'The pragmatics of page-design in nineteenth-century general-interest weekly illustrated news magazines in London and Paris', esp. 682–3.

7 Berker *et al.* (eds.) *Domestication of media and technology* for a recent deployment of Roger Silverstone's concept of domestication, the process by which technologies are adopted and adapted into everyday life; in this case (in the first place) the everyday life of a process-engraving business.

8 The foundational study is by Harris, 'Iconography and intellectual history', pp. 196–211. Beegan, *The mass image* offers a useful recent introduction.

9 In this essay 'artwork' is used in a technical sense, which the *OED* first records from 1926: sketches, photographs and decorative material ready to be reproduced for printing on a page.

10 Definitions and bibliography to be found in Nadeau, *Encyclopedia of printing, photographic, and photomechanical processes* under, for example, 'Gillotage' and 'Comte process'.

11 Nadeau, *Encyclopedia of printing, photographic, and photomechanical processes* under 'Line-block' and 'Swan process' for example. See also Jussim, *Visual communication and the graphic arts*. Wakeman, *Victorian book illustration* remains a useful resource.

12 Nadeau, *Encyclopedia of printing, photographic, and photomechanical processes* also discusses Leggotype, developed in Montreal in the late 1860s; that technology does not seem to have spread south to the USA or across the Atlantic, or to have survived in use for very long.

13 *Graphic*, Christmas Number (December 1882), unpaginated (p. 4).

14 The phrase comes from that same Christmas number of 1882 (p. 2): of the nine men in 'some "Graphic" artists' perhaps three acted primarily as artwork producers.

15 In Shorter, 'Illustrated journalism, its past and its future', C. K. Shorter makes the point that wood-engraving- and line-block-illustrated weeklies need a dedicated 'art editor' independent of the overall (and text-orientated) editor (489).

16 Liddle, 'Salesmen, sportsmen, mentors', 31–68.

17 Their businesses were called 'process engravers', but almost all the work they did was actually photo-etching.

18 The situation was sharply different in equivalent media in Paris, where originators, artwork-producers and wood-engravers were all quite regularly acknowledged in captions.

19 P. de Chavannes, 'The pigeon', oil on canvas, Paris, Musée d'Orsay, 1367 x 865 mm.

20 I have not located a copy of the original prospectus. The complete-volume prospectus from June 1870, which survives in the John Johnson Collection in the Bodleian Library, Oxford (Prospectuses of Journals 26 (2a)) stresses the magazine's artistic achievements with a 'told-you-so' air.

21 J. Tissot 'The warrior's daughter', 1878, oil on panel 362 x 218 mm, Manchester City Art Galleries; G. Clausen 'A morning walk', 1881, oil on canvas, 305 x 203 mm, private collection; both are of much the same size as the *ILN* pictures.

22 Waylon Jennings and Willie Nelson recorded Jimmy Webb's 1978 song 'Mr. Shuck and Jive' for the *WWII* album, released on RCA Victor in 1982.

Bibliography

Adorno, T. and M. Horkheimer. *The dialectic of enlightenment*, trans. E. Jephcott (Redwood City, CA, 2002)

Beegan, G. *The mass image: a social history of photomechanical reproduction in Victorian London* (London, 2008)

Berker, T., M. Hartmann, Y. Punie and K. Ward (eds.) *Domestication of media and technology* (Maidenhead, 2006)

Brown, J. *Beyond the lines: pictorial reporting, everyday life, and the crisis of gilded age America* (Berkeley, CA, 2006)

Clark, T. J. *Image of the people: Gustave Courbet and the 1848 revolution* (London, 1973)

Gretton, T. 'The pragmatics of page-design in nineteenth-century general-interest weekly illustrated news magazines in London and Paris', *Art History*, 33:4 (2010), 680–70

Harris, N. 'Iconography and intellectual history: the half-tone effect', in J. Higham and P. Conkin (eds.) *New directions in intellectual history* (Baltimore, 1979), pp. 196–211

Jussim, E. *Visual communication and the graphic arts: photographic technologies in the nineteenth century* (New York, 1974)

Liddle, D. 'Salesmen, sportsmen, mentors: anonymity and mid-Victorian theories of journalism', *Victorian Studies*, 41:1 (1997), 31–68

Nadeau, L. *Encyclopedia of printing, photographic, and photomechanical processes* (Frederickton, New Brunswick, 1990)

Shorter, C. K. 'Illustrated journalism, its past and its future', *Contemporary Review*, 75 (1899), 481–94

Sinnema, P. *Dynamics of the pictured page: representing the nation in the Illustrated London News* (Aldershot, 1998)

Wakeman, G. *Victorian book illustration, the technical revolution* (Newton Abbot, 1973)

Weiner, M. *English culture and the decline of the industrial spirit 1850–1980* (Cambridge, 1981)

9

True ornament? The art and industry of electric lighting in the home, 1889–1902

Graeme Gooday and Abigail Harrison-Moore

> During the great part of the last century, Art had but little in common with the crafts of the workers in metal and it was reserved for the declining years of the Victorian era to bear witness to that great revival of interest in the applied arts, which we see as a living force to-day. In no direction has this been more marked than in that branch of handicraft which concerns itself with the design and manufacture of metal fittings for electric lighting purposes.[1]

At the turn of the twentieth century the arrival of domestic electric lighting posed major new challenges: safety, economy, reliability and aesthetics.[2] For many householders, as much as for those working in the decorative arts, the last of these was a major concern. This quotation from an *Art-Journal* editorial of October 1904 signals one way in which the tension between art and industry at the centre of this chapter would be resolved. As demonstrated by two of William Morris's key disciples, Philip Webb and W. A. S. Benson, this would be accomplished by looking back to the medieval 'golden age' of metal craft, when crafts were as valued as 'art', and concurrently promoting a skilled craft-based approach to engage with the fresh possibilities of electric lighting.[3] Their anxiety that the ancient metal crafts should be reunited with this newest of technologies illustrates the significance of the aesthetics of electric lighting in exploring the relationship between art and industry (see figure 9.1).

As the *Art-Journal* saw it, the artist-craftsman's application of 'metal forms' to the needs of the electric lighting engineer revealed an important and fascinating new relationship developing between 'one of the youngest of the sciences and the very oldest of the industrial arts'. This topic had previously been neglected by artists, it alleged: throughout the preceding century, the design of the lamps and gas fittings 'which held sway' had received little attention from them. They were instead left to the 'tender mercies' of the trade designer and the commercial makers, whose use of

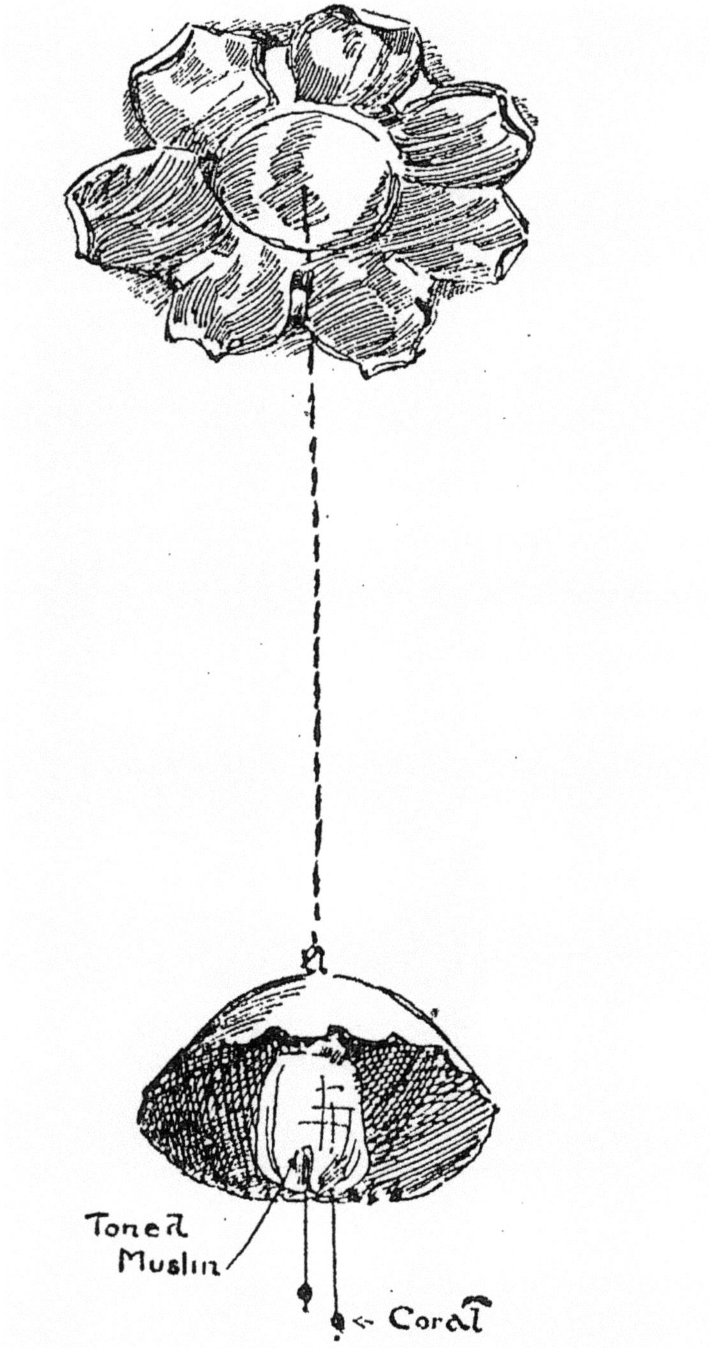

C. R. Ashbee, design for a light fitting, featured in 'Suggestions for electric light fittings', *Art-Journal*, 1895. (Author's collection.) **9.1**

velvet or brocade, and a heap of big soft pillows placed on it. If this divan is placed in the corner of the room, a three-shelved corner bracket should be fixed just above it, and an arm made to spring from the top shelf of this bracket, holding a lamp and handkerchief shade, where Tommy and his mother can have a most comfortable nest in which to study "Struwwel-Peter," or any other nursery classic. A little carved cherub with wings, Fig. 18, can be made to sit on the top shelf, holding from his outstretched hand a pink electric wire cord, and

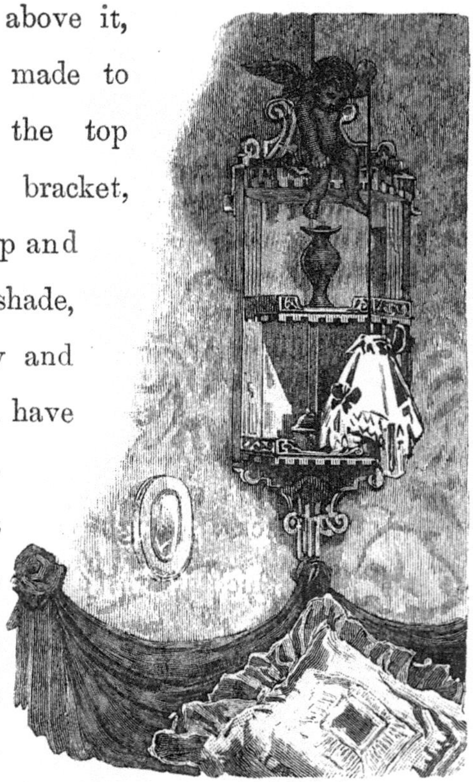

FIG. 18.—CORNER BRACKET WITH CUPID.

9.2 Suggestion for lighting in 'the boudoir', Gordon, *Decorative electricity*, 1891. (Author's collection.)

stereotyped patterns and diverse utilitarian metal articles had produced 'sadly inartistic' results. The *Art-Journal* found this separation of artists from industry surprising, given the 'high order of excellence' attained in metalworking during preceding generations.[4] A revival of the collaborative sort underway was thus sorely needed to guarantee the integrity of the glamorous new technology.

Rather than acquiescing to the *Art-Journal*'s partisan view on the proper development of electric lighting, however, we examine the alternative approaches that it condemned as producing 'sadly inartistic' results. This attack had, we suggest, one particular (implicit) female target, Mrs J. E. H. (Alice) Gordon, whose popular handbook, *Decorative electricity* appeared in 1891, running to a cheaper second edition in 1892. Her amateur use of silk dressings for lampshades to disguise electric light, and recommendations for exotic designs to assimilate the shaded lamps into the late Victorian boudoir, were the antithesis of the Arts and Crafts Movement's focus on foregrounding the art of metalwork (see figure 9.2). One might read this within the wider gendered division of labour in late nineteenth-century society which saw women conventionally represented as primarily responsible for the decorative in the home. In the second half of the chapter, we illustrate Benson's and Webb's approaches to this topic by examining how they extended Arts and Crafts techniques to the electric lighting at Standen, a country house outside East Grinstead, West Sussex. By comparing the commentary in Mrs Gordon's book to the bold statements in both the *Art-Journal* and the designs of Webb and Benson, we show that, although the end results in terms of physical design could not have been more different, Gordon's rhetoric on 'good design' in electric lighting was very similar to that of her critics. However, from the *Art-Journal*'s complete avoidance of any direct mention of her work we infer that its editors would not encourage their readers to think that their discussion of the art–industry nexus had anything in common with the practice of 'false ornament' that they decried in works such as hers. Hence it is to her book *Decorative electricity* that we must first turn to analyse the early development of contested notions of 'artistic' design for electric lighting.

Transformers: the changing aesthetics of electric lighting in the home (1892–98)

> It would be very difficult to over-rate the fascination of the art of electric lighting in its application to beautiful rooms, as exemplified in Mrs J. E. H. Gordon's charming little volume on 'Decorative Electricity'.[5]

What constituted 'artistic' electric lighting in the last decade of the nineteenth century was clearly a somewhat contested matter. The *Art-Journal*, a forum for debate among predominantly male designers and art critics, presumed the status of arbiter of good taste on such matters. By the late

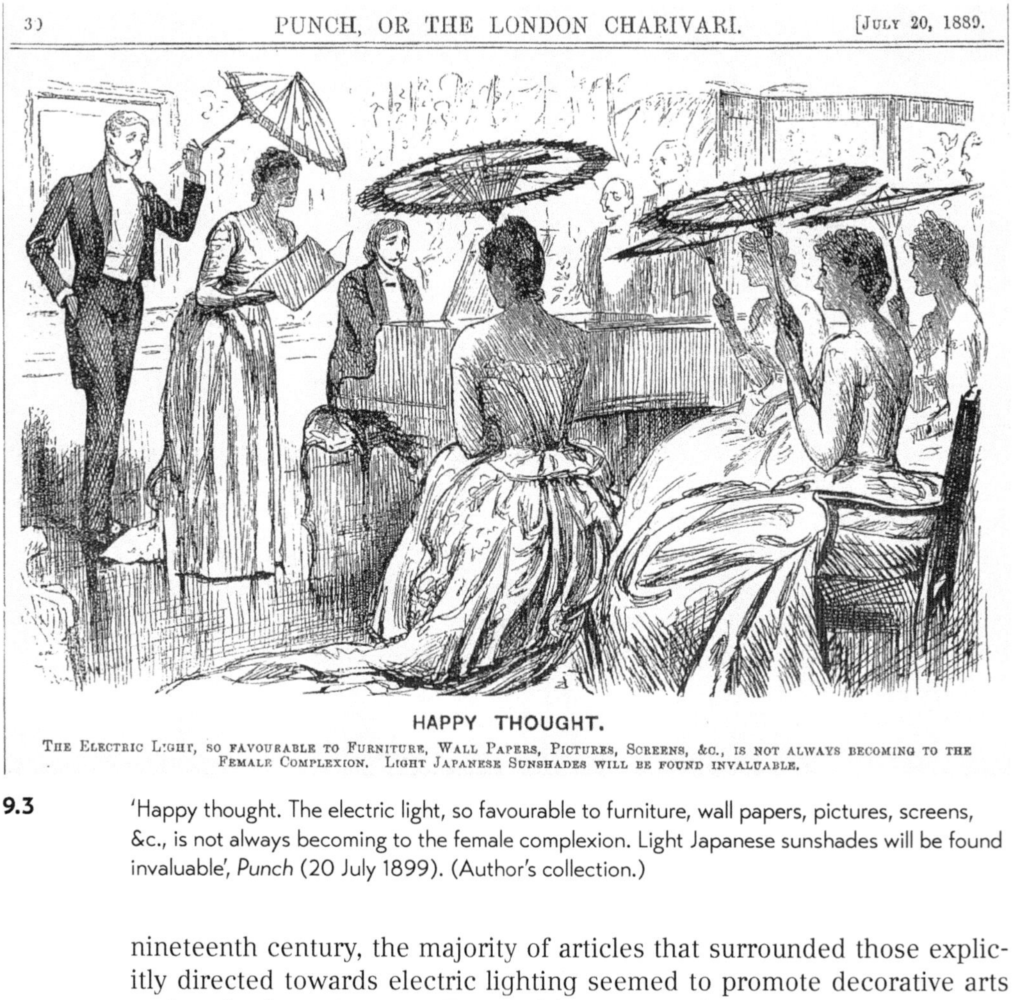

9.3 'Happy thought. The electric light, so favourable to furniture, wall papers, pictures, screens, &c., is not always becoming to the female complexion. Light Japanese sunshades will be found invaluable', *Punch* (20 July 1899). (Author's collection.)

nineteenth century, the majority of articles that surrounded those explicitly directed towards electric lighting seemed to promote decorative arts and crafts from the past. Founded in 1839 as the *Art Union – A Monthly Journal of the Fine Arts*, the journal was aimed specifically at 'fine' artists, but was keen to stress – as one article put it 'The mutual interests of artists and manufacturers'.[6] As George P. Landow has pointed out, the retirement of Samuel Carter Hall as editor in 1880 saw the journal turn away from its previously anti-Ruskinian, pro-art-manufacture rhetoric, which may go some way to explain why so much ink was spilled on electric lighting on its pages in the 1890s.[7] The results, however, which it condemned condescendingly as 'sadly inartistic', were promoted by commercial manufacturers and female authorities, and celebrated in the popular press as being distinctly 'decorative'. Indeed, as we see from the comment in the *Lady's Pictorial* with which we opened this sub-section, for at least one significant reader, the use of commercial fabrics and ornaments to bring decorative electric lighting to the home resulted in much beauty.

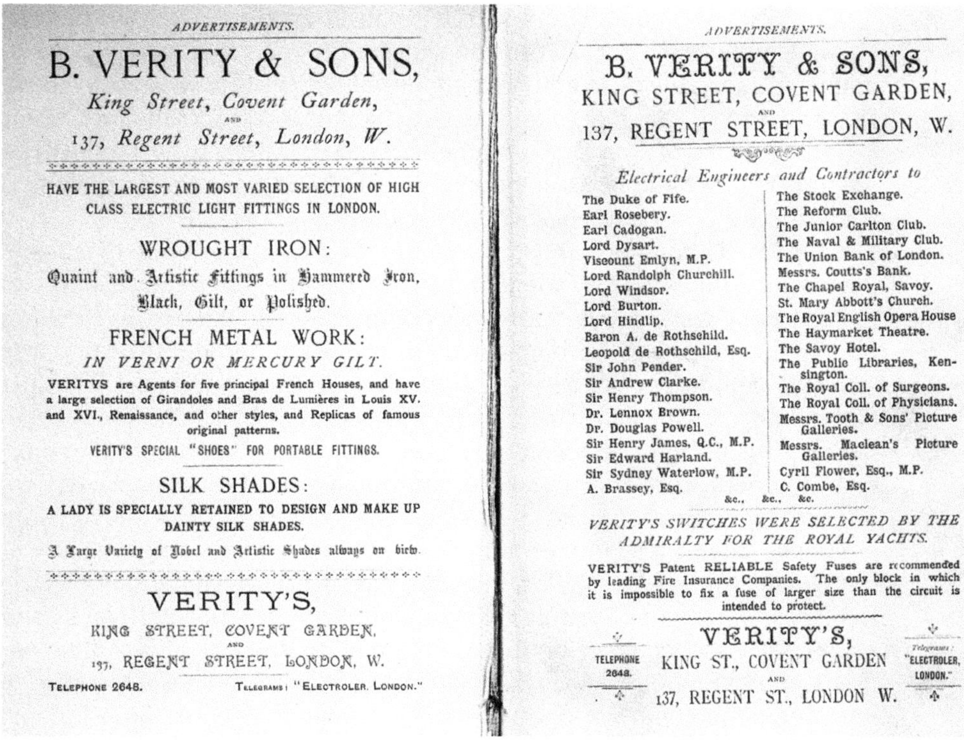

Advert for Verity and Sons' light fittings in Gordon, *Decorative electricity*, 1891. (Author's collection.) **9.4**

As Gooday has argued in *Domesticating electricity*, there was much objection, particularly among female commentators, to the garishly dazzling effect of the first mass-produced electric light fittings available in the later 1880s. Given the enormous expense of early electric lighting in comparison to that of gas lighting, practical forms of the new illuminant had been designed by electrical companies on the grounds of industrial efficiency to give value for money. They thus were unshielded, directed downward and otherwise constructed to have maximum brilliance, wishing both to enjoy the vivid spectacle of the electric light and also its virtuous non-emission of the sulphuric vapours that gas lamps emitted, so often to the detriment of furnishings and artworks. As seen through the characteristically male gaze of *Punch* magazine in 1889, the discomfort of women experiencing such harsh rays prompted them to seek protection in the form of Japanese sunshades which allegedly made the ladies more 'decorative' still (see figure 9.3)

It was precisely this strategy of disguising, deflecting or absorbing the electric light by the judicious use of silk covering material that Mrs Gordon advised to readers of her popular handbook. As the collaborative spouse of an electrical engineer, she had a strong interest in adapting the new technology to 'feminine' values and sensibilities, and as a married house-manager, she wrote as an authority on the matter for other women to follow. Her criticism of garish lighting was trenchant in this work, and argued for a particular kind of fabric and ornament-centred strategy to accomplish the artistry ineptly omitted by some manufacturers and designers (including some that advertised in her own book) (see figure 9.4).

For Mrs Gordon and those working in her tradition of amateur home decoration, the strategy adopted for the beautifying domestication of electric light was a matter of recasting the new illuminants in terms of the familiar. This was accomplished by disguising, hiding, diverting less attractive features, while also using historical design references from the eighteenth century and earlier to lend classical and oriental panache to both the details of ornamentation and the practice of marketing. Commercial designers were very happy to play along with this particular vision. We see this, for example, in the case of one prominent maker advertising in the opening pages of Mrs Gordon's book: the Faraday Company's use of the classically clad female torch-bearer was clearly to signal that electric light was a medium of truthful illumination, bringing trustworthiness and even justice to beams of light that (potentially) brought global illumination (see figure 9.5). Mrs Gordon similarly appealed to a selective past in her promotional work to find new ways to beautify electric light fittings, but a past of fabrics and adornment with non-European ornamentations, not of metalwork. These engagements with the past enabled both sides in the debate about artistic lighting to accuse the other of regressive design. Mrs Gordon accused 'artists' of using too much medievalism – old forms obtruding on the function of lighting, and the *Art-Journal* writers accused her ilk of being too sentimental in ornamentation. The question then was: how to unite the art of electric lighting with its industrial production? Each side effectively accused the other of being incompetent at forging any such unity, instead allowing art and industry to work in opposition.

Far from being an uncritical consumer, Mrs Gordon was scathing about much of the commercial electric lighting that was available (even though this was advertised in the front- and back-matter of her book). For example, she was very critical of the ineptitude of many domestic installations that allowed the harshness of unshaded light to intrude on domestic conversation. When considering the drawing room she reported: 'Much of the electric light we see at present in drawing rooms is not conducive to comfort and repose and hinders instead of aids conversation by its unsympathetic glare'.[8] Her judgment was that, among the broad range of possible electric light fittings available commercially, only a limited range of metal brackets, finishes and design characteristics could meet the criterion of being 'artistic', and indeed only if muted by suitable silk shades or reflected off walls or furnishings.

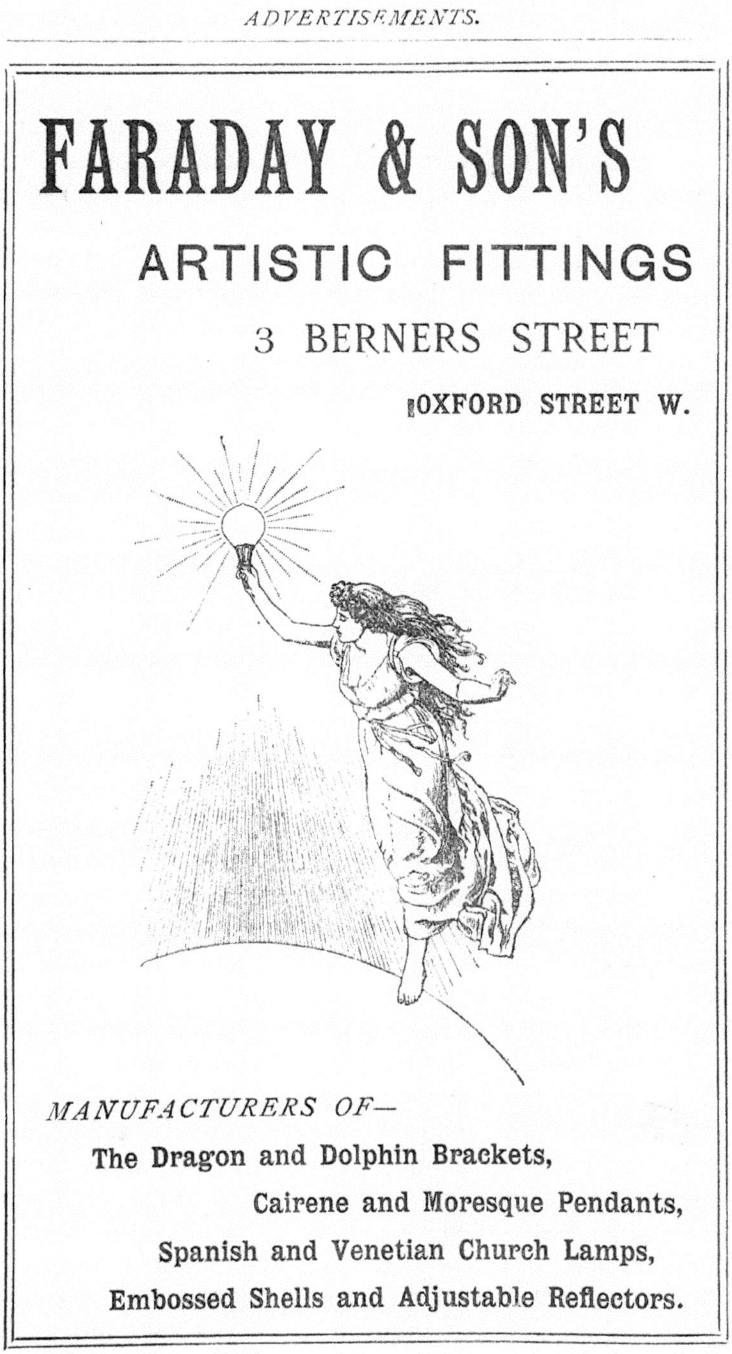

Advert for Faraday and Son in Gordon, *Decorative electricity*, 1891. (Author's collection.) **9.5**

Dedicating most chapters to different parts of the house, she identified other particularly troublesome domains that needed the female householder to be creative with her decorative resources and within her (presumptively) limited budget. Here she identifies one of her shared themes with the designers who responded so positively to John Ruskin's theories of art, such as Morris and Webb: that metalwork should be used with maximised forms of its own innate aesthetic. Staircases were a particular problem area for her: here householders should avoid both 'modern *bright* brass-work' and modern versions of French 'old lamps', with their 'glaring machine-made brass-work' and round dabs of 'common coloured glass'. By contrast she saw the colour of copper as 'delightful', lending itself well to staircase decoration, but so little such lighting equipment available for staircases was suitably graceful that she felt a simple string and pendant was the only option for the 'slender purse'.[9] The boudoir was another domain in which she argued that feminine dexterity and good taste were required against the inelegant results of contemporary commercial production methods. She commented instead that the hand-making of electric light shades was an industry 'very suitable for ladies to take up and develop', especially as these would always be 'more successful and more artistic made one by one', with ladies' personal care and attention devoted to each than anything which could be made by the 'best workmen' in a factory.[10]

Here we see, ironically perhaps, that Mrs Gordon clearly shared one point in common with the Arts and Crafts Movement. This was William Morris's view of the integrity of work done by the skilled craftsmen, as opposed to the mass-manufactured inartistic mechanical replica – albeit in Mrs Gordon's case more by the female hand than that of the male artisan. We must therefore emphasise at least this instance of commonality with the partisans of the *Art-Journal*. Yet as a criticism of those who worked in the domain of the *Art-Journal*, she in turn noted that artists had 'not kept pace with the engineers', criticising most pendants and electroliers (electrical chandeliers) as being 'singularly wanting in imagination and grace: 'They are too heavy and clumsy for the light lamps they support; the lines and curves are ungraceful, and the lamps are often so placed that they shed their light directly in our eyes, instead of reflecting it from the objects that should be illuminated by them.'[11] Following Benson and others she argued that these artist-designers were 'too much the slaves of precedent', derived from their experience of gas, candles, oil and 'other relics of the Middle Ages'. They had carelessly forgotten that the holders for all these lights followed the requirement to have a 'clear space above them for the escape of hot and foul air' and to be reachable by taper or match. Only when they had realised fully their freedom from these two historical 'limitations' would designers begin to appreciate properly the 'artistic possibilities of the new illuminants and give us original design of flying figures, birds, and carved Cupids, delicate chain work, faintly tinted glass, and china powdered with flowers'.[12]

Artistic criticism of Mrs Gordon

Flying figures and carved Cupids were in turn, however, just the kinds of ornamentation rejected by the earnest Ruskinian *Art-Journal* commentators as untrue to the media of modern illumination. Their emphasis was on truth to material: in both classical writings and medieval sources, the authentic use of material for particular purposes, with un-contrived beautification was what was sought. Indeed, writing in the *Art-Journal* in 1892 at the time of the publication of the second edition of *Decorative electricity*, it was on such particularities of design that Aymer Vallance effectively criticised Mrs Gordon:

> What sober-minded person could command extravagant and pretentious devices such as monkey-brackets representing the dawn of the intellect; owl-lamps, representing wisdom derived from light; or Atlases, angels of light, vestals, cupids, tritons etc. all emblematical of some idea or other connected with illumination? Of course the British Philistine, with whom sentiment is everything and intrinsic quality counts for little whose instinct is for having a tale tacked on to everything, says 'how interesting! How charming they are, to be sure!'[13]

But, Vallance reminded his readers, the function of lamps was only the 'humble' one of giving useful light, not preaching sermons: common-sense folk did not want 'philosophical or other truths, however sublime' enforced with the use of electricity. Unlike Mrs Gordon, he argued that the only way to insure the general adoption of the electric light was to 'commend itself to the public on its own merits on the score of practical utility'. That meant electric lighting equipment needed to be designed with intrinsic artistry, needing no additional ornament or veil to maximise its beauty.[14]

By contrast for Mrs Gordon, writing as a domestic authority, the overall context of lighting was key for her, not the intrinsic quality of the lighting design: each pendant, bracket and shade should only be chosen 'after seeing the light behind it', taking into account how different was the effect of electric light from other illuminants 'in its effects upon colours' and similarly with the different shades of colour 'that the same glass and silk will show with transmitted or reflective light respectively'. As judged by the *Art-Journal* the presumptively female designer of household electrical fittings was more concerned with matters of juxtaposition than the 'novel and artistic' designers who worked for the lighting manufacturers Faraday and Son of London. This company's designs for electroliers were illustrated frequently in the *Journal*'s pages, and celebrated for their 'excellence in design', although they were criticised for not following an arts and crafts doctrine of simplicity and truth to materials (see figure 9.6).[15]

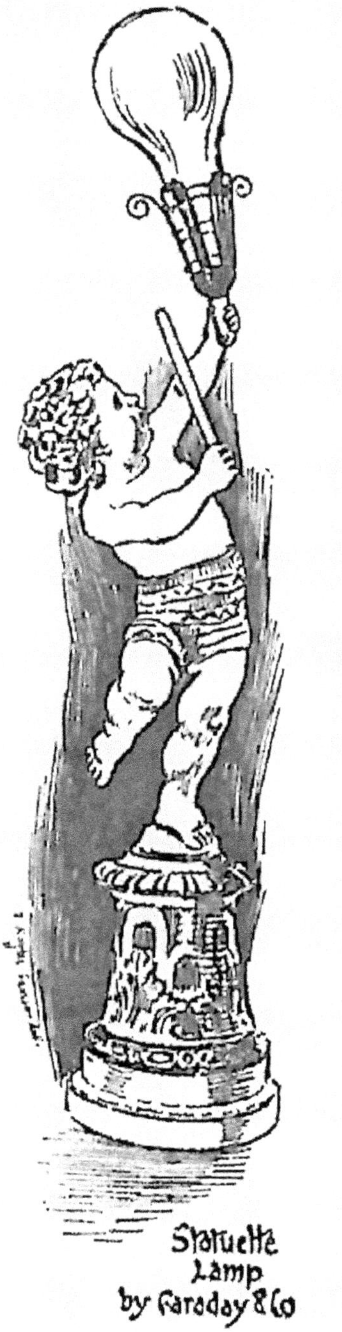

9.6 Statuette lamp by Faraday and Co., illustrated in 'Electric light fittings Edinburgh Exhibition 1890', *Art-Journal*, 1890. (Author's collection.)

And in a further contrast, the artistic commentators on electric lighting were not as committed as Mrs Gordon was (for reasons of harmonious spousal collaboration) to sole use of the newer illuminant. As Vallance discussed in his series on 'The furnishing and decoration of the house' in December 1892: 'Of the older methods, gas may be tolerated on the score of convenience in offices, passages etc. but it should generally be avoided in living rooms, on account of the injurious effects upon the air we breathe.'[16] However, Vallance did at least agree with Mrs Gordon, that, where electric light was to be installed, all previous gas fittings should be removed: 'The problem is not so much how to decorate the incandescent light itself, nor how to mitigate its excessive brilliancy, but rather how to deal with the connecting wire … the truth is the requirements of electric lights are quite different, so that the old gas fittings will not serve'. And when the new technology of the Welsbach incandescent mantle was also introduced in 1892, as the gas industry's alternative to the safety of incandescent electric lighting, there were far fewer decorative possibilities. So naturally the artists joined Mrs Gordon and others in a move towards a prospectively greater level of professional success in the adoption of electric lighting.[17]

Mrs Gordon's suggested deployment of domestic accessorisation to assimilate electric lighting into the home chimes interestingly with the rapidly changing understanding of the art–industry relation from 1892–98, which furnished the first modernist designs for electric lighting. This involved Arts and Crafts architects and designers, often those associated with Morris and Co., who, having embraced the inevitably wider adoption of electric lighting, worked to develop a new aesthetic. W. A. S. Benson is an acknowledged leader in this field, celebrated for his variety of lighting designs that embraced the technological possibilities and celebrated them in metalwork. Less well known, but equally influential was Philip Webb. Their designs can be seen together at Standen, and it is to this house that we will now turn to explore their response to the art versus industry dialectic, and to compare their design credos to that of Mrs Gordon.

From Webb to Benson: designing for electric lighting at Standen

> The growing adaptation of electricity to light private residences has created a demand for elegant fittings which shall worthily compare with other decorations of a room.[18]

Late in the year (1892) that the second edition of Mrs Gordon's book appeared, Vallance already saw an alternative transformation taking place in domestic illumination. In the *Art-Journal* he represented this as a move away from 'extravagant and pretentious devices' that seemed to ignore the technologies of electric lighting – quite obviously a barbed comment on the excesses of Mrs Gordon's style.[19] These excesses were later described in the *Art-Journal* (1904) as being replaced by 'fittings which combine all practical essentials with dignity or grace of form, not sacrificing true ornament to utility, nor utility to mere extravagance or profusion of ornament'.[20] Such a transformation can be mapped through an exploration of the work of Webb and Benson at Standen. In a previous collaborative work we have looked at the project to build electric lighting into this house.[21] In this chapter, we want to explore the designs for the lighting fixtures in more detail and test them against the Ruskinian call for 'honesty' in design.

Standen was designed by Philip Webb in 1891, for James Beale (1840–1910), a wealthy solicitor whose London residence was at 32 Holland Park. From the start of the commission electricity was planned into the house in line with Beale's reputation as a 'progressive', at a time when the majority of the population were still in the process of giving up their paraffin oil lamps and candles in favour of gas lighting.[22] Webb's account to James S. Beale of Hollybush Farm near East Grinstead, Sussex shows that from 1893 onwards he and Mr and Mrs Beale were meeting to discuss electrifying their weekend retreat.[23] On 30 November 1894, Webb 'Paid John Pearson [7s and 9d (and copper drawing room fender 8s)] for 7 embossed copperplates for electric lights in drawing room'. His designs for the drawing room lights have been considered in our previous collaborative work but it is useful to remind ourselves here of the Arts and Crafts aesthetic that Webb employed, where the sunflower designs mapped against the Morris and Co. wallpaper in the drawing room, and celebrated the craftsmanship of Pearson's copperwork, a senior metal worker in Robert Ashbee's Guild of Handicraft. Webb and Pearson together aimed to produce a design for

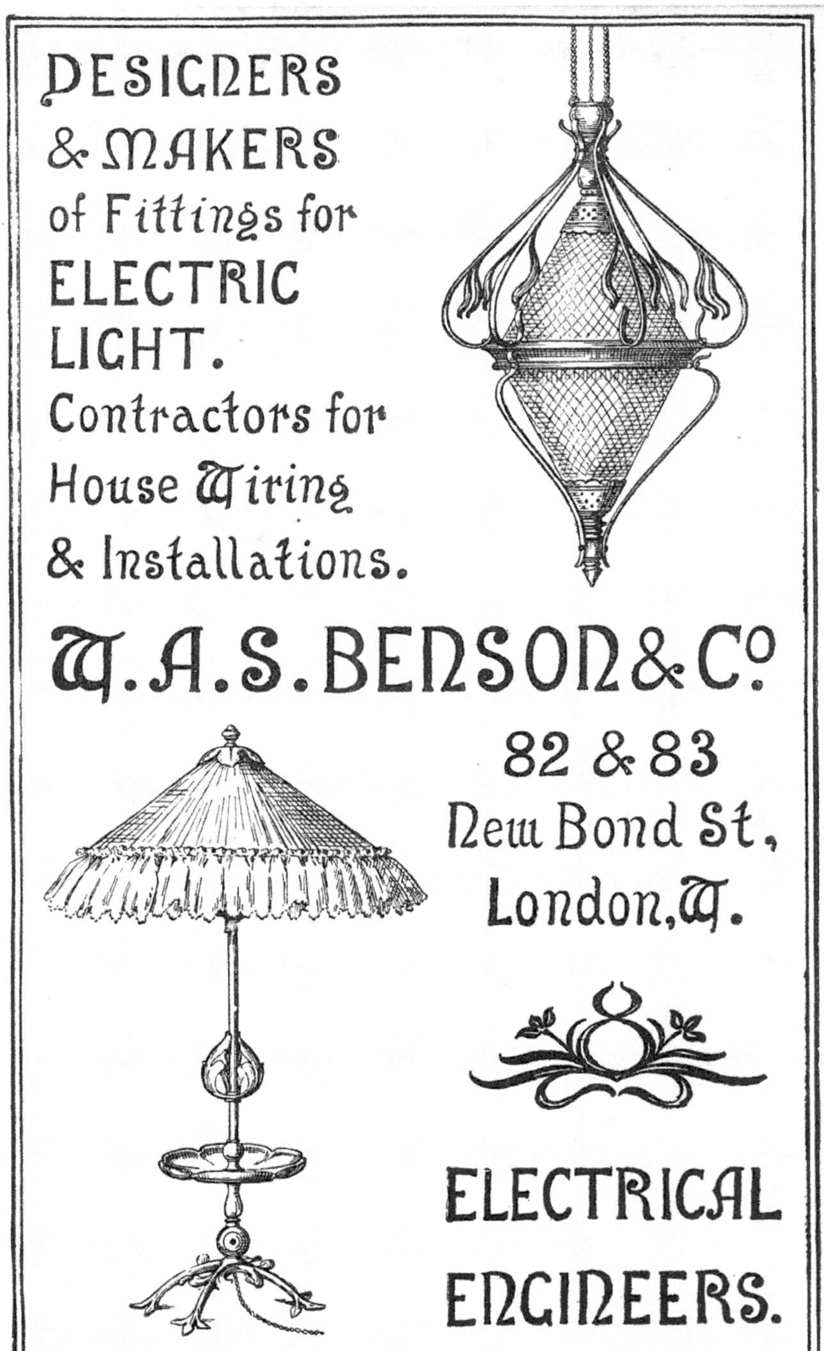

9.7 W. A. S. Benson and Co. Advertisement in Scrutton, *Electricity in town and country houses*, 1891. (Author's collection.)

this newest of technology that celebrated the potential of the metal and glass employed, and the skill of the craftsman. Ashbee had published one of the first full articles in the *Art-Journal* to make 'Suggestions for electric light fittings'. Aimed at the artist and designer, he suggested hammered copper, celebrating the 'extreme simplicity' of designs where 'the bright surface of the copper serv[es] as a reflector, and at the same time as a support' and he published a design that very closely resembles Webb's drawing room lights at Standen.[24]

The celebration of the properties of copper for electric lighting schemes (also shared with Mrs Gordon) leads us to the work of the other designer chosen by the Beales, W. A. S. Benson. His involvement was commissioned by means significantly different to Webb's entry to the project, and this reflects Benson's wider commercial activities as the director of W. A. S. Benson and Co. Benson's lights were used throughout the house.[25] Whereas Webb was specifically commissioned by the Beales to design electric light fittings, in common with many manufacturers including those advertising in Mrs Gordon's book, Benson's fittings were largely constructed from patterns held in stock that could be variously assembled to create the vast range of fittings from which the consumer could choose to buy (see figure 9.7).[26]

This move away from bespoke designs in itself maps against a wider change in consumer behaviour in the late nineteenth century, when England witnessed a significant growth in the high street and the department store. As Thorstein Veblen theorised in 1899, our period of study was structured by consumerism, financial speculation and the rise of Veblen's 'leisure class'.[27] Because at this time consumption was seen as both important yet frivolous, commentators frequently located it in the domestic sphere, where women were expected to consume to express the status of the family, and Mrs Beale was no exception to this.[28] Benson's company benefitted from this rise in consumption and between 1884 and 1887, 'demand and production steadily increased, while the variety of patterns [for lights] designed and carried out came to be reckoned not by the dozens but by the hundreds'.[29] As Maureen Dillon has confirmed, Benson was one of the few manufacturers to produce fittings for all lighting technologies and he designed component parts to be used within and across these technologies.[30]

Dillon has produced a very detailed and carefully researched survey of the lighting at Standen for the National Trust, and in this she has confirmed that Benson wares were employed in the morning room corridor, the hall, and the Larkspur dressing room. The morning room corridor, for example, was lit by three Benson wrought iron lanterns with opalescent glass liners that are the same design as those in the hall and elsewhere in the house. Interestingly the shades were made by James Powell, who also made the Vaseline glassware for Webb's lights in the drawing room, demonstrating the significant interaction between Arts and Crafts designers and manufacturers at the time. Such opalescent glassware also features in the six wrought iron lanterns purchased from Benson for the hall, which appeared as design no. 5515 in his *Catalogue of electric lighting designs* 1899–1900.[31] For the bedrooms, Mrs Beale purchased a number of Benson's most popular designs, his dual purpose wall/table lamp. These lamps were directionally adjustable, making the most of the technological potential of electric light to be re-positioned according to need, in direct contrast to gas light.[32] Here again we can see an interesting analogy between Benson making the most of the freedoms afforded by electric lighting and Mrs Gordon's demand that designers not be 'slaves of precedent', although, of course, her aesthetic response to this was very different.[33]

Benson, art and electricity

The first light fittings produced by Benson and others in the mid-1880s were, in comparison to the fittings produced by other manufacturers, virtually devoid of ornament; Dillon has thus argued that Benson was the first designer of light fittings to break away from historical precedent in regard to decoration.[34] Contemporaries celebrated his work for its truth to function and materials, in line with an Arts and Crafts aesthetic: 'Many of his fittings have no ornament ... but depend for effect on sheer beauty of line or mass, combined with the charm due to correct mechanical construction. For Mr Benson is as good an engineer as he is an artist and designs his fittings, whether rich or simple, with a direct view to their purpose and lasting properties.'[35]

In 1899, Benson commented in a Ruskinian manner that, 'If you would have true ornament you must resolutely refuse all ornament, and just now in this particular branch of work, false ornament is plentiful enough while the real thing for everyday purposes practically non-existent'.[36] In the same year, he reflected on the influence of William Morris on this design turn, concluding that, 'he found the arts of decoration practically dead in England', and as a result produced the 'one vital style of modern days, recognised through Europe as the only school of design which was not an empty echo of passed systems'.[37] It was this desire to learn from the past but to produce a thoroughly modern style to reflect the newest of technologies, that has led many commentators to describe Benson as an innovator of the most significant type, and in 1895, the *Studio* even dared to suggest that he had surpassed his master: 'Mr. Benson's lights could be more influential on public taste than Mr. Morris'.[38] Jope-Slade, in his article on 'Art and electricity' for the *Magazine of Art* in 1897, describes Benson's designs as 'palpitatingly modern ... in a word they are quaint, striking, individual ... the poetry of the mathematical line, evasive of description, and exhausting the beautiful materials in variety and tone'.[39] At the heart of his aesthetic was the doctrine of truth to materials and technology, and Benson spoke strongly about false ornamentation, which he felt was untrue to the nature of the illuminating medium. Many descriptions of his work speak about Benson's innovatory method of combining metals to enhance the aesthetic qualities of his light fittings:

> The charm of quiet contrasts of colour is added by the use of various metals and patinas. Mr Benson has practically re-introduced and extended the association of copper with brass. Brass is employed where rigidity and strength are demanded; copper is used for reflecting surfaces and for those portions of the work where its beautiful colour and peculiar mechanical properties can be utilised to best advantage.[40]

His lamps and their shades used an aesthetic that celebrated the properties of the copper to throw electric light out into the room, and emphasised the industry inherent in the technology of electric lighting. Aymer Vallance, in the *Art-Journal* in 1892, commented on Benson's desire to enhance the technical possibilities of the lighting medium, whatever it may be. For example, while stating that 'Oil gives a far more agreeable light than gas', Vallance complimented Benson's 'ingenious arrangement' for a pendant lamp in which 'the flame is entirely hidden with a metal basin in place of a globe, the light diffused by reflection from a shaped dish attached to the chains above the lamp'.[41]

Benson invented the vaned shade of his lamps at Standen, in order to 'reflect the maximum amount of light without itself becoming overheated'.[42] Likewise, every aspect of the technology of electric lighting was emphasised in the design, including the electric flex, perhaps the most obvious signifier of the technological differences between gas and electric. This Arts and Crafts desire to emphasise function can also be seen in Webb's designs. At Standen, the morning room lamps, supplied by James Powell of Whitefriars glass, have electric flexes decorated with spiral glass cord ornaments that both drew attention to the novelty of electricity and also relieved the plainness of the wiring.[43] As Dillon has reminded us, cord ornaments appeared in lighting manufacturers' catalogues in the late nineteenth century. Both the shades and the cord ornaments drew the eye to the electric lamp and celebrated the new technological possibilities of electricity. In 1897 Benson produced a booklet, *Notes on electric wiring and fittings*, where he was not only selling his products but also educating the consumer in basic electrics with the aim of enabling them to light their homes safely.[44] The booklet was illustrated in colour with examples of his fittings and gave advice, with the aid of room plans, on where lights could be most effectively distributed in the home, and the appropriate fittings to use in different rooms. Although Benson wrote this text in 1897, his views had probably been established by 1894 when electricity was installed at Standen.

The combination of an Arts and Crafts aesthetic and yet also the use of the most up-to-date machinery he could buy has led some to view Benson as the most contradictory of designers. Shirley Bury even called her important article on Benson in *Country Life* in 1965 'A craftsman who used the machine'.[45] He could, therefore, be viewed as a designer who demonstrates most clearly the dialectic of 'Art versus industry'. And yet the products that the firm sold to families such as the Beales seemed to celebrate art and industry, bringing together Morris's call for craftsmanship with an artistry that celebrated the potential of machine production. He designed his metalwork almost entirely for machine production and he used base metal and electroplate as his principal materials, demonstrating a particular liking for brass and copper used in combination. Bury locates the reasons for his embracing of the machine in the influence of his maternal uncle, W. A. Smith, a keen amateur metal worker, who had a workshop elaborately equipped with machinery. Benson, therefore, learned to appreciate the possibilities of the machine, unlike most members of the Arts and Crafts Movement, whose dislike of mechanical production 'rarely sprang from close personal knowledge of the workings of machinery'.[46] In his *Elements of handicraft and design* (1893), published while Standen was being built, he wrote (almost in defiance of the title): 'The mechanics of industry are not mechanical in the baser sense, but full of fine philosophy'.[47] So, for Benson to embrace mechanisation was not to abandon the fine art of design.

Despite his basic differences with his contemporaries over the means of production, Benson still found himself in agreement over several other important issues. He shared their concern for quality, his articles were beautifully made and finished and they were in no sense intended as a cheap alternative to handiwork. As such, his work exemplified the call in the *Art-Journal* for design that recalled the distinguishing characteristics of 'old-world design' with an 'inimitable blending of the utilitarian and the beautiful' in the production of those everyday articles which few still felt 'worthy of time or attention in the making'.[48] In this vein *The Times* obituary of Benson in 1924 highlighted his obsession with using the latest technologies to create designs that pushed the boundaries of artistic possibilities: all of his work was described as resulting from a 'profound study of the capabilities of heavy stamping plant, spinning lathes, and shaping tools which he was able to put down in the large Hammersmith works'. Visitors to the works were described as being 'amazed and almost aghast to find themselves in what appeared to be an engineering workshop, full of large machines, with endless rows of turning and polishing lathes'.[49]

Benson's designs for electric lighting were indeed very influential beyond the United Kingdom. In 1898, the German design commentator Meier-Graefe wrote in *Dekorativ Kunst* that Benson had 'taken the first step' towards a new aesthetic for lamp design. He 'provided the initiative for modern lamps to develop and you will not find anything better from the practical point of view ... his work will count in the history of the modern lamp'.[50] And the great commentator on *Das Englishe Haus*, Hermann Muthesius, wrote in 1904 that:

> Benson was the first to solve the problem of design in metal in the more modern spirit when he created lamps that were later to have a revolutionary effect on all our metalware ... Benson was the leading spirit in electric lighting appliances in England and on the Continent he was a fruitful instigator. He developed not only the most pleasing lines and forms but also many ideas about lighting.[51]

A decade after Mrs Gordon's book on ornamental decorative electricity reached the peak of its popularity, her authority had been entirely eclipsed by the men – especially Benson – that specialised in the application of Arts and Crafts doctrine (but with a pro-mechanical twist) to electric lighting.

Conclusions

This chapter has examined the transition from early improvisations in electrical light aesthetics to the development of a new twentieth-century art form that skilfully produced a material culture for the new illuminant through the time-honoured metal craftwork practices. In the process we saw that even eminent female authors, who, like Mrs Alice Gordon, were critical of the 'inartistic' industry of electric lighting around them, were marginalised and eventually displaced by the Arts and Crafts designers who supported the new aesthetics of electric lighting, notwithstanding the commonality in their requirements for good design even though the aesthetic results were startlingly different. 'Progressive' homes, such as Standen, epitomised this new approach of integrally harmonising design with the qualities of materials used in ornamental lighting. This story then is one about gender shifts in authority, expertise and 'true ornament' as much as it is about the reclaiming of one form of modernity by a form of craft skill. Finally it is about how the *Art-Journal* illustrates the ways in which late nineteenth-century tensions in the art–industry nexus can be mapped in the case of electric lighting. We have shown how the *Art-Journal*'s particular vision of this nexus, celebrating the natural qualities of metal design, displaced others – until this vision in turn was replaced by the arrival of new artificial materials in the Art Deco movement of the early twentieth century.

Notes

1 'Electric light and the metal crafts', *Art-Journal*, 321–8.
2 Gooday, *Domesticating electricity*.
3 Harrison Moore and Gooday, 'Decorative electricity', pp. 363–83. In contrast to that

article's focus on Webb, this piece, our second collaboration, focuses specifically on Benson, and extends our comparison of Mrs Gordon to those writing in the *Art-Journal*.

4 'Electric light and the metal crafts', *Art-Journal*, 321–8.
5 Review in *Lady's Pictorial* cited in Gordon, *Decorative electricity*.
6 Taylor, 'The mutual interests of artists and manufacturers', 69.
7 Landow, 'The *Art Journal*, 1850–1880', 71–6. Landow also points out that 'The *Art Journal* presents an interesting example of a major periodical that appears to have done much to encourage the medieval revival in spite of itself possibly, Hall and others in charge of the periodical simply wished to give their readers what they wanted'. The move towards celebrating the possibilities of electric lighting may also have been linked to the increasing competition in the final years of the century form other journals, particularly the *Magazine of Art*. The *Art-Journal* eventually ceased production in 1912.
8 Gordon, *Decorative electricity*, p. 87 (see Gooday, *Domesticating electricity*). We consider the drawing room in particular in Harrison Moore and Gooday, 'Decorative electricity', 363–83.
9 Gordon, *Decorative electricity*, pp. 40–1.
10 *Ibid*., pp. 84–5.
11 *Ibid*., p. 87.
12 *Ibid*., p. 88.
13 Vallance, 'The furnishing and decoration of the house', 376.
14 *Ibid*.
15 'Electric light fittings Edinburgh Exhibition 1890', *Art-Journal*, 231.
16 Vallance, 'The furnishing and decoration of the house', 374–5.
17 Benson and Co. also converted some gas lights to electric and worked across the range of lighting technologies. This is a theme that has been covered in excellent detail by Dillon in *Artificial sunshine* and by Hammerton and Rose in *W.A.S. Benson*. Our paper builds on their work on Benson by contrasting and relating his practice to that of Mrs Gordon.
18 'Electric light fittings', *Art-Journal*, 3.
19 Vallance, 'The furnishing and decoration of the house', 376.
20 'Electric light and the metal crafts', *Art-Journal*, 321–8.
21 Harrison Moore and Gooday, 'Decorative electricity'.
22 Kirk and Curry, *Philip Webb in the north*. See also Dillon, 'A history and survey of the lighting at Standen', p. 1.
23 On 26 June 1893, Webb went 'To Hollybush, met Mr and Mrs Beale and Mr Robert Beale (electric engineer and settled various things)'. Standen was built on the site of Hollybush, Standen and Stone Farms, and in the accounts the house is still referred to as Hollybush Farm. This meeting is also recorded in Webb's unpublished notebooks, 1891–94, where he lists 'June 26 1893, Met Mr and Mrs Beale and the Electric Engineer, R Beale, arranged with them for wires and lights. Engineers foreman ... to arrange with Hardy'.
24 Ashbee, 'Suggestions for electric light fittings', 91.
25 A bill from the Company dated December 1894 to Beale in the Standen archive records, 'August 29, 1894: 1 table standard No 1079 with green shade, ditto No. 1132, wiring no 1132, case and packing 3 12 6'.
26 See Hammerton, *W. A. S. Benson*.
27 Veblen, *Theory of the leisure class*.
28 A number of authors have examined the role of the female middle-class consumer in the development of a modern commercial world, and particularly at this point in time, in the development of the department store. See, for example Nava, 'Modernity's

disavowal', p. 46. See also Finn, 'Scotch drapers and the politics of modernity'; Rappaport, *Shopping for pleasure*.

29 Church, 'Benson's lamps', 19–20.
30 Dillon, 'W. A. S. Benson designer and manufacturer', Appendix to 'A history and survey of the lighting at Standen'.
31 Dillon, 'A history and survey of the lighting at Standen', p. 15.
32 No. 1139 and 1079, Dillon, 'A history and survey of the lighting at Standen', p. 15. An invoice from December 1894 confirms that two of these lamps (corresponding to catalogue numbers 1079 and 1132) were supplied to the Beales and cost £1 15s.
33 Gordon, *Decorative electricity*, p. 88.
34 Dillon, 'A history and survey of the lighting at Standen', Appendix 1.
35 'Domestic lighting', in Sparrow, *The British home of today*.
36 Benson, 'The embossing of metals', 45.
37 Benson, 'William Morris and the Arts and Crafts', 268.
38 Dillon, 'A history and survey of the lighting at Standen', appendix 1, p. 2.
39 Jope-Slade, 'Art and electricity', *Magazine of Art* (1897), quoted in S. Bury 'A craftsman who used the machine', 624–7.
40 Church, 'Benson's lamps', 21.
41 Vallance, 'The furnishing and decoration of the house', 374.
42 Bury, 'A craftsman who used the machine', 624–7.
43 An invoice from the Company detailing the costs of these and other shades exists dated 9 August 1894 from Whitefriars glass works to J. S. Beale for in total £20 6s 8 ½ d. (Dillon, 'A history and survey of the lighting at Standen', pp. 12–14).
44 This can be compared to the chapter on 'Fire risks' in Mrs Gordon's book that had been written by her electrical engineer spouse, James E. H. Gordon.
45 Bury, 'A craftsman who used the machine', 624–7.
46 *Ibid*., 627.
47 Benson, *Elements of handicraft and design*, p. 627.
48 'Electric light and the metal crafts', *Art-Journal*, 321–8.
49 'Obituary – Mr W. A. S. Benson', *The Times* (9 July 1924).
50 Meier-Graefe, 'Moderne Beleuchtungskorper', 3–20.
51 Muthesius, *The English house*, p. 199.

Bibliography

Ashbee, C. R. 'Suggestions for electric light fittings', *Art-Journal* (March 1895), 91–3

Benson, W. A. S. *Elements of handicraft and design* (London, 1893)

Benson, W. A. S. 'The embossing of metals', *English Illustrated Magazine* (October 1889), 39–46

Benson, W. A. S. 'William Morris and the Arts and Crafts', *National Review* (1899–1900), 268

Bury, Shirley. 'A craftsman who used the machine', *Country Life*, 137:3550 (18 March 1965), 624–7

Church, A. H. 'Benson's lamps', *Portfolio* (1890), 19–23

Daunton, M. and M. Hilton (eds.) *The politics of consumption: material culture and citizenship in Europe and America* (Oxford, 2001)

Dillon, M. *Artificial sunshine: a social history of domestic lighting* (London, 2002)

Dillon, M. 'A history and survey of the lighting at Standen' (unpublished manuscript, January 2010)

'Domestic lighting: the work of W. A. S. Benson and Co. Ltd.', in W. Shaw Sparrow (ed.) *The British home of today* (London, 1904)

'Electric light fittings', *Art-Journal* (December 1901), 3–4

'Electric light fittings Edinburgh Exhibition 1890', *Art-Journal* (August 1890), 231–5
'Electric light and the metal crafts', *Art-Journal* (October 1904), 321–8
Finn, M. C. 'Scotch drapers and the politics of modernity', in M. Daunton and M. Hilton (eds.) *The politics of consumption: material culture and citizenship in Europe and America* (Oxford, 2001), pp. 89–107
Girouard, M. *The Victorian country house* (London, 1979)
Gooday, G. *Domesticating electricity: technology, uncertainty and gender, 1880–1914* (London, 2008)
Gordon, J. E. H. *Decorative electricity* (London, 1891)
Gordon, J. E. H. *Decorative electricity* (London, 2nd edn, 1892)
Hammerton, I. (ed.) *W.A.S. Benson, Arts and Crafts luminary and pioneer of modern design* (Woodbridge, 2005)
Harrison-Moore, A. and G. Gooday, 'Decorative electricity: Standen and the aesthetics of new lighting technologies in the nineteenth-century home', *Nineteenth-Century Contexts: An Interdisciplinary Journal*, 35:4 (2013), 363–83
Kirk, S. and R. J. Curry, *Philip Webb in the north* (Teesside, 1984)
Landow, G. P. 'The *Art Journal*, 1850–1880: antiquarianism, the medieval revival and the reception of Pre-Raphaelitism', *Pre-Raphaelite Review*, 2 (1979), 71–6
Meier-Graefe. 'Moderne Beleuchtungskorper', trans. M. Dillon, *Dekorativ Kunst*, 1 (1898), 3–20
Muthesius, H. *The English house*, trans. J. Seligman (Granada, 1979)
Nava, M. 'Modernity's disavowal: women, the city and the department store', in M. Nava and A. O'Shea (eds.) *Modern times: reflections on a century of English modernity* (London, 1996)
Rappaport, E. D. *Shopping for pleasure: women and the making of London's west end* (Princeton, 2000)
Taylor, W. C. 'The mutual interests of artists and manufacturers', *Art-Union* (March 1848), 69–70
Vallance, Aymer. 'The furnishing and decoration of the house', *Art-Journal* (December 1892), 372–8
Veblen, T. *Theory of the leisure class* (Amherst, 1998)

PART III

Resituating design reform and art education

10

Building a better class of craft practitioner: ideals and realities in sculptural practice and the building industry c. 1880–1910

Ann Compton

Accounts of late nineteenth-century art, architecture and design often connect the progressiveness of the Arts and Crafts' aesthetic with a move to arrest the advance of technology and machines. By contrast, the emergence of modernism in the early twentieth century is linked to a more receptive approach to industry and mechanical processes. Underlying these narratives is an acceptance of art and industry as binary, oppositional systems matched by polarised aesthetic positions.[1] This essay constructs a more textured reading that draws out the complexity of this dynamic by proposing artists are embedded in a web of interconnected production practices shading between the handcrafted and the machine made.[2] It develops this idea through an examination of the experiences of those involved in making sculpture for architectural contexts, and the practical effects of the visionary ideas circulating around 1900 aimed at altering the way architects, sculptors and craft practitioners interacted.[3] Using case studies drawn from art education, sculpture, the stone trades and decorative plasterwork, the text considers how a belief in artistic unity was implemented in the workshop and studio against a backdrop of wider social and economic developments. It traces, from Italian quarries to London buildings, the relationship between supposedly discrete 'artistic' and 'industrial' practices to reveal the impact of aesthetic preferences on manufacturing processes and of technological advances on creative endeavours.

The collaborative ideal

From the early 1880s the Arts and Crafts ideal of achieving 'the Unity, the Interdependence, the Solidarity of all the Arts' by bringing together 'workers in various arts and crafts – architects, painters, designers of all kinds, sculptors and wood-carvers, metal-workers, goldsmiths, and many others' was incorporated into the structure and membership of many art societies and organisations.[4] Pioneers of this vision were the Century Guild (1882), the Art Workers' Guild (1884) and Arts and Crafts Exhibition Society (1888), but many other institutions with allied ambitions were soon established. The founding dates and distribution of these associations is indicative of how rapidly the notion of integrated practice was embraced by groups across Britain and Ireland: the Birmingham Guild of Handicraft (1890), the Sheffield Artcraft Guild (1894), the Northern Art Workers' Guild (Manchester, 1896) and the Arts and Crafts Society of Ireland (Dublin, 1897). 'Art worker' was a key term in the art theoretical lexicon at this time. It was often part of a society's name and still more widely used to describe their membership. Such was the currency of this phrase that *The year's art* added it to the title of its directory of practitioners from 1899. The expression 'art worker' carried a dual meaning which related both to the collaborative spirit in which works were to be produced and the goal of 'effac[ing], as far as possible, the distinction between artist and the artisan'.[5] At its most socially conscious this campaign for merging practitioner identities presented the conventional nomenclature of the arts as hierarchical and divisive. From that perspective old titles like 'painter' or 'sculptor' had a more gentlemanly status than the materials and trade-based descriptions of crafts such as 'silversmith' and 'plasterer'.[6]

The new thinking about art practice was disseminated via meetings that took place at the Art Workers' Guild, Architectural Association, Royal Institute of British Architects and their regional equivalents from the mid-1880s onwards. A still broader audience was reached through the publication of proceedings from some of these events in leading architecture and building journals. Because architecture and sculpture were thought to 'appeal to similar emotions, for each deals primarily with form' these disciplines were frequent topics of debate.[7] Many architects and sculptors shared the artist Albert Hemstock Hodge's aspiration, outlined in a talk to the Liverpool Architectural Association in 1910, to create work 'so enveloped in its surroundings that it is difficult to say which is architecture and which is sculpture'.[8] Although promoting a spirit of unity dominated discussions, the recurrence of divisive language continued to undermine harmony between the sister arts. It was usually architects who tried to take the upper hand, arguing that it was 'absolutely essential when sculpture is allied to architecture that it should be subordinate'. In response, sculptors and carvers demanded to be 'treat[ed] with more confidence and less as machines'.[9]

Such demonstrations of professional rivalry and aesthetic hierarchy might be construed as evidence that the new vision of art practice was more rhetorical than real. Certainly it was ambitious. In 1901 there were over 950,000 people employed in occupations directly associated with construction and many thousands more worked as architects (10,775), artists (13,949) and craft practitioners in each of the principal allied trades such as wood carving (14,739). This was significantly more than were working in the coal mines (640,989) though less than in textiles (1,462,001), making building one of Britain's principal sources of employment and a major industry.[10] Even if a very conservative estimate is made of the people targeted by the ideal of uniting practitioners, such as limiting it to those engaged in fabricating buildings with significant amounts of architectural decoration and sculpture, the number must still be reckoned in tens of thousands. There were, after all, numerous elaborately ornamented buildings erected all over Britain and Ireland between the 1880s and early 1900s and these involved the collaboration of many different specialist practitioners.[11] Amongst these were highly trained metal workers who modelled and cast artistic door furnishings; skilled plasterers who created decorative schemes in relief on the walls and ceilings; and carvers who sculpted elaborate figurative and ornamental compositions in wood or stone. Viewed from this over-arching perspective, the sheer scale of activity suggests that any attempt to influence this mass of people was an impossible task. However if we look beyond the facts and figures to the experiences of practitioners at workshop and studio level, and at the interactions between sculptors, architects and craft practitioners, widespread, sometimes unexpected, responses to the notion of the 'Solidarity of all the Arts' begin to emerge.

This inductive approach corresponds to the practical foundations from which the drive for artistic unity arose. Indeed the range of sculptors and craft practitioners addressed under the umbrella of 'art workers' was not simply a list drawn up in the abstract but reflected facts about production known to all those involved in architecture and building. Construction, like many other nineteenth-century commercial activities, was defined as an industry through its contribution to GDP and labour practices rather than because it was highly mechanised. For much of the century the building industry was dominated by a few huge building firms, notably those owned by Thomas Cubitt (1788–1855), George Myers (1803–75), Thomas Grissell (1801–74) and Samuel Morton Peto (1809–89). Despite this apparent concentration, the majority of work was carried out by small sub-contractors with sculptors and carvers constituting some of the more specialised branches. At whatever scale or cost, most construction undertaken during the nineteenth century was the product of labour-intensive handwork involving limited mechanisation (though this began to change in the early twentieth century).

The complex interconnected pattern of activity in which all small businesses engaged is exemplified by looking at the networks of practitioners involved in creating sculpture in stone for an architectural setting. Here a brief list of the sculptor's possible collaborators included: quarry workers, stone merchants, shipping agents, hauliers, blacksmiths to sharpen chisels, scaffolders and various categories of stone workers. Similar, smaller clusters could be identified in other areas of art practice, but they are especially evident in sculpture because the magnitude and complexity of large three-dimensional works necessitated the participation of many different practitioners. Workers in these specialist trades were normally classified according to varying levels of education, experience and skill. For example, stone carvers and some types of quarry workers and stone merchants were highly trained masters of their chosen craft, whose output might have a fine art dimension; stonemasons and blacksmiths were usually experienced journeymen; scaffolders and hauliers were tradesmen with basic manual skills; while many workers in larger quarries and shipping firms were simply labourers. There seems to have been no expectation that these gradations would disappear in the new world of 'art workers', but the principle of unity fostered more flexible, cooperative working practices.

Educating the 'art worker'

One of the most important means of creating an environment that supported mobility and versatility was re-educating older practitioners and instilling the collaborative ideal in younger, and therefore future, generations of sculptors and artisans through a revised curriculum.[12] The best approach, according to the architect John Dando Sedding (1838–91) in a paper on 'Things amiss with our arts and industries', was for 'all art students, no matter what their ultimate ambitions may be, to study simultaneously during their period of pupilage, architecture, painting and sculpture, and to specialize afterwards'.[13] While few art schools could deliver Sedding's precise programme (which though nominally directed at architects was intended for all), many institutions were very responsive to the principle of providing a broad education. This was facilitated by changes to the legislation governing the financing and management of art education in the late 1880s and early 1900s which made new funding streams available and allowed local authorities to establish or reorganise college education. Under the heading of technical education a range of classes were available in most towns and cities across the country, making training in both fine art and craft techniques readily accessible to the majority of students. Several of these new institutions signalled their sympathetic approach to collaborative practice through their choice of name, for example the School of Architecture and Applied Art in Liverpool (1894), the Central School of Arts and Crafts (1896) and Camberwell School of Arts and Crafts (1898). Scores of other colleges adopted a curriculum influenced by these ideas, notably the offshoot of Birmingham Municipal School of Art called the Vittoria Street Branch School for jewellers, silversmiths and allied trades, which was established by Robert Catterson-Smith (1853–1938). There

YOUNG SWANSEA SCULPTOR.

STRIKING LONDON SUCCESSES.

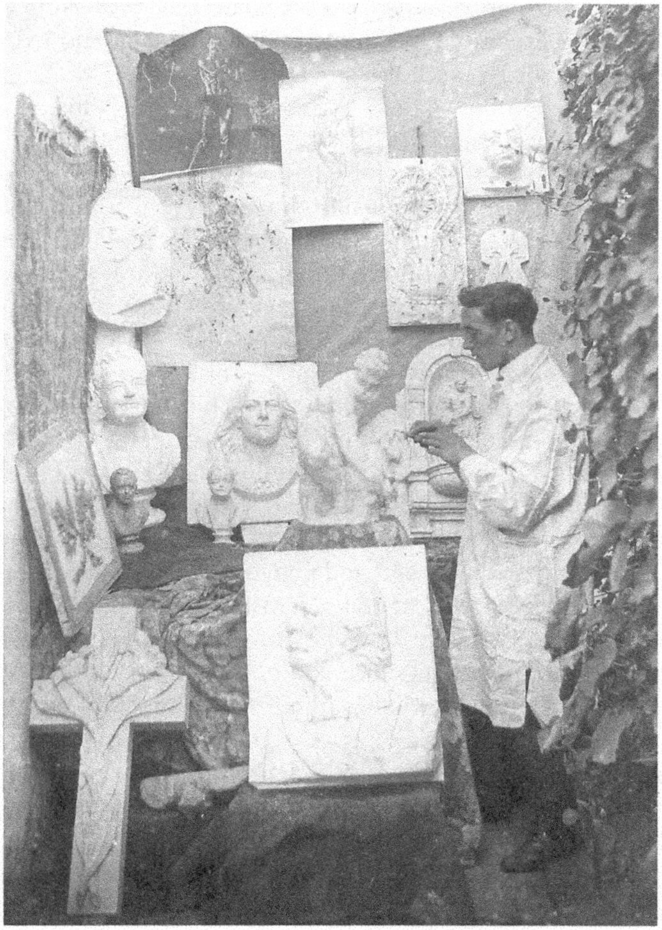

Mr. C. Roberts, a student of the Swansea Municipal School of Arts and Crafts, has been awarded the bronze medal of the South Kensington School of Art, London, for modelling the figure from the antique—figure accepted for the art master's certificate. He also was awarded the second class certificate for head from the antique, and won the first prize at the recent National Eisteddfod for modelling a dog (Great Dane from life, besides having won many other local prizes.

He has been under the tuition of Mr. Grant Murray (Principal of the Swansea School), A.R.C.A., London, and Mr. H. Hall, A.R.C.A., London, modelling master.

'Young Swansea sculptor. Striking London successes', press cutting from the *Wales Daily Post*, (4 September 1911). Clifford Roberts (1888–1965) served an apprenticeship as a monumental sculptor from 1903-9 and attended classes in clay modelling at Swansea School of Art where he won a number of prizes including a bronze medal in the National Competition. (Courtesy of Simon Roberts.) **10.1** were also short-lived but important experimental programmes instituted in Manchester and at the Royal College of Art by Walter Crane (1845–1915) during the mid-1890s. Often these colleges arranged the timetable so that 'the hours of meeting and the fees [were] ... suited to all classes of the community – craftsmen, designers, manufacturers, purchasers, teachers'.[14]

The Acts of Parliament that provided the financial and legal structure for these developments were the so-called 'Whiskey Tax' of 1890 and the Technical Instruction Act of 1889.[15] This latter Act introduced modelling in clay as a mandatory part of the 'manual instruction' curriculum in schools and colleges making the acquisition of three-dimensional, sculptural skills a central part of art study alongside drawing.[16] These modelling classes taught pupils to create geometric, decorative or natural forms in clay. Ambitious students, like Clifford Roberts (see figure 10.1), followed an extended course of study in modelling techniques and progressed through the various stages of the National Competition towards the creation of sculpture.[17] In 1901 courses were available at twenty-eight local colleges in the London area, ranging from the Mile End Road to Putney. Through a national network of similar institutions all over Britain and Ireland, clay modelling became a kind of three-dimensional lingua franca reaching many of the 100,000 students attending art classes each year.[18] Professional sculptors, architects and craft practitioners campaigning for a collaborative approach also valued the technique for its wide-ranging uses in many different areas of practice from fine art to manufacturing. One of the more influential educationalists of the time, John Sparkes (1833–1907), stated that 'the intelligent manipulation of clay into forms that will increase the perception of what is good in art, beautiful and exact is the proper complement to the daily work of the potter and the carver'.[19] This idea was also promoted in 'How To' manuals like Henry F. Ganz's *Practical hints on modelling design and mural decoration* of 1908, which presented this skill as central to a range of art forms from bas-relief murals to carving in stone and marble. The fact that Ganz (1888–1919) was a painter who nevertheless considered himself qualified to instruct readers in the art of clay modelling is indicative of how widely the practice was disseminated.

Modelling and architectural sculpture

In the early 1900s, a decade after these reforms were implemented, clay modelling began to be viewed more critically among those involved in the creation of architectural sculpture. There had always been a strong feeling, articulated by the influential teacher William Silver Frith (1850–1924) that the sculptor's 'work must be firmly rooted in and grow from the architecture, and must not be independent sculpture imposed on the architecture'.[20] Architects were also of the opinion that if this 'rooted' approach was not followed there was a danger that sculpture would appear like figures that have 'climbed out onto tops of windows, or on to the parapets, and continue to recline upon their giddy couches because they are unable to retrace their perilous steps'.[21] In short it was argued that when wrongly applied the fluid, multi-purpose technique of clay modelling could undermine the very unity between art and construction it was intended to ensure. The sculptor Thomas Stirling Lee (1856–1916) was one of those who had pushed back against the promotion of this technique. He considered sculpture was 'divided into two classes – the plastic or modelled, and the glyptic or carved. Treating stone, we have to do with the latter, so must consider the laws that govern that material.'[22] In the early 1900s Stirling Lee's position hardened and he argued that the sculptor 'has to do his work if he possibly can *in situ*, because [then] he is governed by his whole surroundings: his mind is filled with one idea, that his work is to be part of the building, not the mere erection of a modelled figure'.[23]

Most professional sculptors were less doctrinaire than Stirling Lee. However, the upsurge in the number of students who came into the profession in the early 1900s having only attended clay modelling classes led many to reassert the importance of rising through the ranks from stonemasonry or wood carving (practised in the mainstream of the building industry) to fine art. This had been one of the most common career patterns up to the early twentieth century.[24] Indeed in Lambeth, the South London Technical School of Art was founded in 1879 by John Sparkes specifically to serve Doulton's Pottery and train the employees of the many local 'large carving firms which produce work for the whole country'.[25] Out of this setting several influential sculptors emerged in the 1880s: Harry Bates, George Frampton, William Goscombe John and Frederick William Pomeroy. They were responsible for important architectural schemes and their election to the Royal Academy was seen as endorsement of their early career paths. What was particularly valued about a progression from apprenticeship to art school was that the pedagogical foundations for a former carver's sculptural collaborations with architects arose from personal experience acquired on the scaffold rather than being an adopted art theoretical construct. Indeed students with this background knew at first hand the steps described by the teacher, William Silver Frith, between 'masonry and the simpler forms of carving, thence to the most elaborate and the highest sculpture, [or] the series of links graduating from severe restraint to complete freedom'.[26]

However it was not only an increasing number of aspiring sculptors who came from a purely modelling background who caused concern. New educational policies also undermined efforts to sustain and promote this route into sculpture that embodied the collaborative ideal and bridged art and industry in the work of the individual practitioner. Particularly problematic was the Royal Academy Schools' ruling of 1890 that lowered the maximum age on entry to twenty-three. William Silver Frith and John

Sparkes protested that this was especially unfair to apprentice carvers who could not complete their workshop training as well as acquiring basic fine art skills until the age of twenty-four (or later).[27] So the aspiring craft practitioner seeking a more advanced fine art training was blocked from pursuing this ambition at the highest level.

Collaboration in the stone trades

At the same time that tensions surrounded the tier of practitioners transitioning from craft to fine art, a productive fusion between the new ideals for art practice and profitable returns can be found in other sectors linked to architectural sculpture, notably amongst those working in quarrying and supplying stone. Quarries vary considerably based on ease of access to the beds of stone, the hardness of the material, its suitability for carving and resistance to weather, particularly frost. These factors determine a stone's final use, value and, from around 1900, whether it was extracted and processed with simple tools or with cranes, mechanical saws, grinders, polishers and other industrial equipment. Marble, the principal material for sculpture, was extracted and worked in both ways. Italian quarries in the Carrara area were often run on traditional lines employing labour-intensive methods such as inserting wooden wedges into holes drilled in the stone, which were then wetted and allowed to swell to split the stone. But a diversification in usage (such as the promotion of marble as an easy clean surface for use in hospitals), the expansion of new markets particularly in North America, as well as increased demands for aesthetic reasons, notably the creation of decorative, often polychrome finishes for walls favoured by Arts and Crafts designers, generated greater pressure to quarry marble cheaply and in larger quantities.

In the UK imported marble was one of the most sought after materials for architects and builders, as well as sculptors. The supply of marble was discussed every month in the trade press with reports of strikes, wasteful quarrying practices, losses of shipments, and the growth of international demand for marble. To ensure a steady supply and capitalise on a profitable trade, several British marble merchants, like Messrs Anselm Oddling & Sons Ltd and Walton, Goody and Cripps Ltd, bought into the Carrara district.[28] These firms introduced new machinery for cutting stone and constructed modern wharves to increase their edge in the marketplace. This helped secure substantive contracts for architectural and sculptural projects, which could be prestigious as well as lucrative. For example, in the early 1900s Walton, Goody and Cripps Ltd supplied over 3,000 tons of marble for Thomas Brock's monument to Queen Victoria, and a further 1,000 tons for the memorial's architectural and masonry elements designed by Aston Webb.[29] This stonework was cut in the firm's Italian workshop using pneumatic tools (see figure 10.2).[30]

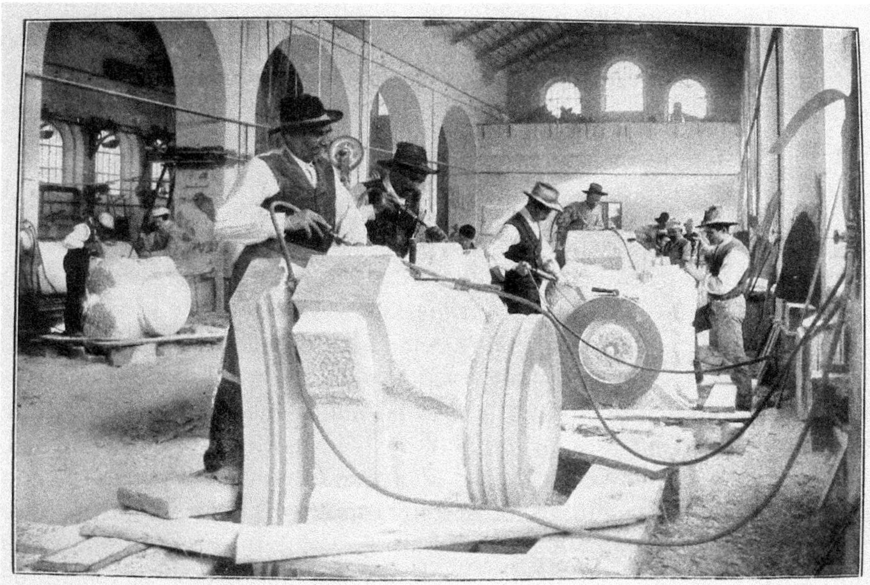

Interior of Walton, Goody and Cripps workshop at Carrara showing the use of pneumatic tools to work marble for the production of architectural sculpture. (Author's collection.) **10.2**

The demand for coloured marbles used widely in Arts and Crafts buildings and to particularly striking effect in such landmark projects as Lloyd's Registry of Shipping in Fenchurch Street (1898–1901, architect Thomas Collcutt), also created new opportunities for diversification amongst practitioners. Leading the field in this regard was William Brindley, who was one half of an outstandingly successful partnership established with William Farmer in about 1868. Farmer and Brindley became one of the leading architectural sculpture firms of the late nineteenth century that worked extensively for the architects George Gilbert Scott, Alfred Waterhouse, Lockwood and Mawson, Bodley and Garner, as well as completing numerous other smaller decorative schemes. After Farmer's death in 1879, Brindley was quick to see the impact of Arts and Crafts' aesthetics on the market for stone, and he travelled extensively in Greece, Turkey and North Africa to research marble and ancient quarries. This led to the reopening of several ancient workings, including those for Cipollino marble on the Island of Evia, Verde Antico near Larissa and Imperial Porphyry at Gebel Dokhan in the Egyptian Eastern Desert.[31] Fitting the ideals of collaborative practice, Brindley produced publications for the trade, gave talks at the Royal Institute of British Architects and Art Workers Guild as well as hosting visits from architects to the yard in Westminster Bridge Road.[32] The benefits of all this activity were public recognition and financial reward. In 1888 he was elected a Fellow of the Royal Geological Society and in

1905 he was able to launch Farmer and Brindley as a private limited joint stock company. As a further measure of his success, at his death in 1920 Brindley's effects were valued at almost three times those of his former partner William Farmer, whose estate reflected only the profits from architectural sculpture.[33]

It was not only in such specialist sectors of the stone trades as the supply of costly marbles that there were signs of commercially successful interactions between the arts. They can also be found in areas of quarrying where extraction utilised industrial equipment, such as the granite trade. From the mid-century British granite was marketed increasingly aggressively as a relatively cheap local product that could be polished like marble but was much more durable and resistant to soot and pollution.[34] The many quarries in Aberdeen (known affectionately as the Granite City) increased their edge against domestic and foreign competitors by introducing pneumatic drills, mechanical saws and electric hoists to ensure cost efficiency in extracting and cutting huge quantities of stone.[35] Architects and sculptors were responsive to the aesthetic and utilitarian claims made for granite and increasingly used it in buildings, for plinths and occasionally as a material for sculpture.[36] To publicise granite's fine art potential, in 1910 Alfred Drury was commissioned to create a statue of Edward VII for Aberdeen (the actual carving was carried out locally by the sculptor and granite carver, Arthur Taylor).[37] Another strategy implemented in the mid-1890s by the Aberdeen Granite Association to enhance granite's cultural status was to launch free classes for stone workers from a well-equipped shed at the back of Gray's School of Art. This programme was intended to make 'art workers' out of employees in the quarrying business because traders saw the potential profits for business in a more highly trained body of craft practitioners, capable of versatile, collaborative practice. The classes were set up with advice from the sculptor Pittendrigh MacGillivray RSA and had the support of two trade unions (the Master Masons' Association and Granite Cutters' Union). Architectural sculpture was one of the subjects students were taught, and standards were high enough to receive a bronze medal at the *Exposition Universelle* of 1900 in Paris.[38]

The challenges of construction work

There is a marked contrast between the comparative responsiveness among certain marble merchants and quarries to the benefits of artistic unity and the more unsettled, tense environment of construction projects. Achieving harmony in these circumstances was particularly difficult because many different categories of practitioners using distinct materials and techniques had to work side-by-side to create a single building. One of the most persistent problems was the impact of new materials and technologies on working practices, which was discussed at some length in an anonymous article of 1898 on 'Progress of the architectural crafts' in the *Building News and Engineering Journal*.[39] The root of the problem was a prolonged slump in the building industry at the start of the twentieth century, which greatly reduced the volume of work available for stone carvers, and placed architects under considerable client pressure to decorate buildings at the lowest possible cost. In these circumstances an increase in the use of powered equipment in the workshop (such as motorised saws, powered drills and even 'sculpture' machines) in the early 1900s to mass produce the simpler forms of architectural detail became a contentious issue.[40] But a far greater concern was the extent to which new materials, techniques and technologies caused widespread antagonism amongst craft practitioners by undermining historic boundaries between crafts. For example, the article of 1898 noted that 'in the decorative trades the various new processes for ... relief decoration in fibrous plaster, and materials like tiles, embossed leathers, wood-veneers, have interfered with joiners, plasterers, paper-hangers and carvers'.[41] In these circumstances 'the principle that every trade shall have the right to earn its bread without the interference of outsiders' had been eroded and so disputes arose because 'it is difficult to fence off every craft from encroachment'.[42]

A detailed account of such problems was given by William Millar (c. 1835–1904) in the 1890s. He was a modeller and decorator in plaster who wrote an encyclopaedic text about his craft entitled *Plastering plain and decorative* (1897). Millar complained that it was becoming increasingly common for stone carvers to obtain contracts from builders to cut cheap moulds and run plaster cornices.[43] In some respects builders were simply taking advantage of the fact that moulds for plasterwork were sometimes carved from wood (rather than modelled and moulded in clay and plaster), and many of the basic patterns, like dentil or egg and dart, were stock-in-trade for makers of all forms of enrichment in architectural settings. But when carvers worked in gypsum or lime plaster, for which they had no training and which entailed specialist skills very different from cutting ornament in stone, it is easy to see that fellow practitioners regarded this as definitely overstepping the limits of their trade. However, it is evident that plasterers were not always the underdog and were capable of poaching also. Indeed Millar described, sometimes with a note of triumph, several instances of modellers engaging in new forms of plasterwork that intruded directly on the stone carver's craft. A notable example of this was the use of cement to fashion exterior architectural decorations like ornamental gateways, pillars and quoins. Plasterers could execute these more quickly and cheaply in cement and so won contracts from stonemasons who naturally took much longer to cut them in stone and who also had the higher cost of obtaining bulky, heavy materials.[44]

In this competitive environment where new processes resulted in trades taking work from each other, it became apparent that the promotion of collaborative practices, though presented as a solution to difficulties in the workplace, often unintentionally increased such dissension. A key instance of this was the importance attached to versatility, which gave certain craft practitioners an additional edge, and thereby created a new form of hierarchy. William Millar noted this development in his account of plastering. He remarked that sculptors and craft practitioners able to 'interpret by their ready pencils the distinctive character of every style, and furnish architects with appropriate and clever designs' had greater success in securing the most lucrative contracts. Millar named Gilbert Seale (1862–1933) as an outstanding example of this type of practitioner.[45] Gilbert's father, John Wesley Seale (c. 1826–85) was a stone carver who established a modest firm of architectural carvers in Lambeth. Under Gilbert Seale's management the business grew into a large architectural sculpture firm that created ambitious carvings for many sites including 70–72 Jermyn Street, London (1902–03) and 41 Holborn, Kingsway, as well as substantial plasterwork schemes for Battersea Town Hall (1892–93), the Old Bailey (1900–07) and Debenham and Freebody's department store, Wigmore Street (1907–08). It is a measure of Seale's success that at his death in 1933 his effects were recorded at a very substantial £82,086 19s. 1d. This sum compares very favourably with the most successful Royal Academician sculptors of this time, such as George Frampton whose estate was valued at £70,316 4s. 2d. for probate in 1928.[46]

Architect-craft practitioners and the building industry

The widening professional and financial divide in the building industry between those who learned to be adaptable and those who did not have the necessary skills or resources to do so was increased by the rise of a subset of craft practitioners who had originally studied architecture. These architect-craft practitioners were a group of makers who believed '*doing* is designing' and put into practice the notion that an architect should be 'manysided', indeed 'He should be an artist, a man of science, and a man of business'.[47] While there had been architects who had practised various arts throughout most of the nineteenth century, the debates circulating on collaboration and unity from the 1880s stimulated a larger number of young professionals to branch out into handicraft.[48] They took inspiration from influential individuals, like John Dando Sedding, who designed embroideries, wallpaper and metalwork in addition to running a busy architectural practice. In some respects this new generation of architect-craft practitioners represented the fullest expression of the versatile, multi-talented 'art worker'. This appears to be affirmed by the fact that many of the craft practitioners who are now considered the most original and influential belong to this group. These include the leading silversmiths and art metal workers W. A. S. Benson (1854–1924), Henry Wilson (1864–1934) and John

Paul Cooper (1869–1933), as well as the furniture makers Ernest Barnsley (1863–1926) and Sidney Barnsley (1865–1926) who ran a business in the Cotswolds with another architect-craft practitioner, Ernest Gimson (1864–1919). Close examination reveals that many architect-craft practitioners enjoyed greater social, financial and professional opportunities than colleagues who arrived from more conventional routes via the apprenticeship system and studying in art school. The influx of this privileged group resulted in a number of inequalities that undermined, and even contradicted, the very principles that prompted them to take up a practical skill.

A typical pattern of study for these architect-craft practitioners was to spend about five years training in an architect's office prior to moving into handicraft. Funding this lengthy period of study limited the type of students who could follow this path, particularly because the fees for entering an architect's office were higher than for apprentices acquiring a manual skill in a workshop. There were also significant practical advantages arising from this experience. A trainee architect could establish a network of valuable connections, at the same time as acquiring an insider's knowledge of the design process and the rudiments of site management. Although any sculptor or craft practitioner working in an architectural context had to acquire some insight into building processes and learn to draw plans, they were unlikely to match a former trainee's ability to talk on an equal footing with architects. A more subtle expression of privilege is evident in an architect-craft practitioner's attitude to handicraft. Fortified by a professional background, many of them approached the acquisition of new skills with a certain freedom, such as studying several different crafts or researching forgotten practices. Such self-determination was less easily available to the traditional craft practitioner who, typically, had been indentured to a master for five to seven years from around the age of twelve to fourteen. Where architect-craft practitioners had access to significant family wealth, as in the case of Ernest Gimson (1864–1919) (his father was an iron founder, engineer and industrial entrepreneur), these funds cushioned practitioners from having to undertake bread and butter work and allowed them instead to focus on more interesting, creative projects.

The benefits of a middle-class background for an architect-craft practitioner are illustrated by the career of Laurence Arthur Turner (1864–1957). He was the son of a churchman and was educated at Marlborough College. Turner was articled to the architect John McCulloch for five years, after which he studied carving and modelling. In launching his career as an architectural sculptor, Laurence received additional contacts from his older brothers, the architect Hugh Thackeray Turner (1853–1937) and the painter Hawes Harrison Turner (1851–1939) who was a Keeper of the National Gallery between 1898 and 1914. From these auspicious beginnings Turner became one of the most respected architectural sculptors of the first half of the twentieth century who collaborated with many of the leading architects of the day. His versatility was a key part of his success, which encompassed carving in stone and wood, modelling in plaster, as well as the more specialised crafts of heraldry and lettering.

Architect-craft practitioners were not only more likely to secure high-profile, profitable commissions compared to their conventional trade-based counterparts but also many of them left an unusually visible imprint on their chosen area of practice. They received a greater number of invitations to speak to societies like the Art Workers Guild than ordinary craft practitioners or sculptors. This in turn led to opportunities to publish papers in professional journals or to write books, as well as to win awards and public recognition from colleagues. Laurence Turner again illustrates this path. Between 1906 and 1940 he delivered upwards of ninety papers at meetings of the Art Workers Guild; he also wrote a number of articles and a book on decorative plasterwork (1927).[49] Turner was given a number of awards, including being elected a member of the Society of Antiquaries, Master of the Art Workers Guild in 1922, and the rare privilege for a craft practitioner of being made an honorary Associate of the Royal Institute of British Architects. Although such success can be accounted for by an individual's industry and enthusiastic engagement with the subject, the loyalty and support of an extended network of colleagues drawn from fellow craft practitioners and architects was equally important.

Taking up a handicraft was not only an enactment of the ideal of unity between the arts but also a means of reclaiming an area of architectural practice deemed to have been lost. In the 1880s and 1890s architects lamented greater specialism in their profession meant that 'in the decorative branches of craftsmanship, the architect is deprived of a good deal of his own work; he is confronted by a host of designers of furniture and decoration which properly belong to him'.[50] Some practitioners went further than viewing handicraft as a means of reconnecting the profession with its past, and claimed their efforts reinvigorated the work of traditional sculptors and craft practitioners. One of those who took this position was the architect-decorative plasterer and lead worker, George Bankart (1866–1929) who 'believe[d] all crafts must draw blood from the ranks of architects to bring about a thoroughly healthy condition'.[51] The son of a Leicester-based merchant and insurance broker, Bankart came from a middle-class family. He trained in the architect Isaac Barradale's office in the 1880s where he met Ernest Gimson. Through him, Bankart was introduced to William Morris and a number of other leading architect-designers, including Mervyn Macartney (1853–1932), Sydney Barnsley and W. R. Lethaby. During the 1890s Bankart put his interest in plasterwork and leadwork into practice whilst also doing some teaching. He worked for the Bromsgrove Guild between about 1899 and 1906 and then set up a business in London. Within a few years Bankart had the opportunity to provide a practical demonstration of an architect 'bring[ing] about a thoroughly healthy condition' in his craft when his business merged with the highly respected firm of George Jackson and Son and he became their principal adviser and designer.[52] Under this new arrangement the Jackson firm (which had been in operation in the upper tier of the building industry since the eighteenth century) increased its range of services to include decorative work in gesso, egg-tempera painting, carving in wood and stone, as well as modelled plasterwork and lead work.[53]

Conclusion: writing out artistic unity

The belief in the pre-eminence of the architect-craft practitioner expressed by Bankart and others was not always so beneficial either for the concept of artistic unity or the work of traditional craft practitioners. A particularly clear instance of this can be seen in the literature on decorative plasterwork. William Millar's monumental volume, *Plastering plain and decorative*, quickly went through several editions, and in the trade acquired the colloquial title of the plasterer's bible. However, around the time of Millar's death in 1904, several architect-craft practitioners, namely Ernest Gimson, Laurence Turner and particularly George Bankart, emerged as new authorities on plasterwork. By the 1920s Millar's substantial contribution to the description and documentation of his craft was greatly diminished because Bankart substantially revised *Plastering plain and decorative*.[54] He cut many chapters, wrote several new ones and added his name as editor. While this radical approach to an existing text is exceptional, Bankart's rewriting exemplifies the important role played by architect-craft practitioners in shaping the history and practice of their chosen craft. These publications not only assured the long-term legacy of their individual careers but also moulded our understanding of the aesthetics and practice of their art at the expense of more traditionally trained colleagues. This reshaping of roles and practical intervention in construction was not so much a case of Arts and Crafts ideals holding out against the advance of industry as pulling off a coup from within.

Notes

1 This polarised view is given by, for example, Cummings and Kaplan, *The Arts and Crafts Movement*, p. 6, and in standard works of reference like Crawford, 'The Arts and Crafts Movement'. A more textured reading is found in Livingstone and Parry (eds.) *International Arts and Crafts* and Adamson (ed.) *The craft reader*.
2 The theme of this essay is drawn from a book by the author and currently in preparation, *A collective art: the makers and methods of sculpture in Britain c. 1851–1940*.
3 'Craftsman' was the term used in this period to signify a master or skilled practitioner such as a stone carver. 'Craft practitioner' is used here to avoid gender specific terminology.
4 Image, 'An address', p. 17, and entry for the Art Workers' Guild in *The year's art*, p. 90.

5 *Journal and proceedings of the Arts and Crafts society of Ireland*, 3, 1901 quoted in 'The Arts and Crafts Society of Ireland', *Mapping the practice and profession of sculpture* (accessed 1 January 2014).
6 Clutton-Brock, *Essays on art*, pp. 110–19.
7 Belcher, 'Sculpture and sculptors' methods', 49.
8 Hodge, 'Architectural sculpture', 773–6.
9 Belcher, 'Sculpture and sculptors' methods', 49–50, and Reynolds-Stephens, 'Sculpture in its relation to architecture', 510.
10 Census 1901. *General Report*. Cd 2174, Appendix A, Table 34, 258, 260, 263 and Table 35, 278.
11 Beattie, *The new sculpture*; *Public sculpture of Britain* series.
12 The idea of disseminating ideas about the re-conceptualisation of art practice through art education was not new, for example champions of the Gothic revival had launched ambitious initiatives aimed at educating stone carvers.
13 'Mr Sedding's opinion', 206–7.
14 *Birmingham Municipal School of Art*, p. 3.
15 An amendment of 1892 to the Local Taxation (Customs and Excise) Act 1890, 53 & 54 Vict. c. 60 (known as the 'Whiskey Tax') allowed local authorities to use duties on the sale of spirits to fund education. Technical Instruction Act 1889, 52 & 53 Vict. c. 76.
16 'The expression "manual instruction" shall mean instruction in the use of tools, processes of agriculture, and modelling clay, wood, or other material', Technical Instruction Act, 1889, 52 & 53 Vict. c. 76, 388.
17 The National Competition was organised from South Kensington by the Department of Science and Art (to 1899) and then by the Board of Education until 1913 when the examination system was revised.
18 Based on annualised figures for the period 1900–03 given in the Board of Education, *Report 1902–3*, p. 59.
19 Sparkes, 'Report, June 1888', p. 5.
20 Frith, 'Sculpture and sculptors' methods', 52.
21 Smith, 'Sculpture in relation to architecture', 380.
22 Lee, 'Sculpture and sculptors' methods', 57.
23 Lee, 'Sculpture in its relation to architecture', 504.
24 See also Compton, '"Art Workers"'.
25 Sparkes, 'Report of the superintendent of studies, June 1888', pp. 4–5.
26 Frith, 'Sculpture and sculptors' methods', 52.
27 Sparkes, 'Report of the superintendent of studies, July 1890' (1889–90), pp. 9–10.
28 'Carrara and its marble industry' and 'Walton, Goody and Cripps Ltd'.
29 'The Queen Victoria Memorial' *Stone Trades Journal*, 30:12 (1911), 786–7.
30 Renwick, *Marble and marble working*, p. 127.
31 Rogers, *The beauty of stone*, pp. 17–19, and 'Farmer and Brindley', *Mapping the practice and profession of sculpture* (accessed 31 December 2013).
32 *Specimens of marble pavements*; Brindley and Weatherley, *Ancient sepulchral monuments*; and *Builder*, 78:2980 (1900), 262.
33 William Farmer's effects were valued at £20,000 in 1879 and Brindley's at almost £60,000 in 1920.
34 'The quarrying industry one hundred years ago', 79.
35 'Machinery at Aberdeen', 226; 'Granite', 237.
36 There are multiple references to this in *Stone Trades Journal*, for example five works listed in 'Sculpture and monumental', 172.
37 Arthur Taylor ran a business in Jute Street, Aberdeen between c. 1890 and 1940. 'The King's statue Aberdeen', 402; 404 and 'Granite statue of King Edward VII', 630.

38 'The granite statuary class in Aberdeen', 182–3.
39 'Progress of the architectural crafts', 1–2.
40 For example: Bale, 'Pneumatic machinery for stoneworking'; 'Sculpture by machinery'; and 'The Wenzel sculpturing and carving machine'.
41 'Progress of the architectural crafts', 1.
42 *Ibid.*, 2.
43 Millar, *Plastering plain and decorative*, p. 353.
44 *Ibid.*, p. 189.
45 *Ibid.*, p. 353. Seale was originally a carver, so he was exactly the sort of craft practitioner Millar urged his fellow plasterers to compete against.
46 'Sir George James Frampton RA, FSA, LLD', *Mapping the practice and profession of sculpture* (accessed 31 December 2013).
47 *RIBA Proceedings*, 7 (1892), 222 quoted by Kaye, *The development of the architectural profession*, p. 139.
48 Lethaby, Powell, and Griggs, *Ernest Gimson*, p. 4.
49 Turner, *Decorative plasterwork in Great Britain*.
50 'Progress of the architectural crafts', 2.
51 Bankart, 'Old stucco and plaster work', 657.
52 George Jackson & Sons Ltd were already trading in 1780 and became a subsidiary of Clark & Fenn Ltd in 1988.
53 'Trade and craft', *Architects' and Builders' Journal*, 32:807 (1910) 82, quoted in 'George Percy Bankart', *Mapping the practice and profession of sculpture* (accessed 17 February 2014).
54 This was the fourth, revised and enlarged edition edited by Bankart.

Bibliography

Adamson, G. (ed.) *The craft reader* (Oxford, 2010)
Bale, M. P. 'Pneumatic machinery for stoneworking', *Stone Trades Journal*, 19:11 (1901), 227
Bankart, G. P. 'Old stucco and plaster work', *Builder*, 85:3177 (1903), 654–8
Bankart, G. P. *Plastering plain and decorative by William Millar* (London, 4th edn, 1927)
Beattie, S. *The new sculpture* (New Haven, 1983)
Belcher, J. 'Sculpture and sculptors' methods in relation to architecture', *Royal Institute of British Architects Transactions*, 8 (1892), 49–64
Birmingham Municipal School of Art. Programme for the Session 1893–94
Board of Education. *Report of the Board of Education for the Year 1902–3*, House of Commons command paper Cd 1763 (1903)
Brindley, W. and W. S. Weatherley, *Ancient sepulchral monuments* (London, 1887)
'Carrara and its marble industry', *Stone Trades Journal*, 21:9 (1903), 203–6
Census of England and Wales, 1901. *General Report with Appendices*, Cd 2174 (London, 1904)
Clutton-Brock, A. 'The artist and tradesman', *Essays on art* (London, 1919), pp. 110–19
Compton, A. '"Art Workers": education and professional advancement in sculpture and the stone trades c. 1850–1900', *Sculpture Journal*, 21:2 (2012), 119–30
Crawford, A. 'The Arts and Crafts Movement', *Grove Art Online. Oxford Art Online*. www.oxfordartonline.com/subscriber/article/grove/art/T004452 (accessed 1 February 2014)
Cummings, E. and W. Kaplan, *The Arts and Crafts Movement* (London, 2002)
Frith, W. S. 'Sculpture and sculptors' methods in relation to architecture', *Royal Institute of British Architects Transactions*, 8 (1892), 49–64
Ganz, H. F. W. *Practical hints on modelling, design, and mural decoration* (London, 1908)

'Granite', *Stone Trades Journal*, 20:10 (1902), 237 'The granite statuary class in Aberdeen', *Stone Trades Journal*, 21:8 (1903), 182–3
'Granite statue of King Edward VII', *Stone Trades Journal*, 24:6 (1914), 630
Hodge, A. H. 'Architectural sculpture', *Builder*, 99:3542 (1910), 773–6
Image, S. 'An address delivered by request in the hall of Clifford's Inn before the Art Workers' Guild on the twenty-fifth anniversary of the Guild's foundation, Friday the fifteenth of January, 1909', in H. J. L. J. Massé, *The Art-Workers' Guild* (Oxford, 1935), pp. 15–21
Kaye, B. *The development of the architectural profession in Britain: a sociological study* (London, 1960)
'The King's statue Aberdeen', *Stone Trades Journal*, 29:1 (1910), 402–4
Lee, T. S. 'Sculpture and sculptors' methods in relation to architecture', *Royal Institute of British Architects Transactions*, 8 (1892), 49–64
Lee, T. S. 'Sculpture in its relation to architecture', *Journal of the Royal Institute of British Architects*, 12:15 (1905), 497–504
Lethaby, W. R., A. H. Powell and F. L. Griggs, *Ernest Gimson: his life and work* (Stratford-upon-Avon, 1924)
Livingstone, K. and L. Parry (eds.) *International Arts and Crafts* (London, 2005)
Local Taxation (Customs and Excise) Act 1890, 53 & 54 Vict. c. 60
'Machinery at Aberdeen', *Stone Trades Journal*, 20:10 (1902), 226
Mapping the practice and profession of sculpture in Britain and Ireland 1851–1951, University of Glasgow History of Art and HATII, online database 2011, www.sculpture.gla.ac.uk
Millar, W. *Plastering plain and decorative: a practical treatise on the art of modelling & craft of plastering* (London, 3rd edn, 1905)
'Progress of the architectural crafts', *Building News and Engineering Journal*, 74 (1898), 1–2
Public sculpture of Britain (Liverpool, 1997–)
'The Queen Victoria Memorial', *Stone Trades Journal*, 30:12 (1911), 786–7
Renwick, W. G. *Marble and marble working* (London, 1909)
Reynolds-Stephens, W. 'Sculpture in its relation to architecture', *Journal of the Royal Institute of British Architects*, 12:15 (1905), 505–10
Rogers, P. *The beauty of stone: the Westminster Cathedral marbles* (London, 2008)
'The quarrying industry one hundred years ago', *Stone Trades Journal*, 21:4 (1902), 79
'Sculpture and monumental', *Stone Trades Journal*, 20:7 (1902), 172
'Sculpture by machinery' *Stone Trades Journal*, 22:1 (1903), 60–1
'Mr Sedding's opinion of things amiss', *Builder's Journal and Architectural Record*, 11:272 (1900), 206–7
Smith, S. C. K. 'Sculpture in relation to architecture', *Stone Trades Journal*, 25:12 (1907), 380
Sparkes, J. C. L. 'Report of the superintendent of studies, June 1888', in *Report of the South London Technical School of Art, 1888, City and Guilds of London Institute for the Advancement of Technical Education* (1888), pp. 1–15
Sparkes, J. C. L. 'Report of the superintendent of studies, July 1890', *City and Guilds of London Institute, South London School of Technical Art, Session 1889–90*, pp. 1–11
Specimens of marble pavements from old examples made by Farmer and Brindley (London, n.d.)
Technical Instruction Act 1889, 52 & 53 Vict. c. 76
'Trade and craft', *Architects' and Builders' Journal*, 32:807 (1910), 82.
Turner, L. A. *Decorative plasterwork in Great Britain* (London, 1927)
'Walton, Goody and Cripps Ltd', *Stone Trades Journal*, 20:7 (1902), 159–64
'The Wenzel sculpturing and carving machine', *Stone Trades Journal*, 22:4 (1904), 138–9
The year's art (London, 1890)

11

'A fraught challenge to the status quo': the 1883–84 Calcutta International Exhibition, conceptions of art and industry, and the politics of world fairs

Renate Dohmen

The spectacular success of the 1851 Great Exhibition unleashed a worldwide craze for international exhibitions and placed this new cultural phenomenon at the heart of Europe's imperial, national and commercial affairs. Furthermore, the performative, consumptive, and participatory acts of visiting world exhibitions fashioned an imaginary of exotic, far-off colonial spaces seen as readily assimilable and firmly part of an integrated, orderly social totality with Europe at the centre. But what if such an exhibition were to be held in one such far-flung exotic space so fancifully represented in these world fairs? How would the representational order of the imperial centre be challenged by the very act of transposing the phenomenon of the world fair to the colonial periphery? And more specifically by transposing the phenomenon to India, that is, a subject rather than settler community such as Australia, which had taken the lead with staging an international exhibition in a non-European location? The success of the Sydney exhibition in 1879 had emboldened Calcutta to follow suit in 1883–84, staging the first international exposition in British India, which was also to remain its last (see figures 11.1 and 11.2). So how are we to understand the Calcutta International Exhibition, and why did it mark the end to British India's world fair ambitions?

The historian Peter Hoffenberg, a prominent scholar in the field of empire and international world fairs, referred to the Calcutta International Exhibition of 1883–84 as 'India's own *Great Exhibition*', that is 'a South Asian version of the first international exhibition at London's Crystal Palace in 1851'.[1] He described the Calcutta International Exhibition as 'the largest, most comprehensive and popular Indian exhibition of its day' and acknowledged it as a 'watershed event'.[2] The colonial government in India, in a similar vein, celebrated the exhibition as a great success and proudly measured its achievements in terms of 2,500 exhibitors, over

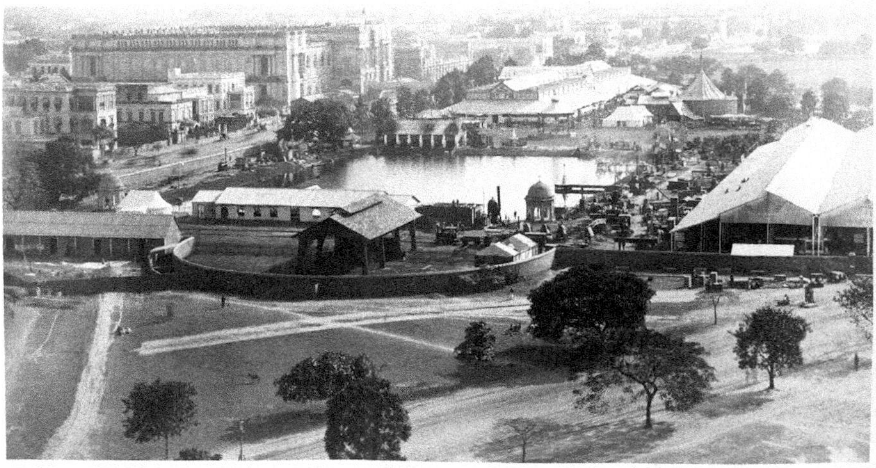

11.1 Bird's-eye view of the Calcutta International Exhibition 1883-4. It shows the Indian Museum on the left, and the 488 foot long Indian Court in the centre of the photograph where the arts of the Indian regions were displayed. The shed to the right housed machinery mainly from Great Britain. Except for the Indian Museum all exhibition buildings were temporary. The exhibition was criticized as lacking an overall visual scheme. (Collection Centre Canadien d'Architecture/ Canadian Centre for Architecture, Montréal.)

100,000 articles on display, 3,142 awards bestowed, and approximately one million mainly Indian visitors, with an average of 6,277 daily exhibition goers.[3] The exhibition was also financially successful. Hoffenberg, however, also makes a case for the subversive potential of the exhibition. Highlighting that the exhibition's regional exhibition committees were predominantly Indian in composition, and that Indian natives were not only involved in sourcing, but also labelling and displaying objects at the exhibition, he proposed that 'it was perhaps only a short step to organise, study, and use the Indian history and its architectural heritage for national rather than imperial or regional ends', and that 'more than one vision of the Indian political community was on view' (see figures 11.3 and 11.4).[4] Hoffenberg points to a jostling over the meaning of the exhibition between the native population and the colonial government.

This chapter seeks to expand but also challenge Hoffenberg's view of the exhibition's lines of contention, and argues that the native population sided *with* the Indian government's and Viceroy Ripon's vision of

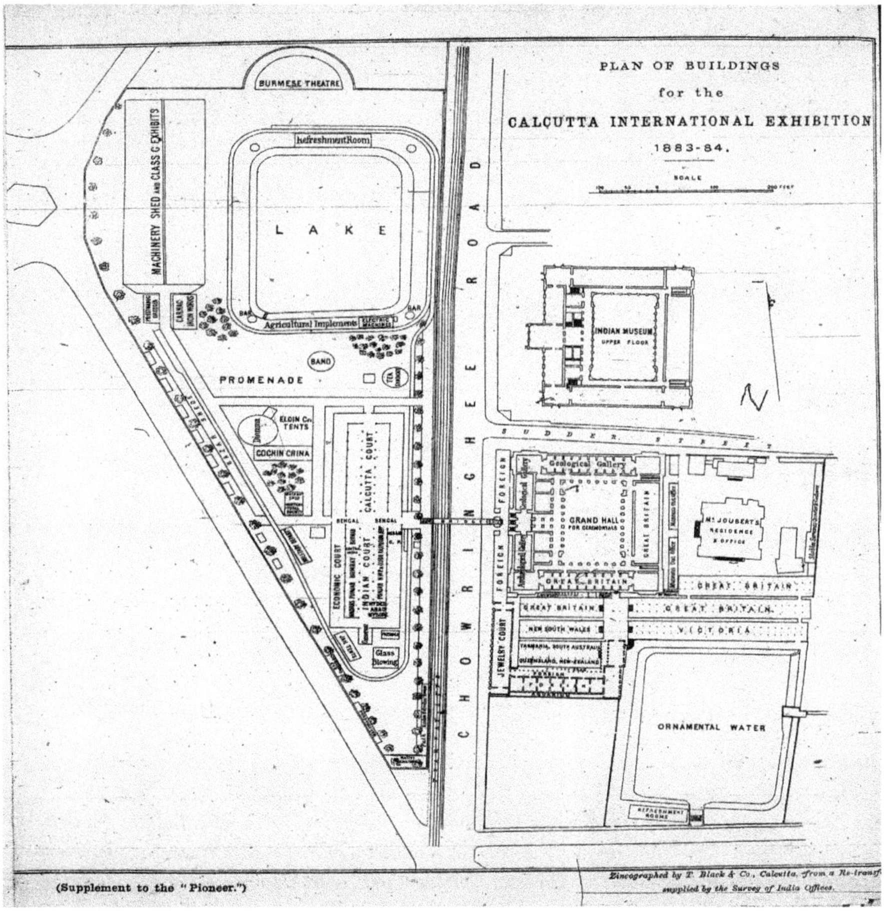

11.2 Ground plan of the Calcutta International Exhibition of 1883-4. The exhibition was divided by Chowringhee Road. Its two parts were connected by a wooden foot bridge between the Indian Museum on the Eastern and the Indian Court on the Western side which often caused congestion. The walls of the Indian court were surrounded by shrubs and life-size clay figures of Indians in regional costumes. The entrance to the exhibition was on the museum side. (© The British Library Board SM147.)

the exhibition, supporting him in his conflict with local British residents and the colonial administration in Britain. It further holds that the posited struggle over the meaning of the exhibition is closely related to issues of art and industry played out between colony and imperial metropole which came into sharp relief through the staging of the Calcutta International Exhibition. The discussion also proposes that the India-centricity of the official exhibition rhetoric needs to be recognised as a climb-down by the government of India after its dressing down by the imperial centre for its world fair ambition. I hence argue that when Rivers Thompson, the

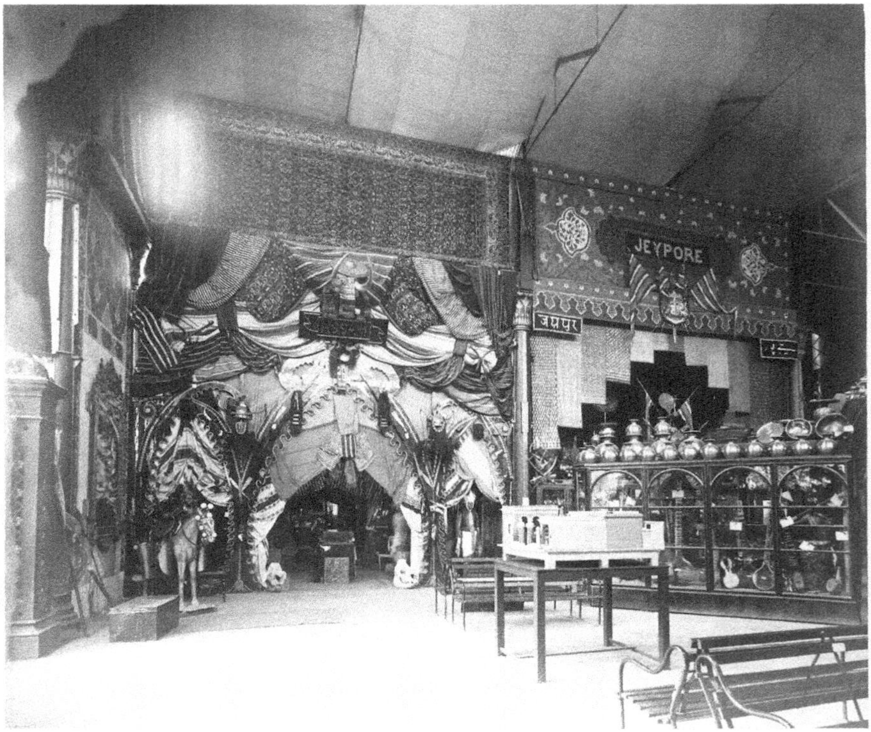

11.3 Interior view of a pavilion showing the Assam section to the left and Jeypore's exhibits to the right at the Calcutta International Exhibition 1883-4. The cloth-draped, arched entrance to the Assam Court refers to the domestic architecture of Assam's Naga hill tribe and the textile industry of the tribes of the region, the only art manufacture in the region. Jeypore Province in contrast has rich and diverse art industries. On view here is Jeypore metal ware. (Collection Centre Canadien d'Architecture/Canadian Centre for Architecture, Montréal.)

Lieutenant-Governor of Bengal, congratulated the colonial administration in his exhibition closing speech 'upon having excited the keen interest of the native population', claiming the native interest in this 'Exhibition for India' as 'primary aim'[5] and stating the furthering of trade with Australia as the exhibition's secondary aim, this cannot be taken at face value.[6] What I want to suggest is that both the native-centric and inter-colonial perspectives that have come to define the exhibition should rather be recognised as a successful face-saving manoeuvre adopted when the original but ultimately unsuccessful ambition of the Calcutta International Exhibition to be a true world fair had failed. The rhetoric shifted to a native-centric and inter-colonial perspective when it became apparent that the world was not only not going to descend on Calcutta in droves as had been anticipated, but that it had decided to ignore the exhibition altogether.

Framed more generally, this discussion considers the adjustments that occur and the difficulties that are faced when the phenomenon of

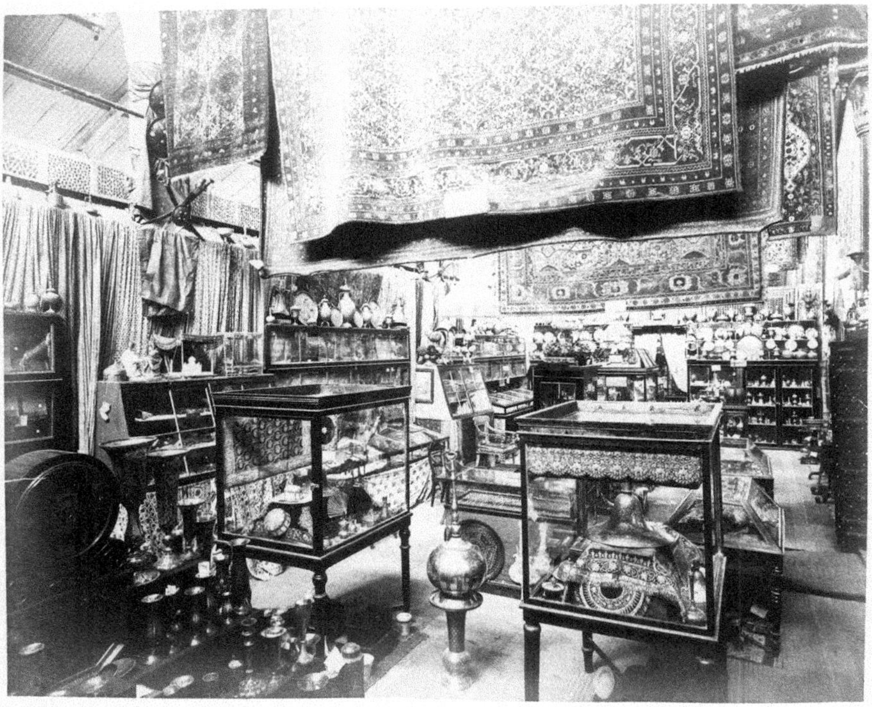

The Court of the Northwest Provinces at the Calcutta International Exhibition 1883-4 shows the extensive traditions of art manufacture of the region. Prominently displayed are brass, copper and bell-metal work, as well as textile manufacture ranging from muslin, plain, embroidered and hand-printed cottons, to silk and carpets among others. The carpets on view were for sale and were produced at Agra Central Prison. (Collection Centre Canadien d'Architecture/Canadian Centre for Architecture, Montréal.) **11.4**

the 'world fair' is transposed to a colonial context. Of importance here, as will be developed, is the distinction between settler community such as Australia, which had taken the lead with staging successful international exhibitions in non-European colonial locations, and a subject colony such as India which sought to emulate Australia's success.

It was the remarkable success of the Sydney exhibition in 1879 that emboldened Calcutta to follow suit in 1883–84 to stage its first international exposition. But despite the publicly voiced aspiration that the Calcutta International Exhibition was 'destined to prove the harbinger of many such exhibitions on a grander scale in time to come', and even though a follow-up exhibition in Bombay was in the works when the Calcutta International Exhibition closed, there were no further world fairs staged in colonial India.[7] This discussion explores what I hold to be the exhibition's ultimate failure of establishing India as a location for staging world fairs. This defeat, I argue, is intricately linked to the crucial distinction between a settler and subject colony, respective associations with the city and progress, and 'the production of handicraft against the backdrop of the timeless village'.[8] In other words, the complex interplay of imperial politics, prominent South Kensingtonian ideas of design reform and the place of Indian art and artefacts in the British empire.[9]

The exhibition

The exhibition was initiated by Jules Joubert (1824–1907), a Frenchman who had adopted Australia as his home. He had overseen the Australian government's hugely successful display at the *Exposition Universelle* 1878 in Paris and had participated as New Caledonia's commissioner for the Sydney 1879 International Exhibition. These prominent involvements allowed him to lay claim to the success of these exhibitions and emboldened him to try his luck in India, suggesting to the governments of Bengal and India that a similar triumph surely lay within their reach.[10] Ominously, however, the Calcutta International Exhibition had a disastrous opening on 4 December 1883. As the Viceroy gave his opening speech the attending public pressed into nooks and corners to shelter from the pouring rain that spilled through the ceremonial awning 'as if it were a sieve'.[11] It was a most 'dismal spectacle' that was crowned by a complete blackout due to an electrical failure as darkness descended and people were ready to leave. But it was not only the weather that dampened the spirits. Rather, the exhibition was overshadowed by a heightened animosity between natives and Europeans, 'in a manner not known since the Mutiny' due to the Ilbert Bill that Viceroy Ripon supported. The measure sought to allow senior Indian magistrates to preside over cases involving British subjects in India. Resident Europeans were up in arms about this bill and campaigned vigorously against it, concentrating their ill-feeling towards the Viceroy. This circumstance, according to the *South Australian Register*, had a 'material effect on the Exhibition itself, as the whole of the European non-official residents made up their minds not to attend any entertainment where the Viceroy would preside, or to do him honour in any way'.[12] This attitude noticeably had not changed by the closing of the exhibition the following March, which was marked by a noted lack of a European presence and a pronounced absence of enthusiasm. A thoroughly troubling picture therefore emerges of the exhibition. The local British residents boycotted the exhibition to demonstrate their discontent with the Ilbert Bill, rejecting any suggestion that India and, by extension, Indians could fully, and increasingly equally, participate in the subcontinent's governance, thereby refusing the very aspirations which underpinned the Calcutta International Exhibition for a modern India to take its place among the nations of the world. The 'white mutiny' as the Ilbert Bill agitation is also referred to, markedly jeopardised the success of the exhibition and is indicative of the battle over conceptions of India in relation to empire that played out through the exhibition. It is proposed here that the Calcutta International Exhibition, by its very existence, muscled in on the territory of representing India that was claimed by the colonial metropole, and sought to disentangle it from the dominant construction of Indianess centred around pre-industrial craft traditions and its placement in an idealised past. Through their support of the exhibition the colonial governments of Bengal and of India arguably made a case for changing the romanticised image of India, and sought to grasp the mantle of commerce, manufacture and progress so comfortably claimed by its sister colony Australia. By doing so, the colonial government inadvertently challenged India's position in the colonial pecking order, as well as its association with the timelessness of a pre-industrial past. In other words, the colony dared to step into the present and had the audacity to claim a place among of the 'benefactors of the human race'.[13] It was Kristo Das Pal, the editor of the English language native newspaper *Hindoo Patriot* considered 'as recognised leader of advanced thought',[14] who poignantly defended this vision of India by drawing on Australia's example. In his speech at the International Exhibition Dinner in February 1884, praised as 'one of the best speeches of the evening',[15] Pal observed how Australians, as descendants of Englishmen, sprang from the same Aryan stock from which Indians were descended, and emphasised how the common ancestors of both colonies were 'the pioneers of civilisation and commerce in the ancient world'.[16] He suggested that 'the example of Australia teaches a most important and valuable lesson to India', lauded Australia's advances in agriculture, commerce and enterprise and presented the colony as role model for India. He furthermore stated that, 'India now feels that she cannot stand where she did, that she must walk and run with the other nations of the world in the race of peaceful progress and civilisation'.[17] Pal's view, largely representative of the Western-educated sections of the Indian population who endorsed the exhibition and its perceived potential for India, also represented a liberal agenda as championed by Viceroy Ripon, who, according to the English language native newspaper the *Indian Spectator*, was referred to as 'Gladstone's best gift to India' and was appreciated by the natives of India 'to the fullest extent'.[18] In a similar vein the *Bengalee*, while critiquing the administration's repeal of duty on cotton goods, acknowledged 'the genuine earnestness of Lord Ripon and his councillors to govern India for the benefit of the Indians', crucially adding the qualification 'with the aid of the Indians'.[19]

While the vision invoked by the Calcutta International Exhibition of an India that endorsed manufacture and industry and joined the forces of 'progress and civilisation' (see figures 11.1, 11.2) was supported by the Indian educated and entrepreneurial classes, as well a liberal administrative agenda, it was stonewalled not just by the resident British in the colony, but also, after a brief period of flirtation with the idea, by the imperial centre. A change in tone in the British press is noticeable from prior to the opening of the exhibition to shortly thereafter. An early, expansive article in *The Times*, reprinted in the *Times of India*, anticipated that the exhibition of English manufacture at the Calcutta International Exhibition would be of 'value for the development of backward regions', and 'there can be no question that the peoples of India must benefit more largely than any one else'.[20] The paper cited the 'further introduction of English capital, knowledge and enterprise into the peninsula', which was assumed to be the benevolent reason why the government of India 'resolved to give the International Exhibition all the support and countenance in its power'.[21] And while the paper warned that 'India is not an El Dorado' it pointed out that 'there are plenty of opportunities of investing moderate sums of money' with a good chance of a respectable return. It also emphasised 'that there is no want of sympathy on the part of Englishmen generally in the matter, or of readiness to contribute towards the consummation of a much-desired result', that is the improvement of India as evidenced by the ready participation of the principal English manufacturers in the Calcutta International Exhibition.[22] Yet barely a month later, the space allocated to reports of the exhibition had contracted markedly. The grand opening of the exhibition was only reported in the most cursory fashion and any subsequent and increasingly infrequent news of the exhibition was limited to a few lines that update on visitor numbers.[23] In a similar vein the familiar buzzwords common for such occasions such as 'peace of the nations', 'industrial progress' or 'improvements of taste' are only invoked on rare occasions such as in the anticipatory *Times* article of 20 September 1883 that referred to the exhibition as a 'Temple of Peace now in course of construction in the capital of British India'.[24] And yet the article tellingly never referred to the Calcutta *International* Exhibition but denigrated the show by consistently calling it the Calcutta Exhibition, a reference echoed across the British press. The article furthermore framed the exhibition entirely with regard to Indian art and artefacts. Ignoring its industrial aspects, the article referred to the successful Jeypore native arts exhibition of the same year and hoped that what 'the Jeypore exhibition did in a small way for one part of India' will be accomplished in Calcutta 'on a much larger scale for the empire'.[25] Tellingly, it further emphasised that this exhibition was not aimed at the world, but the native Indian population, underscoring the benevolence and inspired stewardship of the imperial government by stating that, 'whereas former conquerors appropriated for their own use all the art treasures on which they could lay their hands, we are inducing and encouraging Indian chiefs and merchants to expose their possessions in an exhibition for the benefit and improvement of the less favoured peoples of the country'.[26]

After an initial period of anticipation the Calcutta International Exhibition – or rather the Calcutta Exhibition as it was stubbornly referred to

– was by and large ignored in the British press, as it was considered an inter-Indian, or at best an inter-colonial affair without wider significance. It was the imperial centre that can be credited with initiating an overwhelmingly Indian-centric rhetoric for the exhibition. Of crucial importance here was, as Devleena Ghosh reminds us, that:

> India and the Australian colonies were both important but very different imperial spaces of the British empire in the latter half of the nineteenth century ... they were of different value and status in the Empire. The Australian settler colonies were European and white like imperial Britain whereas the Indian subcontinent was a colony of extraction, the ownership of which was crucial to Britain in terms of its imagination of its own imperial power.[27]

Moreover, British investment in the vision of the happy village artisan representative of a timeless India was a key legacy of the Great Exhibition of 1851, which had generated the highly influential 'South Kensington System', as it became known. The latter championed Indian designs as unadulterated examples of good taste that were, in an abstracted form, taught to aspiring English industrial designers. The hugely influential South Kensington approach to art and design education linked the progress of English manufacture to unadulterated design principles extracted from traditional Indian arts applied to British manufacture. The progress and market viability of British production therefore became intricately linked to Indian pre-industrial craft practices on a conceptual level, which further strengthened the race-based conviction that 'progress in the western sense was inimical to the unchanging arts in India'.[28] A further influence to note is the romantic Arts and Crafts veneration of the craftsman, considered to be nearly extinct in Britain but alive and well in India, who in the view of Arts and Crafts aficionados had to be protected at all costs.[29] Add Social Darwinism and the doctrine of racial essentialism to this equation, and Indians were now not only deemed essentially incapable of modern progress, but the pushing of Indians in the direction of the latter was declared a profound violation of their inalienable racial instincts. The perceived incongruousness of an industrial vision for India was also raised on more practical grounds. The British-Indian newspaper the *Englishman* questioned the position of a colony as exhibitor of manufactures and found the notion peculiar because it assumed that colonies could not compete with Britain or the older countries of Europe in that department.[31] *The Times* was decidedly cynical about the possibility of Western-style industrial development in India. While it declared that the exhibition marked the beginning of 'a new epoch in the industrial history of British India', it was only encouraged in its capacity to 'offer a wider field of expansion to English trade'.[32]

The exhibition's promoters, in contrast, initially envisaged a true world fair and anticipated that 'new branches of trade may thus be opened out, and an impetus given by force of example to manufactures suited to India'.[33] This goal, as they were to find out, would put them in conflict with the imperial centre. While interest by commercial exhibitors was more vigorous than the organisers had expected, this constituted a private response only and 'foreign delegates were appointed only by the government of Austro-Hungary, by the French colonies of Cochin China and Toquin, and by the Dutch colony of Batavia'.[34] This meant that the main players in Europe and North America, such as Great Britain most notably, but also 'France, Germany, Italy, Belgium, Turkey, Japan, and the US', were only represented by private companies and as such had no official representation.[35] Without government representation the exhibition's global aspirations were stymied, a realisation that was reflected in newspaper reports in British India. While in January 1883 the *Pioneer Mail*, another British-Indian newspaper, had confidently pronounced that there was every reason to believe that the Calcutta International Exhibition 'will attract the attention of foreign countries to the great natural wealth of India, and to the opportunities for profitable trade which the country presents', the paper conceded only a few months later that the foreign visitors had stayed at home.[36] This was publicly declared shortly before the opening of the exhibition in a newspaper advertisement in Calcutta where the Great Eastern Hotel Company announced:

> The general expectation of a very large influx of European and Colonial strangers into Calcutta almost necessitated the Company raising their charges very materially. As this expectation is clearly not likely to be realised, the Company have the pleasure to notify that they revert from today to their usual charges for the cold weather.[37]

The lack of European visitors was keenly felt by the organisers, who, after it became clear that their initial expectation for the Calcutta International Exhibition to be an equal player on the world stage would not be fulfilled, adjusted the exhibition rhetoric, adopting a more inter-colonial perspective. The government declared the local Indian population as the primary audience while focusing on relations with Australia with regard to trade and commerce. Now the success claimed for the exhibition rested mostly with the Indian visitors that it was hoped would be attracted to the exhibition grounds. Viceroy Ripon proclaimed in his opening speech 'if this exhibition furthers the development of that trade [between India and Australia], that result alone will be amply sufficient to justify and reward the labours of those who have carried out this undertaking'.[38] He also noted that the 'active co-operation of many of the British colonies was extremely gratifying. Royal Commissions were appointed by Victoria, New South Wales and South Australia, and representatives were sent by Tasmania, Ceylon, the Straits Settlements, Demerara and Mauritius'.[39]

Shortly after the opening of the exhibition the *Indian Daily News* reported that a 'large proportion of visitors are, of course, natives, and many of those are of the poorer classes', and framed the exhibition as an educational tool for these visitors by stating that, 'it is satisfactory to think that this show has not only given these poor men so much gratification but has in a measure helped to educate them regarding the resources of India and the world'.[40] Furthermore, among the Indian audience female visitors were singled out for special attention. In his closing speech the Lieutenant-Governor Rivers Thompson stated that special women-only days allowed the higher-caste Hindu and Muslim women, traditionally confined to domestic women's quarters, to safely see the exhibition. He estimated that 50,000 native ladies attended the exhibition and claimed the exhibition as an 'educational and social reformer' that weakened the 'bonds of caste and exclusiveness'.[41] But Rivers Thompson also emphasised the sense of wonder uneducated Indians, who were described as wandering the courts in a bedazzled state of awe and amazement, must have felt when seeing the displays.[42] H. J. Reynolds, Vice-Chancellor of Calcutta University, also suggested that whereas Europeans visiting world fairs reportedly gazed at Indian displays in wondrous amazement, the Exhibition 'cannot but have made an impression even on the most simple rustic, who regarded it with a kind of stolid wonder, – as a … mere palace of magic'.[43]

But what lessons or messages were imbibed by the locals as they made their way through the wonders on display? What image of India and empire and what notion of their place within it did they absorb? As has been pointed out, world fairs represented 'symbolic universes' staged for Western viewers that allowed them to proceed from 'white civilization to visions of dark barbarity', and gaze in wonder at the world's bounty that could be metaphorically possessed, while absorbing the message of the natural superiority of industrialised nations.[44] Such exhibitions offered progress and civilisation in contrast to the 'irrational babble of backwardness' presented through 'grotesquely sublime exotic' ethnographic displays, which, however, gave the exhibitions their excitement and appeal, while serving the didactic purpose of confirming the place of superiority in the European viewer.[45] As Rydell has argued, 'at the fairs, the idea of technological progress became laced with scientific racism' by 'stressing the diversity of racial "types" and an evolutionary hierarchy'.[46] He calls world fairs 'part of a broader universe of white supremacist entertainments' with 'scientific, artistic, and political underpinnings'.[47] This statement is poignantly underscored by the following description of the Calcutta International Exhibition regarding a scene in the Economic Court where: 'the ethnological specimens of the races of India' were arranged 'in groups, as for example a group of the people of Chota Nagpore, a group of Assamese and another of the natives of the Punjab: these are modelled to the life, and when seen with a number of swarthy natives around them from a distance, the eye is almost deceived into accepting the clay figures as part of the living throng around them' (see figure 11.2).[48]

Did the Calcutta International Exhibition put the local audiences 'in their place', confirming their inferiority and backwardness? The *Indian Daily News* seemed to think so, but also emphasised the potential for development the exhibition represented and the civilising mission of the imperial presence. It reported that in 'the European and Australian Courts, there is more that appeals to the European than to the native mind' and proposed that 'a people, like the people of India, should see and comprehend what makes the wide difference between their own civilisation and that of the west'.[49] The article concluded that 'any intelligent native who goes through the Australian and English Courts will come away impressed with a conviction that India is very far indeed behind Western countries'. In a similar vein *The Times* stated that 'it is to Europe that India must come for the quickening of her torpid civilization. This is the true lesson which the Calcutta Exhibition has to teach, and it is one which the present VICEROY OF INDIA has to all appearance only imperfectly learnt'.[50]

Given that the exhibition was now mainly addressed to the native population, one would imagine there to be a debate about the nature of the Indian exhibition experience in the British-Indian press. But only snippets of information can be gleaned in the form of one or two scattered sentences found in the often extensive exhibition reviews, which ran over several pages. This underscores the argument that the exhibition was initially aimed at a world audience, and that when it became apparent that this goal was not to be fulfilled there was simply no time to think about how to cater for a more or less exclusively native audience. Collating these comments the following picture of Indians in the exhibition emerges: overall, native visitors were described as gazing in wonder at the spectacle the show presented and reportedly displayed a lack of exhibition etiquette and cultural capital to appreciate the articles on show. Indian visitors were said to cause congestion as 'they are apt to congregate before some object especially interesting in their eyes, such as a mechanical doll, or clock, or a mirror, or a more than usually talkative stall-keeper, leaving other parts of the Courts almost deserted', and it was reported that the native exhibition goer 'never thinks of moving aside till he is forced; yet he resents being requested to move on'.[51] Furthermore a British-Indian newspaper asked why 'our native-fellow subjects who throng the courts on four anna days [the cheapest entry fee] persist in asking the prices of things which by no possibility can it be their intention to buy – such things as refrigerating machines, steam engines, glass bedsteads, and crystal fountains'.[52] Native audiences were reportedly equally 'eager to stare' outside the exhibition venue. The *Englishman* reported a crowd of natives on Chowringhee Road 'watching who goes in and out; and as soon as a swell native or European carriage pulls up, it is surrounded by staring eyes and gaping mouths'.[53] This was not the sort of amazement the organisers had had in mind. The Lieutenant-General of Bengal painted the picture of a future industrialised India when the wonder and amazement felt by the ordinary Indian who stood 'aghast at the marvels wrought by the mechanical appliances of Europe constructed for the relief and diminution of manual labour' would, with the help of the education provided by the imperial administration, be transformed into an attainable expertise taught by the exhibition 'for the benefit and advancement of India'.[54]

The expectation and actuality of the native engagement with the show do not seem to coalesce, which is not surprising. Whereas European exhibition goers in the metropolitan centres were amused, entertained, dazzled and impressed by a mix of the exotic and the familiar, the uneducated natives that frequented the show in large numbers were doubly bedazzled by the Eastern and Western worlds on display. And while they most likely could make sense of the jewels of Indian princes on display, they evidently found it rather difficult to relate to the mechanical wonders presented. The *Hindoo Patriot* lamented that the machine court is not popular with Indian visitors as they do not possess the necessary knowledge 'which might make their visit to the machinery court either interesting or instructive'.[55] The periodical made a point of publishing detailed descriptions of the principal exhibits in the Machine Court (see figures 11.1 and 11.2). An ardent supporter of Western-style progress, it sought to bring the machine closer to the Indian population and declared it to be the most important part of the exhibition, as it revealed the source of England's wealth and might. The *Hindoo Patriot* clearly endorsed an industrial future for India which it advocated as the most important message of the Exhibition for the Indian population. It criticised Indian elites for not starting cotton mills in India, but also chastised the government for not protecting Indian mills from the cheap textiles produced in Glasgow and Edinburgh.[56] The *Bengalee* took a similar stance. It lauded the government's efforts to stimulate indigenous manufactures 'seen to be of immense service to the country', but also critiqued the lifting of import duty on cotton as 'injudicious sacrifice of revenue' that has created a shortfall in state revenue.[57]

But what about the Indian art industries that formed the core of India's representation in the world fairs in the imperial centres? How did they fare in the Calcutta International Exhibition, and what was their perceived message to the native populations (see figures 11.3 and 11.4)? As newspaper reports attest, this question was contested. The *Indian Daily News*, for example, presented the improvement of the Indian workman and the public's taste through the display of good specimens of pure Indian art as the aim of the exhibition, which was intended to stimulate a cleansing of Indian art from European corruption.[58] This view was shared by the *Pioneer* which welcomed the fact that, as had occurred after the Great Exhibition, a permanent sample collection of good specimens was envisaged as an outcome of the exhibition.[59] The *Pioneer*, however, also accepted English influence on Indian art and design and argued that Indian crafts could be successfully adapted to European needs. It cited the everyday kerosine lamp as an example, arguing that its often tasteless stand might well be replaced by the elegant simplicity of traditional Indian black and silver bidri work.[60] Yet the colonial administration, despite its endorsement of a modern India, was also invested in securing what they perceived as the purity and authenticity of India's traditional arts. This concern was expressed in the government of India's resolution to initiate the *Indian Art Journal* to be published in England in the aftermath of the Calcutta International Exhibition to promote knowledge of Indian art and to preserve its traditions, even though the official report of the Calcutta International Exhibition stated the administration's desire to further 'the other important objects of an exhibition, – the bringing of distant countries into closer commercial union with India and the development of new branches of industry'.[61] The rationale of the exhibition can therefore be divided into the promotion of Indian arts manufacture, a familiar aspect of colonial exhibitions in India and abroad and already well established in government protocols, as well as the promotion of trade and articles of manufacture and industry, which sought to break new ground.

While the exhibition failed to feature on the world stage and did not fulfil its global ambitions, what was its claim to success after its re-orientation towards the native population? The English language native newspaper the *Bengalee* argued that the exhibition had been a 'cruel farce' that could not possibly benefit 'many millions of our poor and unfortunate countrymen, who really constitute the nation'.[62] And even the well-to-do Indians with mercantile interests, who supported the idea of a world fair staged in India, in the end conceded that the ambition of a true world fair was out of their reach, as evidenced by the largely native backers of the Bombay International Exhibition who in the end pulled the plug on the project. This was in part due to wrangling over funding, but also over exhibition dates that simply could not be settled, as whatever date they envisaged they found themselves in competition with a major exhibition requiring Indian representation in Europe and elsewhere. The year 1885 was rejected because of the Antwerp exhibition; 1887 because of the Australian Jubilee Exhibition; and once 1886 had been settled on, the rumoured 1886 Colonial and Indian Exhibition in London became official and had to be worked around. The official stance at first was to delay the Bombay International Exhibition yet again, and to display the objects that had been shown in London on their return to India, as 'it is thought that many [artefacts] may return to Bombay from London after the close of the Exhibition at the latter'.[63] The Bombay International Exhibition had been reduced to secondary status, and with it Bombay's claim to staging a true and unique world fair that would truly attract an international audience had been shattered, a consequence not lost on the Indian exhibition supporters. The 1886 Colonial and Indian exhibition in London was the final straw for the planned Bombay International Exhibition. The *Times of*

India, quoting the Indian language newspaper *Rast Goftar*, reported that the exhibition was sacrificed 'for the sake of the London Exhibition' scheduled to take place in 1886 under the patronage of the Prince, arguing that 'it is the royal foot that has crushed the Bombay exhibition', and that the Prince of Wales, in conjunction with the London Exhibition Committee, was to blame for this collapse and the serious loss to the Indian public this represented.[64]

In conclusion, the collapse of the Bombay International Exhibition points yet again to the power relations between the metropole and the colonial administration, and to the ultimate failure of the Calcutta International Exhibition to be a true world fair and to establish India as venue for international exhibitions. In the end, world fairs are all about location, a fact the Duke of Connaught evidently understood as he was overheard to remark about the Calcutta International Exhibition 'that if the whole Exhibition could be moved to London, it would make a great sensation there'.[65]

Notes

1 See Hoffenberg, 'Photography and architecture at the Calcutta International Exhibition', p. 176.
2 *Ibid.*, p. 178.
3 'Formal closing of the exhibition', *Indian Daily News (Weekly)* (11 March 1884), p. 27.
4 Hoffenberg, 'Photography and architecture at the Calcutta International Exhibition', pp. 181, 177.
5 'Formal closing of the exhibition', *Indian Daily News (Weekly)* (11 March 1884), p. 27.
6 See 'The exhibition banquet', *Indian Daily News (Weekly)* (26 February 1884), p. 25.
7 The statement is taken from Kristodas Pal's speech reported in 'The exhibition banquet', *Supplement to Indian Daily News (Weekly)* (19 February 1884), p. 3. See also the Viceroy's closing speech 'The Calcutta Exhibition', *South Australian Register* (15 April 1884), p. 5.
8 Spear, 'A South Kensington gateway from Gwalior to nowhere', 916.
9 See for example *Ibid.*
10 After the Calcutta intermezzo Joubert returned to Australia and continued with his career as exhibition manager running joint private sector/government exhibitions in Australia. For further details please refer to Douglas, 'Jules Joubert: Australia's nineteenth-century exhibition impresario'.
11 'The Calcutta Exhibition', *South Australian Register* (8 January 1884), p. 6.
12 *Ibid.*
13 'The native press at the International Exhibition', *Hindoo Patriot* (25 February 1884), p. 93.
14 'The Calcutta Exhibition', *Argus* (19 March 1844), p. 10.
15 *Ibid.*
16 'The native press at the International Exhibition', *Hindoo Patriot* (25 February 1884), p. 93.
17 *Ibid.*
18 *Indian Spectator* (17 May 1885), p. 386.

19 'Financial policy and the encouragement of manufacture', *Bengalee* (6 January 1883), p. 6.
20 'The English contributions to the Calcutta Exhibition', *Times of India* (9 November 1883), p. 6.
21 *Ibid.*
22 *Ibid.*
23 A search for the Calcutta Exhibition in *The Times* digital archive reveals a brief mention on 4 December that the International Exhibition will be opened in the news section, and all following references are under the sections 'News in brief' or 'Latest Intelligence', which are organised by country. In the three months that the exhibition was open, it was mentioned only five more times, and is now only referred to as 'Calcutta Exhibition'. These reports focused on visitor numbers and average between one- and two-sentence entries. The editorial and commentary category shows two inconsequential mentions of the exhibition as part of larger pieces devoted to other subjects, and of the three features that refer to the exhibition one is devoted to the native arts at the exhibition, the other to the English contributions. The short piece that reported on the opening of the exhibition in December 1883, which still referred to the exhibition as 'international', immediately referenced the political context of the Ilbert Bill by commenting on the 'marked absence of non-officials'. It devoted more space to the description of the soaking wet conditions of the opening ceremony, and the large native presence, than the opening proceedings or the purpose of the exhibition. And after these preliminaries it launched into an attack on Ripon's politics that had caused such a rift in the colony.
24 'Native art at the Calcutta Exhibition', *The Times* (20 September 1883), p. 7.
25 *Ibid.*
26 *Ibid.*
27 Ghosh, 'Under the radar of empire', 498.
28 Mitter, *Art and nationalism in colonial India, 1850–1922*, p. 53. See also 'The appointment of Havell', *The Times* (7 November 1883), p. 6.
29 See Tarapor, 'John Lockwood Kipling', 72.
30 See Mitter, *Art and nationalism in colonial India, 1850–1922*, p. 51.
31 See 'The International Exhibition', *Englishman (Weekly)* (14 March 1884), p. 4.
32 *The Times* (5 December 1883), p. 4.
33 Government of India, *Official report*, p. 2.
34 *Ibid.*, p. 6.
35 *Ibid.* The lack of official representation is stated in the Official report, which explained that the exhibition was a private enterprise and not a government affair. Yet the exhibition had the official backing of the Viceroy. Furthermore the 1883 Amsterdam exhibition was a private enterprise and yet all the countries of Europe were officially represented. The British residents in India also clearly did not see the exhibition as a private enterprise, as they boycotted the exhibition in protest at the Viceroy's political agenda.
36 'The International Exhibition', *Pioneer Mail* (24 January 1883), p. 82.
37 'International Exhibition', *Englishman* (3 December 1883), p. 2.
38 Government of India, *Official report*, p. 15.
39 *Ibid.*, p. 5.
40 'The week', *Indian Daily News* (18 December 1883), p. 2.
41 'The exhibition banquet', *Indian Daily News (Weekly)* (26 February 1884), p. 26. The singling out of the native woman by the Exhibition's promoters is a prominent theme in the ideology of the Raj and underscores the central role of the Oriental female in the construction and legitimation of imperialism, focusing in particular on

her liberation from what is considered as stifling oppression by traditional Oriental culture and the tyrannical seclusion imposed on her.

42 See 'The week', *Indian Daily News* (18 December 1883), p. 2.
43 Government of India, *Official report*, p. 18.
44 Berger and Luckmann, *The social construction of reality*, pp. 113–34; Cole, 'Cultural and racial stereotypes on the Medway', *Historia* 17.
45 See Armstrong, '"A jumble of foreignness"', 207.
46 Rydell, *All the world's a fair*, p. 5.
47 *Ibid.*, p. 6.
48 'Calcutta International Exhibition', *Indian Daily News (Weekly)* (1 January 1884), p. 20.
49 'The Exhibition', *Indian Daily News (Weekly)* (4 December 1883), p. 10.
50 *The Times* (5 December 1883), p. 9.
51 'Calcutta International Exhibition', *Times of India* (14 January 1884), p. 6.
52 'Calcutta International Exhibition', *Indian Daily News (Weekly)* (22 January 1884), p. 24.
53 *Englishman* (7 December 1883), p. 5.
54 'Financial policy and the encouragement of manufactures', *Bengalee* (6 January 1883), p. 5.
55 'Calcutta International Exhibition', *Hindoo Patriot* (24 September 1883), p. 466.
56 See 'The Exhibition. Machinery Court I', *Hindoo Patriot* (28 January 1884), p. 42.
57 *Bengalee* (6 January 1883), p. 5.
58 'The Calcutta Exhibition. Jewels and valuable property at the Calcutta International Exhibition', *India Daily News (Weekly)* (8 September 1883), p. 24.
59 'Indian Exhibitions', *Pioneer Mail* (5 August 1883), p. 108.
60 See 'The Jeypore Exhibition', *Pioneer Mail* (17 January 1883), p. 54. Bidri work refers to a traditional Indian metal working technique where intricate silver but also copper inlays are inserted on a black metal surface and the contrast is exploited to stunning effect.
61 Government of India. *Official report*, p. 1.
62 'The close of the International Exhibition', *Bengalee* (8 March 1884), p. 113.
63 APAC, J. Monteath, Esq., 'Bombay Exhibition', pp. 151–2.
64 *Ibid.* and 'The native papers: the collapse of the Bombay Exhibition project', *Times of India* (13 July 1885), p. 6.
65 'The native papers: the collapse of the Bombay Exhibition project', *Times of India* (13 July 1885), p. 6.

Bibliography

Armstrong, M. '"A jumble of foreignness": the sublime musayums of nineteenth-century fairs and expositions', *Cultural Critique*, 23 (1992), 199–250

Asia, Pacific & Africa Collections, British Library, London (hereafter APAC), P/2280 File no. 32, Serial no. 12, Proceedings of the Revenue and Agricultural Department, Government of India, J. Monteath, Esq. 'Bombay Exhibition' (Calcutta: 1884)

Berger, P. and T. Luckmann, *The social construction of reality* (New York, 1966)

Cole, J., 'Cultural and racial stereotypes on the Medway', *Historia* 17 (2007), 12–32

Douglas, L. 'Jules Joubert: Australia's nineteenth-century exhibition impresario', *National Library Magazine* (2012), 27–30

Ghosh, D. 'Under the radar of empire: unregulated travel in the Indian Ocean', *Journal of Social History*, 45 (2011), 497–514

Government of India, *Official report of the Calcutta International Exhibition 1883–4. Compiled under the orders of the Executive Committee* (Calcutta, 1885)

Hoffenberg, P. H. *An empire on display: English, Indian, and Australian exhibitions from the Crystal Palace to the Great War* (Berkeley, 2001)

Hoffenberg, P. H. 'Photography and architecture at the Calcutta International Exhibition', in A. Pelizzari (ed.) *Traces of India: photography, architecture, and the politics of representation, 1850–1900* (Montreal, 2003), pp. 174–93

Mitter, P. *Art and nationalism in colonial India, 1850–1922: occidental orientations* (Cambridge, 1994)

Rydell, P. *All the world's a fair: visions of empire at American international exhibitions, 1876–1916* (Chicago, 1984)

Spear, J. L. 'A South Kensington gateway from Gwalior to nowhere', *Studies in English Literature*, 48 (2008), 911–21

Tarapor, M. 'John Lockwood Kipling and British art education in India', *Victorian Studies*, 24 (1980), 53–81

12

The industry of colour: art, design and dyeing between Britain and India, 1851–96

Natasha Eaton

> It has been an actual necessity in order to obtain power of colouring that a nation should be half savage ... No one can colour anywhere except the Hindus.[1]

British colonial and Indian subaltern genealogies of colour's multivalent, heterogeneous agency are the subject of this chapter. I want to suggest that colour in relation to the subaltern provides us with a critical lens for examining afresh the entanglement between art, craft, dyeing, aesthetics, pedagogy and imperial expansion, precisely because it straddles these boundaries. In their attempts to discipline and to comprehend what they deemed to be 'Indian colour', colonial art administrators and district surveyors tried to separate chromatics (the theory of colour) from dyeing – with varying degrees of efficacy because, after all, colour eludes such rigid divisions. It is my contention that there was a dramatic shift away from British concern with what constituted this chromatics (which through the lens of the South Kensington arts curriculum were rather variously and ambiguously 'applied'), to growing anxiety that although these chromatics might form the ground for the 'reform' of both British and Indian art, colour was ultimately ungovernable; colour was variously subaltern.

Taking a lead from Ranajit Guha and the early Subaltern Studies Collective, I propose that colour's equivocal agency can be glimpsed through certain codes, visual signs, figures and mutterings in the colonial archive, which demonstrate the contradictions, the aporia and the supplementarity of colonial governmentality.[2] To conceptualise colour as supplemental is to think of something added to design to correct a deficiency, i.e. to complete that which is wanting. There was, I contend, certainly colonial anxiety that British art and design lacked judicious or intuitive colour – which an investment in and perhaps even mimicry of Indian colour could offer. The supplement is a 'surplus, a plenitude enriching another plenitude, the fullest measure of presence'; as an adjunct it is 'a subaltern insistence which takes-(the)-place'.[3] The collusions and the tensions of the subaltern and the supplement *qua* the production, circulation and perception of colour form the research trajectory of this essay.

'Subaltern colour' intends to engage with recent debates concerned with the fraught relationship between art, design and industry, resituating these debates in the context of exhibitions, art schools in Britain and India, and colonial prisons. In India it was largely in these spaces that the threshold between art and industry was both theorised and realised in relation to the complex and contested aesthetic and material focus on colour. Although colour is becoming a 'hot academic topic', colour in the colony has been surprisingly ignored. Yet it was largely due to the exceptionally positive reception of the chromatic harmonies of Indian artefacts displayed at the first world's fair, held at Crystal Palace in 1851, that 'Oriental' art was seen to triumph over modern British industry. Here Indian craft traditions presented a 'traditional' or non-industrial alternative to British industrial design. At the same time they offered a potential remedy or supplement for the widely perceived ills of British design. Given the (perhaps redemptive) appeal of Indian crafts – especially their colours – they became a major attraction for both British reform of colonial design and a major incentive for the introduction of art schools in India. As my chapter hopes to show, however, the divisions between celebration and vilification of Indian art and the relationship between what constituted aesthetic discourse and artisanal practice were far from clear cut. In addition to an investigation of what might be the dialectic between art and industry, a focus on colour also allows us to think about the tentative category of the non- or anti-industrial in relation to art, craft and dyeing.

Colour, the Crystal Palace and South Kensington

The Great Exhibition held in 1851 at the Crystal Palace tried to straddle both the museological demand for object lessons and the desire for spectacle. Oriental splendour at the Crystal Palace highlighted the crisis facing British design: reform or perish.[4] Against the shocking disappointment elicited by British industrially produced artefacts, Indian objects, in particular fabrics and an embroidered saddle, imparted wonder not only from the lay public but also from well established art critics.[5] In the *Official catalogue to the Great Exhibition* John Forbes Royle emphasised 'the command the natives of India have over colour', while the architect Matthew Digby Wyatt singled out 'the quiet beauty by the right employment of the most brilliant colouring when broken up into the most minute and properly contrasted forms and arranged for flat surfaces'.[6] As the supplement to the urgent debates on the category of design, colour could not be ignored.[7] This was in part due to British and French debates in the previous decades which sought to harness the material technologies of colour with the perception of chromatic harmonies.[8] Prolific writer and colourman George Field's theory of the importance of the three primaries (blue, red and yellow) would be partially applied by the architect and theorist Owen Jones to the transepts of Joseph Paxton's iron and glass megastructure – the Crystal Palace.[9] For Owen Jones, eastern design came to be framed in terms of Field's three primaries. In fact, he believed eastern design preceded and perhaps influenced the formation of the three primaries then so prevalent in Victorian artistic practice.[10]

Jones's exposure to eastern design on his travels and at the Crystal Palace had such a profound impact on his thought that he sought to codify ornament and colour in his influential book of 1856, *The grammar of ornament.* This aimed to provide an encyclopaedic history and geography of a world ornament, whose principles could be readily ascertained and emulated. *The grammar of ornament* functioned partly as a design manual, partly as an aesthetic treatise, and partly as a luxury art object. It furnished the lexicon for a new imperial culture then seeking to forge a modern style from oriental ornament.[11] The extensive use of the novel technology of chromolithography brought oriental colour to life in ways never before seen in the championing of chromatics on a mass scale.[12] Although he included a section on 'Hindoo' ornament, Jones's attention to colour is confined to his series of plates of artefacts from the Crystal Palace and/or South Kensington Museum all of which he believed showed the dexterous adjustment of detail to ground, often mediated by outlines of black, white or gold. His use of chromolithography demonstrates how modern chemical pigments and print technology were put in the service of imitating non-synthetic, hand-wrought fabrics.

Although Jones firmly advocated that Indian artefacts, fabrics in particular, should provide inspiration for the Schools of Design, he urged that they not be slavishly copied by British artists. Nevertheless, Indian and indeed ancient Egyptian and medieval Moorish colour were for Jones governed by strict rules – a point which he drove home in his South Kensington lecture 'An attempt to define the principles which should regulate the employment of colour in the decorative arts'.[13] Because England had been 'far outstripped by the nations of the East', the genealogy and underlying principles of colour had to be excavated from what Britons termed 'The Orient'. In eastern nations 'the ornaments on a mummy case are analogous with those of the Egyptian temple … It is different with ourselves, we have no principles, no unity' due to the effects of the division of labour, the result being 'novelty without beauty or beauty without intelligence'.[14] To combat this woeful status quo, Jones outlined a set of 'Propositions' which could be made nationally available as guides to the employment of colour in the decorative arts and architecture. These underlying 'Propositions' foreground the role of colour as a guide to form; the use of colour on flat or rounded, high or low surfaces; the balance of tones and the importance of primaries drawn from George Field's *Chromatography* (1835) and Michel Eugene Chevreul's law of simultaneous contrast (1839).

Jones encouraged the British government to purchase as many of the Indian textiles on display at the Crystal Palace as possible, because he believed that they could serve as 'fruitful lessons' for both the cultivated mind of the art critic, and provide much needed inspiration for the art student. Due to the strong system undergirding Indian art and design, Jones argued:

> It would be desirable that we should be made acquainted with the manner in which the education of eastern artists, the management of colour is made so perfect. It is most probable that they work only from tradition and a highly endowed natural instinct for which all eastern nations have ever been remarkable.[15]

If colour in India and Britain were governed by underlying principles then it could be learned, disciplined and possibly replicated and therefore in turn harnessed for industrial art in a way that was intrinsically bound up with the imperial project. There was, however, a tension between replication and intuition (the 'natural instinct' identified by Jones) that remained unresolved between art, art writing and pedagogy in the period this essay discusses, and which I address in more detail below.

Jones's elevation of ornament in relation to colour in Indian design would be partially eclipsed by anxieties surrounding the supposed decline in the quality of South Asian art – which was attributed both to the colonial administration and to a far more sinister discourse on cultural degeneracy epitomised by John Ruskin's 1858–59 lectures published as *The two paths*. Throughout his career Ruskin advocated an idealised chivalric imperialism that vilified modern, industrialised, democratic or mass warfare. Given his hostile views of modernity and modern imperialism in particular, which included art, it would at first appear that Ruskin, like Owen Jones, might admire eastern colour. However, colour for Ruskin occupies a complex and contradictory space in his voluminous writings as can be seen here:

> Observe how in the oriental mind a peculiar seriousness is associated with this attribute of the love of colour; a seriousness rising out of repose and out of the depth and breadth of the imagination, as contrasted with the activity and consequent capability of surprise and of laughter characteristic of the western mind: as a man on a journey must look to his step always and view things narrowly and quickly while one at rest may command a wider view though an unchanging one from which the pleasure he receives must be one of contemplation rather than amusement or surprise. Whenever the pure oriental spirit manifests itself definitely, I believe its work is serious.[16]

During the Indian Uprising of 1857–58 colour came to be treated by Ruskin as a scapegoat. Precisely because it was treated as a scapegoat, Ruskin hoped that the purging of Indian colour (or at least its vilification) would assist in the formation of a more pacific British empire. In response to this political and military crisis, Ruskin delivered his lecture 'The deteriorative power of conventional art over nations' in January 1858 at the South Kensington Museum (later published in *The two paths*).[17] The lecture targeted an audience of South Kensington sympathisers in order to rebuke both Jones's colonial liberalism for its futility, and all Indians from time immemorial for their 'atrocities' carried out during the Uprising.[18] For Ruskin, the Indian objects used for teaching at the Museum may have demonstrated 'subtle design'. But design when viewed through the South Kensington agenda of surface abstraction ran the risk of negating moral responsibility, as it far too easily 'attache[d] itself with the same intensity and the same success to the service of superstition, of pleasure or cruelty'.[19] Pleasure and degeneracy, Ruskin argued, reigned over the rightful search for truth – which was all too clear from the display of despicable Indian art in the South Kensington Museum:

> [In t]he models set before you in this institution and in the others established throughout the kingdom for the teaching of design there are I suppose none in their kind more admirable than the decorated works of India. They are, indeed in all materials capable of colour ... almost inimitable in their delicate application of divided hue ... it attaches itself with the same intensity and with the same success to the service of superstition, of pleasure or of cruelty.[20]

For Ruskin, Indians produce much subtle and seemingly beautiful art. But it is, he believes, degraded and unnatural: 'out of the ivory palace comes treachery, cruelty, cowardice, idolatry, bestiality – whatever else is fruitful is the work of Hell'.[21] At this time, colour was also fast becoming a source of pathological and evolutionary anxiety on other epistemological fronts. The question 'what is colour doing to the subject?', especially to the colonial and colonised subject, was asked with renewed purpose post 1857.[22]

Colour, colonial art schools and the limits of 'liberty'

'Indian colour', through the inculcation of its 'laws', as envisioned by the South Kensington collective, could and did become a colonising device.[23] But even in and beyond colonial art schools, colour could become the site of interdiction, especially when related to the relationship between pedagogy and what colonial officials deemed to be 'liberty'.[24] Liberty in the colony has been much debated by postcolonial theorists who have taken to task the translation of British political principles to the nineteenth-century colony. In colonial India, the purpose in articulating the principle of liberty was to specify the conditions under which, as Mehta puts it, 'the maximization of utility' which could be realised as 'the ultimate indicator of progress'.[25] These ideas of progress Mehta and Gauri Viswanathan have located in relation to the formation of a hybrid pedagogical system which was torn between an Orientalist and an Anglicist position (variously advocated by Bentham, Mill and Macaulay).[26] On the one hand colonial educationalists wanted to reform the Indian education system through the implementation of English utilitarian values; on the other hand they also valued the importance of 'reviving' Sanskrit. Mehta in particular makes the case that liberty (in relation to liberalism) did not contract the project of empire: they were deeply implicated in one another. These debates were also played out in the colonial art school in the art of drawing and copying from European plaster casts as Partha Mitter has shown.[27] I want to suggest that such debates are most prescient in relation to colour in the colonial art school, the dyer's vat and the colonial prison. Unlike drawing, colour could not be so easily taught.

Colour blurred the boundaries between art and industry, art and craft. It also draws attention to the difficulty in translating English notions of liberty to the colony. As supplement, colour in imperial pedagogy operated as a malleable space to be tactically revealed and concealed.[28] Because it was seen to both be governed by and to exceed the laws for art laid out in colonial manuals, colour draws attention to the tensions between the colonial Orientalist and Anglicist positions. It was seen as ancient, and also as a critical tool in the promotion of Indian-produced goods both in South Asia and overseas. Supposedly freed from rigid laws, it could act as a space for experimentation. But as a space for experimentation it could also threaten to undermine the British colonial project relating to art and industry. Supposedly a space ungoverned by rigid laws where Indian artisans and art school students could experiment, colour also became the space for the denigration of both archaic practices and the introduction of modern dyeing techniques and pigments. The rhetoric of liberty in the colony is thus seemingly undermined by an increasingly tight colonial grip on the production of pigments, colour harmonies and crafts. But I will suggest that colour in relation to these colonial debates on liberty also became a space for subaltern resistance.

Informed by his predilection for Indian artefacts in relation to a broader, liberalist/imperial agenda, Owen Jones and his fellow South Kensington instructor, Superintendent of the Department of Practical Art Richard Redgrave, tried to systematise colour in publications that became integral to the British National Course of Instruction.[29] Redgrave played an extremely active role in the pedagogical agenda of the Department of Practical Art (known as the Department of Science and Art from 1853), where he devised a system of art instruction for its schools that included courses in drawing, painting, modelling and composition in design.[30] Nearly the entire DSA course focussed on drawing; only at the final stage, which advanced to theory, design and ornament, could colour be approached and even then it had to be carefully monitored. Redgrave's *An elementary manual on colour* (1853), which relied heavily on Jones, Chevreul and David Brewster's *Optics*, admitted that pigments could only very imperfectly represent the primaries as viewed by the human eye.[31] Redgrave also concluded that laws of colours can never be transferred to art and design with complete satisfaction.[32] His law-driven abstracting ornament did possess its own 'character'; it had to be imbibed with 'fitness', 'proportion' and 'harmony' – a combination that would eventually lead to 'repose'.

But how would this fascination with 'repose' inform Indian and colonial design, especially given the violent contradictions or at least the perceived ambivalence of the colony?[33] Art schools in India modified the National Course of Instruction in favour of what they perceived to be the exigencies of the local status quo. Perhaps in response to the demands of the Bengali elite who made up the majority of the Calcutta School (or his own ambition to break free from South Kensington), the Principal of the School, Henry Locke, shied away from Redgrave's emphasis on industrial design, geometry and abstract ornament in favour of lessons in painting, lithography and photography, which he saw as a more adequate basis for teaching fine as opposed to applied art. Clearly within this specific colonial context there was perceived to be a stark division between what constituted fine art and industry. This division has as much to do with the attempted rejection of the South Kensington curriculum as with the intense rivalry between art school administrators. Locke wanted the Calcutta Art School to resemble more an art academy and less a school of design.[34] Alexander Hunter, Principal of the Madras Art School, initially adopted the South Kensington curriculum and also sent the works of his students for perusal by Forbes Royle and Redgrave in London. But he favoured a pedagogical model that was far closer to the master–apprentice ethic, stating that the 'system of instruction followed in the schools of art in England ... is not quite suited to the requirements of our schools in India'.[35] As well as establishing the Madras Art School, Hunter sponsored the formation of an Industrial College with which the art school would later be amalgamated under the aegis of the government to form the School of Industrial Arts (1852). As an arts administrator Hunter clearly held pan-Indian ambitions, which sought to promote what he understood to be the championing of artisanal-based industry. Unlike Locke, he did not perceive a stark division between art and industry. He acted as government consultant for the newly formed J. J. School of Art in Bombay and he sent several of his students as instructors to the art schools in Jaipur and Calcutta, as well as dispatching advisors trained at his Madras School to work in Lahore and Lucknow, and to oversee craft production in eleven colonial jails.[36] The Madras Art School functioned as the hub in a network of colonial artistic projects in such a way that it 'played an equal if not greater role than South Kensington in shaping the early history of colonial art education' in India.[37]

In Europe, the poor quality of Indian art schools goods at the Paris Exhibition 1878 drew gasps of horror from worried publics. This display of shoddy goods signified as an index of the 'decadent' and 'impoverished' nature of South Asian visual culture under British colonial policy; it elicited a petition from leading art designers and administrators who protested against the further production of such third rate objects.[38] Five years later the government of India drew up a series of 'Resolutions on Museums and Exhibitions', which dwelt on the improvement of museums through trade and the development of commerce in art manufactures. Totally ignoring the issue of pedagogy, the primary resolution highlighted the need for trade museums and a system of uniform numbering of collections at local, provincial and presidential museums.[39] But the government had to concede that its project was 'likely to involve excessive interference and supervision'.[40] The influence that the museum 'would thus exercise over an industrial art would be the indirect one of excluding articles of bad design or workmanship from its collection'.[41] Whilst the Secretary of State for India believed that the 'presidency or provincial museum ought ... to be allowed to grow up gradually', he expressed unease concerning the role of art schools and their officials.[42]

In 1893 the government of India attempted to abolish the art schools for serving no purpose – a policy that was vehemently challenged by officials from these institutions at the Museums Conference, Lahore the following year.[43] As a retort, the Arts and Museums Committee which convened at Lahore 'unanimously agreed that one of the chief objects of every museum should be the preservation of every good example of the art of the past and that such specimens would prove the surest guide to the native workmen of today'.[44] It strongly opposed the imposition of a transregional standard of taste, stressing the primacy of locality. Although several art schools made fundamental changes to their structure and curricula, the sense of impending crisis was never far away.[45] E. B. Havell, former Principal of the Calcutta Art School, conjectured that the innately *un-artistic* nature of colonial governance was to blame:

> In Europe nobody expected Government to be artistic, but in India things are different. The people of India are an artistic people or they were before English men began to educate them and they believed that the Government was artistic. Sometimes even the Government itself believed that it was and that made matters much worse. The real question is whether the British people individually, collectively and administratively are an artistic example to the people of India.[46]

In spite of his own extensive reforms of its curriculum, Havell complained that the Calcutta Art School resembled a 'fourth rate provincial art school in Europe thirty years ago'.[47] And colour was also implicated, as can be seen quite plainly in art administrator George Birdwood's handbook to the British Indian Section of the 1878 Paris Universal Exhibition (1878).[48] Although a leading figure in colonial art pedagogy, Birdwood admitted to the difficulties in discovering 'the secret of the harmonies of the bloom of

Indian textiles, even with the aid of Chevreul's prismatic scale'.[49] In his eyes:

> The Government of India thinking only of how to effect small economies, hit upon the plan of using their jails for the supply of the now lucrative trade in carpets ... The examples exhibited in 1851 ... gained their reputation for the originality and great beauty of their designs, the harmony of their colouring and their special fitness for the houses of the cultivated, the wealthy and the great ... But what did the Government of India do? They handed this great historical craft, this glorious art over to the Thugs in the jails and the Thugs strangled it.[50]

In his analysis of dyeing in Lahore Gaol, Birdwood complained that 'the dyes with which they are coloured are hideous and the arrangement of the colours is harsh and inharmonious ... compounded, I could believe, out of the jail medical stores'.[51]

Many of the brightly coloured Indian rugs shown and sold in Britain were the products of this sinister colonial project. From 1862 these carpets, which emulated the patterns and colours of those previously celebrated at the world's fairs, were transferred to the responsibility of prisoners in the jails and bazaar factories across India.[52] The prison then became a dominant calibrating mechanism for informal labour; jail activities proved critical to the anti-economic rubric of 'tradition' which occupied and shaped the infrastructure of the colonial economy.[53] Clearly the colonial prison as the site of art/industrial production further underscores the peculiar hybridisation and the limits of the English rhetoric of art and liberty in the colony. While the colonial art school failed to impose its ideas of the free artisan who could manipulate colour in the advancement of colonial trade, the failure of colour in the prison (as seen in the over saturated, poorly made pigments and anilines) further emphasises the colonial abandonment of the rhetoric of liberty. Nevertheless I would like to suggest that there are mutterings of subaltern resistance in relation to colonial attempts to 'reform' colour regarding the entanglement of art and industry. This can most clearly perceived when we consider the figure of the dyer.

The *figure* of the dyer: art versus industry?

Central to this rubric of tradition were dyes and what I term the 'figure' of the dyer. I am referring here to 'figure' in relation to Lyotard's idea of the figure as that intensely visual space which cannot be reduced to discourse.[54] The idea of the figure refers to the creation of a domain which is less concerned with producing meaning than as the sentient space where intensities can potentially be felt. Like the subaltern, the figure suggests a silent and potentially revolutionary or at least disruptive agency with which to challenge the vexed art–industry agenda of the colonial state.

The insertion of the figure *qua* the subaltern here with an emphasis on the dyer can allow us to explore a certain unspoken agency that enables us to read colonial accounts of colour and labour for their gaps and fissures. The figure of the subaltern dyer and the contested practice of dyeing in India further complicates the colonial pedagogical debate on the relationship between art and industry.

By the 1880s dyes regularly featured at international and India-based regional exhibitions, as each district was made by the government to investigate what might be its 'singular' cartographic palette. In his report for the Lahore Central Museum following the first major exhibition in Upper India, Punjab, 1884, art school administrator Baden Henry Baden Powell concluded:

> In common with the inhabitants of lower India [the artist in the Punjab] has an instinctive appreciation of colour and though without any knowledge of the principles which should regulate its use, is often more than happy in his combinations than the educated workmen of Europe. His colour is often exaggerated but it is always warm and rich and fearless.[55]

In spite of his call for technological and pedagogical improvements, what is missing from Baden Powell's account is the growing sense of urgency associated with what colonial officials believed to be the dying art of dyeing, and the need to train artists and craftsmen in relation to correct colour harmonies.

Debates centring on the imperial nostalgia for the fragile status of colour production and perception were transacted in newspapers, official reports, colonial art schools, gazetteers, craft monographs, laboratories and museum displays which sought to discipline, politicise and to resuscitate colour. From being strangely fetish-like, almost disembodied and yet instinctive, colour and its absence or paucity became a major colonial preoccupation. Even jail carpets, otherwise so prolific and commercially viable in Britain during the past two decades, had not been sent to the 1884 exhibition from the North West Provinces, precisely because they were too saturated with aniline dyes – anilines being modern European and considered 'garish' by colonialists as opposed to vegetable dyes.[56]

The resolution to undertake a pan-South Asia survey on dyeing resulted from the 1894 Lahore Art Conference where the government agreed to establish a committee that would not only look into dyeing practices across India, but which also aimed to use the reorganisation of the Madras Art School as the space for experimenting with the reform of colour training and production. The committee wanted a separate dyeing school which would be equipped with dye-houses and a chemical laboratory and which would introduce the technologies of European dyeing.[57] It is likely that the government aimed to collate, to distil, to organise and to assemble this data in the hope of formatting an imperial standard for colour.[58]

But what does it mean to map, to survey, to seek out colour? What does it mean for colonialists to see or not see colour? Some of these men were perhaps familiar with the art of dyeing or at least they had studied textiles; others were not.[59] In each designated region the District surveyor (or appointed official) aimed to identify the economic and ethnographic conditions for the decline, survival or proliferation of dyeing by mapping out the colours favoured in their locality. This allowed – at least in theory – the government of India to construct a colour-saturated map of the subcontinent – to study its contours and to try to fathom its (dis)harmonies. Chromatics, once associated with the swatch of fabric or the pages of Jones's *Grammar of ornament*, now become literal patches on the pink background of the imperial map.

The most thorough research conducted on colour was carried out by 'vernacular informants'. Colour is not just an article of commerce but the key to a rich and varied worldview or series of worldviews. N. N. Banerji, Assistant Director of Land Records and Agriculture in Bengal, who became Bengal's dye investigator, highlighted the prominence of *lac*, *tumeric* and *safflower* in this region, which underscores the importance of colour in spices, bazaars, dress, personal adornment and cooking. He listed, in order of preference, the colours he had found to be favoured in Bengal – indigo, light blue/grey, red, yellow, orange, green, purple, chocolate, gold (*sonali*) and *asmani* – sky blue. In spite of this variety Banerji concluded that in most of Lower Bengal coloured cloth was seldom, if ever worn.[60] Clearly he linked colour here to dyeing rather than to the subtle natural gradation of tone in spun thread. Observing that most weavers in Bengal were Muslim, Banerji conjectured that along with prostitutes they seemed to show the greatest demand and liking for coloured cloth. In his account colour hovers on the geographical and social margins of Banerji's economically directed agenda as something transgressive, perhaps even taboo.

Colour, then, could be harnessed to religion, caste and profession: to substantiate these claims, Banerji included information on dyers' caste gleaned from previous district reports and the 1891 Census which he included alongside a series of tables detailing the prices and types of cloth available in Bengal and Bihar.[61] Banerji, like other colour investigators, was here taking a lead from *The people of India*, the extensive photographic project by John Forbes Watson (Reporter on the Products of India at the India Office, London) and John William Kaye, in an attempt to fashion ethnographic insight into the lives, appearance and characters of the elusive figure of the dyer. Watson had initiated a sample museum of fabrics and the Industrial Survey of India, thus demonstrating his professional investment in colour. He reported that dyers were mostly Hindu worshippers of Devi or Bhowani or else they were Sunni sheikhs. While there was 'little to remark' in relation to their habits and customs and he considered them to be generally peaceful and industrious, Watson said they had 'in many localities a reputation for intemperance and it is certain that the use of ardent spirits is not forbidden to them and they have too an indifferent character for morality'.[62] District officers following Watson's lead classified dyers as being very poor, working only on a local, ad hoc basis, and further restricted in their access to regional and long distance markets by their exceedingly low caste status.

The results of the colonial surveys of Assam and Bengal on dyeing suggested that there was no separate dyeing caste and that very few people wore colour at all.[63] Overall, colonial officials voiced disappointment at what they perceived to be the vernacular lack of interest in dyestuffs. How was this possible, given the 'intuitive' talent for colour harmony previously seen at the world's fairs? James Fraser's 1896 account of dyeing in Burma suggested that colour is both socially abject and associated with a backward, isolated, tribal community that is shunned by mainstream society: colour is fit only for 'the savage mind'.[64]

Against this colonial archival drive for authenticity, there are glimpses of the dyer as subaltern. During his tour of India, Arts and Crafts supporter and Advisor to the government of India Thomas Wardle complained that native dyers were unwilling to adapt to changing market conditions; he cited the instance of when he tried to have a piece of cloth stained red, whereupon the artisan:

> Made a very respectful salaam but said very firmly, 'Tell the Sahib that I and my forefathers have dyed blue for thousands of years and that I will dye it only blue. No monetary inducement or the promised information on the processes of dyeing other colours is of any avail' and so I brought two yards of white calico to England undyed.[65]

Vernacular colour production was believed to be infused with magic that colonial officials feared. Wardle objected to the order to remove his shoes at an indigo vat in Lahore, but nonetheless did so for fear of the effects of *nazar* – the evil eye associated with dyeing.[66]

The figure of the dyer's refusal to act as mimic men infuriated these officials: vernacular practice will not be colonised:[67]

> Any improvement in colour or production of a new one has been rather a happy accident than the outcome of the application of rules of chemistry and no better results can be expected till the properties of the various dyestuffs are investigated and the natives are taught how to turn them to practical use ... Until European capital is directed to this branch of industry there is no prospect of improvement.[68]

Indian 'intuition' only went so far; the industrial art of dyeing really needed an injection of European (industrially generated) capital to bring it up to scratch. Colour, through the agency of the vernacular dyer, refuses to speak to colonialism's demands – so much so that it is colonial frustration which is by the end of the nineteenth century voiced from the archive:

'the only way to get native workmen to do anything is to shut them up in a jail!'[69] The colonial rhetoric of liberty which had initially been so pressing at the world's fair of 1851 is by now well and truly undermined and displaced. Indian dyers' resistance to a whole-hearted embrace of the tenets of colonial pedagogy reveals the flaws and frustrations at the centre of the British imperial promotion of art and industry.

Conclusion

In an exemplary study of the role of colour in Western modernism, Briony Fer notes that dreams of a truly universal and scientific colour have often been set against a sensual utopia of chromatic excess, but in reality the oppositions were never so clear-cut: 'the desire for a system often led to the most sensual, impure results just as the myth of colour's much vaunted freedom from rule-bound convention has often produced the most formulaic and exhausted of modernist experiments.'[70] As Fer here proposes, the work of colour in modernity turns out to be *counter-intuitive*.[71] Subaltern, supplementary, the material and aesthetic embodiment of excess and menace, whose technological aporia threaten permanent entrapment and alienation, Indian colour offers us a subtle but sometimes radical path to view anew what might be the limits of colonial mimicry. Subaltern in its supplementarity, colour in India transgressed the boundaries of colonial representation.

This transgression of colonial representation is perhaps best captured in my epigraph drawn from Ruskin: 'it has been an actual necessity in order to obtain power of colouring that a nation should be half savage ... No one can colour anywhere except the Hindus'.[72] This essay has attempted to show how such loaded claims can be unpacked and read against the grain. Colour can be subaltern in a number of ways. In line with the agenda of the Subaltern Studies Collective it can be viewed as mutterings in the archive, attested to by numerous colonialist monographs on dyeing that anxiously sought out its presence, or by the more obdurate figure of the dyer who sometimes refused to do the staining work of empire. The subaltern also merged with ideas of the supplement, by which I mean colour added to whilst supplanting principles of British design, especially in relation to textiles and teaching manuals.

The subalterity of colour is very much apparent at world's fairs and in the pedagogical agenda implemented at colonial art schools. In their very different ways, Owen Jones, Richard Redgrave and John Ruskin all aimed to explain and to regulate what they believed to be 'Indian colour'. In resisting colonial representation, colour's subaltern agency frustrated the imperial promise of reforming industrial design through the lessons of Indian art and craft. As seen in relation to world's fairs, colonial art schools and prisons, the divisions between art and industry were repeatedly complicated by colour. Colour straddles and disturbs the boundaries between tradition and modernity. The figure of the subaltern dyer used almost as much aniline as 'traditional' vegetable dyes, sometimes even combining them. In art schools colour seemed to elude the more exigent discussions of drawing and design. Unruly and refusing to become entirely rule-bound, colour spills out of conventional boundaries, repositioning the relationship between art and industry.

Notes

1 Cook and Wedderburn (eds.) *The works of John Ruskin*, vol. 10, p. 153.
2 Spivak and Guha (eds.) *Selected subaltern studies.*
3 Derrida, 'The dangerous supplement', p. 145.
4 Royle, in *Official descriptive and illustrated catalogue*, p. 936.
5 Royle, 'The arts and manufactures of India', p. 387 notes that very few instances of Indian paintings were on display, the exception being miniatures on talc from Delhi and Trichinopoly which featured dresses, manners and customs and which 'do not attract much attention' although some from Delhi 'are very beautiful, resemble enamels and are frequently worn in brooches and bracelets'.
6 Royle, in *Official descriptive and illustrated catalogue*, p. 936; Wyatt, *The industrial arts of the nineteenth century*, p. 553.
7 See the selection of press cuttings on the Great Exhibition, 4 volumes, National Art Library, London.
8 See Wilkinson, *On colour.*
9 Field, *Chromatography.*
10 Denis, 'The educated eye and the industrial hand'; Department of Science and Art, *Introduction to the drawing book of the school of design.*
11 Jones, *The grammar of ornament.*
12 Ferry, 'Printing the Alhambra'.
13 Jones, 'An attempt to define the principles', pp. 253–301.
14 *Ibid.*, p. 256.
15 *Ibid.*, pp. 271–2.
16 Ruskin, *The stones of Venice*, vol. 2, pp. 162–3.
17 Cook and Wedderburn (eds.) *The works of John Ruskin*, vol. 16, p. 310.
18 The Museum was established in May 1852 at Marlborough House, London. Its collections were largely objects purchased from the Great Exhibition with the assistance of the DSA and included numerous saris, daggers, spice boxes and rosewater bottles.
19 Cook and Wedderburn (eds.) *The works of John Ruskin*, vol. 16, p. 314.
20 *Ibid.*, p. 261.
21 *Ibid.*, p. 265.
22 Massumi, 'Too blue', 180.
23 Barringer, 'The South Kensington Museum and the mid-Victorian moment'.
24 Viswanathan, *Masks of conquest.*
25 *Ibid.*
26 Mehta, *Liberalism and empire*; Viswanathan, *Masks of conquest.*
27 Mitter *Art and nationalism in colonial India, 1850–1922*, chapters 2 and 3.
28 Mehta, *Liberalism and empire*, p. 14.
29 Redgrave's 'National Course of Instruction' was devised and delivered in 1852 and lasted until 1887. He sent a report on art education to India on the request of the

colonial state. In 1857 Hunter adopted the curriculum at the Madras Art School; Hunter, *Correspondence*.

30 Redgrave made regular contributions to the annual reports of the DPA and the DSA and Cole's *Journal of Design*. He was also working with Cole, Pugin and Owen Jones on the Design Purchase Committee selecting objects from the Great Exhibition for the School of Design with the aid of a government grant.

31 Redgrave, *An elementary manual on colour*, p. i.

32 *Ibid.*, p. 7: 'explanations of the laws of harmony are best with many difficulties'. He followed Field by stating that 'to satisfy the eye and to produce harmony of colour, the presence of all the three primaries is required'.

33 Trevelyan proposed the idea of art schools in India in 1853.

34 Mitter, *Art and nationalism in colonial India, 1850–1922*, chapter 2.

35 Hunter, *Correspondence*, p. 13.

36 Dewan, 'Crafting knowledge' notes that the Madras School of Art's influence extended to Travancore, Bangalore, Nagpur, Jubbulpur, Sri Lanka, Mooltan, Murree, Roorkee in addition to Lucknow and Lahore. She also records its influence on the crafts training in the jails at Coimbatore, Bangalore, Bombay, Surat, Mangalore, Pune, Bassimin Berar, Secundra, Assam and Vizinagram.

37 *Ibid.*, p. 89. Hunter's successor, the architect Henry Chisholm, called for the school's closure – which was declined by the government of India.

38 This massive petition was supported by William Morris, Walter Crane and Burne-Jones amongst others.

39 Department of Revenue, Agriculture and Commerce (hereafter DRAC), government of India, 'Resolution on Museums and Exhibitions', 14 March 1883.

40 DRAC January 1884 part B no. 199.

41 *Ibid.*

42 *Ibid.*, no. 198.

43 'Papers relating to the maintenance of schools of art in India as state institutions'.

44 DRAC January 1884 part B no. 199.

45 Burns, 'Functions of schools of art in India', 631.

46 Havell in *Ibid.*, 644.

47 Havell, 'Art administration in India', 123.

48 Birdwood, *Handbook*, p. 116 on the house of Vincent Robinson & co 'the colours introduced are not suited to the floor of a room particularly the green even if they are harmoniously blended'.

49 Birdwood, *Handbook*, p. 120.

50 *Ibid.*, p. 113–14.

51 *Ibid.*, p. 123.

52 Ian Bennett, *Jail birds: an exhibition of nineteenth-century carpets* (London, 1987); Swaminathan, 'Prison as factory'; see also the Asia and Africa Collections, British Library: Judicial Files P/206/65, 657–8.

53 For a fascinating discussion of this case see Mathur, 'Living ethnological exhibits'.

54 Lyotard, *Discourse, Figure*.

55 Baden Powell, *Handbook of the manufactures and arts of the Punjab*, p. 355.

56 Watt, 'Guide to ethnological models and exhibits', p. 245.

57 Thurston, *Monograph on the cotton fabric industry of the Madras presidency*, pp. 40–1. Whilst in favour of the reform of dyeing, Thurston did prefer indigenous dyes.

58 In 1875 Thomas Wardle submitted a report to the Secretary of State calling for more information on dyeing in India. See *Selections of DRAC Dyes and Dyeing*, 1888–190 OIR/V/27/600/16 vol. 2 Pt 1 no. 3; 'Products and trade: dyestuffs' IOR/V/27/624, 1848–1928. Manuscripts records in the India Office Collection, British Library.

59 Ramaswamy, *The goddess and the nation*, introduction.

60 Banerji, *Dyes and dyeing in Bengal*, p. 36. See also *Handbook of commercial products Calcutta, 1982–7* contained in Dyeing IOR/V/27/600/28/6, IOR/V/27/600/29/16; India Office Records, British Library.
61 Banerji, *Dyes and dyeing in Bengal*, p. 3.
62 Watson and Kaye, *The people of India*, p. 352.
63 Duncan, *Assam monograph on dyes and dyeing*, p. 2; Mukherji, *Art manufactures of India*, p. 348.
64 Fraser, *Account of dyes and dyeing in Burma*, p. 1.
65 Wardle, *Tissue or textile printing as an art*, p. 56.
66 *Ibid.*, p. 88.
67 For instance Fawcett's Bombay report quotes H. K. Taravia of the Victoria Jubilee Technical Institute, Bombay who blamed the 'neglect of the Indian dyer' for not using enough soap and salts to produce a longevical uniformity of colour; Fawcett, *A Monograph on dyes and dyeing in Bombay*, p. 10.
68 Fraser, *Account of dyes and dyeing in Burma*, p. 17.
69 Baden Powell, 'On some difficulties of art manufactures', 37.
70 Fer, *Color chart*, p. 28.
71 *Ibid.*
72 Cook and Wedderburn (eds.) *The works of John Ruskin*, vol. 10, p. 153.

Bibliography

Baden Powell, B. H. *Handbook of the manufactures and arts of the Punjab* (Lahore, 1872)

Baden Powell, B. H. 'On some difficulties of art manufactures', *Journal of Indian Art and Industry*, 1 (1886)

Bagal, J. C. *History of the Government College of Art and Crafts* (Calcutta, 1964)

Banerji, N. N. *Dyes and dyeing in Bengal* (Calcutta, 1896)

Barringer, T. 'The South Kensington Museum and the mid-Victorian moment', in *Victoriana: the style of empire, selected proceedings of the 4th annual Decorative Arts Institute* (Toronto, 1996)

Bennett, I. *Jail birds: an exhibition of nineteenth-century carpets* (London, 1987)

Birdwood, George, C. M. *Paris Universal Exhibition of 1878: handbook to the British Indian Section* (London and Paris, 1878)

Breckenridge, C. 'The aesthetics and politics of colonial collecting: India at the world's fairs', *Comparative Studies in Society and History*, 31:2 (1989)

Burns, C. L. 'Functions of schools of art in India', *Journal of the Royal Society of Arts*, 57:2952 (18 June 1909), 629–41

Codell, J. 'Vulgar India from nabobs to nationalism: imperial reversals and the mediation of art', in S. D. Bernstein and E. B. Michie (eds.) *Victorian vulgarity: taste in verbal and visual culture* (London, 2009), pp. 223–40

Cole, H. 'The function of the Science and Art Department', bound with *Introductory addresses on the Science and Art Department and the South Kensington Museum* (London, 1857)

Cook, E. T. and A. Wedderburn (eds.) *The works of John Ruskin* (39 volumes, London, 1903–12)

Denis, R. C. 'The educated eye and the industrial hand' (PhD dissertation, University of London, 1995)

Department of Practical Art, *Catalogue of the articles of ornamental art in the museum of the department* (London, 1853)

Department of Science and Art, *Introduction to the drawing book of the school of design* (London, 1854)

Department of Science and Art, *Instructions in art: directions for establishing and conducting schools of art* (London, 1865)
Derrida, J. 'The dangerous supplement', in J. Derrida, *Of grammatology* (Baltimore, 1976)
Dewan, D. 'Crafting knowledge and the knowledge of crafts: art education, colonialism and the Madras school of arts in nineteenth-century South Asia (PhD dissertation, University of Minnesota, 2001)
Duncan, W. A. *Assam monograph on dyes and dyeing* (Calcutta, 1896)
Duncan, W. A. *Monograph on dyes and dyeing in Assam* (Shillong, 1896)
Fawcett, C. G. H. *A monograph on dyes and dyeing in the Bombay presidency* (Bombay, 1896)
Fer, B. *Color chart: reinventing color 1950 to today* (New York, 2008)
Ferry, K. 'Printing the Alhambra: Owen Jones and chromolithography', *Architectural History*, 46 (2003), 175–88
Field, G. *Chromatography: a treatise on colours and pigments and of their powers in painting* (London, 1835)
Flores, C. A. *Owen Jones: design, ornament, architecture and theory in the age of transition* (New York, 2006)
Fraser, J. D. *Account of dyes and dyeing in Burma* (Calcutta, 1896)
Gage, John. *George Field and his circle* (London, 1988)
Giles, F. H. *Note on dyes and the process of dyeing in Karenni* (Rangoon, 1896)
Handbook of commercial products Calcutta, 1982–7 contained in Dyeing IOR/V/27/600/28/6, IOR/V/27/600/29/16; India Office Records, British Library
Havell, E. B. 'Art administration in India', *Journal of the Royal Society of Arts*, 58 (1910), 274–98
Holder, E. *Monograph on dyes and dyeing in the Madras presidency* (Madras, 1896)
Hunter, A. *Correspondence on the subject of the extension of art education in different parts of India* (Madras, 1867)
Jobbins, W. *Papers relating to the maintenance of the schools of art as state institutions* (Lahore, 1896)
Jones, O. 'An attempt to define the principles which should regulate the employment of colour in the decorative arts', *Lectures on the Great Exhibition* (volume 2, London, 1852), pp. 263–300
Jones, O. *The grammar of ornament* (London, 1856)
Keyser, B. W. 'Science and sensibility: chemistry and the aesthetics of colour in the early nineteenth century', *Colour Research and Application*, 21:3 (1996), 169–79
Kriegel, L. 'Narrating the subcontinent in 1851: India at the Crystal Palace', in L. Purbrick (ed.) *The Great Exhibition of 1851* (Manchester, 2009), pp. 146–78
Leveson, H. G. A. *Note on dyes and dyeing in the South Shan states* (Rangoon, 1896)
Leveson, H. G. and F. H. Giles, *Notes on the dyes and process of dyeing in Karenni* (Calcutta, 1896)
Liotard, L. *Memorandum on dyes of Indian growth and production* (Calcutta, 1881)
Lyotard, J. *Discourse, Figure*, trans. Antony Hudek and Mary Lydon (Paris, 1974; London, 2011)
Massumi, B. 'Too blue: colour patch for an expanded empiricism', *Cultural Studies*, 14:2 (2000), 177–226
Mathur, S. 'Living ethnological exhibits: the case of 1886', *Cultural Anthropology*, 15:4 (2000), 492–524
McCann, D. *Dyes and tans of Bengal* (Calcutta, 1883)
McGowan, A. *Crafting the nation in colonial India* (New York, 2009)
Mehta, U. *Liberalism and empire: a study of 19th-century British liberal thought* (Chicago, 1999)

Mitter, P. *Much maligned monsters: a history of western reactions to Indian art* (Oxford, 1977)
Mitter, P. *Art and nationalism in colonial India, 1850–1922* (Cambridge, 1994)
Mukherji, T. N. *Art manufactures of India* (Calcutta, 1888)
'The Museum of Ornamental Art', *Spectator* (22 October 1853), p. 17
Official descriptive and illustrated catalogue to the Great Exhibition (London, 1851)
'Papers relating to the maintenance of Schools of Art in India as state institutions', in *Selections from the records of the government of India: Home Department*, no. 356 (Calcutta, 1898)
Ramaswamy, S. *The goddess and the nation: mapping mother India* (Durham, 2010)
Redgrave, R. *An elementary manual on colour … prepared for the use of students in the DSA* (London, 1853)
Robinson, J. 'The museum of ornamental art', *Art-Journal* (May 1855)
Royle, J. F. 'The arts and manufactures of India', in *Lectures on the results of the Great Exhibition* (volume 1, London, 1852)
Ruskin, J. *The stones of Venice* (London, 1888; London reprint, 2013)
'The school of ornamental art', *Art-Journal* (July 1852, 227–8
Selections of DRAC Dyes and Dyeing, 1888–190 OIR/V/27/600/16 vol. 2 Pt 1 no. 3; 'Products and trade: dyestuffs' IOR/V/27/624, 1848–1928 – manuscripts records in the India Office Collection, British Library
Sparkes, J. C. L. *Schools of art: their origin, history, work and influence* (London, 1884)
Spivak, G. and R. Guha (eds.) *Selected subaltern studies* (Delhi, 1988)
Swaminathan, S. 'Prison as factory: a study of jails manufactures in the Madras presidency', *Studies in History*, 11:1 (1995), 77–100
Tarapor, M. K. 'An art education in imperial India: the imperial schools of art', in K. Ballhatchet and D. Taylor (eds.) *Changing South Asia: city and culture* (London, 1984)
Thurston, E. *Monograph on the cotton fabric industry of the Madras presidency* (Madras, 1897)
Viswanathan, G. *Masks of conquest: literary study and British rule in India* (London, 1989)
Wardle, T. *Tissue or textile printing as an art* (London, 1890)
Watson, J. F. and J. W. Kaye. *The peoples of India: a series of photographic illustrations with descriptive letterpress of the races and tribes of India* (Bath, 2007)
Watt, G. 'Guide to ethnological models and exhibits shown in the Imperial Court', in *Empire of India: special catalogue of exhibits* (London, 1886), pp. 159–89
Wilkinson, J. G. *On colour and the necessity for a general diffusion of taste among all classes* (London, 1858)
Wyatt, Matthew Digby, *The industrial arts of the nineteenth century* (London, 1851–53)
Young, Paul. 'Carbon mere carbon: the Kohinoor, the Crystal Palace and the mission to make sense of British India', *Nineteenth-Century Contexts*, 29:4 (December, 2007), 343–58

13

Surface deceits: Owen Jones and John Ruskin on the ornament of the Alhambra

Lara Eggleton

Throughout the middle decades of the nineteenth century, Welsh-born designer-architect Owen Jones (1809–74) was instrumental in introducing the Alhambra palace to British audiences, and placing it at the centre of debates around the relative merits of domestic and foreign design traditions. A proponent of the design reform movement, his interest in ancient and medieval ornamental traditions led him to monuments in Italy and Greece and eventually to the Islamic fortress complex near Granada, Spain.[1] The Alhambra palaces date from the thirteenth and fourteenth centuries when they were home to the Nasrid dynasty, the last Muslim rulers of the region known as al-Andalus.[2] Conquered by the Catholic monarchs in 1492, their strategic location along a mountainous outcrop of the Sierra Nevada ensured that they remained remarkably well preserved, and throughout the eighteenth and nineteenth centuries their decorated halls and courtyards came to attract the attention of a great number of European artists, architects and antiquarians.[3] While many were enthusiastic about the site, Jones took an exceptionally strong interest in its patterns in plaster, ceramic and wood, which would come to profoundly influence his own design theory and practice. He admired the versatility and repeatability of Nasrid ornament, and saw within it a rich storehouse of organic and geometric forms that could be broken down and used within new designs. Subsequently, the art of the Alhambra became a familiar motif within the Department of Practical Art under the Board of Trade (called the Department of Science and Art from 1853).[4] It prominently featured in the London International Exhibition of 1851 and the Sydenham Crystal Palace of 1854, and was the main inspiration behind Jones's famous pattern book of 1856, *The grammar of ornament,* which was reprinted numerous times and circulated in design schools in Britain and abroad.[5]

Designers, critics and general audiences encountered the Alhambra's patterns through the technical language of Jones's schematic drawings, prints and architectural reproductions. The 'Moresque' style, as he called it, would also strongly influence his design and architectural practice, with elements making their way into patterns for wallpapers, textiles, book illustrations and biscuit tins. Not all would approve of this Oriental turn within British decoration, particularly within architectural circles where gothic or classically derived examples were preferred.[6] Among the critics of the Nasrid style, the prominent writer and polymath John Ruskin (1819–1900) would dismiss it as an inferior, derivative branch of a longer Arabic tradition. Following his appraisal of 'Arabian' ornament in *The stones of Venice* (1851–53), he made a point to exempt the art of the Alhambra in an appendix footnote:

> I do not mean what I have here said of the inventive power of the Arab to be understood as ... applying to the detestable ornamentation of the Alhambra (I have not seen the building itself, but Mr. Owen Jones, work may, I suppose, be considered as sufficiently representing it for all purposes of criticism). The Alhambra is no more characteristic of Arab work, than Milan Cathedral is of Gothic: it is a late building, a work of the Spanish dynasty in its last decline, and its ornamentation is fit for nothing but to be transferred to patterns of carpets or bindings of books, together with their marbling, and mottling, and other mechanical recommendations. The Alhambra ornament has of late been largely used in shop-fronts, to the no small detriment of Regent Street and Oxford Street.[7]

It is of significance that Ruskin's negative view of Nasrid art is based solely on his encounters with Jones's reproductions. This fact is often brought in to support a historicising narrative that pits Ruskin against Jones and the design reform group, often at the expense of exploring the nuances of their respective theories and bodies of work.[8] The tendency within recent scholarship to 'rescue' Jones from the shadows of his more recognised contemporaries such as Ruskin and A. W. N. Pugin arguably reinforces this polemic.[9] Rather than lingering on the differences between their positions (of which there are many), my aim here is to closely examine some of Jones's reproductions in relation to Ruskin's reflections on abstraction, in order to highlight a problem of representation at the core of the mid-nineteenth-century concerns about the moral value of ornament. Taking this art historical shift into account, it is possible to see Ruskin's objections to the Alhambra as both a direct response to Jones's mechanical translations (or more precisely, his use of synthetic mould-making and print-making technologies associated with industrial process), and the result of his growing distrust of the abstract in wider formal and philosophical terms. Ruskin's opposition to the Alhambra was not just a symptom of his Western-centrism, but emerged from contingent associations between theories of abstraction and Jones's commercial re-deployments of the Alhambra's design.

The historical implications of the pairing of 'world ornament' with industrial achievement at the mid-century have been explored by a number of scholars.[10] Mark Crinson has observed that the contention between Ruskin and the design reform group centred on links between 'the empire, the education of the designer and the role of art (whether conventionalised or naturalistic) within manufacturing', and was underpinned by disagreements about what constituted Islam, and its relative worth, within the context of International Exhibitions.[11] Richard Redgrave and Gustav Friedrich Waagen developed the idea of surface propriety in the 'False principles of design' exhibition at the Museum of Manufactures in 1852, and in 1854 Jones promoted the utilitarian potential of Islamic art (especially for the decoration of flat surfaces) in a series of lectures, his principles promptly adopted in Cole's Department of Practical Art. The resulting proliferation of rationalised patterns would cause Ruskin to intensify his Western-centric views and to articulate his criticisms from a position of racial and ethnic superiority. Believing that artists should be inspired only by the 'true' examples created by God and made visible within the natural world, he developed his own rationalist theory of architectural ornament, which linked the beautiful to permanent and unchanging principles of religion and morality.[12]

It is in relation to these theories of ornament and national character that Ruskin's mineralogical writings prove insightful. An avid collector of mineral and crystal specimens, he gave two public lectures on the subject in 1876, and wrote the peculiar *Ethics of the dust: ten lectures to little housewives on the elements of crystallization* in 1865, followed by a collection of mineralogical studies that he published in parts under the title of *Deucalion* between 1875 and 1883. They reveal his continued struggle to understand the 'right lined' in nature through the descriptive study of crystal and mineral formations, and to provide a metaphorical platform from which to explore the contours and dimensions of the human spirit. Marcia Pointon writes that geology and mineralogy were mediated both through his interest in ornament and also through his 'perception of historical and contemporary artifice'.[13] She explains that the character of rocks, and particularly the qualities of crystals, permitted Ruskin to 'conceptualise the inanimate world in human terms', thereby creating a 'poetics of mineralogy' that lay outside the confinements of orthodox Christianity and scientific naturalism.[14]

I here consider Ruskin's exploration of crystal formations in relation to his aversion to utilitarianism within artistic practice, of which the Alhambra became archetypal. In ordering and assigning value to the forms of the earth, Ruskin might be said to have shared Jones's desire to develop a universalising theory of form, even if it was this very tendency that led him to associate the art of eastern cultures with negative characteristics or behaviours. From this perspective, Jones's and Ruskin's very different responses to the ornament of the Alhambra do not represent a straightforward case of adverse tastes or open versus closed attitudes toward Oriental design or cultural difference; their views at times overlapped or became intertwined over notions of the representational and the abstract as they applied to decorative practice. While Ruskin's intolerance provides a strong foil to the so-called cosmopolitanism of Jones and the reformist circle, such a simplistic view of their political agendas overlooks the important role that industrial and commercial forces would play within cross-cultural interpretations of art and design, and the effects this would have on the methodologies of both.[15] These conditions help to explain how the Alhambra's patterns triggered multiple concerns for Ruskin, not only with regard to the increased visibility of a range of foreign traditions, but also in terms of the effects that industrialism would have on artistic practice. Jones's reproductions of the Alhambra were used to demonstrate the principles of ornamental 'fitness' (subservience to function), and 'conventionalisation' (the abstraction or stylisation of representational forms), as a direct response to the demands of commerce and industry. I argue that not only would this complicate Ruskin's conception of naturally inspired ornament, but it would also increasingly lead him to associate abstract forms with the perceived evils of mechanical production.

Before turning to the respective arguments of Jones and Ruskin on the underlying principles of nature and their relationship to ornamental production, I first provide an overview of Jones's reproductions of the Alhambra. I return to his Alhambra Court at the Sydenham Crystal Palace in the final section, where his reproduction of the *muqarnas* or 'stalactite' ceiling of one of the palace's original halls is shown to have particular relevance to the study of these philosophies of nature and ornament. The majority of this chapter, however, is dedicated to unpacking the complex and often contradictory aspects of their thinking around the relative merits of representation and abstraction more generally, and considering how this impacted on their understanding of Islamic art. At different times the ornament of the Alhambra proves problematic to both their approaches, resulting in a series of mistranslations and subsequent misinterpretations of its patterns and underlying principles.

The nature of representation: Owen Jones's reproductions of the Alhambra

Michael Darby wrote in 1983 that the abstract, experimental and conceptual concerns of advocates of Islamic art during the mid-nineteenth century are difficult to interpret, with more examples surviving from gothic and classical revivalist movements.[16] However, as Kathryn Ferry has rightly pointed out, Jones did not set out to 'peddle a Moorish Revival', and the very fact that he chose not to pursue this option in light of the aims

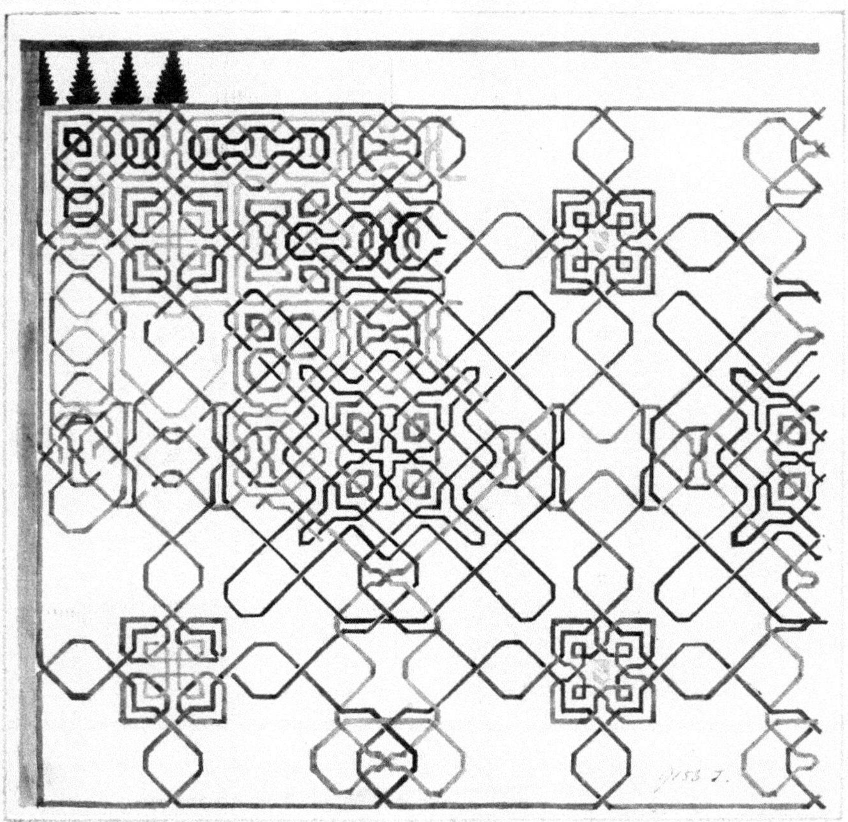

Owen Jones, Original drawing of wall decoration from the Alhambra, for *Plans, sections and details of the Alhambra*, 1842–45. (© Victoria and Albert Museum, London.) 13.1

of his contemporaries is notable.[17] It is important to recognise that his reproductions of the Alhambra span a number of formats and functions, from analytic documentation to commercial application, and that his primary aim was not to copy historical styles but to learn from their underlying principles. His work on the Alhambra began with the painstaking project of documenting a large portion of its palatial buildings and ornament, resulting in the lavish two-volume publication, *Plans, elevations, sections, and details of the Alhambra*, which he privately published between 1842 and 1845. It contained over one hundred drawings and prints based on tracings, schematic drawings and paper squeezes (a process of imprinting whereby wet paper was pressed against relief carvings), taken by Jones and the French architect Jules Goury in 1834 (figures 13.1 and 13.2).[18] Jones developed a new chromolithographic printing technique in order to accommodate the intricate designs of the Alhambra's interiors, producing

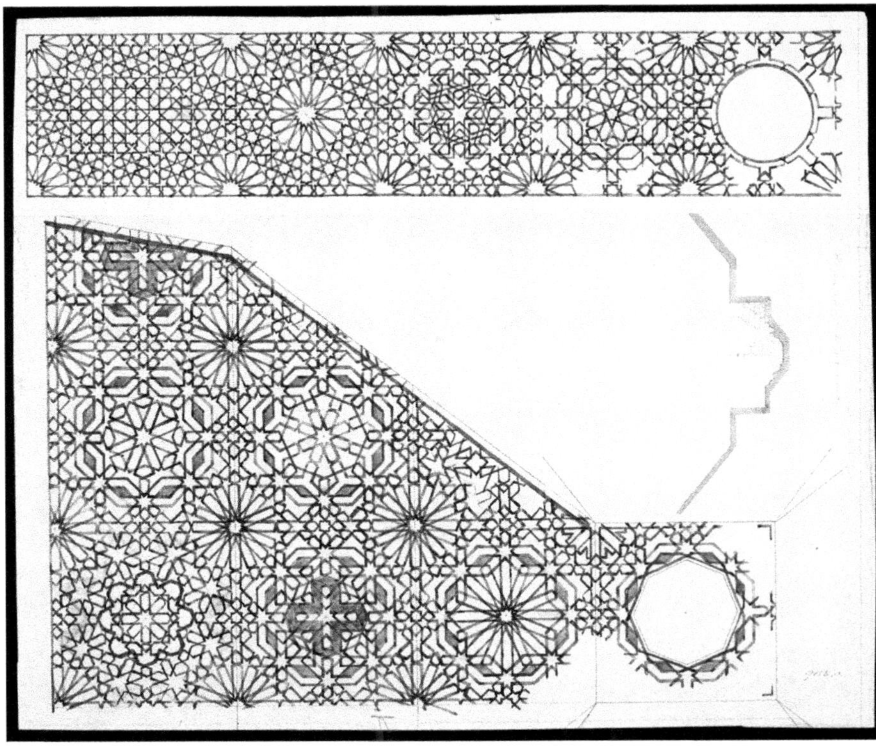

13.2 Owen Jones, Original drawing of wall decoration from the Alhambra, for *Plans, sections and details of the Alhambra*, 1842–45. (© Victoria and Albert Museum, London.)

detailed prints alongside cross-sections and plans of its buildings.[19] This meticulous reproduction of the Alhambra's surfaces nevertheless involved a series of adjustments; he edited out nearly all signs of decay and all evidence of Christian alterations or additions, and liberally applied a primary colour scheme to the majority of prints. Despite these translations and omissions, the accuracy purported by these early reproductions made Jones an uncontested expert on the monument.

As a result of this initial publication, Jones was granted permission to reproduce a section of the Alhambra in three dimensions as one of the 'Fine Art Courts' at the second Crystal Palace at Sydenham (figure 13.3). The 'Alhambra Court' was loosely based on the courtyard and adjoining buildings of the Palace of the Lions, what he refers to in the handbook as the 'Casa Real'. Built on a smaller scale than the original (a fact he makes explicit within his accompanying handbook, even including comparative floor plans), he chose only 'examples of importance' to decorate its surfaces, based on plates from *Plans* and a collection of plaster casts and impressions taken directly from the Alhambra.[20] Jones had the entire Court painted in bright polychrome, and controversially gilded the slender

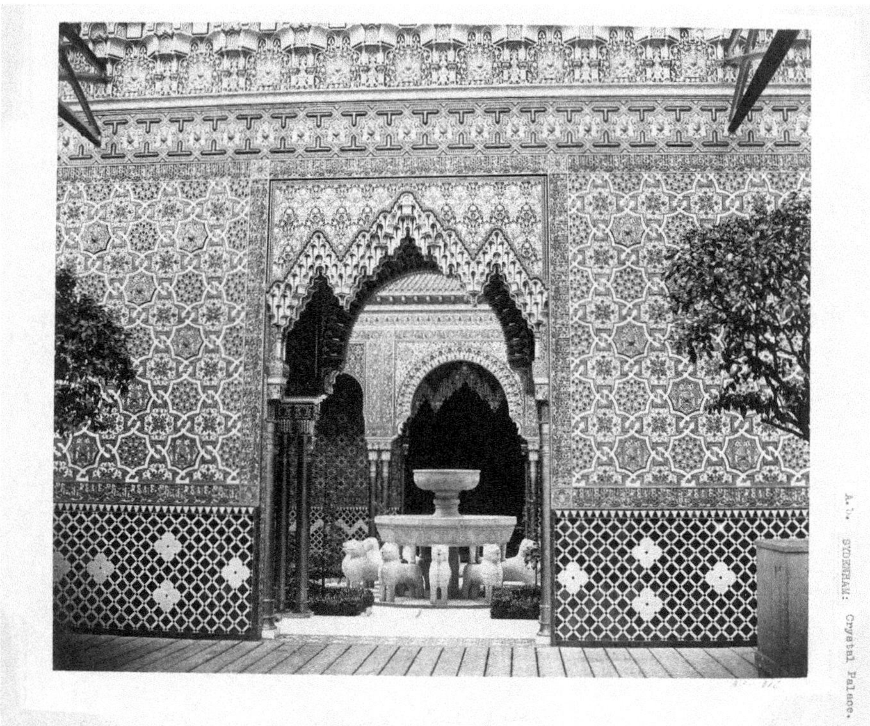

13.3 Philip Henry Delamotte, 'The Alhambra Court – Court of Lions', albumen print from collodion negative, c.1855. (© Victoria and Albert Museum, London.)

columns that bordered the central courtyard (there is no evidence of gilding on the original marble pillars). The quality and precision of its plaster ornament was in keeping with the diagrammatic style of his prints and drawings, from which he also ambitiously chose to recreate the elaborate *muqarnas* ceiling of the Alhambra's Hall of Abencerrajes. For the purposes of efficiency he developed a moulding process using gelatine to assemble groups of individual 'stalactite bricks', which were then adhered to the ceiling in large blocks.[21] Despite his efforts, the Court was still under construction at the time of the opening ceremony in 1854 and would take a further year to complete.

Jones did not intend his Court as a facsimile of the original, but rather as an 'aid' to viewers studying his design principles, and referred to it in his handbook as 'a fragmentary reproduction of the real Alhambra'.[22] Here he provided instructions for how to 'read' its patterns alongside a series of underlying formal principles. In its pedagogic tone the handbook anticipated *The grammar of ornament*, in which he dedicated an entire section to the 'Moresque' style (figure 13.4) and further elaborated his design principles in relation to a universal grammar of form that could be used

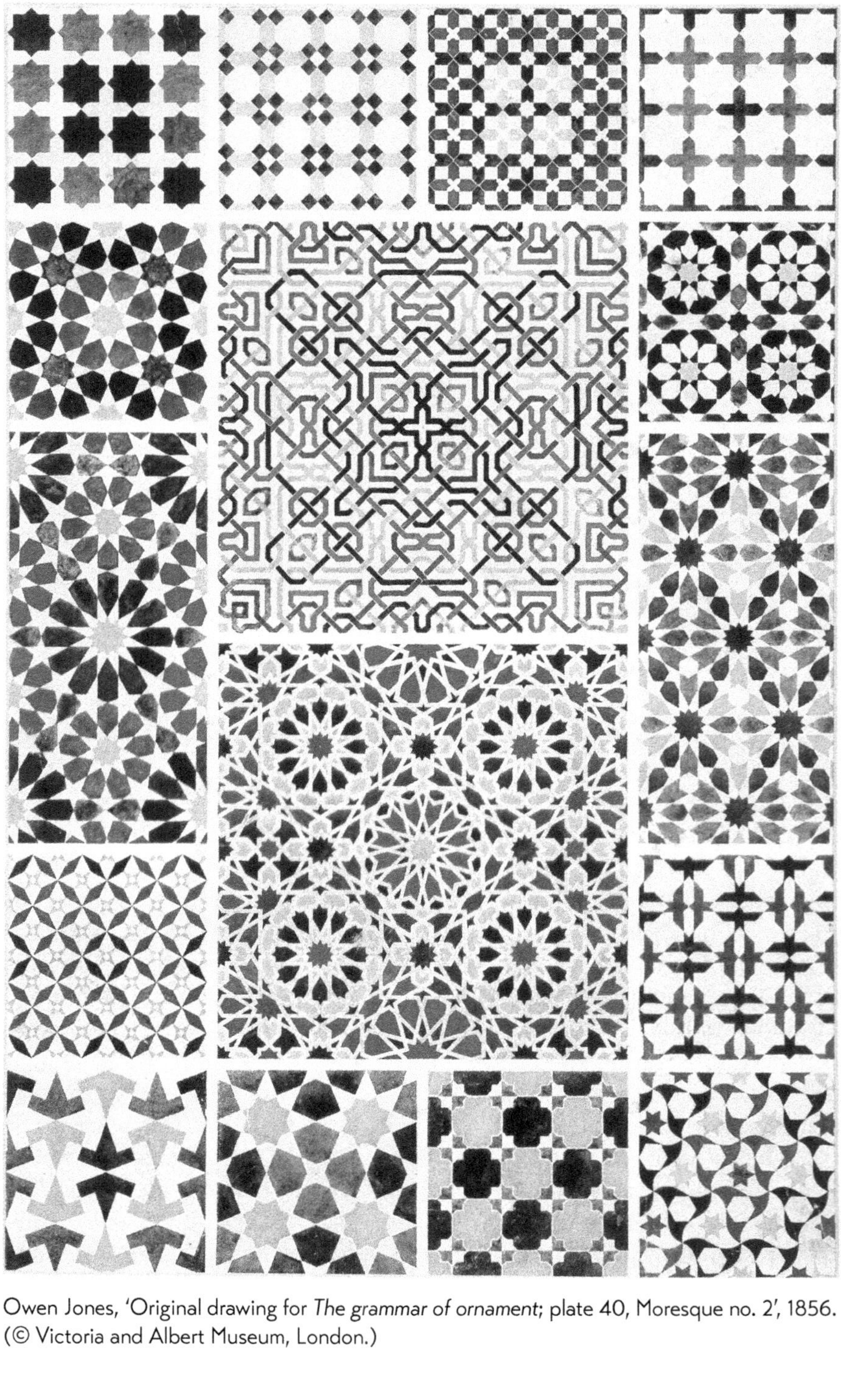

13.4 Owen Jones, 'Original drawing for *The grammar of ornament*; plate 40, Moresque no. 2', 1856. (© Victoria and Albert Museum, London.)

to understand a broad spectrum of ornamental traditions. The section allocated to the Alhambra was sizeable, considering that the Nasrid period was regionally isolated and relatively short-lived compared with 'Indian' or 'Turkish' traditions. He also sees the palace as sufficiently representative of 'Moorish' art in general, ignoring a number of other distinct periods of artistic production in the region.[23] Jones's pattern book was a commercial success, presenting a selection of 'world' ornament with remarkable precision, whilst simultaneously promoting the design theories he had developed as a teacher and practitioner.

In tandem with his pedagogic work, Jones used the Alhambra as a source of inspiration in his own architectural and design practice. His involvement with the Architectural Society (to which he gave his lecture 'On the influence of religion upon art' in 1835), and his numerous entries into national competitions as well as exhibitions at the Royal Academy, gave him some notoriety in the field of architecture, although many of his designs were rejected or received mixed reviews (with the exception of a number of Alhambra-style interior schemes for private houses, including Kensington Palace Gardens and 16 Carlton House Terrace, London).[24] His designs for wallpapers, textiles, furniture, carpets and tiles for a range of commercial companies and private patrons were on the whole more successful. These included a commission for Moorish floor tiles in the Houses of Parliament in 1834 (mysteriously replaced at some later stage by neo-gothic designs by Pugin and Charles Barry, which remain today), and a large selection of wallpaper designs produced for John Trumble & Sons, Jeffrey & Co. and Jackson & Graham from 1858 onwards (ten volumes were donated by his sister in 1877 to the South Kensington Museum, now the Victoria and Albert Museum). He also designed a number of 'illuminated' gift books, beginning with *Ancient Spanish ballads* in 1841, all of which contain some trace of Islamic influence, often alongside naturally depicted flowers and following the format of illuminated gothic manuscripts.[25] As Darby has observed, in the 1840s and 1850s Jones increasingly came to see gothic naturalism as the true inspiration for design, 'eventually to the exclusion of recognisably Moorish forms'.[26] His eagerness to combine Nasrid motifs with other styles also led to a gradual dilution of its cultural or historical specificity, which would have implications for how it was received by both popular audiences and critics.

The representation of nature: Ruskin and the abstract forms of the earth

At the time of writing *The stones of Venice* (1851–53), Ruskin was still relatively tolerant of Islamic art and architecture, admiring the 'transitional style' of early twelfth-century Venetian design in which he identifies a strong Arabic influence.[27] Later, in a series of lectures given between 1858 and 1859, published as *The two paths: being lectures on art, and its application to decoration and manufacture*, his views on the superiority of Western examples had become fully articulated; the political contexts of Ruskin's views are explored by Natasha Eaton in Chapter 12 above.[28] Ruskin felt that the imaginative or conventionalised rendering of forms found in the natural world was an act of ignorance, a moral transgression he increasingly associated with the art of 'Oriental' nations, as well as earlier stages of Western production such as ancient Greek architecture. He contrasted this regressive tendency with the virtuous qualities of the craftsmen of the late gothic period, who were directly inspired by the imperfect beauty of nature and therefore loyal to God's creation. Ruskin's devotion to the Protestant church was a major factor in his preference for naturally occurring forms (though distinct from Pugin's High Church Anglicanism), and throughout his writings piousness became inextricably tied to fidelity within representations of nature in art and architecture.[29] So strong was his belief in the inspirational forms of the earth that he stated: 'No great school ever yet existed which had not for primal aim the representation of some natural fact as truly as possible'.[30] It was his abhorrence of machine production, however, that ultimately cemented his dislike for Eastern art forms. As Debra Schafter has succinctly put it, to Ruskin, 'precision equalled inhumanity; unique, inconsistent, and unpredictable traits, on the other hand, provided evidence of life'.[31]

Ruskin's preference for the flexibility, spontaneity and diversity of the late gothic style had its origins in what Schafter identifies as a 'vision of architectural synthesis guided by a predominantly medieval perception of the order of nature'.[32] She explains that at the core of Ruskin's aesthetic theory (especially as it applied to medieval Christian architecture) 'was the belief in an integrated mode of perception that read signs of transcendent power in natural fact'.[33] This led him to separate the truthful from the deceitful within examples of ornament, where the organic curves of flora symbolised the ordered and virtuous sensibilities of the West, while straight, geometric lines were the product of the 'unrestrained' minds of Arabs and Indians. In *The seven lamps of architecture* (1849) he attributed abstraction to an early stage of artistic development in societies, much like the drawings of a child, whereby 'curved and complex lines are represented by straight and simple ones; interior markings of forms are few, and much is symbolical and conventional'.[34] Crinson traces the beginnings of Ruskin's evolutionary model even farther back to the second volume of *Modern painters* (1846), where he contrasts a pleasure-seeking, sensory mode of perception ('aesthesis') with a virtuous moral sensibility ('theoria'), the latter being grounded in natural theology.[35] Later, in *The two paths*, he returns to this dichotomy as the basis for his assault on the art of 'cruel nations', especially that produced by 'Moorish, Indian, Chinese [and] South Sea Islanders' (which, as Crinson notes, are the same traditions that are given special attention in Jones's *The grammar of ornament*).[36] Ruskin claimed that the people who practised abstract ornamentation were 'cut off from all possible sources of healthy knowledge or natural delight; that they have wilfully sealed up and put aside the entire volume of the world, and have got nothing to read, nothing to dwell upon, but that imagination of the thoughts of their hearts'.[37]

Ruskin's theory of sensory perception has a number of interesting parallels with his studies of minerals. Barbara Keyser has observed that Ruskin used a crystal-versus-plant metaphor in his defence of naturalistic as opposed to stylised plant form (it was a design reformer and student of Jones, Christopher Dresser, who would fully develop a botanical model for design pedagogy and practice).[38] In the fifth volume of *Modern painters* (1856), for example, he contrasts the corruptive potential of mineral growth patterns with the noble lines of leaves:

> The mineral crystals group themselves neither in succession nor in sympathy; but great and small recklessly strive for place, and deface or distort each other as they gather into opponent asperities. The confused crowd fills the rock cavity, hanging together in a glittering, yet sordid heap ... But the order of the leaves is one of soft and subdued concession ... Each awaits its appointed time, accepts its prepared place.[39]

Despite Ruskin's objections, he made a number of allowances for abstract lines in gothic art when it is not possible to render forms distinctly or imitatively, particularly in the case of adapting them to architectural forms.[40] By conceding that even abstract forms are naturally inspired, Ruskin includes 'forms of the earth' in his list of 'proper materials of ornament', explaining that crystalline form is 'the completely systematised natural science of the earth ... an endless element of decoration, where higher conditions of structure cannot be represented'.[41] These are followed by examples in increasing order of representational complexity: water (waves); forms of fire (flames and rays); forms of air (clouds); organic forms or shells; fish; reptiles and insects; vegetation A (stems and trunks); vegetation B (foliage); birds; and finally, mammalian animals and man.[42] According to Ruskin, this hierarchy of elemental forms should be mirrored within ornamentation, so that the 'lower forms' (i.e. mountains and waves of the sea) should only be applied to architectural or structural elements viewed from far away, while the more noble elements (i.e. living plants and organisms) were reserved for the finer details of a building and beckoned closer observation.[43] According to his formula, the use of abstract or geometric forms in the surface decoration of a building was an inversion of this natural hierarchy, therefore indicating an earlier stage of sensory development, or worse, an outright rejection of the laws of nature.

While Ruskin distinguishes between the representation of things visible to the eye and the abstract musings of the mind, he maintains that all beautiful ornament, 'however invented', is always either an intentional or unintentional copy of some constant natural form. For example, he suggests that the architectural mouldings of the 'middle Gothic' style were, 'little more than representations of the canaliculated crystals of the beryl, and such other minerals'.[44] Rather confusingly, he denies that these forms were consciously inspired by nature and claims that the artists 'not knowingly' adapted them. He writes, 'I do not suppose a single hint was ever actually taken from mineral form; not even by the Arabs in their stalactite pendants and vaults'.[45] It is on the point of visibility that Ruskin's typological approach to assigning moral value to naturally occurring forms begins to break down. Having established that the compositional logic of the subterranean world of crystals was 'unfinished' (much like the underdeveloped musings of the mind), he deduces that 'all perfectly beautiful forms must be composed of curves; since there is hardly any common natural form in which it is possible to discover a straight line'.[46] Curved lines are associated with the 'finished work of nature', whereas straight lines can only be found in the subterranean world: 'to find right [straight] lines in nature at all, we may be compelled to do violence to her finished work, break through the sculptured and coloured surfaces of her crags, and examine the processes of their crystallisation'.[47] In suggesting that earlier or 'primitive' societies could not access these forms directly, he was not only implying that they lacked the scientific knowledge and technological means to do so, but that they also possessed a kind of primordial, unconscious link with the underdeveloped forms of the earth. Thus, Ruskin's instruction to artists and designers is that they observe the finished forms of nature whilst avoiding its internal workings, which he links through the use of anthropomorphism to the raw, unrefined quality of the primitive mind.

His mineralogical studies often take on the structure and tone of dramatic narratives, wherein independent formations are significantly altered or corrupted by external forces. He describes the transformation of mineral and crystal specimens within lava silica in *Deucalion* as follows: 'we have essentially three different minerals, passing into each other it is true; but, at a certain point, changing their natures definitely, so that *hyalite, becoming wax chalcedony, gains* the power of prismatic crystallization; and *wax chalcedony, becoming true chalcedony, loses* it again!'[48] In a study from 1867 titled, 'On banded and brecciated concretions', Ruskin sets up a similar tension in his description of chalcedony: 'a free mineral in open cavities it is actively stalactitic, not merely pendent or accumulative, but animated by a kind of crystalline spinal energy, which gives to its processes something of the arbitrary arrangement of real crystals, modified always by cohesion, gravity, and (presumably) by fluid and gaseous currents'.[49] His distinction between the 'actively stalactitic' and the 'mere pendentive' is revealing, for it identifies a kind of human agency within the former, whereas the latter takes on a mechanical, accumulative character.

Crystals adopt anthropomorphic qualities within a number of Ruskin's works, indicative of their problematic, intermediary place between the representational and the abstract. In one of his ten lectures intended as summaries of mineralogical studies 'as explained to children' in *Ethics of the dust* (the lectures were originally given at a girls' school in Cheshire, which would largely determine its moralistic and patronising tone), Ruskin's narrator describes a quartz crystal as 'opaque, rough surfaced, jagged on the edge, distorted in the spine, it exhibits a quite human image of decrepitude'.[50] He explains to his group of 'little housewives' that minerals exhibit the 'same varieties of temper that human creatures might', sometimes yielding to each other to form 'fantastic, but exquisitely finished, groups', while other times fighting furiously for their place, 'losing all shape and honour, and even their own likeness'.[51] Rather than celebrating these irregularities as he does within the world of organic form, here inconsistencies are associated with the impurity of the human spirit, causing mineral forms to lack a clear and noble purpose. The imbalanced, indeterminate character of crystal growth patterns acts as a metaphor for the instability of the human spirit, while the more perfect or 'finished' crystals reflect a strong will and ordered direction of growth. The angular forms of nature posed a problem for Ruskin's aesthetic and moral sensibility, causing him to contradictorily favour arrangements that exhibited signs of regularity. He pauses at one point during his analysis to say, 'the more I endeavour to read Nature patiently, the more I find that she is always trying to deceive us while we are impatient, by pretending to do things in ways in which they never were done, and making things look like one another, which have no connections with each other'.[52] Ruskin's thwarted attempts to rationalise the geological world and explain its inconsistencies ultimately leads him to see a deceitful side of nature within her abstract forms.

'Stalactite vaults' and the conventionalisation of form

While both Ruskin and Jones maintained that ornamental forms should be based on a set of underlying natural principles, Jones argued for a typological system of growth patterns that left room for stylistic interpretation. For the design reformers, ornamental elements need only suggest their natural origin rather than resemble them exactly, so that resemblance never compromises the unity of a pattern or effect of a surface. Rather than the 'realistic' imitation of things in the natural world, they promoted the conventionalisation or abstraction of natural forms with the goal of achieving a greater level of refinement. However, Jones's and Ruskin's views on the subject of 'direct' inspiration are not as antithetical as they initially appear. Jones explains that as the 'Mahometan religion and civilisation' reproduced and elaborated on existing styles, they applied to them 'their own peculiar feelings' and thus gradually departed from the original model.[53] Arguing against the direct copying of forms from nature in the final section of *The grammar of ornament*, 'Leaves and flowers from nature', he states,

> In the best periods of art all ornament was rather based on an observation of the principles which regulate the arrangement of form in nature, than on an attempt to imitate the absolute forms of those works; and that whenever this limit was exceeded by any art, it was one of the strongest symptoms of decline: true art consisting in idealising, and not copying, the forms of nature.[54]

Rather than seeing the stylised vegetal forms of Nasrid ornament as disconnected from the natural world, he saw them as originating from the foundational laws of nature, so that, 'all lines flow out of a parent stem: every ornament, however distant, can be traced to its branch and root ... following the principle of radiation in the human hand or leaf'.[55] Schafter writes that in taking natural laws as his starting point, Jones 'shared Ruskin's interest in combatting the ill effects of industry on design', despite the fact that he based his principles on natural science rather than biblical laws.[56] Jones saw the Moresque style as being grounded on these principles, but with the important difference that they avoided the exact copying of examples found in the natural world. He argued that a mature style of ornament such as that found in the Alhambra could only emerge through the reworking of the same elements over generations, eventually resulting in 'a Grammar of Ornament as that in which every ornament contains a grammar in itself'.[57] It was this level of sophistication which

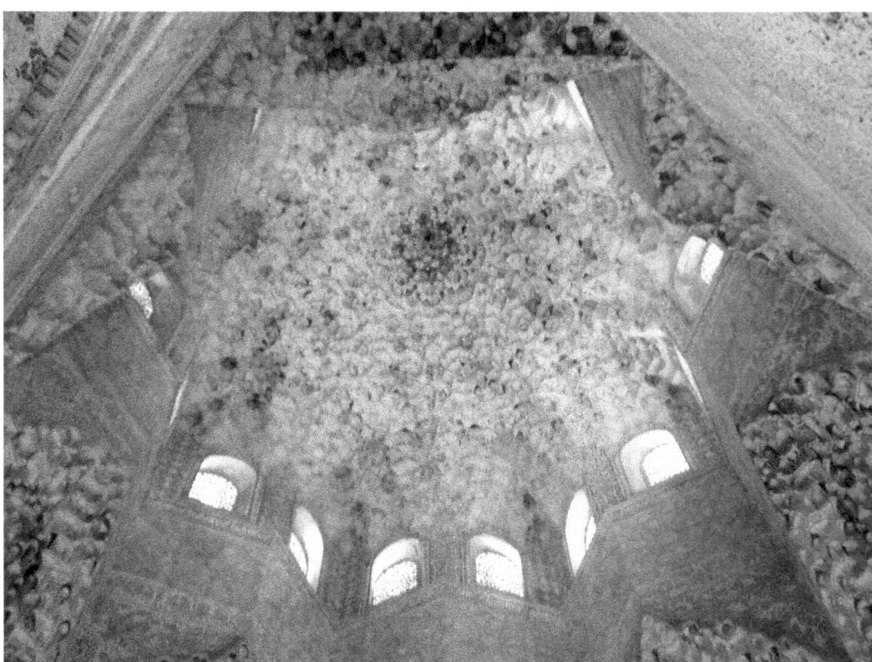

13.5 Muqarnas ceiling, 'Hall of the Two Sisters', Nasrid palaces of the Alhambra, Granada. (Photograph by the author.)

he encouraged British designers to strive toward, through a two-pronged practice of elaborating existing designs whilst adhering to the underlying laws of natural science.

As a final point of comparative analysis, I would like to return to the domed *muqarnas* ceiling of the Alhambra Court. Jones had originally intended on reproducing the even more complicated ceiling of the Hall of Two Sisters, which proved too difficult for his team of workers.[58] His insistence on reproducing this challenging feature suggests that he saw it as essential part of the Court and a central 'lesson' amongst its ornamental features. Owing to three centuries of development in Islamic art, *muqarnas* (or *mocárabes* in Spanish), reached a remarkable level of refinement during the Nasrid period, adorning arcades, cornices and entranceways throughout the Alhambra palace, and most notably within its elaborate ceilings (figure 13.5).[59] Through the multiplication of small geometric elements, *muqarnas* appeared to grow naturally from the structure itself, invoking the central design reform imperative, 'to decorate construction, never to construct decoration'.[60] In a lecture given in 1852 Jones explained that, 'it was reserved for the Moors to carry this principle to its utmost limit; and we see [that] in the Alhambra capitals of columns, arches over large openings, and ultimately the ceilings of their halls, were covered with the stalactite roof, which are not more remarkable for their elegance and beauty than for their scientific construction'.[61]

The vaulted dome at Sydenham can be understood as Jones's decorative *tour de force*, for which he applied a process of 'piece moulding' using gelatine. He describes this as a 'more economical and rapid process which modern invention has placed at our disposal', and muses at what the Moors would have achieved had they had access to the same technology.[62] Furthermore, in successfully reconstructing the complex geometric language of the *muqarnas* he was also demonstrating his analytical prowess. He based his replica on a series of section drawings originally developed in *Plans* (figure 13.6), alongside a textual breakdown of their geometric formula: 'composed of numerous prisms of plaster, united in their contiguous lateral surfaces, consisting of seven different forms, proceeding from three primary figures on plan'.[63] Ferry has written that in reducing the *muqarnas* dome to its underlying geometric principles in plan and section, Jones and Goury broke new ground, 'not least because their plan actually represented the structure in a way that would have been comprehensible to the original craftsmen who visualised such designs on a single plane'.[64]

The Court ceiling is interesting for another reason, which I would like to take up as a final point. To many visitors to the Alhambra over the centuries, its *muqarnas* resembled the natural form of the stalactite cave, with its 'dripping' crystalline formations, a likeness that could not have been lost on Ruskin. Indeed, he had previously cited the 'stalactite pendants and vaults' of the Arabs as an example of ornament conceived by the uncontrolled imagination, while unconsciously based on the subterranean world of crystals. In *The stones of Venice* he mourned the Arab artist's inability (or refusal) to represent natural form: 'Much he achieved; and yet, effort of his overtaxed invention, restrained from its proper food, he made his architecture a glittering vacillation of undisciplined enchantment'.[65] Even at this early stage, he read in the abstract ornament of the Arabs a kind of moral decrepitude, just as he would come to see ignoble qualities within crystal formations. Ruskin's difficulty in ascribing value to abstract form would prove equally as problematic within his analysis of minerals as within his theories of architectural ornament. Jones's reproduction of the *muqarnas* ceiling, which in the absence of photographic evidence we can only assume was as calculated and precise as the rest of the Court, would reinforce Ruskin's conviction that the tendency toward abstraction belonged to 'cruel'

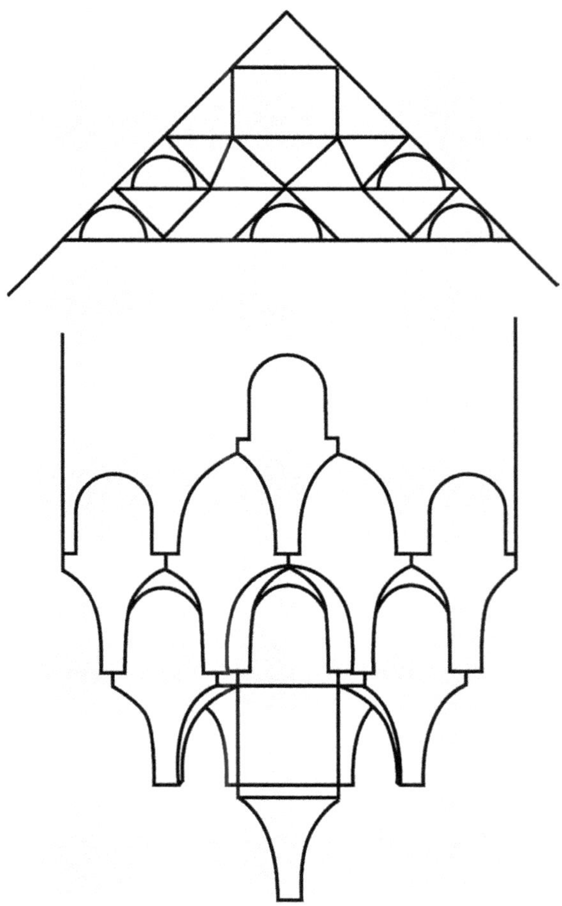

13.6 From Owen Jones, 'types, elevation and plan of muqarnas', *The Alhambra Court in the Crystal Palace*, 1854. (Illustration by the author after Owen Jones.)

societies lacking in their ability to connect with the natural world around them. Jones's mechanical reproductions of the Alhambra, which reached its viewers through international displays, design handbooks, and a range of commercial contexts, would further remove the Nasrid ornamental tradition from the realm of 'true' representation.

It was on the issue of conventionalism that Ruskin's theory of representation fully departed from that of Jones, on the basis that by not directly observing nature the artist's interpretation failed to convey a sense of 'human care and labour'.[66] Along with other naturalists at the time, Ruskin feared the obsolescence of human agency in the wake of new technologies and standardised modes of production. Ultimately this led him to condemn a wide range of artistic traditions that lay outside his ever-changing definition of naturalistic representation, so that the perceived evils of industry became aligned with a selection of Oriental design traditions. Yet Jones's and Ruskin's views on natural representation were not entirely opposed. They agreed that artists and designers should follow the laws of nature, and interpret rather than copy its forms directly. It was precisely this principle that presented a fundamental problem for Ruskin when it came to the 'right lined' forms of the geological world, which he struggled to place within his hierarchy of architectural ornament.

Ruskin saw mechanical production as the enemy of pure inspiration and expression, and as artificiality and abstraction became synonymous in his mind he would increasingly associate Eastern ornament with the 'shopfronts of Regent Street and Oxford Street'. It is no coincidence that he singled out the Alhambra as a monument of a culture in decline, as he warned of a similar fate for Britain in the wake of the Industrial Revolution. I have suggested here that Ruskin's conflicted response to the crystal forms of the earth reflects these wider social and political anxieties. Kate Flint has argued that for the Victorians, the idea of dust – the foundational material from which the earth is made to which it may return – 'chimes with a wider fear of reversion, of history not moving in a confident forwards direction, or alternatively sinking as a result of catastrophe or degeneration'.[67] Ruskin's forays into the mineralogical world can in this way be understood as a way of confronting these fears, and of negotiating non-representational forms on moral and conceptual grounds.

To conclude, there is little doubt that Ruskin's criticism of the Alhambra was rooted in his distrust of industrial processes and the dangers these presented to manual craft and individual expression. However, as I have argued here, his response should be understood not simply as a reaction to Jones's technical reproductions, but also as part of his ongoing discussions of abstraction in relation to the human spirit. The forms of the earth served a symbolic and metaphoric function within his writings, hovering somewhere between the referential and the abstract, not unlike Jones's *muqarnas* ceiling in the Crystal Palace. It was Jones's further dilution and homogenisation of the Alhambra's patterns within his commercial design work that led Ruskin to condemn them to 'patterns for carpets or binding of books'. Taken together, and in light of their respective agendas, Jones's and Ruskin's responses to the Alhambra complicate the notion of an art inspired by industry, and of a universal theory of ornamental form.

Notes

1 See Ferry, 'Awakening a higher ambition'.
2 Eggleton, 'History in the making'.
3 Raquejo, *El Palacio encantado*; Raquejo, '"The Arab cathedrals"'; Heide, 'The Alhambra in Britain'; Lundström, 'Experiencing the Alhambra'.
4 See Lubbock, *The tyranny of taste*; and Kriegel, *Grand designs*.
5 See Jespersen, 'Owen Jones's *The grammar of ornament*'.
6 e.g. Freeman's description of 'Saracen' architecture in *A history of architecture*, pp. 270–1.
7 Ruskin, *The stones of Venice*, p. 409 (appendix 22).
8 e.g. Gombrich, *The sense of order*, p. 53.
9 e.g. Flores, *Owen Jones*.
10 See Crinson, *Empire building*; Levell, *Oriental visions*; Moser, *Designing antiquity*.
11 Crinson, *Empire building*, p. 61.
12 See Schafter, *The order of ornament, the structure of style*, pp. 17–22.
13 Pointon, *Brilliant effects*, p. 321.
14 *Ibid.*, pp. 344–5.
15 See Sloboda, 'The grammar of ornament'.
16 Darby, *The Islamic perspective*, p. 6.
17 Ferry, 'Awakening a higher ambition', p. 3.
18 Goury died of cholera during their six-month stay in Granada, and Jones returned to the Alhambra in 1837 to complete his preparatory studies.
19 See Ferry, 'Printing the Alhambra'.
20 Jones, *The Alhambra Court in the Crystal Palace*, p. 4.
21 *Ibid.*, p. 86.
22 *Ibid.*, p. 30.
23 See Rosser-Owen, *Islamic arts from Spain*.
24 See chapters 3 and 4 of Flores, *Owen Jones*.
25 Darby, *The Islamic perspective*, p. 77.
26 *Ibid.*, p. 62.
27 Ruskin, *The stones of Venice*, p. 22.
28 Ruskin, *The two paths*, pp. 11–12.
29 Chitty, 'Ruskin's architectural heritage', p. 39.
30 Ruskin, *The two paths*, p. 19.
31 Schafter, *The order of ornament, the structure of style*, p. 17.
32 *Ibid.*, p. 18.
33 *Ibid.*, p. 18.
34 Ruskin, *The seven lamps*, pp. 120–1.
35 Crinson, *Empire building*, p. 60.
36 *Ibid.*, p. 60.
37 Ruskin, *The two paths*, p. 12.
38 Keyser, 'Ornament as idea', 135.
39 Cook and Wedderburn, *The works of John Ruskin*, vol. 7, p. 49.
40 Ruskin, *The stones of Venice*, p. 215.

41 *Ibid.*, p. 219.
42 *Ibid.*, p. 215.
43 Schafter, *The order of ornament, the structure of style*, pp. 19–20.
44 Ruskin, *The stones of Venice*, p. 219.
45 *Ibid.*, p. 219.
46 Ruskin, *The seven lamps*, pp. 98–9.
47 *Ibid.*, p. 99.
48 Cook and Wedderburn, *The works of John Ruskin*, vol. 26, p. 239 (Ruskin's emphasis).
49 *Ibid.*, p. 47.
50 Ruskin, *The ethics of the dust*, p. 86.
51 *Ibid.*, p. 109.
52 Cook and Wedderburn, *The works of John Ruskin*, vol. 26, p. 72.
53 Jones, *An attempt*, pp. 454–6.
54 Jones, *The grammar of ornament*, p. 154.
55 *Ibid.*, pp. 68–9.
56 Schafter, *The order of ornament, the structure of style*, p. 25.
57 Jones, *The grammar of ornament*, p. 66.
58 Rosser-Owen, *Islamic arts from Spain*, p. 124.
59 Tabbaa, *The transformation of Islamic art during the Sunni revival*, p. 128.
60 Jones, *The grammar of ornament*, p. 67.
61 Jones, *An attempt*, p. 456.
62 Jones, *The Alhambra Court in the Crystal Palace*, p. 86.
63 Jones and Goury, *Plans, elevations, sections, and details of the Alhambra*, pl. X.
64 Ferry, 'Awakening a higher ambition', p. 69.
65 Ruskin, *The stones of Venice*, p. 228.
66 Ruskin, *The seven lamps*, p. 48.
67 Flint, *Victorians and the visual imagination*, pp. 52–3.

Bibliography

Chitty, G. 'Ruskin's architectural heritage: the seven lamps of architecture – reception and legacy', in R. Daniels and G. K. Brandwood (eds.) *Ruskin and architecture* (Reading, 2003), pp. 24–54

Cook, E. T. and A. Wedderburn (eds.) *The works of John Ruskin* (39 volumes, London, 1903–12)

Crinson, M. *Empire building: orientalism and Victorian architecture* (London, 1996)

Darby, M. *The Islamic perspective: an aspect of British architecture and design in the nineteenth century* (London, 1983)

Eggleton, L. 'History in the making: the ornament of the Alhambra and the past-facing present', *Journal of Art Historiography*, 6 (June 2012) http://arthistoriography.wordpress.com/number-6-june-2012-2/ (accessed 21 April 2014)

Ferry, K. R. 'Printing the Alhambra: Owen Jones and chromolithography', *Architectural History*, 46 (2003), 175–88

Ferry, K. R. 'Awakening a higher ambition: the influence of travel upon the early career of Owen Jones' (PhD dissertation, University of Cambridge, 2004)

Flint, K. *The Victorians and the visual imagination* (Cambridge, 2000)

Flores, C. H. *Owen Jones: design, ornament, architecture, and theory in an age in transition* (New York, 2006)

Freeman, E. A. *A history of architecture* (London, 1849)

Gombrich, E. *The sense of order: a study in the psychology of decorative art* (2nd edn, London, 1984)

Heide, C. 'The Alhambra in Britain: between foreignization and domestication', *Art in Translation*, 2:2 (2010), 201–22

Jespersen, J. K. 'Owen Jones's *The grammar of ornament* of 1856: field theory in Victorian design at the mid-century' (PhD dissertation, Brown University, 1984)

Jones, O. *An attempt to define the principles which should regulate the employment of colour in the decorative arts* (London, 1852)

Jones, O. *The Alhambra Court in the Crystal Palace* (London, 1854)

Jones, O. *The grammar of ornament* (1856) (London, 2nd edn, 1868)

Jones, O. and J. Goury, *Plans, elevations, sections, and details of the Alhambra: from drawings taken on the spot in 1834 by the late M. Jules Goury and in 1834 and 1837 by Owen Jones* (2 volumes, London, 1842–45)

Keyser, B. W. 'Ornament as idea: indirect imitation of nature in the design reform movement', *Journal of Design History*, 11:2 (1998), 127–44

Kriegel, L. *Grand designs: labor, empire and the museum in Victorian culture* (Durham, 2008)

Levell, N. *Oriental visions: exhibitions, travel, and collecting in the Victorian age* (London, 2000)

Lubbock. J. *The tyranny of taste: the politics of architecture and design in Britain, 1550–1960* (New Haven, 1995)

Lundström, M-S. 'Experiencing the Alhambra, an illusive site of oriental otherness', *International Journal of Islamic Architecture*, 1:1 (2012), 83–106

Moser, S. *Designing antiquity: Owen Jones, ancient Egypt and the Crystal Palace* (New Haven, 2012)

Pointon, M. *Brilliant effects: a cultural history of gem stones and jewellery* (New Haven, 2009)

Raquejo, T. '"The Arab cathedrals": Moorish architecture as seen by British travellers', *Burlington Magazine*, 128:1001 (1986), 555–63

Raquejo, T. *El palacio encantado: la Alhambra en el arte Británico* (Madrid, 1990)

Rosser-Owen, M. *Islamic arts from Spain* (London, 2010)

Ruskin, J. *The seven lamps of architecture* (London, 1849)

Ruskin, J. *The stones of Venice* (London, 1851–53)

Ruskin, J. *The two paths: being lectures on art, and its application to decoration and manufacture, delivered in 1858–9* (London, 1859)

Ruskin, J. *The ethics of the dust: ten lectures to little housewives on the elements of crystallization* (London, 1900)

Schafter, Debra, *The order of ornament, the structure of style: theoretical foundations of modern art and architecture* (Cambridge, 2003)

Sloboda, S. 'The grammar of ornament: cosmopolitanism and reform in British design', *Journal of Design History*, 21:3 (2008), 223–36

Tabbaa, Y. *The transformation of Islamic art during the Sunni revival* (Seattle, 2001)

Index

EU authorised representative for GPSR:
Easy Access System Europe, Mustamäe tee 50,
10621 Tallinn, Estonia
gpsr.requests@easproject.com

www.ingramcontent.com/pod-product-compliance
Ingram Content Group UK Ltd.
Pitfield, Milton Keynes, MK11 3LW, UK
UKHW051912100926
8556IPUK00006B/858
* 9 7 8 0 7 1 9 0 9 6 4 6 4 *